WORKMEN'S COMPENSATION

OXFORD UNIVERSITY PRESS
AMEN HOUSE, E.C. 4
LONDON EDINBURGH GLASGOW NEW YORK
TORONTO MELBOURNE CAPETOWN BOMBAY
CALCUTTA MADRAS
HUMPHREY MILFORD
PUBLISHER TO THE UNIVERSITY

WORKMEN'S COMPENSATION

BY

Sɪʀ ARNOLD WILSON, M.P.

AND

Pʀᴏꜰᴇꜱꜱᴏʀ HERMANN LEVY

VOL. I. SOCIAL AND POLITICAL DEVELOPMENT

VOL. II. THE NEED FOR REFORM

VOLUME II

THE NEED FOR REFORM

OXFORD UNIVERSITY PRESS

LONDON NEW YORK TORONTO

1941

PRINTED IN GREAT BRITAIN

FOREWORD

THE manuscript of *Workmen's Compensation*, Volume II, was finished in the first days of September 1939. No statistical material exceeding this date could be considered, although it has been possible to insert, where space allowed, some Notes relating to material published at a later time. Under normal conditions this volume would have been published in the spring of 1940. As, in fact, the Workmen's Compensation Statistics annually published by the Home Office do not show great changes from year to year it should not be of material importance to our findings that those used for the purpose of this book were published in 1939 and relate to the figures available for 1937. It was possible, however, to utilize a large part of the Minutes of Evidence of the Royal Commission on Workmen's Compensation for the purpose of this book.

The necessity of paper economy during the War is responsible for the lack of appendixes which we should have wished to add to our work as further documentation. As, however, the Royal Commission on Workmen's Compensation has published most valuable Memoranda on the subject, the reader may consult those where facts and figures supplementary to our own are required. I may refer in this respect to the exhaustive Memoranda by various Government Departments, in particular to that prepared by the Home Office, as also to that presented by the International Labour Office, whose work in the matter of social services deserves highest praise. It may also be mentioned that the authors themselves were among those who presented Memoranda to the Royal Commission, which may be consulted where the lack of an Appendix is felt (cf. Royal Commission of Workmen's Compensation, Papers 9 and 9A, 1939). While war conditions had thus no decisive material effect upon the publication of our work, personal loss fell hard upon it. When war broke out Sir Arnold Wilson was granted a commission as Pilot Officer for General Duties (Air Gunner), R.A.F.V.R. In the spring of 1940 he was reported missing. In spite of his absorbing military duties he had been able to read the first hundred pages of the first proofs. When the war brought our collaboration to a sudden stop, he wrote to me: 'I shall not ever forget the years of fruitful partnership in constructive research in almost unexplored territory. It has brought me as much satisfaction as anything I have ever attempted.'

One of the first things Sir Arnold said to me when we discussed the possibilities of our common labours was that he wanted our books to be objective, complete, and comprehensive. What better guarantee could have been given to an economic and social investigator? In collaborating with me Sir Arnold did not feel himself tied to any party principles; indeed, if party principles could have influenced us, our co-partnership would have been less harmonious than it was, for I came from a decidedly Liberal school of economic thought. But from the inception of our work Sir Arnold felt that, as far as it lay in our power, we were bound to the duty of following the path of truth wherever it might lead us, and his undaunted courage enabled him to abandon any previous views or convictions as soon as he thought himself able to replace them with others of more validity. It is this courage and loyalty that true science demands from her followers. Sir Arnold's loyalty to scientific truth fitted him to become a great British social reformer. That in regard to a real and effective reform of industrial accident insurance in Britain such reformers are sorely needed the formidable evidence laid before the Royal Commission on Workmen's Compensation abundantly shows. For it may be hoped that reform will not content itself with measures of partial efficiency. Former improvements, so called, of existing legislation have revealed themselves as tragically defective. Reform must go much deeper. 'War never leaves where it found a nation', said Edmund Burke. More than ever this truth will relate to matters of social reform when this War is ended. Fate—having destined Sir Arnold to a service certainly of no less value—has denied him a place in the front line of those who, after this war, will fight for a better and happier social England. Sir Arnold Wilson,—farewell.

HERMANN LEVY

CONTENTS

PART I

THE INJURY

PART II

COMPENSATION

PART III

RESTORATION TO HEALTH AND REHABILITATION

PART IV

THE ADMINISTRATION OF WORKMEN'S COMPENSATION

THE LEGAL SIDE

THE MEDICAL SIDE

CONTENTS

THE ECONOMIC AND SOCIAL SIDE

PART I

THE INJURY

B

CHAPTER I

SOME FUNDAMENTAL STATISTICS

The statistical regularity of accident data . . . raises the question as to whether the causes that lead up to accidents depend merely on random chance or, in other words, whether the majority of accidents are really accidents in the sense of being—to use a legal phrase—'acts of God'.

EDGAR W. COLLIS and DR. MAJOR GREENWOOD,
The Health of the Industrial Worker, 1921.

ACCIDENT prevention and Workmen's Compensation in Britain have hitherto followed separate lines of development. Under the British (but not the German) system the former is enforced by a large and growing body of Inspectors under the Factories and Mines Acts, with the co-operation of unofficial bodies, such as the 'Safety First' Association and of official organizations such as the Industrial Health Research Board[1] and the Miners' Welfare Fund. On the other hand, compensation for an injured workman or, in the event of a fatal accident, to his dependents, has remained, subject to the current Workmen's Compensation and Employer's Liability Acts and to the Common Law, a personal and private responsibility of the employer.

The existence of the sharp line of demarcation thus drawn between the two matters in this country, for historical reasons expounded in a previous volume, does not absolve us from the necessity of examining the modern significance of injuries and accidents, as well as of industrial diseases, before dealing with Workmen's Compensation at the present day. The medical literature on this aspect of the subject is as abundant as that relating to Workmen's Compensation is scanty, for the problems of accidents and diseases seem to have attracted some of the keenest minds of the medical profession and of sociologists. Workmen's Compensation has interested lawyers, a few distinguished members of the medical profession, and social workers, but as a rule their studies and contributions have been limited in scope. The incidence of accidents and industrial diseases is closely connected with the general problems of National Health. Workmen's Compensation is commonly regarded as a form of compulsory charity, as an awkward liability to be insured against as cheaply as possible, and of little if any personal concern to the ordinary employer. But it is not the problem of accidents and industrial diseases as such which interests us here, although a comprehensive inquiry into its social and economic signi-

[1] A branch of the Medical Research Council.

ficance seems to us overdue, but rather that part of the problem of accidents which directly relates to, and is indeed inseparable from, Workmen's Compensation.

Our historical review started with a description of the dreadful increase of accidents which was an aftermath of the industrial revolution. Men were slow to realize that such accidents were largely unavoidable and that the incidence would vary but little over a period of years. Legislators, so far as they felt inclined to deal with the question, which has only once been an important electoral issue, and judges, so far as they had an opportunity to pronounce upon related matters, were apt to consider all industrial injuries as 'accidental' unless evidence could be adduced to prove that they were due to individual carelessness, either of employer or employee. It is, of course, true that no accident can be wholly independent of the acts or behaviour of some individual, just as some persons do and others do not contract a contagious disease which may be epidemic. If A had not gone to school, or B, who was not in good health, had stayed in bed, or C had not reduced his powers of resistance by over-indulgence, all three might, like D–Z, have remained immune from it. In practice A, B, and C would doubtless regard themselves as the victims of an unlucky 'accident'. Yet it is well known that epidemics, in general, fall with greater force on some age-groups and some classes, rather than upon others, in conformity with a law of averages in which 'individual' cases are merged without distinction.

This knowledge, securely based upon statistics covering some eighty years, is of highest importance. So soon as industrial injuries are stripped of their 'accidental' character and are recognized as an unavoidable occupational risk which measures of safety and prevention can mitigate, but not remove, the workman's claim for compensation has the same moral basis as that of the victim of sickness. This view of the matter became, as we have shown, the driving force of the Workmen's Compensation movement in its early days. The same is true of industrial disease. Statistical regularity deprives a disease of its 'accidental' character and is a prima-facie reason for its inclusion among those scheduled for compensation purposes. The number and frequency of accidents is thus an essential element in the elaboration of compensation and disability schedules. Deficient as are available statistics, except in mining, there is ample evidence that its significance is greater than is usually believed. The incidence of accidents and industrial diseases may properly be stated in comparative terms, but the greatest caution is necessary in doing so. The amount of compensation paid for death or injury appears trifling when compared with the number of accidents per million men employed who incur no injury, or the number per £1,000 of commodities produced, but such comparisons serve merely to obscure the gravity of the problem. It is probably on this account that a recent publication of the International Labour Office stresses the fact that '*the frequency with which industrial accidents occur is much greater than is generally supposed* and that they are so numerous as to constitute a tremendous toll, not only on the health and happiness of the industrial classes, but on the economic production'.[1] Statistics have raised accidents to what Germans call *eine Gesetzmässigkeit*.[2] But appreciation of the important part played by the statistics as to the frequency of accidents must not blind us to the even greater significance of individual experience. The statistical 'law of the big number' has indeed deprived social phenomena, here as elsewhere, of their 'accidental' character and placed them in the category of unavoidably recurring conditions, to be dealt with systematically and methodically. It is not without significance that it has been in many cases the horror and tragedy of the single accident and the single case which, even with greater force than figures, has prompted the necessity for action. It is not by chance that Joseph Chamberlain came from a highly industrial area, and that the late Samuel Lever (afterwards Lord Leverhulme) first inaugurated the 'Safety First' movement in England after he had witnessed an accident at his soap works in 1892.[3] Mr. Joseph A. Parks, Chairman of the Department of Industrial Accidents of Massachusetts, stated recently in an address that when he was a boy of 11 he happened to witness an accident in an English cotton mill and was appalled to note that so little was done for the injured man. He had 'never been able to eradicate this profound impression'; in 1905 he introduced a Workmen's Compensation Act in Massachusetts, which became law in 1912.[4]

One of the present writers was brought up in the centre of a great industrial town in Lancashire, of which his father was vicar. The frequency of accidents to his own schoolfellows, as half-timers, and in later life, and the sights of the accident ward in the Hospital to which he was sometimes taken by his mother, made a profound impression upon his mind which, supplemented by his personal contacts as an M.P. with injured workmen in his constituency, gave rise to the pre-

[1] Cf. I.L.O., *Occupation and Health*, vol. i, 1930, p. 10.

[2] There is no English equivalent; regularity does not quite exhaust its meaning which contains the element of a fundamental and scientifically discernible law (*Gesetz*). The classic statistical essay of the late Prof. von Mayr, a pioneer of statistical science in Germany, was entitled *Die Gesetzmässigkeit im Wirtschaftsleben*. In our case statistical science has raised the conception of accidents to that of a *Gesetzmässigkeit im Wirtschaftsleben*.

[3] Cf. H. M. Vernon, *Accidents and their Prevention*, Cambridge, 1936, pp. 254 sqq.

[4] Cf. *Discussion of Industrial Accidents and Diseases*, U.S.A. Department of Labor, Division of Labor Standards, Washington, 1935, pp. 1–2.

sent work. So, too, Mr. Geoffrey Lloyd, when Under-Secretary of State for Home Affairs, speaking of his first experience of an industrial accident, said, 'it cured me of any tendency I might have had for taking such matters lightly'.[1]

Imagination can seldom transcend experience and the effect upon the mind of a single serious accident brings home to most people the necessity of accident compensation far more effectively than any figures. Nevertheless, the importance of statistics and general observations relating to the accidents will always be an important factor in the progress of accident prevention as well as Workmen's Compensation. Two sets of such statistics are in general use. The one relates to the occurrence of accidents as recorded by the Chief Inspectors of Factories and of Mines and elsewhere; the other to the amounts disbursed annually as compensation to workers of all kinds.

Accidents may be fatal or non-fatal. For the former we have complete and satisfactory figures, but the figures for non-fatal accidents are incomplete and, as now presented, often misleading. The number of persons reported killed in industrial accidents in the United Kingdom was:[2]

	1913	1923	1932	1936	1937
Grand Total	5,087	3,304	2,098	2,483	2,709
Main Groups:					
Factories and Workshops (industries proper) .	996	701	417	683	729
Factories and Workshops total . .	1,309	884	613	938	1,026
Coal Mines	1,753	1,297	881	790	859
Shipping	1,400	763	306	398	457
Railway Service	463	252	214	246	238

These figures only give a rough idea of the trend of fatal accidents, and admit of no far-reaching conclusions. Statistical revisions of the industrial groups make accurate comparisons between 1913, or even 1923 and 1937, impossible: the number of workers employed in successive decades has risen in some cases and fallen in others. Changes in industrial methods have altered the incidence of accidents. A smaller proportion of men, for example, are employed at the coal face in the mining industry, and more above ground. New methods have reduced the danger in some industries, but may have increased it in particular processes. New materials may have given rise to new industrial diseases. The figures are no more than a fair indication of the

[1] Cf. *Debates H.C.*, vol. 317, 1936–7, p. 1294.
[2] Cf. *Statistical Abstract*, December 1937, pp. 158–9. The special notes therein given as to each of these groups are important.

general trend. Taking the Census of Production figures, the average number employed (except out-workers) for all industrial trades (factory trades, building and contracting, mines and quarries, public utility services and government departments) in the United Kingdom was steady at 7,298,115 in 1924 and 7,141,434 in 1930; fatal accidents between these dates fell from 3,177 to 2,714, viz. by 9 per cent. But it remains true, in the words of Sir Duncan Wilson:[1]

Accidents still exact far too heavy a toll, though there are signs that (leaving out of account the last two years in which trade depression has materially affected the figures) the general level of fatal accidents is lower than formerly.

Statistical comparisons are even more difficult in the international sphere, and figures merely indicate general trends. A recent publication of the I.L.O. gave the following data in regard to the mining industry in different counties:[2]

	Number of workers (annual average)	Number of fatal accidents per 1,000 workers
Belgium 1920–7	163,040	1·038
France 1920–6	250,034	0·981
Great Britain 1920–8	1,137,982	0·997
Netherland 1920–8	29,219	1·127
Prussia 1920–8	569,555	2·156
U.S.A. 1920–6	511,580	4·464

Here, again, many factors apart from that of the relative safety in mines and the effectiveness of legislation may affect the statistical results. A single big disaster may affect the comparative figures for a decade. The structure and character of mines differs from country to country and affects the frequency of fatal accidents. The number of hours worked a week and the proportion of men employed above ground is bound to affect the figures. Yet, excluding the U.S.A., the figures show a certain uniformity, the yearly number of fatal accidents in mines lying between somewhat under 1 and somewhat over 2 per 1,000 workers.[3]

[1] Cf. *Report of the Chief Inspector of Factories and Workshops for 1932*, 1933, p. 8.
[2] Cf. I.L.O., *Occupation and Health*, vol. ii, Geneva, 1934, p. 260.
[3] A recent publication by the I.L.O., *Industrial Accident Statistics*, Geneva, 1938, has taken great pains to elucidate the difficulties of comparing industrial accident figures on an international basis. The Report tries to eliminate the difficulties of comparison of non-fatal accident frequency rates by utilizing so-called 'severity rates' (number of days lost) and 'man-hours of employment' as a comparative measure. The Report reaches the conclusion that 'in a field where so many defects are present in the source materials as is the case with industrial accident statistics, conclusions as to the relative risks in different countries are extremely hazardous', cf. p. 19. For our purpose the absolute, and not the comparative,

Great as the industrial death-rate by accident still is, in spite of the progress of preventive measures, non-fatal accidents are of even greater social importance. Deaths by industrial accident do not in general give rise to the disputes associated in the workman's experience with non-fatal accidents. Once the liability of the employer for compensation has been settled by legislation, assessment presents no difficulty. Non-fatal accidents involve legal and medical problems, questions of jurisdiction and administration, related to such matters as lump sum payments, assessment of damage, unfair settlements, rehabilitation of health. But for non-fatal accidents and their effects upon the life and social conditions of the injured, the question of state versus private insurance would not arise. In many cases, as we have shown elsewhere, legal controversy arises in regard to injuries, their nature, cause, and further developments, in particular in the case of industrial diseases. It is here that Workmen's Compensation and the character of accidents are closely related, as an increasing and more detailed knowledge of the frequency and nature of non-fatal injuries is bound to have a great effect upon the progress of compensative legislation.

Official statistics relating to non-fatal accidents are unfortunately so defective, except in mining, that it is not possible to make in regard thereto even the cautious generalizations possible in relation to fatal accidents. Sir Duncan Wilson stated in his Report for 1932 that 'any comparison of non-fatal accidents similar to that of fatal accidents would be invalidated by comparison with any date before 1923 as the Notice of Accidents Act, 1906, and the Workmen's Compensation Act 1923 have brought about changes in the standard of notification'.[1] He compares total accidents with fatal accidents for the period 1924–36,[2] but adds that no decisive conclusions can be drawn therefrom except that 'the risk of accident has tended to decrease, but this tendency has hitherto been masked by wide fluctuations from year to year', and that 'the credit for this improving situation can only be approximately distributed'.

Various abiding factors may contribute to a favourable trend, such as the activities of Factory Inspectors and educational measures among employers and employed. But these factors may be neutralized by disparate causes. In time of war or prosperity hours of work are longer and speed of production greater, more inexperienced young workers

---

magnitude and frequency of industrial accidents in various countries is what matters; but a study of this valuable treatise is indispensable to all those who wish to master the statistical intricacies of the matter.

[1] Cf. PEP, *Report on the British Health Services*, 1937, p. 71, where this has not been taken into account, and *Annual Report of the Chief Inspector of Factories for 1932*, 1933, p. 8.

[2] Cf. *Report for 1936*, pp. 6–8.

and more previously unemployed workers, long out of practice, are
absorbed and new machinery and materials with unknown risks
are installed.[1] Conversely, in times of depression, working hours are
shortened, production is slowed down, and accident- or negligence-
prone individuals tend to be displaced. If, as Sir D. Wilson says, 'a
rising toll of death and injury must still be regarded as a penalty to be
paid for increased prosperity', there would appear to be a strong case
for the more generous treatment of injured workmen, who alone pay
the penalty, by those who reap the reward or by the state.

While we prefer to attempt no statistical treatment of 'accident
rates', much may be learned from a detailed study of the non-fatal
accident figures, though these again are very incomplete. The figures
given by the Chief Inspector of Factories refer only to accidents under
the Factory and Workshops Act, 1901, and 'accident' means 'an
accident which is either fatal or disables the workman for more than
three days from earning full wages for the work at which he was
employed'. We do not know what the figure for all accidents would
have been. The figure of non-fatal accidents was 175,470 in 1936, but
to this the non-fatal figures in mines should be added.[2] The total
number of persons injured in mines was 137,163 in 1936, of which
135,329 cases in coal-mines (including shale and fireclay mines) under
the Coal Mines Act. The corresponding figures for 1937 were 141,936
and 139,951. The 'factory' figures include docks, buildings, warehouses, and railways. These figures, taken together, give a total for
1936 of 312,633 and for 1937 of 334,475 non-fatal injuries, which
may be accepted as a fair measure of the total of non-fatal accidents in
industry proper, subject to the reservation made in regard to the
meaning of 'accident'.[3]

But there is more to be said. The persons employed in factories
(the term 'Workshop' is obsolete under the new legislation) in 1935
was 5,197,643; the average number of persons employed at all mines
under the Coal and Metalliferous Mines Regulation Acts and at
quarries under the Quarries Act was 862,080.[4] Taken together this

[1] Cf. in particular *Report for 1937*, p. 25. Cf. also *Report for 1938*, 1939, p. 44. Widespread activity in the building trade coincides with an increase of 20 per cent. in the number of reported accidents; but no rash conclusions should be made: 'this increase is, no
doubt, in part due to a better standard of reporting and also to the extension of accident
notification requirements of the new Act to building operations generally.'

[2] This has not been done by PEP in its *Report on British Health Services*, 1937, p. 71.
N.B. The injured persons is the unit.

[3] Cf. *Report of Chief Inspector of Factories for 1936*, p. 81, and *Mines Department,
Annual Report for 1936*, p. 183. See also *Report for 1937*, p. 189. Non-fatal accidents are
such which disable the persons injured for more than three days.

[4] Cf. *Factories Report*, loc. cit., p. 99, *Mines Report*, loc. cit., p. 139.

would amount to about 6 million workers; if we take, according to the
last Census figures, the number of workers employed as builders,
bricklayers, and stone workers as about 750,000, that of railway
workers as about 300,000, and that of warehousemen as about 300,000,
leaving out dock workers, for whom no figures are available, we might
say that the non-fatal accident figures given above would relate to probably not more than 7,500,000 persons employed in factories, 'places',
and mines in Great Britain. These figures are not sufficient for our
purpose, for the Holman Gregory Report estimated at 15 million the
number of workers within the scope of the Act.[1]

Impressive as are the official accident figures, they do not elucidate
the whole incidence of non-fatal accidents upon the insured population
of 14–15 million people, nor do the Annual Home Office Reports on
Workmen's Compensation help us to do so; for the statistical information afforded is neither authoritative nor complete. The figures given
relate only to seven groups of 'industries'—a misleading term, for
while the Annual Report of the Chief Inspector of Factories excludes
such occupations as shipping and mines, Workmen's Compensation
statistics, surprisingly enough, include them as 'groups of industries', although former Acts and statistics have more appropriately
spoken of 'factories and workshops', and the Inspectorate Statistics
refer to docks, buildings, warehouses, and railways as 'places in which
accidents occur'. Of the 'seven groups of industries', viz. shipping,
factories, railways, docks, mines, quarries, and constructional work,
only four are 'industries', namely, factories, mines, quarries, and
constructional work. As factories and mines and quarries and constructional work are treated separately, we regard 'factories' in these
statistics as 'industries proper', a distinction which, as the reader will
later see, is not merely verbal.[2] These 'factories' again comprise the
following groups: Cotton Wool, &c., other Textiles, Wood, Metals
(extraction), Engine and Ship Building, other Metal Work, Paper and
Printing, China and Earthenware, and 'other factory industries'.

The difficulties of Workmen's Compensation statistics are not
exhausted when we state that they only relate to seven groups of occupations employing in 1937 only 7,959,063 persons.[3] Of the compensation paid, 82·6per cent. was paid by 144,571 employers who made
so-called 'collective returns', i.e. return supplied by Employer's Mutual

[1] The Census of Great Britain for 1931 reported a figure of 14,789,586 for occupied
persons and the estimated number of workpeople under the Unemployment Insurance
Acts were 13,338,700 in July 1936.

[2] In regard to this point, cf. the Census of Production in which Building and Contracting,
Mines and Quarries, are ranged as 'other trades' in contrast to 'Factory Trades'.

[3] Cf. for this and the following, *Workmen's Compensation Statistics during the Year 1937*,
Cmd. 5955, 1939.

Indemnity Associations and Insurance Companies who are under an Agreement with the Home Office to make returns on behalf of the employees belonging to or insured by them.

It should here be explained that whilst the great majority of the Mutuals undertake to cover all classes of risk under the Acts, some of them have hitherto indemnified their members against a part only of liabilities. For example, several important Associations, while indemnifying their members against the whole of the risks in fatal cases, have not shouldered the liability in disablement cases, except after the first six months. In these cases, the liability for the first six months has been met by payments made either by the member himself, or, less frequently, on his behalf by the Association acting not as insurers but as agents, the cost of compensation being recovered from the member. It appears that during 1937, the payments made in this way by members of the Associations, or by the Associations in the capacity of agents, amounted to £756,087 of which £722,111 was paid in the coal-mining industry. It is evident that these conditions tend to increase the statistical difficulties of some uniformity in the matter. Further, it should be remembered that no compensation is payable in Great Britain unless liability lasts three days; the figures relating to compensation, even only in the seven groups, cannot therefore be taken as indicating accidents in total. Dr. Norris states that the total number of industrial accidents involving personal injury in Great Britain may well be about 15 millions per annum.[1]

These minor injuries are, however, not our main concern. The 1937 Report stated that 15,525 returns were received from uninsured employers. Of these 2,456 gave particulars of payments of compensation under the Workmen's Compensation Acts, while 13,069 were to the effect that there had been no cases of compensation. It is well to remember here that the *Holman Gregory Report* estimated that the total number of uninsured employers within the Act then in force could not be less than 250,000.[2] There is no reason to suppose that the figure would be substantially less to-day. This figure contrasts painfully with the 15,525 returns to which the Report refers. The defect lies in the fact that, while under § 42 of the 1923 Act (which corresponds to § 12 (1) and (2) of the former Act) the Home Secretary is entitled to include 'any industry' in an obligatory scheme, in which case it would be under legal obligation to make returns, such regulations have only been applied to specified employments, viz. the 'industries' mentioned above. The regulations now in force date from October 17th 1913 and are certainly ripe for overhaul and extension. Every

[1] Cf. Dr. Norris in the *British Encyclopaedia of Medical Practice*, 1938, vol. vii, pp. 119–20.　　　　　　　　　　　[2] Cf. *Holman Gregory Report*, p. 17.

employer, covered by the Workmen's Compensation Acts, whether factory or small employer, might reasonably be obliged to make a return, thus enabling the Home Department in its Annual Report to give more information than merely that which relates, in its own words, to 'certain industries'.[1] Domestic servants might perhaps be excluded for administrative reasons.

The figures, nevertheless, are impressive. The number of cases were:

	1931	1933	1934	1935	1936	1937
Total . . .	398,886	362,043	403,688	425,339	461,557	488,865
Fatal . . .	2,315	2,072	2,229	2,640	2,286	2,370
Non-fatal . .	396,571	359,971	401,459	422,699	459,271	486,495

These figures relate to all industrial injuries, i.e. by accidents or disease, for which compensation was paid. Taking accidents alone, the figures for 1937[2] were: Total number of cases 470,584, of which 2,345 were fatal and 468,239 disablement cases. Not all these cases occurred in one calendar year, for we have to distinguish between:

	Accidents	Industrial disease
Those continued from previous years.	58,589	6,518
First payment made during year	409,650	11,738

The total is certainly great enough to illustrate the vast importance of the accident as an economic factor. They show how great is the toll of industry and other occupations on working-class life and health. The trend since 1937 is upward especially as regards fatal accidents.

Viewed as a whole, the figures falsify the anticipations of the framers of the Workmen's Compensation bills. It was calculated by the Home Office, in estimating the probable effect of the passing of the 1897 Act that 150,000 accidents a year would fall within its scope. To-day, the figure is more than three times as great. The late Sir John Collie, who could claim an experience of over thirty years in the matter, declared that the 'disparity between anticipation and realization' remains striking, even if due allowance is made for the extensions made by subsequent Acts, and for the possible increase in the numbers employed. Changes in the methods of presenting the statistics on the subject made it impossible for him to give exact comparisons; but 'it is not a question of an increase in thousands of cases, but of hundreds of thousands'.[3]

[1] Cf. also H. M. Vernon, *Accidents and Prevention*, Cambridge, 1936, p. 13. 'We know comparatively little about the frequency of the uncomparable accidents.' He stresses the fact that 'minor accidents' are not reported.

[2] Cf. *Workmen's Comp. Statistics*, loc. cit., p. 19.

[3] Cf. Sir John Collie, *Workmen's Compensation. Its Medical Aspect*, 1933, pp. 1–2.

The vast number of industrial accidents led to a change in the treatment of employers' liability and workmen's compensation. Its significance once realized, the early notion of 'accidental' happenings, partly attributable to the fault of employers, but mostly to that of workmen, partly to fate or 'Acts of God', was relegated to the limbo of outworn dogmas. It became clear that accidents and injuries were bound to occur in great numbers and that it was in vain to regard every single case as an exceptional occurrence. The principle of 'occupational risk' superseded in every country the principle of 'employer's liability' as a basis for the right of compensation, as the risks inherent in work came to be regarded as the consequence of the normal development of human activity.[1] Statistical investigation has lately gone much farther. Taking the 'great number' of accidents and injuries as the starting-point and assuming them to be an unavoidable corollary of some 'law' (*Gesetzmässigkeit*), statistical investigators set themselves to analyse the various facts on lines which might enable them to place a constructive interpretation upon the differentiations revealed by such an inquiry. Once more fundamental study took the place of casual experience: these studies are still in their early stages but deserve every encouragement.

[1] Cf. the very appropriate remarks to this matter in I.L.O., *The International Labour Organization and Social Insurance*, Geneva, 1936, pp. 26–8.

CHAPTER II

PSYCHO-PHYSICAL ASPECTS

But as the unthought-on accident is guilty
To what we wildly do, so we profess
Ourselves to be the slaves of chance, and flies
Of every wind that blows.

SHAKESPEARE, *A Winter's Tale*, Act IV, Scene 3.

If you can bring influence to bear external to the workman (i.e. one over which he can exercise no control) you will be successful; and, if you cannot or do not, you will never be wholly successful.

SIR THOMAS LEGGE, *Industrial Maladies*, 1934.

INDUSTRIAL accidents and injuries are generally due either to some subjective failure in the human element, to an objective failure of machinery, or to cognate fortuitous causes beyond the subjective control of the worker. The witty phrase *Die Tücke des Objekts*—'the perversity of the inanimate'—is a popular slogan in the German tongue, reminiscent of Swinburne's reference to 'the malice of things'.[1] It is specially applicable to accidents and injuries not directly ascribable to a failure of the human element, such as earthquakes and tidal waves; boiler and other explosions in mines and factories and the sudden and unpredictable failure of some vital part of a great machine are almost in the same category. No hard-and-fast line can be drawn, but the human element plays no part in many and is only a subsidiary factor in most industrial accidents. In the words of Professor Sargant Florence:

Industrial accidents are usually neither wholly humanly circumstanced nor yet wholly mechanically, but arise most commonly from the fact that potentially errant human nature is employed on potentially dangerous occupations.[2]

That is the issue: to third parties in general, including employers and inspectors, the human element appears, in most cases, to be at fault. 'The reasonable man', as he appears to those versed in our Common Law, is thus apostrophized by Mr. Justice Farrow, that delightful creation of Mr. A. P. Herbert's imaginative genius:[3]

Devoid of any human weakness, with not one single saving vice, without ill-nature, avarice, or absence of mind, as careful for his own safety as for that of

[1] Swinburne, *Hymn of Man*, line 81.
[2] Prof. P. Sargant Florence, *Economics of Fatigue and Unrest*, 1924, p. 291.
[3] A. P. Herbert, *Misleading Cases in the Common Law*, 1927, p. 11.

others, this excellent but odious character stands like a monument in our Courts of Justice, vainly appealing to his fellow-citizens to order their lives after his own example. I have called him a myth, in so far as there are few if any of this mind and temperament to be found in the ranks of living men, the title is well chosen.

It is tacitly assumed that 'a reasonable man' should be able, in the course of his daily work, to incur a risk in the performance of his duty a hundred, or a thousand times a day for years on end without once transgressing the rules of safety. Should he make a slip, and be injured, the fault is his alone.

Carelessness certainly plays an important part in industrial hazards. 'It is appalling to note the number of accidents which could have been avoided by ordinary care and forethought.'[1] In the woollen and worsted industry 15 per cent. of the total accidents were caused through cleaning machinery in motion. 'Nothing seems wholly to overcome the British worker's dislike of what he considers timidity and fussiness. The old school accept industrial risks as inevitable, while with boys a contempt for danger is part of their heritage.'[2] This attitude of mind probably increases the incidence and cost of sepsis, consequent on neglect of trivial injuries, but excessive anxiety about trivial cuts may well make workmen nervous and do more harm than good. The belief, sedulously fostered by advertisement, that danger can be avoided by dabbing the cut with a proprietary disinfectant has little justification unless the treatment is applied by expert hands. Sir John Collie ascribed the majority of accidents to the failure of the human element and not to machinery. Dr. Donald C. Norris quotes Greig (1937) and the Industrial Safety Survey (1937) of the International Labour Office which estimates that 72·2 per cent. of industrial accidents are attributable to the 'human factor', i.e. causes intrinsic to the individual injured.[3]

To accept this point of view is not to condone the existing gaps in the technical defences of employers and workmen against accidents, or against injury arising from defects which may be altogether beyond the operator's control. We need only to quote a passage out of the Chief Inspector's *Report for 1936* (p. 21):

The prevention of accidents at transmission machinery or 'mill-gearing' is a subject to which Inspectors have for years given special attention, both by verbal instruction and distribution of official precautionary leaflets. Accounts of distressing fatalities appear from time to time in the press; prosecutions have been undertaken with fair regularity. Safety Committees have discussed the matter and posters have been exhibited, yet driving belts and revolving shafts continue to take their grim toll. Most employers and persons in charge appear to be aware of the danger,

[1] *Report of Chief Inspector of Factories for 1936*, 1937, p. 20.   [2] Ibid., pp. 20–1.
[3] Cf. Greig, E. C., *Industrial Welfare*, 1937, pp. 19 and 29. Dr. Norris in the *Brit. Encyclop. of Medical Science*, 1938, vol. vii, p. 121.

but while substantial progress has been made in fencing and exhibiting rules forbidding approach to mill-gearing in motion, there is much to be done. Idle belts are quite commonly seen hanging loosely upon the revolving shafting where belt perches or hangers should have been provided for safe support, comparatively few machine belt-mounting appliances are in use, and belt-mounting poles are viewed with suspicion by workpeople.

Here again, the line between the 'human element' and the 'perversity of the inanimate' is difficult to draw. Another example, showing a danger inherent in a technical appliance is the following:[1]

A fatality during the painting of a hangar roof illustrates the difficulty of protecting men on the average large area of floor below. The painters had placed planks along the roof trusses and when one was moved to the next position, it fell upon a man 50 feet below. The proper course in this class of work is to supplement the protection afforded by tarpaulins by employing a man on the floor to warn persons against passing under the particular section.

Though the human element plays its part in most accidents, the victims are very frequently third parties whose acts and omissions in no way contribute to the accident.

Another field where the human and non-human causation of the accident may both be active is that of explosions. Here the occurrence may be entirely dependent on the action of a workman.[2] Some types of accidents may be prevented, as in the case of vessels containing steam or gas under pressure by testing, fitting safety valves, and periodic inspection. When, in spite of all precautions, accidents occur, they are in general due to some hidden and unrecognizable flaw in the appliances themselves.

Attempts to allocate the causes of accidents to human and non-human factors should therefore be viewed with the greatest reserve. Subject to this proviso, we set forth below the tentative analysis of an American writer, based upon general experience, as to the various groups of causes which may be responsible for an accident.[3]

    1. Machinery.
    2. Vehicles.
    3. Explosives, electricity, fire, heat, corrosives.
    4. Poisons, occupational diseases.
    5. Falls.

---

[1] Cf. *Report for 1936*, p. 23.

[2] For example cf. *Report of Chief Inspector for 1932*, pp. 95–7; *Report for 1936*, p. 26; and *Report for 1938*, pp. 46–7.

The explosion of an economizer caused the death of four persons and injuries to four others. Inquiry showed that it was due to the failure of the foreman mechanic to close a flue damper after the water inlet and outlet valves had been shut, the economizer thus becoming a closed vessel in which steam ultimately was generated.

[3] Cf. J. D. Hackett, *Health Maintenance in Industry*, Chicago, 1925, p. 281.

6. Stepping on or striking against objects.
7. Falling objects, not being handled by the injured.
8. Hand tools, flying nails, chips or particles.
9. Animals.
10. Miscellaneous.

The above analysis[1] corresponds approximately to the American Accident Form in current use. It should be studied in the light of the official figures of the Chief Inspector of Factories[2] from which we have prepared the following summary:

Causation of all Reported Accidents in Industry, 1938

Total of all accidents (the injured person is the unit)	180,103
Machinery moved by mechanical power	32,767
Transport (whether moved by Power or not):	
(a) Railways	1,616
(b) Other vehicles	1,573
Handling goods, &c.	56,716
Persons falling	12,795
Struck by falling body	19,930
Use of hand tools	17,802
Stepping on or striking against objects	12,795
Molten metal or hot or corrosive substances	8,129
Machinery not moved by mechanical power	3,540
Electricity	560
Fires (not dangerous occurrences or explosions)	340
Gassing	190
Explosions (including boiler back-draughts)	1103

The number of 'dangerous occurrences'[3] was 722 and related to seven kinds of such accidents consequent upon bursting of revolving vessels, &c., collapse or failure of cranes, &c., explosions or fire, electrical short-circuits or failures of electrical machinery, explosions or fire, due in particular to the ignition of dust, gas, or vapour, or the ignition of celluloid, &c., and explosion of a receiver or container used for the storage of gases.[4]

This careful analysis of accidents in a wide field relates, for the most part, to injuries attributable to technical factors and not to any act or omission of the injured worker. A particularly tragic case affecting 81

---

[1] Cf. also Prof. S. Florence, loc. cit., *passim*.

[2] Cf. *Report for 1938*, pp. 124–5 for more detailed figures.

[3] As notified to Inspectors in accordance with the Dangerous Occurrences Notification Order, 1935, made under § 5 of the Notice of Accidents Act, 1906. See § 159 of Factories Act, 1937.

[4] For further details see *Report of Chief Inspector for 1938*, p. 127.

of 150 workers in an ice-cream factory is reported under 'Ammonia' in the *Report for 1938*,[1] where a large volume of ammonia escaped when the nozzle of an ice-cream making machine was forced off; inflammation of the respiratory passages and burns were caused, 60 people had to seek hospital treatment, 2 died.

Mining exacts a heavy toll of fatal and non-fatal injuries. The number of persons injured by accidents below and above ground during 1937 in mines and quarries under the Coal Mines Act, 1908, so far as particulars are available, was 140,645, equivalent to 175·1 cases per 1,000 persons employed in mines, as compared with 152·1 in 1932. and 181·4 in 1929.[2] They may be conveniently summarized thus:

	1935	1936	1937
Total accidents below ground . . .	123,124	125,034	128,922
„ „ above ground . . .	10,632	10,934	11,723
(a) *Principal causes below ground:*			
Falls of ground	47,156	47,535	48,269
Haulage accidents	34,352	33,649	33,668
Shaft accidents	196	238	337
Explosions of firedamp or coal dust .	59	56	55
Miscellaneous.	41,361	43,556	46,593
(b) *Principal causes above ground:*			
On railway sidings or tramways .	3,639	3,537	3,617
Other accidents	6,993	7,397	8,106

The accident rate for 1937 per 1,000 persons employed in the United Kingdom above and below ground on occupations covered by the Coal Mines Act were:

Killed . . . . . 1·07
Killed and seriously injured . . 5·26
(*Report of Chief Inspector for 1937*, p. 87.)

Of 803,359 persons *employed under the Act* 3,363 were seriously injured, of whom all but 314 were underground. The Inspector's reports make it clear that, excluding an unduly large category of 'miscellaneous' accidents, each group has its underlying types of human and technical failures which cannot easily be distinguished. The Inspector of the Midland and Southern Division regards 84 per cent. of haulage accidents as 'avoidable'. Of these he assigns one in four to the 'human element' and the remainder to various causes including in-

---

[1] Cf. p. 77; also *Annual Report of the Secretary for Mines for 1936*, p. 203, and ibid. for 1937, p. 207.
[2] Cf. ibid., p. 207.

adequate facilities or faulty conditions. The Chief Inspector is satisfied that:

There can be little hope of improvement unless the conditions under which
haulage operations are carried on are improved; unless stop-blocks and other
similar apparatus are provided and maintained in working order; unless persons
are prohibited and actually prevented from travelling on haulage roads whilst the
haulage is in motion; unless heavier and better rail-tracks are laid and unless
stricter supervision is exercised by the management.

It seems clear that the fault here lies with the 'object'; in other cases
responsibility is divided, 'neither the management nor the workmen
are free from blame'. An Inspector reports of the Swansea Division,
that 'derailments were the primary cause of 30 per cent. of all the
mechanical haulage accidents' and in this connexion makes several
suggestions for technical improvements. The Inspector of the Scotland Division suggests that over 75 per cent. of derailments 'were
avoidable by the use of ordinary common sense, better haulage gear and
more commodious roads'. The hazard of the 'human element' is not
to be underrated.

The personal factor is one of the most important, as well as perhaps the most
baffling, connected with the subject of accidents. Is the prevalence of accidents
classed as 'unavoidable by ordinary caution' due to an attitude which accepts
inevitability of accidents, the forgetfulness and indifference, or to inability to adapt
oneself to rapidly changing conditions?

In connection with the latter possibility it is perhaps not out of place to remember the very low accident rate in winding and the use of explosives, where conditions are not liable to change unexpectedly and to compare them with accidents
from falls of ground and haulage, where the reverse is the case.[1]

He also notes that a large turnover of labour goes hand in hand with
a high accident rate and that accidents to new-comers are out of all
proportion to their numbers. Two out of three non-fatal accidents
connected with the use of explosives were due to foolhardy or negligent failure to take proper shelter. Given stricter supervision and
proper discipline, nearly all such accidents could be prevented, as in
the case of the Wharncliffe Woodmoor Nos. 1, 2, and 3 Colliery,
Yorkshire, where on August 5th 1936, 58 lives were thus lost. 'Lack
of discipline', as the Chief Inspector called it, here entailed the death
of men with no more responsibility for the explosion than the passen-
gers on a ship which meets with disaster.

'Falls of ground' entail more serious injuries than any other group
of mining accidents. Inspectors find it hard to decide the relative

[1] Mr. H. J. Humphrys, Divisional Inspector of Mines (Yorkshire), in a statement submitted to the Royal Commission on Safety in Coal Mines of 1936. *Evidence*, Monday,
March 5th 1936, p. 136.

importance of causative factors. The rapid change from hand- to machine-mining has not led everywhere to a higher rate for fatal and serious accidents,[1] but there is little doubt that in some mines the din of the mechanical cutters drowns the warning noises that presage a fall of ground. The comprehensive recommendations of the Chief Inspector of Mines in his *Report for 1936* for the better safeguarding of men against this risk suggests that whilst much of the hazard is due to the non-human factor, the human element must be better protected against its weaknesses.

This is equally true of surface accidents. Year after year, several persons[2] are killed when oiling moving machinery. Warning notices are exhibited and penalties provided; both are ignored. If machinery must be oiled when it is running, the provision of lubricators placed outside the fencing should be compulsory.[3]

The necessity of fencing was recognized almost a century ago, but there is still room for improvement. Examples of machinery guarded by simple post and rail fences still exist.[4] Four men were killed during 1936 after they had deliberately climbed through fencing erected for their protection. Sixty years of compulsory education has not been accompanied by a corresponding growth in intelligence, and carelessness was never commoner. 'Such fences are not enough,' says the Chief Inspector: it would seem that the only real protection against the 'human element' is to make accidents technically as well as humanly impossible. Hoist accidents teach the same lesson. The total number of such accidents was 490 in 1936, of which 20 were fatal. Of the 490 accidents, 230 were due to 'crushes'; viz. a person was crushed between the cage and some part of the structure of the well. This can be prevented by the installation of gates automatically interlocked with pickets so spaced that no limb can protrude, thus incidentally eliminating accidents by falling down the well. The new Factory Act includes stringent provisions: many old hoists and almost all new ones are so fitted, but sometimes only after an accident. The fact that many, indeed most, accidents are due to human carelessness does not diminish the responsibility of employers to do or the State to require whatever is possible to protect fools from the results of their folly even if, as Herbert Spencer predicted, the consequence should be to fill the world with fools. Herbert Spencer did not work in a factory, and in his voluminous works and elaborate note-books there is no indication that he had ever even entered one or was acquainted with industrial hazards.

---

[1] Cf. *Report on Mines for 1936*, p. 83.

[2] 6 in 1936.   [3] *Report for 1936*, p. 83.

[4] A special pamphlet of the Mines Department was published giving advice in the matter in 1928: *Fencing and other Safety Precautions for Machinery in Mines*.

When a process involves an element of danger, the men employed on it are selected with care, and work with caution: in proportion as it becomes 'fool-proof' it tends to be worked by less intelligent and less experienced persons. The incidence of accidents in various occupations differs widely. The accident rate of professional chauffeurs, for example, is far lower than that of owner-drivers. But there is no simple distinction between safe and dangerous occupations. Assuming that the whole body of occupied (and retired) civilian males has a comparative mortality figure of 1,000 from all causes of death combined, Dr. Vernon[1] has shown that in the period under review (1921–3) 4·9 per cent. were due to accidents.

			Comparative mortality rate	
			All causes	Accidents
All occupied and retired civilian males			1,000	49
Coal-miners			1,126	157
	All causes	Accidents		
1. Conveying material to shaft . .	1,204	211		
2. Making and repairing roads. .	1,192	161		
3. Hewers and getters . . .	983	98		
Average . . .	1,126	157		
Barge and boatmen			1,290	146
Iron-ore miners			954	98
Building trade labourers			1,060	66
Shop assistants and salesmen			973	28
Gardeners and their labourers			707	21
Cotton weavers			1,048	11

These figures, though not up to date, are of some significance. The death-rate of coal-miners from fatal accidents is three times as high as that of the general male population, but their general mortality rate is only 11 per cent. higher. The fatal accident rate for iron-ore miners is double that of the general population, but their general mortality rate is lower.

Dr. Vernon concludes from these figures that non-industrial occupations are not necessarily safer than industrial. We cannot endorse this claim unreservedly: the average age of iron-ore miners and shop assistants is certainly lower than that of cotton weavers, and gardeners' labourers are usually young. But the table shows that the fatal accident

[1] Cf. H. M. Vernon, *Accidents and their Prevention*, Cambridge, 1936, pp. 18 and 19. Cf. also Chap. IV where the Registrar-General's *Decennial Supplement on Occupational Mortality* is cited.

rate is only one and not invariably the most important element in the general mortality rate of men in a given occupation.

An interesting comparison of occupational mortality rates is found in the recent Registrar-General's *Decennial Supplement* as regards coal-mining:

Death-rate per 100,000 living: 1930–2

	Ages				
	16–20	20–25	25–35	35–45	45–65
All males	268	328	346	559	1,114
Coal-miners	342	381	417	645	1,146

The Report in general bears little relation to our purpose, as the causes of death as related to the particular disease-probability in the different trades are only occasionally mentioned or treated. But it may be noted that, for instance, as regards skilled glass workers, the Report states *for certain groups of them* 'a significantly high mortality from respiratory tuberculosis' and probably significant 'excess from bronchitis and asthma'. It also mentions the high mortality rate of potters due solely to a specific factor in their work, which is productive of a particular disease, viz. silicosis, 'which, if it could be removed, would leave them with the normal mortality of their class'. The normal mortality of their wives indicates that the occupation involves no special social and environmental handicaps. In this respect 'it contrasts strongly with such an occupation as that of a coal miner, whose unsatisfactory total mortality rates seem to arise not from occupational risks but from the unsatisfactory general environment of coal mining areas'. The latter statement reaffirms our opinion that it is not advisable to draw too definite conclusions from occupational mortality figures in general as regards the incidence of industrial disease.[1]

Mark Twain's humorous warning against lying in bed in view of the heavy death-rate in that posture must ever be borne in mind by students of statistics.

Agricultural conditions in the U.S.A. will not bear comparison with those in Europe where mechanization is less prevalent. But the figures show that manufacture and mining had not the heaviest toll of fatal accidents. The 'frequency rate' per 1,000,000 man-hours of exposure to risk in 1934 was, in all industries, 15·29, reaching 83·83 in the lumber industry, and falling to 3·13 in tobacco manufacture. But between these two extremes the intermediate rates showed a greater regularity, most of them ranging between 10 and 30.[2]

[1] Registrar-General, *Decennial Supplement*, Part IIa. *Occupational Mortality*, 1938, pp. 81, 89, 90.
[2] Cf. *Handbook of Labor Statistics*, Washington, 1936, pp. 279–80.

More statistical information tends to reveal an ever-increasing range of occupations, which though non-industrial, are liable to a fairly heavy accident risk.[1] The accident rate will, of course, vary in different industries and occupations. But we should not be led thereby to confine our attention to the most dangerous trades. The regularity of accidents makes itself felt in every branch or group of occupation, as English statistics, if they existed, would show as clearly as do the American figures. The Frequency of Accident is largely due to what may be called the psycho-physics of work, a term first introduced into economics and analysed in detail by the late Professor Max Weber.[2] The term relates to certain psychological and physical circumstances and factors influencing the efficiency of work, such as environment, hours of work, fatigue, and external distractions. Collis and Greenwood have noted certain groups of facts which may affect occupational risks and accident ratios. They speak of the accident being, to some extent, due to 'reaction to environment influence', viz.:[3]

- (*a*) Fatigue.
- (*b*) Psychical influences.
- (*c*) Illumination.
- (*d*) Temperature.

Prof. Florence, who in 1921 studied the effects of fatigue and over-strain upon the accident rate, has devoted particular attention to the 'hours of work',[4] as has also the Chief Inspector of Factories. It is unlikely, however, that a further general shortening of the hours of work would now noticeably affect the accident rate. The custom of rest pauses of 10–15 minutes about the middle of the working spell appears to be increasing, and several instances were quoted to the Inspectorate where no reduction in output has resulted in spite of the loss of working time—a result which well corresponds to the early experiences of Earl Brassey and Prof. Chapman.[5]

Recent research has corroborated the pioneer conclusions of Prof. Florence. In an article published by a medical specialist in *Mine Disasters* it is stated 'that chronic over-fatigue will cause inco-ordination

---

[1] A special investigation in the U.S.A. showed that there occurred 1,570 accidents to telegraph messengers during 1931, involving absence from work, of which 735 were serious, including 6 cases of death, and 12 of permanent injuries. Cf. Ellen Nathalie Mathews, 'Accidents to Telegraph Messengers', in *Monthly Labor Review*, 1934, p. 14.

[2] Cf. Max Weber, 'Zur Psychophysik der Arbeit', *Archiv für Sozialwissenschaft*, 1908 and 1909.

[3] Cf. Edgar W. Collis and Major Greenwood, *The Health of the Industrial Worker*, London, 1921, pp. 176 sqq.   [4] Cf. Sargant Florence, loc. cit., pp. 292 sqq.

[5] Cf. *Report of Chief Inspector of Factories for 1932*, p. 109.

of the muscles and a greatly increased tendency to accident'. An investigator in this field found that 82·8 per cent. of a certain group of accidents were the result of personal factors, of which fatigue was one of the most important. The conditions of work in the pits, such as ventilation, temperature, humidity in the air, the method of lighting, may greatly contribute to the greater or lesser existence of fatigue.[1] A good description of 'fatigue' in its effect on accidents is given by Eric Farmer, *The Cause of Accidents*, London, 1932, p. 11: 'Fatigue plays a large part in accident causation.'[2] The effect of shorter or longer hours of work is difficult to assess. When business is slack the shorter hours of work may be responsible for a decrease in accidents in times of prosperity[3]—absolutely or relatively—whilst speeding up and overtime tend to increase accident-proneness. But the nature of the work and many other factors are involved. A tired taxi-driver is more likely to have an accident than a jaded girl in a cigarette factory. Once it is accepted that fatigue may be a cause of accidents, it follows that fatigue is a psychopathic source of accidents beyond individual control.

The effect of fatigue caused by long hours upon the accident rate was recognized nearly a century ago. Mrs. Gaskell referred to it in 1849 as an established fact in her novel *Mary Barton*. Her discerning references to over-solicitation by undertakers and to lapses of insurance policies due to unemployment show her to have been well informed as to the social evils of her day. It is a book which deserves to be read by every student of the consequences of the Industrial Revolution.

Recent researches have shown that, apart from the 'hours of work', 'time' has still other effects on the risk of accidents. There is the 'length of employment' which plays a not inconsiderable part in the morphology of accidental risk. An investigation into the average number of employees injured daily in the metal trades of the U.S.A. gave the following results:[4]

---

[1] Cf. *Mine Disasters*. Special Supplement to *Compressed Air Engineering*, Dec. 1937, pp. 15–16. Also a valuable series of studies by Prof. Neville Moss of Birmingham University in the *Proceedings of the Institute of Mining Engineers*.

[2] A particular problem arises in regard to 'meal time accidents' of juvenile workers. Care should be taken that young workers should not have access to prohibited places during meal times. Cf. *Report of Chief Inspector for 1937*, pp. 49–50.

[3] Cf. Florence, p. 283: *English Experience*. 'The accident rate probably fluctuates with business activity, but in recent years the deterring event has undoubtedly been the reduction of hours.' Cf. also E. L. Macklin (Superintending Inspector of Factories), *Report for 1936*, p. 20.

[4] Cf. *Cause and Prevention of Accidents in the Iron and Steel Industry*, Bureau of Labor Statistics, Bulletin No. 298, Washington, 1922. Also J. D. Hackett, *Health Maintenance in Industry*, Chicago, 1925, p. 283.

Length of employment	Male	Female	Total
First day	166	294	460
Second day to end of week	38	45	83
Second week to end of month . . .	11	6	17
Second month to end of sixth month . .	1	5	1·5

It is to be noted that from this particular experience 81·4 per cent. of the accidents occurred on the first day of employment, and over 96 per cent. happened within the first week of employment. Cases like this demonstrate as Hackett writes: 'The vital need in certain occupations for instructing and supervising the new worker.'

An interesting statistical comparison has been worked out by Mr W. E. Harding (Superintending Inspector) as to the relation of length of employment and young workers' accidents. He, too, found that greater liability to accidents prevails during the initial stages of employment: 10·4 per cent. of the boys and 24·4 per cent. of the girls who were injured during the first six months in a sample set of seventy-seven factories (about 55,000 workers) were injured during the first week of the first six months. In the German works of the Friedrich Krupp AG, figures relating to this sociological phenomenon gave the following results:

	Accidents Per cent.
First year of employment. . .	38·4
Second ,, ,, ,, . . .	11·5
Third ,, ,, ,, . . .	6·4
Fourth ,, ,, ,, . . .	5·4
Fifth ,, ,, ,, . . .	5·4[1]

The accident-proneness of the new worker is thus fully recognized by the English inspectorate,[2] and the National Safety Council in the U.S.A. has long paid particular attention to the problem of safeguarding new entrants into industry.[3]

Day and night work. 'There is a definite relation between accident and time', writes Hackett,[4] 'more accidents are apt to occur at night

[1] Cf. R. Schwenger, *Die betriebliche Sozialpolitik in der westdeutschen Großindustrie*, München und Leipzig, 1934, p. 85.

[2] Cf. also E. L. Macklin in *Annual Report of Chief Inspector for 1936*, p. 20 under 'Accidents': '. . . the considerable influx into industry of persons who, by reason of long inactivity had lost temporarily some of their skill and alertness, while others endeavoured to make good by taking risks or making efforts beyond their capacity.' Cf. also Hackett, loc. cit., p. 299: 'Numerous statistical investigations have demonstrated the increased risk of accident run by the inexperienced, newly hired "green hand".' Cf. also for the same point Sargant Florence, loc. cit., pp. 300–1.

[3] Cf. *Teaching Safety to New Employees*, Safe Practices Pamphlet No. 65, n.d. Cf. also Collis and Greenwood, loc. cit., p. 201.   [4] Cf. Hackett, loc. cit., p. 284.

than by day, principally because the light is bad, but also because the
worker himself is not apt to be in as good a mental or physical condition
and there is less supervision than in the day-time. Were it not for the
fact that there is less congestion, less speed in work and that there are
more experienced workers, it is probable that the night accident rate
would be much higher than is generally the case.'[1] A statistical investigation carried out by the Departmental Committee on Lighting in
Factories and Workshops in 1915 indicated that accidents of certain
types occur more frequently during the winter months when daylight
hours are short.[2] According to Farmer,[3] however, the accident rate
during night is, according to some statistical tests, highest in the first
hours of a shift, and gradually falls to a minimum in the last hour.
Farmer, agreeing with Vernon, suggests that this is due to night
workers getting up some hours before they start work and spending the
time in amusements and having substantial meals.

On the other hand Sir Richard Redmayne, then Chief Inspector
of Mines, in giving evidence before the Sankey Commission, alluded
to the tendency for accidents to occur in the *early* portion of a shift,
and said that this was what might be expected when a working place
had been standing for any period, e.g. during the night.[4] Such factors
tend to obscure the line dividing 'hourly incidence between accidents
in day and night shifts' and between night and day accidents. But if
the worker is more liable to accidents after his evening's distractions he
should be less so in the morning after a night in bed. In this connexion
the efficiency and sufficiency of lighting is of first importance. Due
consideration has been paid to it by the Inspectorate for some time,
and since 1931 inquiries have been made, during the winter months,
into the conditions in the basic industries of Sheffield with special
regard to the fact that bad lighting increases the danger of accidents,
and the risk of night work in particular.[5] Sufficient and suitable
lighting is now required in factories by § 5 of the Factories Act, 1937,
and the Secretary of State is empowered to prescribe general standards
of lighting for factories and special standards for any class of factory
or for any process.[6]

Max Weber's studies show that the workman's efficiency varies

[1] Cf. also Florence, loc. cit., p. 298. Night work as a cause of increased accident risk is
also mentioned by Vernon, loc. cit., pp. 29 sqq.

[2] Cf. vol. i, of *First Report* (Cd. 8000), 1915, p. xii. The second *Report* was published in
1921, the third in 1922, the fourth in 1938 (see p. 19). The subject is under constant
consideration of the Home Office. Cf. *Lighting in Factories and Workshops*, Welfare
Pamphlet No. 7, issued by the Home Office, 5th edn. 1937, pp. 17–18 and *passim*.

[3] Cf. loc. cit., p. 19.   [4] *Sankey Commission Evidence*, Q. 5202.

[5] Cf. *Report of Chief Inspector for 1936*, pp. 91–2.

[6] Cf. also the statement in ibid. *1937*, pp. 22–3.

appreciably during the week. The accident rate varies likewise. In German mines, for instance, the percentage of accidents between 1894 and 1915 was:

Per cent.

on Monday	.	.	.	15·47
Tuesday	.	.	.	16·90
Wednesday	.	.	.	16·28
Thursday	.	.	.	16·20
Friday .	.	.	.	16·33
Saturday	.	.	.	16·87
Sunday .	.	.	.	2·05

This table does not reveal the number of man-hours worked on each day: the low figure for Monday may be due to smaller numbers then at risk. The high figure on Saturday, when in general fewer hours are worked, is certainly not accidental and the drop at midweek is significant.[1] While there is apparently no general agreement as regards the lesser frequency of accidents on Mondays,[2] it is unanimously agreed that peak comes at the end of the week.[3] Accidents which may be regarded as due—so far as the human element is concerned—to casual negligence assume a new significance if such carelessness appears to be regularly enhanced on certain days of the week.

The same consideration applies to the weakening of the workman's mental alertness by exhausting temperatures. Dr. Vernon quotes the following example:

Accident Rates of Miners in Relation to Dry Bulb Temperature

Temperature range (in degrees Fahrenheit)	Accident frequency per million hours worked (1927–8)
Coal-face workers:	
under 70°	133
70–79° . . .	144
80° or more . . .	173
Others underground:	
under 70°	57
70–74° . . .	81
75° or more . . .	92

The relation between heat-accidents is manifest.[4]

A last factor to be mentioned as having its effect upon the different

[1] Cf. I.L.O., *Occupation and Health*, Geneva, 1934, vol. ii, p. 259.

[2] Cf. Florence, loc. cit., pp. 292 sqq. and 296, who arrives at a different result in respect of Mondays.

[3] Cf. Hackett, loc. cit., p. 284. Of a number of 34,886 accidents 13·5 per cent. occurred on a Monday, while the percentage gradually increased to 18·2 per cent. on Friday.

[4] Cf. loc. cit., p. 79.

degrees of accident proneness is the age of the worker. Here, the fact of the young worker stands in the foreground. The toll which accidents take year by year from young workers is appalling. 'Age', writes Hackett,[1] 'affects the frequency and severity of injuries. As people get older the rate is found to decrease. Youth is unskilled and careless, and older persons are found in skilled trades.' Of all reported accidents in 1938 numbering 179,159 non-fatal and 944 fatal, no less than 30,652 and 73 related to 'young persons'.[2] The fatal rate is comparatively small, but about every fifth or sixth person who meets with a non-fatal accident is a young worker! In some trades the figures are even more disquieting. Hoist accidents in 1938 showed a total non-fatal figure of 403: of this figure 117 accidents related to young persons.[3]

Mr. Harding (Superintending Inspector) notes that many injuries to young workers are not due to machinery (arising for example, from the movement or handling of goods, falls of persons and articles, and similar causes), and are not serious, but 'the number is far too high and . . . accidents to juveniles are commonly in higher proportion to the number employed in factories than the accidents to adults are to the number of workers employed'.[4] 'In common with many aspects of safety in industry, the question as it applies to young workers presents its own problems, ranging from psychological considerations in the individual boy or girl to the machinery plant, devices and practices at or among which he or she may work, with their points of potential danger often more real than apparent to the inexperienced.' Here is foreshadowed the obstacle to any scientific analysis of the real causes of accidents which seeks to distinguish psychological from technical causes.

The consoling fact that most accidents to younger workers are relatively slight is offset by the depressing particulars of single cases, of which the Chief Inspector in his *Report for 1936* gives some examples. A boy aged 14 was killed on shafting while attempting to replace the belt of a pulley. He had been told to do so. A boy of 17 lost two fingers and parts of two others on an unguarded press after ten minutes' experience. A girl of 17 lost three fingers on a power press. She had previously drawn the attention of the foreman to the inadequacy of the guard. A boy of 14 was killed after a few days' experience on a slotting machine through his shirt sleeve being caught by a small circular saw which severed a vein in his arm-pit. A boy of 15 was killed on falling into a rope-drive through a defective railing. A boy of 16 lost part of a finger when operating a treadle-driven guillotine. The

---

[1] Cf. loc. cit., p. 283.   [2] Cf. *Report for 1938*, p. 113.
[3] Cf. Chief Inspector's *Report for 1938*, p. 97.
[4] Cf. W. E. Harding's 'Accidents to Young Workers' in ibid. *1936*, pp. 33 sqq. Also ibid. *1937*, pp. 41 sqq.

firm had previously been warned to provide a guard. A few months later in the same factory a girl of 16 lost part of a finger when working an unfenced power press.[1]

These are random examples from a dreadful list which has been continued in the *Report of Chief Inspector of Factories* published in 1938: itself but a summary of a far longer catalogue.

Juvenile accident rates are probably higher in small than in large factories, for the presence of many young people in the same factory tends to increase the danger. 'The herd instinct renders it more difficult to maintain discipline and attention to work', writes a Superintending Inspector, 'no system of supervision can be considered satisfactory unless it provides for this important factor.'[2] An investigation has been made to apportion the responsibility as between the employer and the victim, with the following results:

	Percentage of accidents	
	Boys	Girls
	Per cent.	Per cent.
Firm mainly responsible	40·0	47·4
No blame attached to any party . . .	16·9	15·8
Young worker mainly responsible . .	43·1	38·8[3]

It is not our object at this stage, and only to a limited extent ultimately, to deal with the very interesting proposals and suggestions made by Messrs. Harding and I. N. Bennett for more effective prevention of injuries of juveniles. They deal with the education of the young worker,[4] to enable him to realize the risk attaching to his work, with supervision and training during initial periods of employment, and with the selection of the work on which juveniles are employed. In this connexion Mr. Harding has considered how far scarcity of juvenile labour in busy times results in employers being faced with the choice of an inferior type of boy or girl or none at all, and how far inducements to speed (offered by inappropriate bonus systems) may lead to accidents, as also other points which explain the high rates of juvenile accidents.[5]

---

[1] Cf. Chief Inspector's *Report for 1936*, pp. 9–10; ibid. *for 1937*, pp. 48–9.

[2] Cf. ibid. *1937*, pp. 48–9.   [3] Cf. ibid., p. 43.

[4] We may call attention to the very useful work done by the Miners' Welfare Fund in regard to the assistance of proper training of pit boys in safety principles. The actual instruction is the responsibility of the Local Education Authorities, but the Fund is to assist the defraying of expenses, principally the cost of 'safety badges' for those satisfactorily completing their course. The idea has been adopted in 13 mining districts. The numbers of boys enrolled in safety classes in the session commencing in the autumn of 1936 was more than 10,000 and the number of classes was over 40. The instruction is generally given by a colliery official either at the colliery or at a school. Cf. *Miners' Welfare Fund 1934, 1935; Thirteenth Annual Report*, p. 26; *Fifteenth Annual Report*, 1937, p. 60.

[5] Cf. loc. cit., pp. 35–6.

All this, important as it is, does not directly touch the problem of Workmen's Compensation with which we are mainly concerned. But we are directly concerned by the fact that from 26 to 32 per cent. of the injuries to minors are ascribed to the carelessness of employers. As to the other percentages, the allocation is inevitably superficial. Yet if in about 23 per cent. of cases no blame can be attached to anyone—this, at any rate shows that only about half the accidents were the fault of the victim.   (See Harding, loc. cit., p. 33).

Mr. Harding holds that an unhappy state of mind can be an important factor: two girls, for instance, began to meet with slight mishaps, one after the death of a parent and the other after her family had been evicted from their home—another example of the psycho-physics of work which it is difficult, perhaps impossible, to include in any scrutiny of the worker's responsibility. A girl who fears her approaching confinement, a youth who fears that he has lost the affections of his fiancée, will probably not reveal the fact. This being the case, the need for attacking the evil of such accidents from the angle of a better technical protection of the young worker certainly becomes more urgent. It should, however, not be forgotten that inexperience, carelessness in the young worker, has a surprising counterpart among experienced workers. The latest investigation of the I.L.O. states that old and experienced workers may become accident-prone by being too sure of themselves. 'After a certain length of service, the worker is apt to neglect paying the same attention to his work as at first. His movements become automatic, unconscious, especially where it is a case of machine work.'[1] But, apart from this, the young workers are certainly the most liable to meet with accidents if groups of age are considered.

As a last problem of accident proneness we may refer to the so-called 'multiple accidents'. It is proved that when a number of persons engaged upon a specific task are observed over a period of some weeks or months, they are often found to have sustained a certain number of casualties. If such casualties are so trivial as to permit the injured to continue work, it may also be observed that the same person is injured more than once. The subject was first investigated by Major Greenwood (*Lister Institute of Preventive Medicine and Research: Subsection, Ministry of Munitions*) and Hilda M. Woods (*Ministry of Munitions*).[2]

[1] Cf. *Occupation and Health*, vol. i, 1930, pp. 18–19.

[2] Cf. *Reports of the Industrial Research Board*, no. 4: *The Incidence of Industrial Accidents upon Individuals with special reference to Multiple Accidents*, 1919. Further interesting material on this may be found in the following publications: *Contributions to the Study of the Human Factor in the Causation of Accidents*, Medical Research Council, Report no. 34, 1926. Further, Ethel M. Newbold, 'Practical Applications of the Statistics of Repeated Events particularly to Industrial Accidents', *Journal of Royal Statistical Society*, 1927, pp. 487 sqq. Also ibid., 1920, pp. 255 sqq.

The authors concluded that 'varying individual susceptibility to "accident" is a factor so important that, given the experience of one period, it might be practicable to foretell with reasonable accuracy the average allotment of accidents among the individuals in a subsequent period'. They suggest that by weeding out susceptibles the accident would be greatly diminished. For our own purposes the following statement is particularly interesting:[1]

The naïve interpretation is of course that of carefulness or carelessness; as one says there are people whose fingers are all thumbs and there are others who are neat fingered; or again some people are scatter-witted and others circumspect . . . . Industrial accidents are usually held to be a function of output, and also a function of fatigue; the faster one works the greater the number of accidents, and the more weary one is when working at the same rate the greater the risk of misadventure.

The Home Office Memorandum to the Hetherington Commission dealt briefly with 'accident proneness' which we have treated under 'merit rating'.[2]

Reports on industrial accidents show that a very high percentage of them is due, not to defects of machinery and plant, but to what has been called the 'personal factor'—in particular to lack of care or errors of judgment on the part of the workers themselves, or to what has been termed 'accident proneness' and the chief hope of a substantial reduction in such accidents in future seems now to lie in the education of the workers themselves.[3]

Whilst well aware of the need and value of education in these matters we cannot endorse this conclusion. On the contrary, we have tried to show that what appears, in an individual case, as personal carelessness no longer wears this aspect when viewed in the light of ever-recurring accidents in great numbers of a like nature. To us 'accident proneness' is less the fruit of individual carelessness than an unavoidable, though reducible, predisposition, which may be enhanced by defective safety measures. It would be dangerous to interpret this term otherwise and, by the back-door of 'negligence', to reintroduce the idiosyncrasy of the individual workman as a personal factor.

References to 'accident proneness' are a regular feature of the Annual Reports of the Industrial Health Research Board. 'Given equal exposure to risk, roughly three-quarters of recorded accidents happen to one-quarter of the people exposed to risk.'[4] The 'accidents' recorded were not, however, all or mostly 'injuries'. How far this term is synonymous with or complementary to the conception of 'negligence proneness' deserves more consideration than it has yet received. Negligence may be casual: or it may be inborn, in which case it may be pro-

[1] Cf. loc. cit., p. 9.   [2] Chapter XX. Also our vol. i, p. 169.
[3] *Memorandum*, §§ 464–7.   [4] *Eighteenth Annual Report*, June 30th 1938, p. 28.

perly described as negligence proneness which indeed may be induced by the very nature of the work itself. The point has an important legal bearing; undue insistence by an employer upon speed may, for example. induce or stimulate accident proneness in a driver. If negligence can be assessed in 'degrees', the employer should be required to obviate all temptations which might lead to rashness on the part of the workman, and the repeated statement of the Chief Inspector of Factories as to the influence on accidents of 'the speeding-up of operations' during times of business expansion gives further weight to such considerations.[1] The judgement of the House of Lords in *Harris* v. *Assoc. Portland Cement Co., Ltd.*, 1938, has whittled down the defence of 'added risk' to a degree which renders action on these lines by employers even more important than before. The Ministry of Health is also concerned with the problem, as is shown by the following excerpt from a recent report.[2]

The Causation of Accidents

At a meeting of the Royal Society on 24th March a discussion took place on the 'Application of Quantitative Methods to Certain Problems in Psychology', in which mathematicians, statisticians, physicians, psychologists and industrialists took part. The title hardly implies a subject of more than remote interest to the Ministry of Health, yet some of the matters discussed were directly relevant to the practice of preventive medicine, for instance, the causation of accidents. In this country, the *possibility* of actually measuring the individual factor of accident causation, of discovering *why* some people are 'all thumbs' was suggested by purely statistical studies published nearly 20 years ago. Since then, investigators of the Industrial Health Research Board have made progress in defining and measuring 'accident proneness'. In 1936, 13,380 males died between the ages of 5 and 25 years, i.e., in the period of life with the lowest rate of mortality. Of these deaths 4,654 were due to *all* forms of infectious and parasitic diseases taken together and 2,534 to accidental violence. In other words, simple violence killed more than half as many males as all the infectious diseases taken together, and a very large proportion of those violent deaths occurred on the public roads. If the methods now under consideration can eliminate from the factory or the driving seat even a small proportion of accident prone persons, their justification will be obvious.

Further, just as there are accident prone persons there are sickness prone persons, i.e., persons whose contributions to the total time lost by sickness in industry is abnormally great, although on merely physical grounds no reason can be assigned and malingering can be excluded. This is an even larger field for investigation and its connection with the subject of national fitness is close. It is not claimed by even the most enthusiastic workers, either that *all* accidents or *most* forms of minor illness are due to some quality of proneness, still less is it claimed that present means of assessing proneness are infallible. But enough has now been done to make it no idle dream to hope that psychological fitness may, like physiological

[1] *Annual Report for 1937*, p. 25.
[2] *Annual Report of Chief Medical Officer of Ministry of Health for 1937*, p. 171.

fitness, be quantitatively defined and measured. Such researches will, therefore, continue to engage the close attention of the Ministry; the statistical staff are frequently concerned in testing the accuracy of such results as can be expressed in arithmetical form. At the same time progress is being made with the assessment of dietary sufficiency and the general quantitative problems raised by dietary and nutritional surveys.

All our investigations into the number and the distribution according to certain psycho-physical and social distinctions thus lead to the same results. Accidents can no longer be regarded as individual, accidental, a random chance. They recur with depressing regularity as a certain percentage, changing with prosperity and depression periods, variable in different industries or occupations—but only within narrow limits. The same result is reached if accidents are considered as being connected with particular conditions, such as hours of work (fatigue), length of employment, age, machinery or manual labour, weekdays, day or night work, temperature, and so forth.

Accidents recur 'constantly'. However individual the single accident may appear, viewed from the angle of mass conditions, it recurs with machine-like regularity. Recognition of this fact led to the introduction of Workmen's Compensation, but the popular assumption that the workman is, in general, partly responsible for most accidents remains, and gains some support from the terms of the Act and from the arguments employed when it is cited in Court. The Act gave legislative recognition to the fact that accidents might be due to the carelessness of employers, as well as of workmen. It might also be an Act of God. In neither case, however, was the workman free from all share of responsibility; though free from blame, he was not to be compensated for the whole of his material loss. Hence the importance and relevance of this attempt to analyse 'accidents'. In earlier days an imaginary 'contract of labour' was invoked to prove that the workman had deliberately entered into an agreement binding him to take certain risks. When this doctrine could no longer be upheld, the workman's right to compensation was only partially recognized, because injuries, fatal or non-fatal, were still regarded as accidents for which the employer should not be made wholly responsible.

Many accidents were notoriously due to 'carelessness' or 'default' of the worker; the idea that such carelessness was inherent in mass production was never even discussed. The Legislature still regards carelessness as an individual factor as in each particular case it doubtless is, but in view of the steady incidence of accidents, individual responsibility is merged in the massive incidence of accidents to the great mass of workers. Yet the doctrine that in any case the workman should bear his share in the damages inflicted remains.

The principle of an equal division of the pecuniary loss between the employer and the workman which was deliberately adopted in the first Act of 1897 and continued in that of 1906, after full consideration and discussion, is equitable; and while representatives of the workmen, in giving evidence before the Committee, expressed their desire for a largely increased proportion, some proposing full wages, and in certain cases further benefits beyond that, they placed before the Committee no evidence in support of such a departure from the principles embodied in the existing Act.[1]

The original idea of the Employers' Liability Act in 1880 was doubtless as characteristically here stated by Mr. Guthrie, but there is no justification for this conception to-day. The existence of accident proneness and accident liability—conditions familiar to our forefathers, though the terms are new—can no longer be disputed, although science has still to analyse their full significance.[2] Workmen's Compensation assumes a different aspect once the idea of the individual guilt in industrial accidents is discarded—though this should not influence us when considering the single case, judicially or otherwise, from the point of view of individual causation. Accidents then become a recognized and ineluctable consequence of industrialism. When an injured workman receives half his pay whilst temporarily disabled, the employer is not bearing a moiety of the economic loss involved. It is seldom that he bears any share at all. The workman is not paid for surgical and medical necessities or for extra food or other expenditure necessary to rehabilitate him.[3] But the idea that the workman should bear a moiety of the 'accidental' damage inflicted is so deeply entrenched in the mind of even great English authorities on the subject, that Sir John Collie recently expressed the hope that 'the limit to which compensation is applicable has now been reached, and that any future legislation will tend to be restrictive; although one realizes it is easier to give than take away what has once been given.'[4] This from a surgeon with unique experience of individual industrial accidents and diseases!

Those who have paid particular attention to the statistical aspects of accidents here put forward, and have considered how far the incidence regularity, frequency, and causation of accidents may be attributed to the action of the individual worker, are unanimous in their conviction that the degree if any of such responsibility should not affect calculations of the compensation due. The opinion of the Chief

[1] Mr. Reginald Guthrie in a Memorandum to the Holman Gregory Committee. Cf. Report, p. 75.

[2] Cf. Farmer, loc. cit., p. 59. He draws attention to the distinction of both terms. 'For instance, an individual employed in a dangerous occupation will have a higher accident liability even if he is not very prone to accidents, but if he is prone to accidents, then his liability will be further increased.'

[3] Cf. Cohen, *Workmen's Compensation*, 1923, p. 191.   [4] Cf. Collie, loc. cit., p. 4.

Statistician of the U.S.A. Bureau of Labor Statistics, Mr. Sidney W. Wilcox,[1] deserves wide attention:

For a long time New York . . . has published bulletins in the 'causes of accidents' but in fact the subject-matter is scarcely on the cause of accidents It is mostly on the cause of injuries. The accidents are classified, for example, 'falls'. But a fall does not cause an accident—it is an accident. It causes a broken kneecap or some other injury. The cause of the accident was faulty illumination, worn treads on the stairs, too clumsy a load to be carried, or some other reason. . . . The great reform of workmen's compensation was to do away with the question 'Who is to blame?' and substitute the question 'Who has been hurt and how badly?' The compensation benefits are exactly the same whether the injured party was primarily at fault or whether he was not at fault.

The question 'Who is to blame?' was done away with under Workmen's Compensation, except perhaps in . . . the more or less mythical case of self-inflicted injury. . . . An important practical consideration grows out of the old association of 'Who is to blame?' with the money settlement. There is a certain amount of hold-over in the minds of employers, especially of the less informed, and on the part of new referees who have not fully grasped the philosophy of workmen's compensation to the effect that it does make some difference as to who is to blame. Therefore neither this question nor any other on the fundamental cause of the accident should be on the compensation accident report form. To ask the cause of the injury is as far as it is wise to go. Even if employers and their insurance companies were willing to answer frankly, it takes too much time to make sure of the true cause of the accident and prompt reporting should not be sacrificed. The questions on causes should be on a separate piece of paper and there should be an assurance that the form will not be seen by the compensation division, but only by those engaged in accident prevention.[2]

Here the border-line between accidents and workmen's compensation under an organization which deals with each separately becomes fairly evident. We deal with the point when, at the final stage of this inquiry, we consider how best to bring accident prevention and workmen's compensation under some common administration. But we have already satisfied ourselves and, we hope, our readers, that it is a waste of time to seek to relate the causation of an accident to the rudimentary facts which, in general, characterize it. True analysis should begin where this process ends. Should a workman be so negligent as to disregard the precautionary regulations made for his safety and thereby lose a hand, we may say that 'it was his fault', meaning that it was not that of the employer nor 'an Act of God'. But what deduction follows from an admission of negligence or carelessness if speeding-up is to be taken into consideration, or the youth of the worker, or some hidden

[1] At the 1934 Convention of the International Association of Industrial Accident Boards and Commissions.

[2] Cf. *Discussion of Industrial Accidents and Diseases*, United States Department of Labor, 1935, pp. 230–2.

neurosis due to personal worry of some kind or other, or to insufficient experience or to overwork? This question can seldom if ever be answered. We can only repeat that accidents of all sorts are inherent in the modern industrial processes even where individual negligence is a proximate superficial cause.

We may conveniently conclude this chapter by some reference to the relation of accidents to the national welfare—a point of direct interest as improved systems of compensation might help to reduce the heavy toll of accidents while, on the other hand, a reduction of accidents by improved systems of accident prevention might lessen the direct and indirect costs of Workmen's Compensation.

Statistics showing the amount of compensation paid during a year are of little significance. Such figures cover in the case of Great Britain only seven 'groups of industries', which is only part of the field actually affected by compensation payments of all kinds. Nor do compensation figures include other elements which represent economic damage and national losses connected with injuries to workmen. The expenses the workman incurs, the cost of interruption in factory routine, legal expenses, &c., are excluded. Yet this very incomplete figure amounted to about £8 millions in 1937. After making allowance, so far as possible, for many unascertained and unascertainable items, it is estimated by the Home Office that the total charge of compensation to all industries and employments under the Acts would be something under £13 millions.[1]

Accident statistics in this country are, however, as incomplete as in 1924. Many accidents are not registered either by ignorance or, in the case of minor injuries, by indifference, and a workman may fear loss of employment if a claim is lodged. The statistical position is very defective. The International Association of Industrial Accident Boards and Commissions[2], in order to facilitate and to standardize comparisons laid down certain convenient units of measurement relating to at least one factor of the national economic loss incurred. There is a 'frequency-rate', viz. the number of lost-time accidents (a lost-time accident might be taken to be an accident involving the loss of time beyond the day or shift in which the accident occurred) occurring in each million of hours worked, while the severity rate is the number of days lost per thousands of hours worked. These definitions are adequate for temporary disabilities. They cannot, however, aid in establishing the time-loss involved in fatal accidents and permanent disabilities. An arbitrary period has therefore been fixed for the measurement of the time-loss involved in these casualties, which provides a basis for an estimate of wage-loss. So death might be taken as representing 6,000

---

[1] Cf. *Workmen's Compensation Statistics for 1937*, p. 5.   [2] In U.S.A.

days lost, the same in case of permanent disability, while the loss of an arm above the elbow may represent 4,500 days lost, two fingers 750 days, one ear with loss of hearing 3,000 days, &c. It is well known that the majority of cases of temporary disablement represents a short period only; but the percentage of days lost increases rapidly with the length of disablement.

The following table given by Professor Florence illustrates this:

Classification of Cases of Industrial Accident according to Length of Disability and Comparison of the Proportion of Days lost in each Class of Cases[1]

| | Percentage of cases lasting specified length | | Average duration of cases (American experience), days | Percentage of days lost by cases of specified length |
| | I | II | | |
	American experience	European experience		
Temporary disablement:				
of less than one week . .	40	37	3·1	6·8
a week to 1 month . .	40	43	14·4	34·3
month to half a year . .	15	14	70·6	58·9
Fatalities and disablement over 6 months	5	6	..	..

The conditions of the average periods of disablement vary greatly from industry to industry, but the percentage of relatively short-dated accidents, that is of something like 4–6 weeks, is overwhelmingly great. These are the periods of disablement caused by injuries received in 1936 in or about mines under the Coal Mines Act in Great Britain:[2]

Number of persons disabled for the following periods		Per cent. of total for which period is known
3–7 days	18,787	15·0
8–14 days	28,099	22·5
2 and under 6 weeks	59,476	47·6
6 and under 13 weeks	14,396	11·5
13 and under 26 weeks	3,547	2·9
26 weeks and longer	599	0·5
Period unknown or not recovered at end of year . . .	10,425	..
	135,329	100·0

[1] Cf. Sargant Florence, loc. cit., p. 198.
[2] Cf. *Report of Chief Inspector*, 1937, p. 199. Also PEP, *Health Service*, 1938, p. 76.

The 'hidden cost' of accidents is difficult to determine and has only been done in special cases. When thirty-six injuries incurred in a typical wood-working plant were worked out in detail, it was found that medical treatment represented only 18 per cent. of the total costs. The 'hidden' costs making up the remaining 82 per cent. were found to be:[1]

	Per cent.
Cost of time lost by injured employees, paid for by the employer . . .	15
Cost of time by other employees	36
Cost of time lost by foremen and superintendents	25
Spoilage of material broken and damaged tools	6
	82

The time lost by other employees was due to their stopping work out of curiosity and sympathy, and in assisting the injured worker, investigating the cause of the accident, arranging for the work of the injured worker to be continued by some other employee, selecting and training the substitute, and preparing a State accident report or attending before the industrial commissioners.[2] An American investigation relating to 17,000 accidents showed that the ratio of direct costs was 17 per cent. and indirect costs 73 per cent. of the total expenditure.[3] Vernon deduces from generalized figures that the gross cost of accidents to industry in Great Britain amounts to about £30 millions per annum.[4] This figure is no more than an intelligent estimate, but suffices to show that the economic burden of the accident bill to the nation's economy cannot easily be underrated.

Looking at the problem from the point of view of what is called 'total sickness absenteeism', a recent Report of the Medical Research Council stated that while the most important single cause of such absenteeism was in respect of two large organizations, the cold and influenza group, with 26·3 and 33·2 per cent. of men, and 28·9 and 38·4 per cent. for women, the next important group was accidents with 10·2 and 12·1 per cent. for men and 6·5 and 4·4 per cent. respectively for women.[5] It is clear that much more methodical information, collection, and substantiation of facts relating to accidents and injuries will be necessary in the future.[6]

There is not much hope that improved protective legislation, in-

---

[1] Cf. Vernon, loc. cit., p. 16.   [2] Cf. also *Industrial Welfare*, Feb. 1931, p. 160.

[3] Cf. ibid., May 1933, p. 15.

[4] Cf. Vernon, loc. cit., pp. 16–17. In this connexion it is useful to read those passages of Sargant Florence's investigation in which he deals with 'Absence from Industry'. Cf. loc. cit., pp. 197–200, 274 sqq. and *passim*.

[5] Cf. Medical Research Council, *Sickness Absence and Labour Wastage*, 1936, p. 16.

[6] On this subject see R. M. Woodbury, *Workers' Health and Safety; a Statistical Programme*, New York, 1927, Chapters IV and V.

creased safety propaganda, and better technical education of the working classes will greatly abate the frequency of industrial accidents. In so saying we do not underrate the tireless services of the Home Office Inspectorate, supported by the Industrial Health Research Board, the Safety First Council, the Industrial Welfare Society, and other bodies.[1] There are also private efforts in other directions. The Royal Eye Hospital has formed an Industrial Eye Committee to make employers conscious of the necessity of safety measures, and to combat prejudice or negligence among workmen whom certain appliances (as goggles, veils, guards for grinding machines, &c.) are intended to protect. Mr. Joseph Minton has estimated that throughout Great Britain some 250,000 eyes are injured every year through industrial causes, which, according to the French authority Trousseau, are responsible for 20 per cent. of uni-ocular blindness. It is claimed that 85 per cent. of these injuries are preventible.[2]

In a lecture to the Ophthalmological Congress on April 22nd 1939, on 'Eye Injuries in Industry', Mr. Minton noted with surprise, 'how little is known about the recent development in the production of goggles. As old and inefficient types are still used in many factories, there is no wonder that workmen refuse to wear them. There are now a number of goggles on the market, almost ideal in their design. They are light, do not impede vision, and can be used with anti-dimming compounds, which prevents condensation of moisture on the lenses.'[3] The recent expansion of the engineering and metal trades, as well as the vast rearmament programme which has led to a large increase of industrial eye injuries, lends added importance to preventive measures.

Mention must also be made of the existence of Safety committees in certain classes of factories in connexion with a draft order made in 1927 which, however, has remained in abeyance on the strength of undertakings by the different industries that they would voluntarily take the necessary steps. In 1937 there existed 1,246 such committees but the Chief Inspector's estimate of their value is not very encouraging. Their progress has not been rapid; keen interest on the part of the management is sometimes lacking, and many 'exist in name only'— a point to which we shall revert when discussing the organization of the German corporative mutual indemnity associations and their statutory activities in the matter of safety organization.[4] The Factories Act of

---

[1] Cf. *Report of Industrial Health Research Board*, 1931, pp. 52–3.

[2] A recent exhibition has demonstrated industrial devices for the prevention of eye injuries. Cf. *The Times*, June 23rd 1938, p. 12; cf. for this point and other problems dealt with in this chapter the very instructive article by Dr. Donald C. Norris, 'Industrial Accidents', in the *British Encyclopaedia of Medical Practice*, vol. vii, 1938, pp. 118–35.

[3] Cf. *Transactions of the Ophthalmological Society of Great Britain*, 1939.

[4] Cf. *Report of Chief Inspector for 1937*, pp. 34–5. When asked about precautionary

1937 which came into force on July 1st 1938 will mitigate many evils[1] yet, in spite of all measures, private and official, 9 per cent. more accidents occurred in 1937 than in 1936—thanks 'in the main to greater industrial activity'—not a reassuring explanation! As regards young workers, 'there is no indication of any general improvement'.[2] The *Report for 1938* shows indeed some improvement of accident figures; for manufacturing industries alone the reportable accidents decreased by over 10 per cent. for fatal accidents. It is too soon as yet to judge whether this improvement of one single year justifies optimism. The Chief Inspector hints that the rapid growth of Safety Committees, from 1,246 in October 1937 to 1,449 in December 1938, may have a permanent influence upon the general trend of industrial accidents; but 'it is clear, however, that there is still room for a far bigger reduction'.[3]

Great efforts are being made but every decade sees the birth of fresh industries with new dangers of their own, which can seldom be foreseen. '. . . accident prevention discloses an ever recurrent series of problems to be met. Coincidentally with improvement in technique of safeguarding, new machines and new sources of power each with special risks are introduced, and in this sphere especially it is doubtful whether finality can ever be achieved.'[4] Finality is, indeed, as the legendary Irishman said, the last thing to be looked for. The increasing use of machinery on farms entails fresh risks to agricultural workers, who are not protected by the Factory Acts. The handling of artificial manures has its dangers, both by infection of food and, in a recent case, of the eyes. It is alleged, probably with truth, that belt-driven machines were often unguarded, and worn out. A proposal to extend the Factory Acts to agriculture was laid before the Home Secretary by the T.U.C. on May 16th 1939. This is probably not the best line of approach, but accident prevention is a many-sided science calling for a progressively higher standard of efficiency. The rising risk can be counterbalanced only by greater watchfulness and an increased measure of precaution. How to link up such endeavours with the organization and administration of Workmen's Compensation is a problem upon which we touch elsewhere.

measures against silicosis such as the use of mist sprays during boring operations, and on dusty roads, which according to Mr. J. Griffiths, M.P., were 'only in use at some of the collieries' of the Swansea area, Mr. Geoffrey Lloyd had to reply (*Debates H.C.*, Aug. 1st 1939, col. 2190) that Inspectors had 'at present no power to enforce the use of mist sprays', but did not fail to urge their use in suitable circumstances. Matters would be different if responsible bodies of mine-owners would decide to bring pressure on individual employers to adopt such measures.

[1] Cf. for an abbreviation of the most important items of this new piece of legislation, *A Guide to the Factories Act 1937.* Price 6*d.*   [2] Cf. *Report for 1938*, pp. 11 and 30 sqq.
[3] Cf. ibid., pp. 6–7.   [4] Cf. ibid., *1932*, p. 7.

CHAPTER III

LEGAL CONCEPTIONS

It is a hard thing to torture the laws so that they torture men.
FRANCIS BACON, *De Augmentis Scientiarum*, Pt. I, Book VIII (13).

COURTS of justice in England, as in other countries, have in their own way and in their own good time co-operated with the legislature in extending progressively the meaning in law of the term 'accident'. As explained in our first volume the scope of claims for compensation for occupational injuries has been greatly enlarged since the passing of the first Workmen's Compensation Act in 1897. To sustain a claim to compensation it was originally necessary to prove that the accident resulted from no fault or carelessness of the employee, whereas an employer is now liable to compensate a workman who has sustained injury while acting in direct violation of his orders.[1] This revolutionary change, dictated by purely practical considerations, has profoundly affected the whole course of subsequent legislation. The Holman Gregory Committee considered whether the legal ambit of the term 'accident', should not be further extended by omitting the words 'arising out of', so that an accident should be within the scope of the Workmen's Compensation Act if it arose 'in the course of' employment. In the event, however, tradition and considerations of legal expediency won the day and no change was recommended.

The Holman Gregory Committee did not regard the legal definition of the time of 'accident' as defective, but cited a great number of 'hard cases' which showed that whether what an ordinary workman would term an accident was so regarded by the courts depended upon the views taken by individual judges, who often differed profoundly among themselves, ' . . . so John Smith may find out that he's outside the Workmen's Compensation Act before he's ever been in it'.[2] Sir John Collie, who 'hoped that the limit to which compensation is applicable has now been reached', seems to agree with 'John Smith':

It is a very sound principle that Judges should confine their attention to the facts of the particular case before them, and apply what they find to be the intentions of Parliament as expressed by their Acts, irrespective of what the consequences may be in other cases. I have no doubt whatever that if some cases had

---

[1] Cf., for a number of cases showing the extended meaning now placed upon the words 'by accident', Sir John Collie, loc. cit., pp. 14–15, and the whole chapter: 'What is an accident?'   [2] Cf. *John Smith has an Accident*, Anon., p. 3.

come before a tribunal not bound to proceed on these rigid lines, but able to function on a broader basis, many of the decisions would have been different, and their application to, and extension in, other cases would have been avoided.[1]

'Hard cases', which are as numerous as ever, are said to make bad law, but *exceptio probat legem*—the test of a good law is the extent to which it gives rise to hard cases, viz. to legally sustainable decisions which give rise to evil consequences and offend the social conscience. The effect of such 'hard cases' is always negative, and their effect on the victims is heightened by the psychological and financial consequences of protracted litigation. In this connexion we read in the *Law Journal*:[2]

> An impartial critic reading the Report of the House of Lords' decision last week in Ellison v. Calvert and another might be tempted to make some caustic remarks about our judicial system. A County Court Judge, with medical and other evidence before him, concludes that a man has died from an accident arising out of and in the course of his employment. A strong Court of Appeal reverses this judgment by an unanimous decision, declaring that there was nothing before the learned judge on which he could have reached that conclusion. The workman's widow appeals, and a still stronger House of Lords, consisting of five of the first lawyers in England and Scotland unanimously reverses the unanimous decision of the Court of Appeal.

Until 1903 it was generally accepted that the term 'accident' involved in law as in common parlance the idea of something fortuitous and unexpected. When a workman strained himself whilst carrying on his ordinary occupation, the Court of Appeal held in 1900 that, in the absence of any fortuitous element, there was no accident.[3] When, in 1903, the House of Lords overruled this decision, Lord Macnaghten pointed out that its effect was that if a man did his best for his employer he would be told that his injury was outside the Act because he had exerted himself deliberately! This historic decision effectively enlarged the scope of the Act in the injured workman's favour, but possibilities of similar injustices are still numerous. A workman may find that he is refused compensation because he added to his ordinary employment a peril which that employment does not normally possess, unless he can justify it as necessary or reasonable, or recognized by practice, or due to emergency.[4] An employee, having reported for work at the employer's depot, was ordered to proceed to work at a point on a public road about a mile and quarter distant; no conveyance

---

[1] Cf. Collie, loc. cit., pp. 2–3.
[2] Cf. *Law Journal*, Nov. 7th 1936; cf. also *Debates H.C.*, Nov. 13th 1936, p. 1219.
[3] Cf. *Hensey v. White*, [1900] Q.B. 481.
[4] Cf. W. A. Willis, *Workmen's Compensation*, 1936, pp. 44, 53, 57, and 60.

was provided for him and no directions were given to him as to his method of progress. The evidence seemed to indicate that he had been injured by an accident while journeying on a motor-bicycle. In conformity with this rule, this mode of progress was held to be an added peril not contemplated by the terms of the employment.[1] The legal position may not be open to challenge, but it is certain that the workman in question never thought that by using his motor-bicycle, instead of walking, he would deprive himself of the benefits of Workmen's Compensation 'in the course of his employment'. If it is claimed that the use of a motor-bicycle was not contemplated in the terms of the employment (though not expressly prohibited), it is pertinent to observe that upon the date of the judgment over half a million such motor-cycles were in daily use, largely by men going to and from their employment. Would permission to use it, or a motor-car, have been refused him in view of a possible added peril or was such 'added' peril merely raised as a subterfuge after the accident had happened?

The saving of employer's time was about half an hour.

In the Court of Appeal in Ireland compensation was refused to a girl, a domestic servant, who was injured while drying her hair after washing it, even though she was at the same time attending to a baby; but it was held by the Court of Appeal in England (in 1933) that the proper inference in law was that the act of the servant in drying her hair by a gas fire in the kitchen was incidental to her employment because it was her duty to keep clean.[2] The ideal course would be to hand to every insured person within the scope of the Workman's Compensation Act, a memorandum specifying the risks which are respectively covered and excluded. A workman should know what is meant by 'added risk' and what he should avoid in this connexion. There is in existence a Home Office Memorandum on Workmen's Compensation, apparently drawn up for the information of employees;[3] though it has had in fact a very restricted circulation. Section 2 deals with 'injuries to which the Act applies' and explains in general terms the legal conception of an 'accident'. It has, of course, no legal force and throws little light upon the borderland where the words 'out of' or 'in the course of' become a matter of doubt and dispute.

How difficult is the workman's legal position may be judged from the following recent cases. A fireman, employed in the appellant's coal-mine, slipped and injured his knee whilst taking a bath after coming up from a mine at the end of the night-shift. The baths, which stood at the pit-head, were erected by the employers, but maintained

---

[1] Cf. Willis, loc. cit., p. 56. *Hetherington v. Dublin Tramway Co.* (1926).

[2] Cf. Willis, loc. cit., p. 57.

[3] *Memorandum on the Workmen's Compensation Acts*, 1925–31, 1936, 23 pages. Price 3*d*.

jointly by coal-owners and miners and were managed by a Welfare Committee. All men were instructed to take baths, but failure to do so did not entail dismissal. The County Court judge gave his verdict in favour of the fireman on the grounds that it was his duty to obey the instructions to take a bath and it was 'while performing the duty his employers had placed upon him that he was injured'. The employers appealed. The Court of Appeal held that the order was not a term of the contract of employment. Lord Hanworth said that the man when bathing was no longer 'in the course of his employment'. Lord Justice Slesser said

... there is no evidence that there was an enlargement of the contract of service and, assuming in the man's favour that the order was given, it is an order without standing, which the man could properly dispute without breaking the terms of the contract, which many of them did, and therefore was not a duty.

Their Lordships agreed that in taking a bath it could not be said that the fireman was 'doing something in discharge of a duty to his employer directly or indirectly imposed upon him by his contract of service'.[1] The decision, whatever be its legal merits, is inconsistent with the social intentions of Parliament and with the 'spirit' of Workmen's Compensation legislation. The judges apparently took for granted that a pit-head shower does not differ in nature or kind from the kind of bath, the existence of which (h. and c.), attached to every bedroom in a modern hotel, is regarded by its clientele as an additional attraction. In point of fact, pit-head baths have for forty years been standard practice abroad and, in their Spartan simplicity, may more properly be regarded as an officially provided and widely recognized adjunct to health.[2] Indeed, the County Court judge stated in this case that after the baths had been opened claims of workmen at the colliery in respect of incapacity from slight injuries had decreased in number. Men working in collieries are specially liable to small cuts and abrasions. These are revealed by a bath and treated in the ambulance room and they are thus prevented from becoming infected and so causing incapacity.[3]

At the end of 1938 over 450,000 miners were able to use pit-head baths, and the number is increasing by 50,000 a year.[4] That the case might have been viewed differently was shown by a similar case which happened in Germany in 1935. There it was decided that an accident

[1] Cf. Court of Appeal before Lord Hanworth, Master of the Rolls, Slesser and Romer LL.J., 27 B.W.C.C. 22, 1935.

[2] Cf. *Miners' Welfare Fund*, pp. 12–16. Cf. also *Report of Chief Inspector of Mines for 1936*, pp. 34–6.

[3] Cf. *Butterworth's Workmen's Compensation Cases*, 1935, vol. xxvii, p. 35. *Gaskel* v. *St. Helens Colliery*.   [4] Cf. *Report of Chief Inspector of Mines for 1937*, pp. 36–7.

in a public bath after the conclusion of work does not constitute an industrial accident, but the judge added:[1]

Bathing may by way of exception be regarded as an insured activity in connection with an undertaking only where the necessity of bodily cleansing results from the nature of the undertaking, and that in such a manner that an immediate cleansing becomes an urgent requirement going far beyond the general desire of cleansing and refreshing. In such cases, moreover, there must be, besides the casual connection, a local connection with the undertaking. In such cases washing arrangements are usually available on the premises of the undertaking itself (for example, in mines and smelting works) which permit the workers to carry out the necessary cleansing.

This reasoning might well have been applied to the English pit-head bath case, but the German decision was not that of a regular law court, but of the Federal Insurance Office. This difference in outlook is perhaps significant. Trustees of pit-head baths are now required to insure against their liability under the Workmen's Compensation Act.[2]

Another case illustrative of the difficulties which may beset injured workmen is that of a boy of 15, employed in motor-car manufacture. When first engaged he had been told to take directions from a particular workman. Some weeks later another workman, without any authority to do so, told him to work on a power pressing machine, despite a notice posted up 'Boys under seventeen are not allowed on power press'. After working the power press for two hours the boy was injured by an accident, which resulted in the loss of the tops of his two fingers on his left hand. The County Court judge held that he was working outside the scope of his employment when the accident occurred and was not entitled to compensation. The Court of Appeal was approached in respect of § 1 (2) of the 1925 Act which, however, as the Court of Appeal made clear, applied only when the injured workman, although disobeying a prohibition, was doing something within the scope of employment. In this case it was decided that the boy had done something which was not only prohibited, but was not his job at all.[3] This is doubtless good legal reasoning, but to the lay mind the outstanding picture is that of a boy leaving his home in a perfectly healthy state in the morning, returning from hospital some weeks later, maimed for life, without having consciously overstepped any regulations. He had merely obeyed an order given him by an older hand; yet he was refused compensation for a lasting injury. What

---

[1] Cf. *Entscheidungen und Mitteilungen des Reichsversicherungsamtes*, vol. xxxvii, 1935, p. 279, also *Juristische Wochenschrift*, 1935, p. 270, and I.L.O., *International Survey of Legal Decisions on Labour Law*, Geneva, 1937, p. 266.

[2] *Debates H.C.*, March 3rd 1939.

[3] Cf. *Privett* v. *Darracq Motor Engineering Co. Ltd.*

would have happened had he flatly refused to do as he was told? Had he no reason to fear dismissal? Can a boy of 15 be aware of the 'departmental' regulations as to the authority exercised by one workman and not by another? Can he be expected to know that in obeying a workman other than the one set over him he places himself legally outside the scope of his employment? This is an extreme example of the *Führerprinzip* (principle of leadership) in English law. No such conditions were mentioned by the judges of the Court of Appeal whose sole concern was whether at the moment of the accident the boy was 'in the course' of his employment or not.[1] If not covered by the Workmen's Compensation the case might have been treated under the Common Law. But here the doctrine of common employment would, in practice, bar the way. Thus a case of extreme hardship arose through strict fulfilment of the letter of the law, which in this case was wholly alien to the spirit of Workmen's Compensation. A Workmen's Compensation Commissioner, as proposed by the Holman Gregory Report, might have found such cases worthy of his special attention, as it was intended that he should make annual recommendations for the Amendment of the Act or improvement of its working.[2]

A workman was told by his employer's surveyor to convey certain instructions to the foreman before work was resumed next morning. The workman said that he would deliver the message in the morning but in fact went the same evening *ex abundante cautela* to the works and delivered the message to the night watchman: in doing so he met with an accident. The County Court judge found that the workman delivered the message as an act of courtesy to the surveyor and not under his contract of employment. His appeal was dismissed on the same grounds.[3] Whatever be the legal merits of the decision it is one ill calculated to strengthen good relations between master and man, and offends the lay idea of justice.

In perusing the annual volumes on Workmen's Compensation cases one is particularly struck with the number of such cases upon the

---

[1] Cf. *Butterworth's Workmen's Compensation Cases*, 1935, vol. xxvii, pp. 163 sqq.

[2] Cf. *Holman Gregory Report*, p. 69. With respect to the case *Privett v. Darracq* it should be noted that compensation had been awarded in 1910 to a boy machinist who was told by a superior to take an imperfectly moulded article to another part of the factory to be remoulded. The operator of the moulding machine was temporarily absent. The boy attempted to remould the article and was injured. There was a general order that machinists were not to change from one machine to another, but there was no order expressly forbidding the boy to work this particular machine. The Court of Appeal reversed the decision of the arbitrator and awarded compensation, cf. *Tobin v. Hearn*, [1910] 2 I.R. 639. In another case, *Marshall v. Rodgers*, [1918] a boy got compensation, although he had not been on his regular work, but it was considered as 'within the extension' of his employment.

[3] Cf. Butterworth, loc. cit., 1937, vol. xxix, p. 32. *Rossiter v. Constable Hart & Co. Ltd.*

terms 'arising out of' and 'in the course of the employment'. These words are a constant stimulus to litigation. The following cases all relate to the year 1937:

1. A labourer employed in road-making helped a driver, employed by the same firm. The County Court judge found it was out of his employment. The workman appealed. The Court of Appeal found that the County Court judge had misdirected himself and allowed the appeal.

2. A labourer attempted during the lunch-hour to mend a leaking pipe without orders. The County Court found in his favour, declaring that the act was unnecessary but reasonably incidental to his employment. The employers appealed. Their appeal was dismissed.

3. A land drainer known to suffer from epilepsy was told to leave work early to take tools on a bicycle to a new site. He was later found dead on the road by the bicycle. The County Court judge had found that the workman's death was the result of an accident and that the accident arose out of and in the course of his employment. The employers' appeal was dismissed.

4. A platelayer had been called at night to help in an emergency, overtime being payable from the time of leaving home. He met with a street accident on his way to work and died as a result. The Court of Appeal found that there was no evidence that the deceased workman's employment commenced at the time he left home, but the House of Lords restored the verdict of the County Court judge, in favour of the widow, holding that the workman was actually engaged in the performance of his contract at the time he left home.[1]

In some of these cases a new principle may have been involved and a final decision by the highest court may have been desirable. In general, however, as these cases indicate, insurance offices seem very ready to make the fullest use of the machinery of the law in order to limit the legal liability of the employer and, *pro tanto*, to increase the liability of the workman, *who cannot by any form of insurance cover himself against the residual liability*.

The cases we have quoted give an idea, though by no means a complete picture, of the notional significance, in legal phraseology, of the words 'accident' and 'arising out of and in the course of employment'. The headings under which these difficult matters may be treated may be stated as follows:

A. *In regard to 'in the course of the employment'*.
   1. 'During . . . the time of employment'.
   2. Continuous and intermittent employment.

[1] Cf. *Butterworth's Cases*, 1938, pp. 351 sqq., 132 sqq., 99 sqq., 364 sqq.

3. At place of work.
4. Provision of transport.
5. Access to place of work.
6. Attendance before starting-time.
7. Returning to employer's premises.
8. Compulsory use of premises provided by employer.
9. Legitimate interruptions of work.
10. Absence from work or premises for employer's purposes.
11. Absence from employer's premises with leave.
12. Absence from employer's premises without leave.

B. *In regard to 'arising out of the employment'.*
1. Acting contrary to rules.
2. Ambiguous instructions.
3. Express limitations of duties—prohibited acts.
4. Shot-firing.
5. Haulage roads in mines.
6. Acting in accordance with customs and practice.
7. Arrogated duties.
8. Acting under a superior's orders.
9. Workmen acting for his own purposes.
10. Working or being in unauthorized places.
11. Workmen as mere licensee.
12. Added perils. Unnecessary or unreasonable acts.
13. Acts necessary or reasonable.
14. Acting in an emergency.
15. Workmen 'larking'.

Every one of these headings has given rise to a great number of difficult cases, each differing in some respect from others. As the author of Willis's *Workmen's Compensation* himself remarks:[1]

> There is room for divergent views on the same facts. No principles of general application can be gleaned from the cases, which can only be regarded as illustrations of the operation of the words of the Act upon a particular set of circumstances.

Apart from these categories, which relate to the conditions which may attach to the term 'arising out' and 'in the course' of the employment, there must be considered what is generally called 'risks incidental to employment'.

This expression has no place on the Statute Book, but has often been used in the courts to indicate the dangers to which a workman's em-

---

[1] Cf. Willis, loc. cit., p. 38.

ployment subjects him, so that an accident resulting therefrom may be said in law to arise out of the employment.[1] Here again, the sphere of the possible claim of the employed has been greatly widened by successive judgments of the courts. An important case was *Trim School* v. *Kelly* (1914). A teacher in an industrial school was the victim of a conspiracy among the boys to assault him, as a result of which he received two fatal blows whilst on duty. Did the 'assault' arise out of his employment? Was it not an accident—an occurrence which was to be expected and which should be accepted as in some way inherent in the character of the employment? The Law Lords were in outspoken disagreement. Viscount Haldane, L.C.J., Lord Loreburn, Lord Shaw, and Lord Reading construed the expression 'injury by accident' as meaning an injury and any mishap 'unexpected by the workman, irrespective of whether or not it was brought about by the wilful act of someone else'. Their lordships agreed that the word 'accident' must be construed in its popular and ordinary sense but, as Lord Shaw put it, 'is surely part of that popular and ordinary signification that for seventy years in England the word "accident" has been publicly and descriptively used as inclusive of occurrences intentionally caused'. Lord Loreburn said:

Whether a particular mishap is likely to occur or likely to be feared or foreseen seems to me a different inquiry. In inquiring whether or not an injury by accident in fact arises out of employment, it surely is unnecessary to ask whether such a thing has ever happened before or is likely to happen again, within, say, a hundred years or, for that matter for ever. It may happen, and has happened because the poor man (!!) was a schoolmaster. The event has proved that it was a risk of his employment. I can see no reason for saying that there is to be compensation only when the misadventure was one which could be foreseen as probable, or contemplated as possible, or otherwise apprehended either by the workman or by his employer, or by a County Court judge. All this has, in my view, no conclusive bearing on the simple question: Did it in fact arise out of employment?[2]

The words *popular and ordinary signification*, and *publicly and descriptively used*, are of importance. Lords Dunedin, Atkinson, and Parker, in minority judgments, took the opposite view, holding the fatal occurrence was not an accident in the legal sense.

Legal practice has to a great extent followed the text of this humane judgment, which prevailed by the narrowest possible margin. The definition of 'risks incidental to employment' continues, however, to give rise to many disputable questions, and to protracted proceedings,

---

[1] The Court of Appeal in Ireland preferred to use the term 'risks reasonably in the contemplation of the parties'. Cf. Willis, loc. cit., pp. 78 sqq.

[2] Cf. *Trim School* v. *Kelly*, [1914] A.C. 677; 7 B.W.C.C. 274; 34 *Diges* 270, 2300; also Willis, pp. 8. and 78.

exposing injured men to long uncertainty as to the legal decision in what appears to them an evident case of accident.

The same difficulty arises where the proximate cause of sickness or death is not immediately or directly connected with the circumstances of the accident. Illness may follow and aggravate the consequences of the accident; an accident may, after many years, aggravate an existing though dormant predisposition. Scores of unsuccessful claims in this respect are recorded.[1]

Dr. Donald C. Norris[2] thus underlines the importance of this point:

> If a fracture has healed in a faulty position, or has involved a joint, there may be a period during which the patient can resume his ordinary occupation, following which he may become disabled again owing to osteo-arthritis developing in the injured part, perhaps several years later.

There may be a declaration of liability if there is a 'reasonable probability' of such disability arising.[3] And much will depend upon the diagnosis of the doctor. The liability of the employers, if further extended, might easily stimulate their desire to settle the case by a lump-sum payment and refuse further employment to the injured man. Proposals for a statutory prolongation of liability for compensation should be studied with this possibility in view.

The Chairman of the Royal Eye Hospital and others[4] have been led by long practical experience to take the same view.

> The present position is unsatisfactory in case of an eye injury in which recurrence of trouble may be expected from time to time, or which might conceivably affect the second eye by the dreaded complication of sympathetic ophthalmia. In such a case the workman has to obtain a declaration of liability from his employers, a matter always of considerable difficulty and much legal argument. Would it not be better to abolish the present machinery of these declarations of liability and make the employer automatically responsible for any remote consequences of the accident which could be proved, disregarding the fact that the workman may have signed, on receiving his last payment of weekly compensation, a receipt in final settlement?
>
> The additional risk, spread over the whole body of workmen, should only involve a slight additional insurance premium. It would remove an incentive which exists in these cases for the workman to stay away from work till his case is settled, even if he has to magnify his symptoms to get the necessary certificates.
>
> At present the declaration of liability, which is the workman's only protection against the future consequences of his accident, can only be obtained on the ground that there is a likelihood of future incapacity to earn. We suggest that if the declaration of liability must be retained, the basis for obtaining it should be shifted and

---

[1] Cf. Willis, pp. 115–22.

[2] 'Some Medical Problems in Accident Insurance', *Trans. Hunterian Society*, 1937–8 (Presidential Address).   [3] Willis, loc. cit., p. 286.

[4] Sir Patrick Hannon, M.P., and Mr. F. E. D'Alton, Secretary, Royal Eye Hospital, St. George's Circus, London, S.E. 1, in a letter to *The Times* of Dec. 21st 1938.

made to cover loss of earning capacity arising from the accident, irrespective of the fact that the injury will have no 'medical' after effects. As an example, a man with one blind eye suffers a huge handicap in the labour market, but cannot obtain a declaration of liability unless he can prove that there is a risk of e.g. sympathetic ophthalmia.

Dermatitis is a fruitful source of litigation, owing partly to the liability of sufferers to further attacks. In an Appeal case of 1937 a workman who had suffered from dermatitis had compounded all claims against his firm for the lump sum of £260. Later in another employment he again developed dermatitis; his new employers, not unnaturally, contended that this was merely a recurrence of the original disease as he had become more susceptible thereto.[1] In another case[2] Greaves-Lord J. described dermatitis as 'a disease which is intermittent and results very often in the person who suffers from it becoming more susceptible by reason of the fact that he has suffered from it'; he also mentioned that the medical referee in this case came to the conclusion that, at the time he was certifying, the man was not actually suffering, 'but he altogether omitted to deal with the note which was upon the form of certificate dealing with the possibilities of the future. I think the matter would have been clearer if the note had said that the medical referee must in dealing with the present condition of the man state whether or not the man's susceptibility to disease has been altered.'

In an address on the subject in October 1937 Mr. Erskine Hill, K.C., M.P., explained that medical referees have to scrutinize the questions

(1) of original susceptibility;
(2) of the effects of the schedules process; and
(3) of some neurotic condition.

This was also required of certifying surgeons and others who are not specialists. He also stressed the fact that the Codifying Order of 1932 relating to this disease was complicated by its ambiguity. In many cases it was not fully understood by medical referees in regard to the question whether the workman 'is physically able to work in some trade or business other than the process on which the disease has been contracted'.[3]

On the question of 'final settlement' mentioned in the first paragraph of the letter of the Royal Eye Hospital Governors cited above the judges of the Court of Appeal were at pains to express their views

[1] *Eaton* v. *George Wimpey & Co. Ltd.*, [1937].   [2] *Scruttons* v. *Radonicich*, K.B. 1937.
[3] *The British Journal of Dermatology*, 1937, pp. 428–9; a case which well illustrates the remark was that of *Blades* v. *Wool Exchange and General Investments Ltd.* before the Court of Appeal, Nov. 3rd 1937.

when delivering judgment upon a case in which this issue was raised.[1]
The Report, which we here summarize, reads as follows:

The Court of Appeal dismissed the workman's appeal saying that they were
bound by authority to hold that a man by accepting one weekly payment under an
award was precluded from appealing on the ground that the award was inadequate.

The workman, S. W. Lisseden, appealed from an award in his favour of 12s. 3d.
a week compensation. Lisseden suffered from dermatitis while employed by
C.A.V. Bosch Limited, of Acton, W. After the compensation award was made
by the County Court Judge a cheque for the amount due to date under the award
was sent to Lisseden by the firm's solicitors. The applicant accepted that cheque
and gave a receipt for it.

It was contended in the Court of Appeal that the applicant was not now
entitled to say that this award was inadequate, because he had accepted the money
payment and had thereby approbated the award.

Lord Justice Slesser, in giving judgment, said that he was constrained by
authority to say that Lisseden had approbated the award, and his rights, which
otherwise existed, could not be exercised. Such a result might work grave injustice to a poor man, but that was a matter which could not be corrected by the
Court of Appeal. Leave to appeal to the House of Lords had been given in other
similar cases, but did not seem to have been utilized. It had been suggested that
there ought to be legislation to deal with the matter. He believed that a Royal
Commission was to be appointed to consider the whole of the working of the Workmen's Compensation Acts and perhaps the matter would be considered by them.

Lord Justice Clauson said that it had come as a shock to him that a man who
might be dependent on a weekly compensation payment was precluded, by taking
one weekly payment under an award, from having the award reviewed. But the
Court of Appeal was quite helpless in the matter.

Lord Justice Goddard said that he also was shocked. He remembered that
Lord Justice Scott had said in another case that he hoped that there would be
legislation to remedy the matter. He (Lord Justice Goddard) had always understood that there was some Government Department which watched the administration of the Workmen's Compensation Acts. Considering that the point was not a
new one but had arisen in other cases for a number of years, he thought that
injustice to workmen might have been put right, and he hoped that the day was
not far off when it would be put right, and that the Court of Appeal would be
able to review an award which was not so favourable to a workman as one to which
he was entitled.

Leave to appeal to the House of Lords was given.

Such cases turn in general upon issues of fact,[2] but a more general issue

[1] *Lisseden* v. *C.A.V. Bosch Ltd.*,

'Acceptance of One Payment Under Award: Precluded from Appeal. Before LL. J.
Slesser, Clauson and Goddard.' (*The Times*, Dec. 8th 1938.)

[2] Cf., for instance, the case *Ewers* v. *Curtis*,[1933] 27 B.W.C.C. 553, where dependents
of a farm labourer who died from broncho-pneumonia recovered compensation. The
labourer had met with an accident, which resulted in melancholia, which again, as the
County Court judge found, made him more susceptible to broncho-pneumonia. While,

arises where a moral or psychic depression apparently develops out of a certain external injury. Does mental derangement, if proved to be a result of an accident, entitle the sufferer to compensation? Although suicide could not, in any circumstances, fall within the expression 'injury by accident' it may be consequential upon an injury arising out of and in the course of employment; if so, dependents of the workman are entitled to compensation under the Act in respect of his death as if the original injury had itself terminated fatally.[1] The question is one of great importance. Here again there are on record, for our guidance, decided cases of great subtlety, of which we here cite only two. In the first case[2] the Master of the Rolls entertained no doubts as to what should be the ruling of the Court of Appeal under the Workmen's Compensation Act.

I have no doubt that an accident may be of such a nature that there is a lesion of the brain, a structural injury to the brain itself, which accident may lead to an unsoundness of mind which may directly lead to suicide. He said that in the particular case there was 'no physiological injury' to explain the suicide. It had not been proved that the man's brain was injured. He warned that, if compensation would be given in cases of suicide wherever we find an accident which involves, as so many accidents do, depression of spirits in the case of a man who has been leading an active life as a labouring man or artisan, depression at being kept from his work and idling about at home, the neurasthenia and the suicide can all be traced directly to the accident.

If we were to say that, we should be opening a door which we ought not to open. I think there must be some direct evidence of the insanity being the result of the accident; something more than a subsequent occurrence.

The point was again raised in the case of *Dixon* v. *Sutton Heath Colliery*.[3]

If you cannot find that the accident has caused any physical derangement, but can only find, that, there being an accident with a physical result, the man when faced with it, thinking it over, brooding over it, loses his moral courage to face it and thinks that the only way out is to kill himself, that is not a consequence of the accident.

Lord Justice Scrutton added:

The line runs very fine, and one is always likely to be influenced, or there is a danger of one being influenced, by sympathy for the widow.

The employer's appeal was dismissed.

however, the judge did not feel justified in finding that the broncho-pneumonia was the result of the accident, the Court of Appeal gave judgment for the widow, holding that 'having found as a fact the melancholia was a result of the accident and that melancholia made the deceased more susceptible for broncho-pneumonia, the County Court Judge was bound to find that death resulted from accident'. Cf. also Willis, loc. cit., pp. 209–10 for further examples.   [1] Cf. Collie, loc. cit., pp. 15 sqq.
   [2] *Withers* v. *London Brighton and South Coast Railway*, [1916], 9 B.W.C.C. 616
   [3] Cf. (Nr. 2) (1930), 23 B.W.C.C. 135.

This particular case which is of general importance, was that of a miner who was suffering from nystagmus. He had been a cheerful man before the onset of the disease, but gradually became depressed and ultimately showed signs of marked nervous and mental derangement. He walked unsteadily and failed to recognize his friends. On the evening of October 12th 1928 he attended a certifying surgeon and was afterwards put on a tram. A friend found him crawling on his hands and knees at a spot about 400 yards from the tram terminus and at an equal distance from his home, and led him to a point near his house. He drowned himself later. The County Court judge decided in the favour of the widow, assuming the act of suicide to be due to mental derangement. Lord Justice Scrutton, upholding the County Court judge's decision, sharply distinguished between the causation of the suicide as being merely the consequence of 'brooding' or, as he assumed in this case, 'a result of instability of the nervous system'. Eight years later the Stewart Committee reported that:

The course of the malady (Nystagmus) thereafter depends almost entirely on the question whether the patient obtains light work as soon as he is able to undertake it. If he obtains such work his symptoms (meaning nervous symptoms like: Headache, photophobia, blepharospasm, nausea, giddiness, tachy-cardia and insomnia) may be expected gradually to subside; but if he fails to get it the consequences may well be serious, for left to his own devices, the man remains at home to 'brood'; he oftens becomes progressively more introspective and neurotic with the result that he may become unemployable.[1]

It appears to us that if the onset of nystagmus should so seriously derange normal mental behaviour as to imbue the sufferer's mind with ideas commonly considered as at least on the border-line of madness then suicide should be regarded as due to the accident, particularly in cases where, as in the case of nystagmus, a malady in its progressive stages is notoriously prone to cause such mental disturbances.[2]

Much fresh light has been thrown on this aspect of neurosis by Dr. W. A. Brend whose book, *Traumatic Mental Disorders in Courts of Law*,[3]

[1] Cf. *Stewart Report*, p. 10.

[2] An American case of a similar type is reported in *International Survey of Legal Decisions on Labor Law*, 1934–5, p. 420. A man was in receipt of compensation on account of severe disablement and disfiguring burns received in an accident in his employment. He was extremely nervous and restless, slept poorly, becoming morose, sullen, and utterly unreasonable at times, but with lucid intervals. About three years after the accidental injury, he took his life by shooting himself with a revolver. The Indiana Industrial Board found that death was inflicted during a period of mental aberration, and allowed claims for compensation submitted by dependents, this award being confirmed by the Court which declared that 'the medical testimony supports the idea of irrationality and incapacity to form judgments and that the shock and poison from the injury had unbalanced his central nervous system'.

[3] Heinemann, 1938, see pp. 7 and 28–43 as to differing medical opinions in regard to neurosis.

is of outstanding value to all students of the subject, whether from a sociological, legal, or medical point of view. He notes the significance of 'brooding', observing that 'medicine would not hold a man responsible for maniodepressive insanity, but the law may regard it as within man's own control'.[1] (The word itself is eloquent of enforced inactivity, the consequence of some physical disability or psychological disorder.)

A sufferer from neurosis cannot be expected to make his case in public court especially when under examination by opposing counsel. Referring to a particular case, Dr. Brend says 'this man would never have been allowed to talk in court so unrestrictedly as he did to me: he would have been constantly pulled up for irrelevancy and would have been required to limit himself to answering specific questions'.

This is only one of the medical aspects of accidents which has many complex ramifications. Psychotherapy has as yet reached only the threshold of insight into the reactions of industrial diseases and accidents upon adolescents and adults, male and female, in varying conditions of health and with varying capacities of resistance. As the law relating to Workmen's Compensation has grown in complexity, so has the importance and complexity of the facts to which medical men must testify and which they must seek to clarify in court. An injured workman may suffer, unknown to himself, from a pre-existing internal malady; another may be the victim of a *novus actus interveniens*, viz. a subsequent injury entirely unconnected with the first.[2]

The test applied in the two cases[3] was: 'Is the condition which is the subject of the complaint in fact due to the original injury, whatever it was, aggravated by infection and disease? or, to some infection or malady, independent of the original disease?' An affirmative answer to the first question entitles the applicant for Workmen's Compensation to judgement in his favour; an affirmative answer to the second question means that the injury is due to a *novus actus interveniens*, and the applicant cannot succeed. In such cases the necessary medico-legal investigation forms a new field for judges which may well increase in scope and importance as the horizons of knowledge extend.

Of recent years American jurists have devoted much thought to these problems. Thus, for instance, the effect of physical exertion on

---

[1] Dr. Brend in this connexion cites the decision of a County Court judge in *Withers* v. *L.B.S.C. Ry.* [1915], upheld on appeal, that the workman was at the time medically but not legally insane, and that the injury was not proved to have been the physiological cause of the insanity which led immediately to the suicide; death did not, therefore, result from the injury. In this case the injured workman became depressed as a consequence of the repeated failure of a wound, received in the course of his employment, to heal.

[2] Cf. Collie, loc. cit., pp. 67 and 74 sqq.

[3] Cf. *Doolan* v. *Hope*, and *Laverick* v. *Gray*. Cf. also Willis, loc. cit., p. 213.

an already diseased heart comprises almost limitless possibilities of danger, ranging from a slight increase of functional disability to sudden death. In an address before the convention of the International Association of Industrial Accidents Boards and Commission, Boston, Mass., Dr. Cadis Phipps, Professor of Medicine (Tufts College, Medical School), gave the results of his statistical investigations from 500 selected cases showing that roughly 60 per cent. of these had been aggravated by work and in all of these cases the aggravation was attributable to some sudden or unusual exertion. He had borne in mind that from the point of view of heart pathology all exercise is not harmful and some kinds of exercises are beneficial and stressed the fact that each case had to be studied individually.[1]

A workman with organic disease of the heart dies in his sleep or in his chair after some hours at his employment. Is it possible to prove in court that the man had done some work too heavy for him? Is it possible to demonstrate that the nature of his employment caused or accelerated death? Such questions may defy solution. In the case of *Mitchell* v. *T. W. Palmer*,[2] the claim of the widow was dismissed by the County Court; the Court of Appeal reaffirmed the judgement. It was, as Lord Hanworth emphasized, an accident not arising out of and in the course of employment, although the deceased with his weak heart had lifted, with the aid of a boy, iron stringers of 162 lb. A doctor might conceivably have advised him not to risk his health or life by undertaking such labour, but the man might have been loath to risk the loss of his employment by disclosing the fact. On the other hand, the nature of the work may have had no effect upon his death, in which case it would have been 'hard luck' had the employers been required to pay compensation. But it would be harder luck still for the widow if she were deprived of her right to compensation, for the residual risk is not one against which she could in practice have insured. If there must be 'hard cases', it is better that the sufferer should be the insured employer.

Bacteriological tests are sometimes invaluable. A man, employed for many years as a woolsorter in an American factory, died as a result of a lung infection, clinically diagnosed without bacteriological tests as anthrax. Autopsy disclosed lobar consolidation of the lung. Although the body had been buried for nearly two years, cultures from the lungs were made; they showed a growth of the pneumococcus and streptococcus with few contaminating organisms. But no anthrax bacilli appeared.[3] Cases of this kind give an idea of the difficulties surrounding medico-legal judgement. Injustice may arise to the employee as

---

[1] Cf. U.S.A. Dept. of Labor, *Discussion of Industrial Accidents and Diseases*, Bulletin, no. 2, 1935, p. 177.   [2] Cf. Butterworth, 1935, pp. 159 sqq.   [3] Cf. ibid., pp. 181–2.

well as to the employer. The elaboration of medical science will not alleviate but rather increase the burden of the courts and the attendant costs. Conditions which might have given rise to no dispute whatever twenty years ago because the medical aspect was then free from dubiety may to-day become the object of acute scientific controversy. Much may depend upon the attitude of a medical witness. He may or may not be abreast of current theories and ascertained results. In either case he may be reluctant to accept current views without question or to be guided by popular medical opinion when asked for his opinion. In a case *Dawson* v. *Agwi Petroleum Corporation*[1] a doctor who performed the post-mortem examination found no evidence of heart disease: examination by a borough analyst was also negative. A pathologist, however, found definite evidence of it, and was supported by another expert.

A great number of recent recorded cases illustrate the difficult position of judges or arbiters in such matters.[2] It is not our task at this stage of our inquiry to discuss what steps should be taken in future to ensure that the best medical opinion may have full juridical weight in cases under the Workmen's Compensation Acts. We are concerned at this stage only to show how great are the complications attendant upon any decision as to the significance of the word 'accident'. The medical side is only one aspect, though perhaps the most difficult, of the whole problem. It is one of several factors which make it increasingly difficult for the workman or even his legal adviser to provide, without great expense, legal proof that the 'accident' arose out of and in the course of the employment. We shall discuss later how far pre-existing conditions and second injury cases should be taken into account in any future reform of Workmen's Compensation, and how far certain American examples of legislation merit general acceptance. We are here concerned not with the amount of compensation to be paid, but with the extent to which the legal meaning of accident under existing conditions of law entitles the worker to claim compensation. The relation between first and subsequent accidents is another point of great difficulty.[3] The Supreme Court of Minnesota went so far as to decide that compensation was due in respect of the aggravation of a second injury even though the previous disability did not result from an industrial accident.[4]

The question whether decisions relating to pre-existing conditions

---

[1] Cf. *Dawson* v. *Agwi Petroleum Corporation* (nr. 2), 27 B.W.C. (1934) 456.

[2] Cf. for particulars Willis, pp. 115–22, where a very full account of such cases is given.

[3] Cf. Willis, loc. cit.; for particular cases pp. 233–4.

[4] Cf. Walter F. Dodd, *Administration of Workmen's Compensation*, New York, 1936, p. 676.

of health did not show some 'inconsistency'[1] was discussed in evidence before the Royal Commission. The witness cited the case of a man suffering from aneurysm who ruptured it by ordinary exertion and got compensation as for an accident. Another man, who had suffered for some years from heart disease, died while in employment and got none. The present judicial practice does not in our view show logical inconsistencies in this respect. The rule laid down by Lord Loreburn gives a clear and fair guidance:[2]

> In each case the arbitrator ought to consider whether, in substance, as far as he can judge on such a matter, the accident came from the disease alone, so that whatever the man had been doing it would probably have come all the same, or whether the employment contributed to it. In other words, did he die from the disease alone or from disease and employment taken together, looking at it broadly.

Under German law where, as we shall later show, the legal side of the problem 'in the course and out of' is dealt with on lines more favourable to the worker than in Britain, such cases are no less frequent than in Britain.[3] But the difficulties are mainly of a medical nature and are accentuated by disagreement between medical experts. How far

(a) an 'injury' might have been caused by a pre-existing condition of health not related to the work,

(b) recurrence or a second injury might have been due to it and to what extent (loss of the second eye more likely after loss of the first one, see p. 50);

(c) another malady, quite different from the original one, developed out of an injury (rheumatism after local strains, f.i.),

are medical problems on which it may be most difficult to give an opinion for the judge's guidance. Particular stress should therefore be laid on the protection of the workman's future right to compensation. Mr. Buckland (Home Office) explained to His Honour Judge Stewart, as a member of the Royal Commission:

> If there is a reasonable probability of breakdown, you are given a suspensory award or an award of some nominal sum a week. That is, broadly speaking the line, but there seems to be slight blurring of the lines. I speak with deference before the Judge and that is why in this particular sentence I put it negatively and talked about, 'It is not sufficient to say that there is an unlikely possibility of recurrence'.[4]

Further, as Judge Stewart explained to the Commission, the practice of

---

[1] Royal Commission on Workmen's Compensation, 1939 (hereafter referred to as the Hetherington Commission), *Evidence*, Q. 251 sqq.   [2] Willis, p. 17.

[3] *Reichsversicherungsordnung mit Anmerkungen*, Berlin, 1930, pp. 106–8, for a great number of cases where compensation was granted in such doubtful cases and where not.

[4] Hetherington Commission, *Evidence*, Q. 372.

making awards of a penny a week has been dropped and 'it is now usual
to have a 'declaration of liability in form', which does not involve payment or supposed payment, of a penny a week.' The primary object of
any Workmen's Compensation Legislation is to safeguard the injured
workman against any loss due to far-reaching effects of his injury
which were not or could not be recognized or foreseen early enough,
and increasing attention should be paid to the expert views of exponents
of the several branches of medicine concerned. At a later stage we
shall revert to the problem when dealing with the effects which final
lump sum payments may have in this matter.[1]

The Workmen's Compensation Bill sponsored by the Trade Union
Congress and presented by Mr. Mainwaring on November 6th 1936,
but rejected on second reading, eliminated the words 'out of and in the
course of employment' and substituted 'in connexion with his employment'. This phrase already appears in § 1 (2) of the Statute, where
it is said that the act causing the injury of the workman must not only
be 'in connexion with' but also 'for the purpose of' the employer's
trade or business. Willis suggests that the former expression is really
unnecessary, because every act which is done for the purpose of the
business must be done in connexion with it.[2] We do not think that
the substitution of 'in connexion with' would substantially lessen the
legal difficulties arising as just described, though it may widen the
scope of the Act. It is questionable whether the expression would
alleviate the difficulties of injured persons, for employers might as
readily found a legal argument on these words as on those they displace.
The act of the workman might be related to some interest—real or
assumed by the workman—of the employer: a miner, for instance,

---

[1] An interesting example of the different cases which may arise in this respect, which are
some index to the difficulties with which the judge might be faced is furnished by the conditions attached to hernia. A recent publication of the Accident Insurance Office of
Victoria states three different possibilities:

(1) There are no grounds whatever for awarding compensation simply because a
    hernia developed in the course of employment;
(2) Aggravation of a pre-existing hernia is possible as a result of accident and strain; the
    worker is to be given the benefit of the doubt and he should get compensation;
(3) Recurrence of hernia after operation (usually a slow process) following a 'severe
    effort'; compensation should be given. (A. J. Trinca, M.D., F.R.C.S., *Hernia and
    the Workers' Compensation Acts*, Melbourne, 1939, pp. 5–6.)

The difficulties in regard to ruptures were revealed before the Hetherington Commission by
Mr. Baird. He declared that 'in respect of rupture it is a matter of greatest difficulty to
prove actually the happening of an accident whereby the rupture was caused'. Cf. Q.
2656-7. He mentioned the 'theory' of one medical referee that 'rupture is constitutional',
and drew attention to the large number of claims refused. The way this matter is dealt
with in Victoria shows the advantages of uniform rules covering such matters made by a
Workmen's Compensation Commissioner.   [2] Cf. Willis, loc. cit., pp. 76–7.

acting against the Coal Miners Order 1913 was found by an arbitrator to have acted outside the scope of his employment just 'to save himself trouble'. This judgement was reversed by the Court of Appeal which held that the arbitrator had taken too narrow a view of the scope of the dead man's employment and held that he was in fact engaged in furthering his employer's business.[1] It would, however, not have been disputed that the workman who gave the order to the watchman at night and not to someone in the morning (see p. 46) would under such a ruling have succeeded in his claim, as he certainly acted with the object of furthering his employer's business.

The adoption of the phrase 'in connexion with the accident' was also recommended by the T.U.C. Memorandum to the Hetherington Commission.[2] The alternative of making the industrial plant or unit and the employment of the worker within such units the test for his compensation claims, as suggested by us[3], was not taken into account by Sir Walter Citrine, when he was questioned on the T.U.C. proposal, but was mentioned by the Chairman.[4] A typical case showing the inconsistencies of the present phrase was mentioned by Mr. Russel-Jones,[5] where a roller man was injured by a detonator which was thrown into the rolls and led to some 'fooling about', which again resulted in explosion. The injured man was denied compensation as apparently the matter was considered to be a case of larking and the injury as not arising out of or in the course of his employment. If a workman is injured by 'larking' in which he himself participates he must be considered, in the parlance of German jurisprudence, to 'separate himself' from the unit.[6] But German law recognizes a right to compensation where the injured person is the victim of 'larking, by others, as he would not have been injured had he not been in the factory or place of work. British law has not taken this view,[7] and the position arising through this legal attitude is sometimes viewed with regret by non-legal writers.[8]

The T.U.C. Bill contained another passage which is relevant to this chapter. It proposed that an accident to a workman should be deemed to arise in connexion with his employment should it occur while the workman is travelling to or from his place of work in, or is waiting for, any means of transport directly or indirectly provided by his employer, whether the workman pays for travelling therein or not.

---

[1] *Stokes* v. *Mickley Coal Company*, [1928] 21 B.W.C.C. 70 and Willis, loc. cit., pp. 76–7.
[2] Loc. cit., p. 413.
[3] Wilson and Levy, *Memorandum to Hetherington Commission*, pp. 325–6.
[4] Q. 3764–5. See also p. 492.   [5] Cf. A. 3874.
[6] Cf. *Reichsversicherungsordnung mit Anmerkungen*, 1930, pp. 60 sqq.
[7] Willis, loc. cit., p. 61.   [8] *The Lancet*, Jan. 21st 1939, p. 129 sq.

The present rule is that employment does not in general begin until the workman has reached the place where he has to work or the ambit, scope, or scene of his duty, and it does not continue after he has left it; periods of going and returning are generally excluded, except cases like the one quoted above (p. 47).

But there are inevitable exceptions:[1] a fruit picker was injured by the overturning of her employer's lorry driven by the employer's son who took the applicant to her working place eight miles distant from her home: it was proved that the applicant would not have taken the employment except on the condition that the employer would provide conveyance. The arbitrator held that there was no material upon which it could be held that the applicant was contractually bound to use the vehicle or was directed to use it. The Court of Sessions, by a majority, decided that the arbitrator was entitled to hold that the accident did not arise out of or in the course of the employment. Lord Morison reversed the decision, holding that the applicant was, at the time of the accident, travelling on the lorry in pursuance of the duty which she owed the respondent as her employer.[2] Future legislation should certainly safeguard injured persons from legal sophistries such as those demolished by Lord Morison.

A workman employed by the Bath Corporation was killed by lightning while at work on June 25th 1935. During the afternoon of June 25th a violent thunderstorm passed over Bath and work only proceeded at intervals. The deceased had a steel shovel with a wooden handle in his hand, and was in a stooping position with the shovel slightly raised. Another workman was within a few inches of him similarly employed, whilst a third was $1\frac{1}{2}$ yards away. There was also a wooden wheelbarrow within a few yards of the workmen and there was a steel rim to the wheel. The workman was undoubtedly killed *during* his employment. But the risk of being struck by lightning while at work is, in law, only considered as a common risk from the forces of nature. The question for the judge appeared to be mainly whether the character of the employment was such as to create or intensify the risks that arise from extraordinary natural causes; if not, it could not be held that in such circumstances the accident arose out of the employment. Much evidence was heard. The judge, His Honour Kirkhouse Jenkins, decided that the lightning which struck the deceased was a direct blow, and was not lightning which had established contact by any other object. Having formed this opinion, he found that the deceased was not exposed to more than the normal risk of being struck by lightning and there was nothing in his employment which added in any way to the risk of being struck. The lightning

[1] Cf. Willis, loc. cit., pp. 22–5.   [2] Cf. *Craw* v. *Forrest*, 1931.

which killed the workman had no kind of connexion, direct or indirect, with his employment. *'He was in no greater peril than any other inhabitant in the city of Bath or immediate neighbourhood.'* The claim of the widow was therefore rejected. We do not question the verdict,[1] but the words italicized ignore certain relevant factors. During a heavy thunderstorm people in general seek shelter in houses. They are warned not to shelter under big trees. The workman continued to work in spite of the thunderstorm—for it was not the first lightning flash which killed the man, though the rain had stopped. Was not this an additional risk arising out of his employment? Others not so employed would probably have waited till the storm had passed. Had the workman declined to work under such conditions he would probably be considered as a coward. While the judge took into account all the technical factors which might have caused the death of the workman through lightning,[2] he did not apparently inquire whether, as a matter of precaution, the workmen ought to have been forbidden to work in the open and whether the lack of such an order was not to be considered as adding risk of an extraordinary character to their work. The words of Russell L.J. seem to us to be applicable:

If the accident has occurred to the workman by reason of his employment bringing about his presence at the particular spot and so exposing him to a danger which in fact is proved to exist at that particular spot, then the accident arose out of the employment.[3]

Can there be therefore any doubt that the workmen, but for the nature of their work, would have taken shelter during a heavy thunderstorm?[4] Under German legislation no such technicalities arise. A worker struck by lightning while in the precincts of a factory which comes under the Workmen's Compensation is entitled to compensation and there is no other connexion with his work required than that he has been in the workshop. The factory owner would be clear of liability[5] only when the destructive agency operated widely, e.g. an earthquake or hurricane. The 'accident' need not relate to the works or to conditions therein. The worker must simply establish that he was there when the accident occurred.

The whole conception of 'accident' within the German Insurance

[1] Cf. for a similar interpretation of the law *Thom* v. *Sinclair*, [1917]; cf. further Willis, loc. cit., pp. 81 and 88.

[2] The correctness of the fact that the instruments mentioned above did not cause the death by making contact has been questioned. Cf. *The Lancet*, 1936, p. 221.

[3] Cf. Willis, loc. cit., p. 88.

[4] Cf. for details of the case: *Bath and Wilts Chronicle*, June 28th 1935, and ibid., January 16th 1936. The case is not dealt with in Butterworth's Compilation.

[5] Cf. *Handkommentar zur Reichsversicherungsordnung*, AN. 1914, p. 411 (gr. Senat.)

Law[1] differs from the British in that it relates to the *Betrieb*, i.e. the unit of production or establishment. Every injury to the worker which is related causally to the *Betrieb* or to the presence or action of the worker therein falls within the scope of compensation insurance and justifies a claim, except, as in England, in cases of serious and wilful misconduct. The mere fact that, had the worker not been employed in or by the *Betrieb*, the accident might not have occurred is sufficient to establish a claim. Hence a workman struck by lightning, injured by an insect-bite, or by a chance bullet has a valid claim. The meaning of *Betrieb* is wide, and that of *Betriebsunfälle* even wider, comprising accidents happening on the way to work, in contrast to the English law under which such cases are but rarely eligible for compensation.[2] The German law also comprises accidents arising in connexion with the care of transport, repair, or renewal of implements and utensils so far as they are used in connexion with the establishment in which he is employed[3] even if provided by the worker. The difference in the English system which only relates to injuries in connexion with 'employment', a term liable to many technical intricacies, should be evident and not be overlooked in any coming reform.

An attentive reader will by now have realized that an injured workman cannot feel sure that he will receive compensation. He has no means of knowing whether he is protected by the Act which purports to protect him. Even if he belongs to a powerful trade union, efficiently managed, and is competently advised, he may find his position doubtful, and only one insured person in three belongs to any sort of Trade Union. He may find that his title to compensation depends upon the answers which he or others give to nice questions whose significance to him is obscure, and upon consequential theories and deductions which he is wholly unable to appreciate but which mean economic life or death for him or his dependents.

He will hear physicians of the utmost fame contradicting each other upon the interpretation to be placed upon evidence, and judges of the highest eminence in successive courts differing from each other in the process of reasoning upon and deduction from the same body of evidence.

He will often find that the majority decision turns upon the opinion of a single judge or doctor, upon a necessarily doubtful point. He will readily agree that the letter of the law must be obeyed, but will find individual interpretations of the letter of the law vary greatly. In any

---

[1] Ibid., ss. 537–44 and 545 *a* and *b*.
[2] For the five exceptions of this kind cf. Willis, loc. cit., pp. 22–32.
[3] *Reichsversicherungsordnung*, section 545 *b*, in conjunction with 922 and 1055 *a*. See also note on next page.

case legal assistance at every stage is indispensable to the injured person, and he cannot often get it without paying for it, though much is done under Poor Persons Rules. Great delay must in any event occur before his claim is dealt with in the courts, and during this period he will usually be in receipt of less than half his normal wages—which, if he is a married man with a family, will be less than he would get from the Public Assistance Committee.

Is it possible to remedy these admitted deficiencies within the present legal and administrative structure of Workmen's Compensation? If not, what changes are required? These are the fundamental questions which we must try to answer at a later stage. Much will depend upon full understanding of the legal conception of accidents, which we have here sought to analyse.

NOTE

THE far-reaching effect of the difference between the German and the English definition of 'industrial' injury was apparently not fully appreciated by some members of the Hetherington Commission. German law requires no definition of the accident, the sole criterion is that the employed must not have 'separated' himself from the establishment (*Lösung vom Betriebe*). Mistaking the word '*Tätigkeiten*' in German Law (§ 544) for 'activities' of the workman, whereas it relates here to certain establishments of employers and not to the work of the employed person, Mr. Bannatyne (cf. Hetherington Commission, 3124–5) deduced that the German law in this respect was vague. It seems to us that by excluding the possibility of disputes about 'in the course and out of employment' German as well as Swiss law is far less complicated than British law. While the insistence upon some connexion of the worker with his particular employment, work, or 'job' narrows the sphere of compensable injuries in Britain, the German formula widens it. It makes the non-payment of compensation dependent upon 'separating' oneself from the establishment, i.e. upon a negative factor, while in England the 'positive' factor, that the injury happened in connexion with the worker's occupation must be proved. If under German law a workman falls asleep in the night, or if he falls asleep during lunch-time in a room which he is allowed to enter, he remains protected by accident insurance; if, however, he leaves his work at some irregular hour to sleep, or if he does so at a dangerous or forbidden place in the works he has separated himself from the establishment for a private purpose and will get no compensation.

CHAPTER IV

OCCUPATIONAL DISEASE

The question of health, so important a factor in the existence of all of us, assumes still greater importance in the lives of the workmen ... The advice to 'take care', that vague medical admonition that is so often a euphemism for a definite verdict of a more discouraging kind, is here but a mockery, for with most of the workmen such care is impossible.

LADY BELL, *At the Works*, Chapter IV: Illness and Accidents.

TWO hundred years elapsed before the attempts of the generous minded Italian Professor Ramazzini to call attention to the social evils of occupational disease took legislative shape and then only by way of Compensation rather than by way of Prevention or Cure, which are later growths.[1] Remedial or preventive measures in relation to occupational disease are so intimately linked up with the progress of medicine and pathology that every decade has brought to light new factors which have enlarged the scope of Workmen's Compensation. This tendency will certainly continue, for the subject is still in its infancy: many aspects are obscure, few have received adequate attention. Existing statistics are of limited value and serve as no more than a general indication of the extent of occupational disease. Industrial accidents are normally traumatic, and immediately apparent; statistical enumeration is vitiated only by failure to report, which in serious cases is very rare. Occupational disease is often hidden and often unrecognized by general practitioners who cannot be blamed for failing to correlate the symptoms observed in a panel patient with his working conditions, of which the practitioner often has no knowledge whatever. The occurrence of epitheliomatous ulceration among shale workers and oil refiners had been noted and the disease made notifiable in 1920. In 1922 Dr. Southam and Dr. Wilson showed the high incidence of scrotal epithelioma among cotton-mule spinners admitted at the Manchester Royal Infirmary. Dr. Henry subsequently demonstrated that the introduction of mineral oil into the lubricant for self-acting mules, allowing for the time-lag, coincided with the increased incidence of this horrible and painful form of cancer. A Departmental Committee appointed to inquire into the disease and its prevention supported the view that the disease is caused by mineral oil and it is now well

[1] Vol. i, pp. 13–15. Cf. also two interesting articles by the late Sir Thomas Legge, who is the only English writer who, so far as our knowledge goes, has paid full tribute to Ramazzini and viewed his work from the angle of the modern social hygienist, in the *Journal of Industrial Hygiene*, vol. i, no. 10, Feb. 1920, pp. 475–85, and no. 11, March 1920, pp. 55.

established that sufficient exposure to pitch, tar, mineral oil, and to compounds, products or residues thereof will, in a certain percentage of persons, produce cancerous skin.[1] These avoidably perilous conditions had probably existed for nearly half a century before attention was drawn to them, when they were soon rectified. Had the condition been disabling but not fatal it might have escaped notice, for the individuals concerned did not, and could not, connect the effect with the particular cause.[2] The number of cases in a particular industry within a period of years in a given locality may not suffice to give the most observant doctor a clue to causation, and few voluntary hospitals are equipped with statisticians or with men competent to interpret the figures. Even after medical men are substantially agreed as to causation, many years may elapse before the evidence is considered strong enough to justify an addition to the legislative schedule. New industries may give rise to new occupational risks or increase liability to existing diseases. The manufacture of artificial silk, for instance, gave rise to a new source of poisoning, viz. by diethylene dioxide (dioxon)[3], and to conjunctivitis from the hydrogen sulphide evolved in the spinning room. Chromium plating has increased the risk of chrome ulceration.[4] It is often many years before such conditions are recognized, meanwhile the workman cannot claim compensation: he often does not even suspect that his occupation is the cause of his ailment. Unless the process is one upon which large numbers of persons are employed in one factory or one area, he may not hear of anyone else who has had the same sickness experience. Employers may be equally unaware of the incidence of a new disease unless its onset is sudden, and almost spectacular. Many years elapsed before the elementary facts of lead poisoning were admitted.

The toxicity of industrial solvents and of volatile organic substances used with increasing frequency in industrial processes is not fully known, as is shown by occasional and unexpected deaths.[5] Occupational diseases are, in fact, for the most part beyond the victim's control. 'The employee can seldom contribute anything to the prevention of occupational disease, nor does he acquire it from carelessness',[6] though it may be aggravated by neglect in the early stages of the malady as so

[1] John C. Bridge, F.R.C.S., M.R.C.P.E., in *Report of the Chief Inspector for 1932*, pp. 56–7.

[2] Cf. Collie, loc. cit., p. 111, who speaks of 'diseases which occur often insidiously as the result of employment in certain trades'.

[3] See Workmen's Compensation (Industrial Diseases) Order, May 28th 1937.

[4] Cf. John C. Bridge, loc. cit., p. 57.

[5] Industrial Health Research Board, *18th Annual Report*, 1938, p. 38.

[6] Cf. Industrial Commissioner of Wisconsin, U.S.A., in discussion of Industrial Accidents and Diseases, Washington, loc. cit., 1936, p. 39.

often happens in the case of industrial accidents.[1] The incidence of epitheliomatous ulceration, though still high, has fallen in certain industries, doubtless as a result of better provision for periodical examination.[2] But years may elapse before the victim realizes that some malady has an occupational origin. A biscuit packer in a recent case[3] first suffered in 1932 from a rash on her hand. Her employer's doctor gave her ointment, and treated her for a considerable time. Not until four years later did it become clear that she would not be able to work any more. Up to that time she had hoped 'to get better' by taking a holiday after her marriage, and so on.

Lady Bell, in her classic study *At the Works*, has devoted some very pertinent remarks to the reluctance of workers to safeguard their health. The workman dreads any interruption of his work for fear of supervision or dismissal and therefore avoids or defers the initial step towards recovery: '. . . physical discomfort and wretchedness, the inconvenience of having daily life interrupted, so keenly felt and complained of by the man who cannot afford to be idle, are intensified tenfold, in the case of the workman, by anxiety at his pay being stopped at a moment when he needs it most.[4] The workman frequently scoffs at the idea that he is displaying symptoms of disease; he does not realize what is happening to him until it is too late. In this development the employee usually contributes nothing as a causative factor. He is working in a place of employment provided by his employer. He does not know the ingredients of the materials with which he works and to the effects of which his skin, lungs, or eyes are exposed. These diseases come to him as a result of doing his work in the place and manner prescribed by an employer. In the case of accidents, the employee may be justly chargeable with at least a part of the cause, but in the case of disease, the causative responsibility is primarily that of the employer, unless he can prove that adequate precautions, ordered to be taken, were wilfully and repeatedly neglected without reasonable excuse. The full burden for freeing employment of any sort, so far as is humanly possible, from the hazards of disease must rest with industry. 'In the absence of such protection industry should meet its compensation burden.'[5]

In practice, however, such logical arguments are of little avail. The extent to which a given disease should be classified as occupational is one upon which there is seldom general agreement. Divergent views

---

[1] Cf. vol. i, p. 200. Also *Report of Chief Inspector for 1937*, p. 71.
[2] Cf. *Report of Chief Inspector for 1936*, p. 10.
[3] For further particulars cf. *Insurance Mail*, May 4th 1938, p. 289.
[4] Cf. Lady Bell, *At the Works* (1911), pp. 129–30.
[5] Industrial Commissioner of Wisconsin, U.S.A., loc. cit.

on this subject were expressed in evidence before the Holman Gregory Committee[1] and still exist. There are the scheduled diseases, due to the nature of the employment, which are attributable to the sufferer's occupation and employment. Apart from these, any disease which can be shown to be the result of an accident arising out of and in the course of employment is a personal injury within the meaning of § 1 of the Act, the right to compensation for which is expressly preserved by § 43 (4). But it has always been held since the classic *Anthrax Case*[2] that the disease must be the result of some external and visible effect or action of the workman or, as Lord Halsbury put it, it must not be 'idiopathic disease'; 'some affection of our frame induced by an accident'. A disease of the eye, for example, may develop because an object strikes a man, while at work, on a delicate or tender spot of the eye, thus predisposing the organ to attack by a germ. The list of diseases subject to the provisions of the Act is comprehensive and will shortly include most recognized industrial diseases.[3] But every new process in industry, and every new chemical employed, brings new dangers to be dealt with under § 43 (3) of the Act and in many cases impose new and onerous tasks on the Medical Inspectors of the Home Office.

Schedules distinguish between:

1. The disease: e.g. a localized new growth of the skin, papillomatous or keratotic, due to mineral oil, and
2. The process: in this case cotton spinning by means of self-acting mules.

Important as diseases are as a source of occupational injury, statistics indicate that they are a source of less sickness and death than industrial accidents. In 1937 there were 468,239 disablement cases arising from accidents, but only 18,256 from disease, including 11,738 new cases and 6,518 cases continued from previous years. At the end of 1937 5,617 cases were outstanding and 12,639 had terminated. Outstanding cases included 3,720 which had lasted one year or more and 632 which had lasted ten years or over; of the latter all but 31 cases were in the mining industry. It is of interest to compare the duration both of accident and disease compensation:[4]

Cases terminated by payment of a lump sum are not taken into account in this Table. In such cases disablement has usually lasted for

---

[1] Cf. vol. i, p. 124.

[2] Cf. *Brintons Ltd.* v. *Turney*, [1905] A.C. 230; cf. *Grant* v. *Kynoch*, [1919] 12 B.W.C.C. 78.

[3] For full list cf. *Workmen's Compensation Statistics for 1937*, pp. 24–5, and the particular Orders of the Secretary of State quoted ibidem in footnote (3), also cf. Collie, loc. cit., p. 111.   [4] Cf. *Compensation Statistics for 1937*, p. 10.

a considerable period, so that if such cases were included, the proportion of cases of disablement of longer duration would be higher than

	Percentage of cases terminated in which compensation had lasted	
	Accident	Disease
Less than 2 weeks	43·62	26·36
2 weeks and less than 3 . . .	16·50	16·01
3 weeks and less than 4 . . .	7·18	7·24
4 weeks and less than 13 . .	27·44	33·17
13 weeks and less than 26 . . .	3·51	5·93
26 weeks and over	1·75	11·29

the figures in the last two sections of the above table. It is clear, however, that industrial disease entails longer disablement periods than industrial accidents. Of every 1,000 cases of disablement arising from accidents terminated during 1937, including cases settled by lump sum payment, 34·7 had lasted for 26 weeks or more, while the corresponding figure for diseases was as high as 185·5.

Payments for compensation in the seven groups of industry within the scope of Workmen's Compensation Acts totalled £454,096, against £6,184,428 for accidents. Compensation paid for disease is about twice as large a proportion as that paid for industrial accidents. On the other hand, while £662,927 was spent in compensation for fatal accident cases, fatal cases of occupational disease cost only £5,637. The main causes of compensation payments for disease are as follows:[1]

	Cases in which first payment was made during the year 1937
Beat knee	4,962
Dermatitis	2,610
Beat hand	1,419
Miner's nystagmus	1,165
Beat elbow	715
Inflammation of wrist joint and tendon sheaths .	566
Lead poisoning or its sequelae	109
Total cases	11,748

It will be seen that, with the exception of dermatitis and beat hand and knee, the mining industry accounts for the most frequent cases of

---

[1] Cf. ibid., pp. 24–5, for further details.

occupational diseases in the above table.[1] From the point of view of social justice and humanity the single case is all important; but cases must not be merely counted, they must be weighed. The compensation paid in one single and exceptional case may outweigh that paid in a score or more of minor cases. The total compensation paid in the seven groups of industries in respect of industrial disease in 1936 was £3,741 for fatal cases and £552,121 for disablement cases, of which £450,000 was for nystagmus.[2] If a separate *ad hoc* régime could be devised for the mining industry, the problems of occupational disease in all other industries would be of such dimensions as to be easily manageable by a central authority. The payments in disablement and fatal cases were, during the year 1937:

	Fatal cases	Disablement cases
	£	£
Shipping	..	129
Factories	5,337	94,769
Railways	..	2,130
Docks	..	1,134
Mines	300	347,529
Quarries	..	312
Constructional work . .	..	3,456

Viewed, therefore, not by cases, but by the amounts payable by way of compensation, occupational disease resolves itself mainly into the problem of disease in mines and, in particular, of nystagmus, inquiry into which was one of the principal tasks of the Stewart Committee.[3]

C. Turner Thackrah, writing in 1832 of colliers, notes that their eyes were often intolerant of full light and that eye trouble caused many to leave the mines. Nystagmus (derived from the Greek νυσταγμός, meaning a nodding of the head as in sleep) was recognized in Sheffield in 1854, and a case was described in 1861 in a technical paper dealing

[1] Compensation cases resulting from silicosis and asbestosis are treated separately in the official statistics and are not contained in this table, apparently because compensation for these diseases is payable under the Special Schemes of compensation made under § 47 of the Workmen's Compensation Act, 1925, as amended by the Act of 1930. The total number of such cases in which compensation was paid was 2,425 in 1937. See also later pp. 81 sqq. We are well aware that when first scheduled the description was and still is of miner's nystagmus 'whether occurring in miners or others', but the latter cases must be negligible in practice, and indeed in the 1936 statistics not a single case of compensation is mentioned.

[2] Cf. *Stewart Report*, p. 2, for the latter figure.

[3] The terms of reference were 'to enquire into the operation of the Workmen's Compensation Acts (including any Orders or Regulations made thereunder) in relation to workmen affected by miner's nystagmus, and to make any recommendations, whether by way of amendment of the law or otherwise, as having regard to the special character or effects of the disease or any special circumstances connected therewith, they may think desirable'.

with nystagmus generally. A German doctor described cases between 1860 and 1863, and in 1875 a British ophthalmologist, in a paper entitled 'Miner's Nystagmus, a new disease', ascribed the condition to the overburdening of the eye-muscle and to sustained effort to see *in a deficient light*. The same view had been adopted by some continental experts from 1878 onwards. This view is now almost universally held and has been adopted by every authoritative investigating body since the *First Report of the Miners' Nystagmus Committee* (1922).[1] But miners themselves are convinced that other factors of primary importance are involved, and some experts agree with them. It is noteworthy that no case of nystagmus arising from work in coal or other mines in South Africa has been recorded. The very few cases that have occurred have been imported from Britain. Snell and Drausart from 1875 onwards claimed that the disease was due to the constrained position assumed at work and the upward direction of vision. Nieden held deficient light to be the primary and the constrained position of the miner a secondary cause: this view was likewise taken by Jeaffreson from 1887 and by Rutten from 1908 to 1922 and later, as well as by Christie (1906), who, like Rutten, regards nystagmus as a neurosis brought about by fatigue which follows the disassociation of movements normally combined, e.g. a flexion of the head with the elevation of the eyes.

Poisoning of the human system by absorption of gases given off by the coal was suggested by Pechdo (1893) and tentatively by Harrison Butler (1912), Coulter (1914), and Leighton Davies (1920), but finds little or no support to-day. The late Dr. J. S. Haldane, M.D., F.R.S., on the other hand, after a full discussion on this point,[2] concluded 'with complete certainty, that the abnormal constituents in ordinary mine air have nothing whatever to do with the production of miner's nystagmus'. On the other hand, he records that

Nystagmus *is* sometimes produced by acute poisoning with carbon monoxide, and cases are described in Glaister and Logan's *Gas Poisoning in Mining*, 1914. These cases had marked mental symptoms and the nystagmus itself is described as horizontal. On p. 262 is described '*a remarkable oscillation of the eyeballs* following afterdamp poisoning, in which the movement is incessant and continued over a few days. This phenomenon has been noticed in a most exaggerated degree in cases of producer and illuminant gas poisoning.' It is certain that acute poisoning by carbon monoxide can produce a nystagmus or the irregular oscillation of the eyeballs described above, *but these movements are not comparable with the oscillation of the eyes found in miners' nystagmus.*

Alcoholism was at one time regarded as a predisposing factor.

[1] Medical Research Council, *Special Report Series*, no. 65.
[2] *First Report of Miners' Nystagmus Committee*, 1922, p. 49.

Ohm found that large doses of alcohol lessen and even arrest the oscillations of the eyes. He added that in Germany the miners know this and make use of the fact when they wish to be declared fit for work, but the effect is transient, lasting no more than an hour. On the other hand, 'when the miner is in the acute or convalescent stage, alcohol has a marked harmful influence and a vicious circle is formed in which loss of work leads to drink and drink to prolongation of incapacity'.[1]

Age is a factor of great importance. In the series of cases examined for the Report of 1922 the average age of the workman at time of failure (through nystagmus) was 42·3 years, average duration of underground life 26 years. The youngest patient was 15 and had been 20 weeks in the pit.[2] In other words, the majority of sufferers had reached the age when they might normally be expected to find their eyesight beginning to be less acute and to feel the need for glasses.

Accident was the determining factor in 10 per cent. of the same series. 'The connexion in many cases is striking, and a man perfectly free from all symptoms of the disease presents a typical clinical picture shortly after an accident to his eye. Injuries to the eye in particular and to the head, shock, and acute illnesses, are frequently followed by the appearance of symptoms (of nystagmus).'[3]

The authors of the *First Report* suggest that these conditions 'probably' act by aggravation of a previously existing latent stage which was causing no incapacity. This, of course, is a frequent result of accident which 'brings out' other latent diseases, and is in no way peculiar to nystagmus. But it may well be that the accident set up a neurosis which in its turn gave rise to or, at least, brought out, nystagmus, which is latent in an incipient form in a large proportion of men in certain pits.

There is some evidence of hereditary predisposition, probably through the transmission of ocular defects: it is not a factor of importance. 'Sons follow their fathers' occupation and cases would occur in families in accordance with the working of the general law of averages.'[4]

A great difference of opinion exists as to the influence of refractive errors and the most diverse results have been reported: it is reasonable to suppose that the strain of working in a dim light is greater in men with defective vision and would increase with age, as it in fact does. In the series of cases examined for the purpose of the *First Report* there was a preponderance of fair, blue-eyed individuals. The Report does not comment upon this fact, but it is well known that such persons are more susceptible to heat and sunstroke, the eye here presumably plays an important part. 'Nystagmus is always found in the complete albino'—who suffers always from the sun in eastern coun-

---

[1] *First Report of Miners' Nystagmus Committee*, 1922, p. 50.   [2] Ibid., p. 51.
[3] Ibid., p. 52.   [4] Ibid., p. 53.

tries. It is not therefore surprising that the incidence of nystagmus is seasonal, occurring more frequently in summer.

After considering all these subsidiary or alternative causes of nystagmus, it is clear that the relation of the disease to illumination is of great importance though probably not the sole factor. A candle has been shown to possess great advantage over a safety lamp. It can be placed nearer the working area, gives an all-round light, remains constant through the shift, and casts no shadows. 'A collier in a naked light pit works in an illumination ten times as great as in a safety lamp mine.' These words were written in 1912: the discrepancy is now not so great as oil lamps and electric cap lamps have greatly improved lighting, but all available figures indicate that improved lighting is the best preventive measure that can be adopted and nothing that has been written or done in the last twenty-five years weakens or invalidates this claim.

Yet the improvement consequent on the widespread adoption of electric cap lamps has been slower than might reasonably have been anticipated. The number of men in receipt of compensation for nystagmus has indeed fallen from 11,083 in 1931 to 6,218 in 1937, and the percentage from 1·61 to 1·00, and of new cases from 0·39 to 0·19. Too much reliance should not be placed on these figures: those for 1931 were abnormally large owing to continued depression in the industry (the relative percentages in 1927 were 1·18 and 0·22). Since then the proportion of men employed at the coal face, who have always been most liable, has decreased and far fewer men are working in a constrained position owing to the increased use of mechanical cutters. Some miners take the view that the reflected light from 'bright' coal is an important factor, that the brilliant light in other men's caps is hard on the eyes of their neighbours, and predisposes to nystagmus. They are convinced that if deficient light were the only, or the only important factor, the decline in the incidence of the disease would have been far more substantial and they point to the apparently arbitrary distribution of the disease in support of their contention.

Miners, and those who advise them, agree with many ophthalmologists and doctors that neurosis of one kind or another is so closely associated with nystagmus that no clear line of distinction can be drawn. In December 1938 a private Member introduced a Bill, sponsored by the Home Office, which gave effect to the recommendation of the Stewart Committee that actual oscillation of the eyeball was necessary for a diagnosis of nystagmus,[1] all members of Parliament

---

[1] When in 1908 nystagmus was first scheduled as an industrial disease, it was defined as denoting only oscillation of the eyeball. In 1912 the definition became 'miner's nystagmus, whether occurring in miners or others and whether the symptom of oscillation of the eyeball is present or not'.

representing mining areas opposed this proposition and the Bill was withdrawn.

A Medical Referee, with thirty years' experience of nystagmus, wrote to a Member of Parliament on the following day:

The majority of the cases that come before me for award have not this sign, and were we to follow the recommendation hundreds of miners would be forced to work underground who were quite incapable of doing so without terrible suffering.

Again a board consisting of two men is unworkable. Who would decide when the two, the physician and the ophthalmic surgeon, could not agree? The question of the award is so difficult that I am quite sure that this disagreement would be very frequent. I have never any real difficulty in coming to a decision in the case of ordinary accident cases that come before me, but every case of miners' nystagmus presents problems that are intensely complicated, and often it is very hard to be fair and just to both parties. There is one great advantage in dealing with miners; malingering is practically absent, whereas in the ordinary accident case it has to be taken into consideration occasionally.

The question is an urgent one, but I do not think that it is fair to have no confidence in the Medical Referee. It is true that some of us like myself think that once a man has had severe nystagmus he is unfit for further work underground, whereas others tend to think that many recover completely, but I am sure that *the majority of us*[1] try very hard to strike a really judicial balance, and that our awards are based upon more knowledge than a Judge can possibly possess. I always give the miner the benefit of the doubt, and I find that my awards are about 50 per cent. each way.

I cannot, after 30 years' experience of the disease, feel that the cause is really known. I am not really satisfied that lack of illumination is the prime cause. . . . Something ought to be done of a fundamental character. I am constantly giving the award that the man 'is unfit to work underground, but that he is fit for work on the surface that does not involve much bending or exposure to bright light, and that work on the screens is impossible'. What is left? The men do not recover mooning about at home, some work is essential, and there ought to be some means of providing it out of a fund set apart for the purpose. The real cure is to get work apart from mining, and this is generally impossible. My sympathies are wholly with the miner, who when he gets nystagmus has a really 'raw deal'.

This spontaneous expression of opinion from a man whose high authority is everywhere recognized well illustrates the fundamental difficulties of those concerned with diagnosis. It may be contrasted with the view of Dr. H. M. Vernon, a former University lecturer on Chemical Physiology at Oxford and from 1919 to 1932 an Investigator for the Industrial Health Research Board.

Writing in 1936, he holds nystagmus to be a form of neurosis:

The tendency of considerable accident risk to induce or reinforce neurotic symptoms is suggested by the experience of coal miners.

---

[1] The italics are ours.

He points to the great increase in the 'number of compensation cases' after the Compensation Act came into force—forgetting that the sole object of the Workmen's Compensation Act was to widen the range of injuries for which compensation would be legally claimed. He 'observes, pontifically that . . . in the U.S.A. *where miner's nystagmus is not compensated,*[1] the disease is practically unknown'.

The statement does not do justice to the facts. Nystagmus is not scheduled in the U.S.A. because it is non-existent, as Dr. Vernon could have ascertained had he studied the available American technical literature on the subject. Thus Kober and Hayhurst declare: 'Safety lamps, fortunately, with their imperfect illumination (the potent cause of nystagmus in British mines) are not required for work in Ohio or Illinois mines because these mines, being ventilated, are non-gassy, so that naked lamps are safe.'[2]

'In the U.S.A.', writes Dr. Frank Shuffleton, 'the adequacy of illumination probably explains the absence of nystagmus.'[3] The same author 'regrets that, although the cause is known, nothing has been done effectively to prevent the disease in British mines'. We note with surprise that the B.M.A. has given fresh currency to this legend in a special Report on Nystagmus in which it is stated that 'In America, where compensation is not payable, no cases are reported'. This statement is presumably an insinuation that there was no nystagmus in the U.S.A. *because* Workmen's Compensation was not paid. If this is not the meaning it would have been better to indicate the probable reason for the absence of nystagmus in American mines which is certainly not the lack of compensation.[4] Ignoring foreign views and experience (a fault to which British academic writers are prone) Dr. Vernon has concocted his own theory, viz. that sufferers from nystagmus are neurotics who, 'in the absence of compensation, would usually return to work with very little delay, and ignore or overcome their neurotic symptoms'.

The Stewart Committee took a more scientific view: but it is premature to regard their Report as conclusive,[5] for the evidence was given in confidence and those who appeared before the Committee were not subject to expert cross-examination. Nystagmus in general represents a more or less harmless disease, **if properly dealt with at the beginning, and if at a later stage light work is obtainable.** 'The course of the malady thereafter depends almost entirely on the

[1] The italics are ours. Cf. loc. cit., pp. 25–6.
[2] G. M. Kober and E. R. Hayhurst, *Industrial Health*, Philadelphia, 1924, p. 151.
[3] Cf. *Journal of Industrial Hygiene*, Nov. 1920, p. 254.
[4] British Medical Association, *Report of Committee on the Diagnosis and Certification of Miners' Nystagmus*, 1936, p. 5.   [5] Cf. *Stewart Report*, pp. 9–10.

question whether the patient obtains *light* work as soon as he is able
to undertake it', failing which incapacity for work may supervene.
The Memorandum of Evidence by the Federation of Colliery Deputies
Associations of Great Britain reported very definitely to the Hetherington Commission in 1939[1]: 'It is common knowledge that once a
miner has been certified as suffering from Miner's Nystagmus he is
doomed and debarred from again becoming employed except in rare
circumstances.' Dr. Vernon attributes much of the disease to psychoneurosis, existence of which is not open to dispute.[2] On the other hand,
many workers affected by nystagmus or its early symptoms 'carry on
their work as best they can until either they become accustomed to the
condition, or until developments supervene which preclude their
carrying it on any longer'.[3]

Men who act thus are not neurotics by nature: Dr. Vernon seems to
be unaware of their existence, but he wrote while the Stewart Committee was still sitting. There is apparently a long course leading from the
first and in some cases harmless symptoms to grave mental derange-
ments and even suicide.[4] A neurasthenic disposition may indeed make
the workman inclined to overestimate his malady—a matter which we
shall have to discuss when dealing with 'malingering' and related problems—but there is no reason to think that this frame of mind is more
common than the sanguine and courageous temperament which
makes a man 'carry-on' till his condition becomes incurable. It is not
unreasonable, moreover, to regard this 'psycho-neurasthenic' condition
itself as an industrial disease, particularly if the nystagmic workman
was normal in this respect before he contracted the disease. 'He had
been a cheerful man before the onset of the disease', noted Lord
Justice Scrutton in respect of the suicide case connected with nystagmus, apparently laying stress upon this from a legal point of view.[5] In
a Report published in 1932[6] the Medical Research Council suggested
that the psychological conditions connected with nystagmus should be
regarded as analogous to 'shell shock', and denied that psychological
symptoms can be a direct physical result of the oscillation of the eyeball.

[1] Cf. *Hetherington Commission*, p. 697.

[2] Cf. *Stewart Report*, p. 4, where the *Haldane Report on Miner's Nystagmus* is quoted
(1923) which stated among others: 'The increase in duration of cases in Great Britain is due
to the dragging on of cases in which the workman is suffering from hysteria or psychoneurosis'.

[3] Cf. *Stewart Report*, p. 9.

[4] *Dixon v. Sutton Heath and Lea Green Colliery Limited*. There are many unrecorded
cases: this tendency is familiar to all persons with practical acquaintance with the problem.

[5] See p. 54.

[6] Cf. Medical Research Council, *Third Report of the Miners' Nystagmus Committee*, 1932,
conclusion no. 4

From the evidence and *Report* of the Stewart Committee the following important points emerge:

1. The main cause of the disease is deficient illumination.[1] In conditions of low illumination an object can be seen better by looking, not directly at it but a little to one side of it. Hence the miner's eyes are constantly 'wobbling' in the effort to find an optimum point of vision, and this, continued over lengthy periods of time, gives rise to oscillations which tend to become perpetuated by habit spasm. There can be no doubt that 'if sufficient illumination could be provided the miner would use his central vision and the tendency to eye movement would be eliminated'. Improvements in mine lighting could eventually greatly reduce the disease. The Committee received evidence that in certain areas there have been few or no cases of nystagmus in pits where the lighting has been considerably improved. But the prevalence of nystagmus is apparently influenced by the structure of the mines itself, so that where the coal seams are thin, the cramped position of the miner at work may well make him more prone to nystagmus than he would be if he could perform most of his work in an upright position. This is what the *Stewart Report* calls 'the positional theory of causation'.

2. Miner's nystagmus should not, in general, lead to incapacity: **this can be easily avoided if the miner is restored to some work as early as medically advisable,** and **thereby forestalling psychoneurosis.** The decision whether the workman's condition is such as to entitle him to compensation and as to the degree of his incapacity, should, in the view of the Medical Research Council, be entirely in the hands of medical men having special experience of the disease and cases should be reviewed at suitable intervals.

3. As employers are afraid of the recurrence of nystagmus and the emergence of new compensation claims they do not re-employ former sufferers underground. Most colliery proprietors not only refuse further underground work to men demonstrably susceptible to miner's nystagmus, but exact a declaration from men seeking employment underground that they have not previously suffered from nystagmus. Failure to disclose previous liability to nystagmus was till recently held by the courts to disqualify a miner from claiming compensation for a second attack of the same disease.

Can the nystagmic workman find light work or work on the surface?

[1] Cf. *Stewart Report*, p. 12. 'The Swansea area ... was mentioned in evidence as one in which the incidence of nystagmus had for years been heavy, and it was realized that in order to improve matters better lighting was desirable. In a certain colliery in that area where the conditions have been thus improved there have been no new cases of nystagmus recorded during the last few years. But when the coal itself reflects light in brilliant glistening facets, as is the case in certain seams, certain types of artificial light may increase eyestrain. Miners themselves hold that excessive heat in mines is a predisposing factor.'

In many cases there is no prospect of such work. The *Stewart Report* emphasizes that

The adoption by the owners of the policy referred to, made the position of workmen in these districts well nigh hopeless so far as their own industry is concerned.

This is confirmed by Reports made lately to the Unemployment Assistance Board.[1] The Hanley District Officer reported that in April 1937 an analysis was made at the Ministry of Labour Employment Exchange of the registered 'ex-colliery workers'—including labourers whose last employment had been in the coalmining industry. Of a total of 2,798 no less than 2,039 were classified as unfit, in addition to 565 men who had received lump-sum compensation and who were consequently unable to resume employment at the mines; only five were found to be fit to be skilled underground workers (and of these four were over 45 years of age); only forty were registered as unskilled underground workers and of these thirty-nine were classified as unfit. This analysis shows, as the Hanley District Officer emphasized, 'that it is unlikely that many applicants to the Board will obtain employment in the coalfields'. It was also stated for two areas (that of Cinderford and the Bath area) that men who have suffered from affections of the respiratory system[2] have during recent years 'been regarded' as unfitted for further underground occupation owing to the potential risk of silicosis.

Miss Ward's Bill of December 1938 made no provision for finding work for miners suffering from nystagmus in its early stages; on the other hand it would unquestionably have made certification more difficult. It presented special treatment for men under 30, who could be dismissed on payment of thirteen weeks compensation—a salutary if harsh provision which could only have been justified if the Bill included adequate provision for finding alternative employment. In cases where weekly compensation had been paid for two years the Bill empowered Medical Boards to recommend redemption of weekly payments by a lump-sum payment. This, too, might have been salutary if accompanied by effective measures to provide alternative employment. In the circumstances it is not surprising that the Miners' representatives opposed the Bill, though it might have been greatly improved in Committee in this and other respects. It was further stated that in these areas with a comparatively high number of unemployed men registered as miners there was little prospect of their return to mine work even when trade was brisk.

[1] Unemployment Assistance Board, *Annual Report for 1937*, pp. 109 and 117.
[2] Cf. later under silicosis, pp. 85 sqq.

The words 'regarded as unfit' were doubtless carefully chosen in order to avoid any expression of opinion why or by whom these men were so 'regarded'. It is fair to assume that refusal to employ such men is based primarily upon the desire to avoid possible claims for compensation—a matter beyond the scope of the Unemployment Assistance Board. In this connexion a miner is sometimes placed in a legal dilemma. If he has entirely recovered from an attack of nystagmus, but is unable to find underground employment by the just-mentioned arrangement between the coal-owners, nor light employment, should he be treated as totally incapacitated as a result of the disease? In one case it was decided that the attack of nystagmus was a *causa sine qua non* of the miner's inability to obtain work, but not the *causa causans*.

Such a decision operates very hardly on the miner whose inability to find work is attributed not to disease but to the discretionary action of an employer against whom he has no remedy. It is hard to decide whether a man who had been suffering from the disease still harbours 'a proneness or susceptibility'[1] or whether such predisposition was merely due to his 'idiopathic disposition'. In 1934 the House of Lords allowed an appeal of a miner, who had falsely declared that he had not previously suffered from miner's nystagmus and, after it had been detected, was discharged and claimed compensation afresh. The County Court and Court of Appeal dismissed his case, but his appeal to the House of Lords was successful. The Stewart Committee was apprised of the difficulties which this decision would bring upon employers, particularly in cases where a nystagmic miner had already received a substantial lump sum, as also where the liability has not been finally ended, and made recommendations to overcome this difficulty.[2] On the other hand, the *Stewart Report* itself called attention to 'existing uncertainties' in the matter. To remove these uncertainties by some more comprehensive and defined legal enactments, coupled with effective measures of rehabilitation and compensation administration is as necessary as disease prevention itself and should not await leisurely discussion by a Royal Commission charged to investigate the whole field.[3] While the Stewart Committee was sitting, an agreement was reached by a Mutual Indemnity Association in the South and West Yorkshire districts providing *inter alia* that a workman who has suffered from nystagmus and is certified recovered from the disease, will, in the case of the first time of having suffered, be allowed to return to his old work; in the event of his old work not being available he will be found other suitable work temporarily in accordance with the principles

[1] Cf. Willis, *Workmen's Compensation*, 1936, p. 518.
[2] Cf. *Stewart Report*, p. 39.
[3] Cf. *Debates H.C.*, Nov. 3rd 1938.

obtaining at each colliery as regards men restarting work.[1] This is a hopeful sign.

Another occupational disease which during the last decade has given rise to wide research and discussion is silicosis and certain diseases related thereto. As it is not our task to review this and other occupational diseases other than for the purpose of our inquiry into the conditions of Workmen's Compensation, we cannot undertake anything like a detailed analysis of the medical opinion and controversy on the subject. It is admirably summarized by Dr. A. J. Lanza, Assistant Medical Director, Metropolitan Life Assurance Company, in his recently published *Silicosis and Asbestosis* (Oxford Medical Publication), 1938, which comprehensively reviews the whole subject for the first time. It includes an authoritative chapter on Occupational Preventive and Legislative aspects in Britain by Dr. E. L. Middleton, Medical Inspector of Factories, Home Office.

Unlike nystagmus, which is a 'harmless' disease, silicosis, formerly known as 'miner's phthisis', 'grinder's rot', 'potter's' or 'stonemason's phthisis', is a 'killing' disease of the lungs due to the inhalation of flinty siliceous particles. The incidence of silicosis is heavy and widespread: it is often accompanied by tuberculosis. The possibility that some other minerals may play an important part, if not the only part (e.g. sericite, as suggested by W. R. Jones), cannot, however, be entirely excluded. In the words of the Report of the Royal Commission on Safety in Mines 1938 (p. 456):

Whether the irritant in the dust is free silica or something else, there is no doubt that exposure to dust, and particularly to fine dust, is the fundamental element in the causation of the disease. It is also generally agreed that the irritant property of the dust does not arise from physical characteristics . . . but from the fact that the dust particles dissolve in the lung, and the harmful solution thus produced initiates the process of fibrosis. It is for this reason that bronchitis, bronchopneumonia and other diseases which impair the dust-eliminating function of the lungs are often thought to be contributory.

Over a period of $6\frac{1}{2}$ years, 1931–7, 411 men were certified as partially, 1,003 as wholly, disabled by the disease, and there were 317 deaths.[2]

Up to 1936 the number of cases certified rose continuously: it is too early to say whether the slight fall recorded in 1937 has any significance. The disease is prevalent in Germany (Ruhr), in the anthracite region of Pennsylvania, in Belgium, and northern France.[3]

Lanza and Vane, on a rough but, in their view, very conservative estimate, assess the number of workers exposed to silica dust to a

---

[1] Cf. *Stewart Report*, p. 29.   [2] *Safety in Mines Report*, p. 458.
[3] Dr. Middleton in Lanza, op. cit., p. 383.

harmful degree in the U.S.A. at upwards of 500,000, or say 3½ per cent. of industrial workers: others have put the percentage at a higher figure.

Silicosis is not a new disease: the Elder Pliny describes the devices used by refiners to prevent inhalation of 'the fatal dust'.[1] Hippocrates in the fifth century B.C. recorded the symptoms of a metal-digger which differ little from those observed among present-day miners suffering from dusty inhalation. Agricola (1556) and Paracelsus (1567) recognized dust as the cause of lung disease. Dimerbrock in 1649 made the first section of a stonecutter's lung which revealed 'lung vesicles completely clogged with fine dust'. Ramazzini noted[2] the effect of dust on the respiratory organs and the connexion between dust inhalation and consumption.

A patent for grinding flints by a wet method was granted to Thomas Benson of Newcastle-under-Lyme early in the last century. Previously, flints were pounded dry, the process proving so fatal that 'any person, ever so healthful and strong, working in that business, cannot possibly survive over two years'.

Thrackrah (1831) noted that not all dusts are perilous to health. Dr. Greenhow, the first Medical Factory Inspector, collected lung specimens of workmen who had died from dust diseases, and as a result of his work the first Royal Commission was appointed in 1861 (Lord Palmerston being Prime Minister) to make a thorough investigation of health conditions in mines. The interest of medical men was awakened, none too soon, for mining continued to employ increasing numbers of men in every part of the world, particularly in South Africa, where pulmonary dust diseases caused great havoc in the last quarter of the nineteenth century, as the quartz content of gold-bearing ore bodies contained from 80 to 90 per cent. free silica. But silicosis was not scheduled as an industrial disease under the Workmen's Compensation Act until 1918 some fifty years after the disease and its cause had been recognized.

The disease is not peculiar to mining. It is not infrequent among men engaged in sand-blasting, a process of projecting sand, crushed flint or other grit, by means of compressed air, against a surface, in order to remove adherent sand from castings and to produce a surface of metal or other articles suitable for coating with enamel or another metal. It is also used to apply sand to the surface of bricks and tiles in the plastic state.

Abrasives which formerly included a high proportion of free silica are now being replaced by metal grit or other abrasives containing no free silica: this obviates the risk to workmen from the abrasive itself,

[1] Pliny, *Nat. Hist.*, bk. ii.   [2] See vol. i, p. 14.

but does not affect the dust hazard from the moulding sand which is being removed in this way.

Elaborate safety regulations have been framed, but, 'even with improvements in sand-blasting apparatus, the margin of safety is so narrow in this hazardous process that the workers cannot yet be said to be fully protected. The only solution of the problem at present in sight is the abolition of siliceous abrasives in sand-blasting and the removal of moulding sand from castings before shot-blasting.'[1]

Another process entailing risk of silicosis is the grinding of metals, where dust is produced by the attrition of the grindstone. The change from grindstones containing free silica to artificial abrasives has been rapid and has beneficially affected mortality rates. Metal grinding is subject to an elaborate code of preventive regulations and has its own scheme under the Workmen's Compensation Acts.[2]

The Refractories Industries, which have been subject to special regulations since 1919, are a group of industries handling material containing not less than 80 per cent. total silica, including the quarrying or mining of the raw materials, usually sandstones of the coal measures called 'ganister' in open quarries or mines, or sands or clays. The material is crushed, and made into bricks, cement, and similar products for use as refractories in the manufacture of metals and the lining of gas-retorts and flues.

Abrasive Soap Powders.

These products include a proportion of finely ground free silica and in connexion with their manufacture some of the most rapidly developing cases of silicosis on record have occurred before adequate measures could be taken to deal with the danger. Some of the victims were quite young. This is a typical case of an industry which developed very rapidly and where employers, through ignorance, exposed workmen to very serious risks. Since 1931 it has been covered by the Various Industries (Silicosis) Scheme.

The Sandstone Industry.

In this industry, in which silicosis has long been recognized as an industrial hazard, the risk is greatest under cover or in a closed yard and least in the open air. The stonemason who dresses stone by hand is most liable, and preventive measures are not easily applied nor readily adopted by masons who dislike wearing respirators. Localized exhaust draughts applied to the point at which the stone is being dressed, have been devised and are increasingly used.

---

[1] Dr. Middleton in Lanza, op. cit., p. 351. [2] Middleton, ibid., pp. 352 sqq.

A special scheme is in force for this industry similar to that of the Refractories Industry.

The Granite Industry.

The Granite industry also gives rise to cases of silicosis, and men employed in dressing granite, but no others, are covered by the Various Industries (Silicosis) Scheme, 1931.

Slate Quarrying and Dressing.

Slate quarrying and dressing is not specifically covered by the Workmen's Compensation (Silicosis) Acts, though during 1930–6 twenty-three deaths from silicosis occurred among slate quarry men and dressers. Lanza holds that 'in view of the ages reached by many of the workmen while still remaining fit for work, it may be assumed that there is no general disability among them from exposure to dust'. We would add a caveat; any new development, such as the commercial use of 'expanded slate' with a suitable binding agent, might so increase the hazard as to make special regulations necessary.

The Pottery Industry.

Exposure to flint dust in the pottery industry in addition to the preliminary processes of preparation of the flint, occurs among those manipulating the earthenware body in its semi-manufactured states: in these processes the incidence of silicosis is highest, the average annual mortality being as high as 16·4 per thousand in some processes. The industry is covered by the Pottery (Silicosis) Regulations, 1932. The growing use of alumina to replace flint in various processes is likely to reduce mortality.

Tin-mining.

Silicosis killed 140 tin-miners in the seven years 1930–6, a mortality rate of twelve per thousand. The Various Industries (Silicosis) Scheme covers all workmen employed *underground* in tin-mines.

Haematite Iron-ore Mining.

This industry which is concentrated in north Cumberland and north Lancashire involved little risk of silicosis until machine superseded hand-drilling: during the six years 1931–6 fifty-seven deaths have occurred among haematite miners, an average of about ten per annum. At one time the management and workmen were alike sceptical of the danger from dust. The danger is now recognized: preventive measures are enforced. The industry is covered by the Various Industries (Silicosis) Scheme.

Coal-mining.

The danger of silicosis has long been recognized and was noted by the Royal Commission on Mines in 1909. It follows especially those processes underground which expose the worker to siliceous dust. The distribution of the disease is very unequal. The number of fatal cases, calculated on the number of wage earners, is 22·37 for Great Britain; 4·13 for England and 112·59 for South Wales and Monmouth. 'No completely satisfactory explanation of the distribution of the disease has yet been reached.'[1]

Sir A. Faulkner (Permanent Under-Secretary, Mines Dept.) stated in evidence before the Royal Commission on Safety in Coal Mines, 1936: 'There are cases where it is not possible to trace the silicosis to silica.' You may have two pits in apparently identical circumstances, one of which has much, the other no, silicosis, and nobody can explain why.[2]

Mine-owners and trade unions are alive to the importance of preventive measures, and are co-operating with the Mines Dept. The urgency of the matter is emphasized by the fact that cases of disablement by silicosis rose from 285 in 1936 to 437 in 1938.[3] The whole question is under active examination by the Industrial Pulmonary Diseases Committee of the Medical Research Council.[4]

Byssinosis.

In 1937 the Home Secretary appointed a Committee under the chairmanship of Sir David Ross[5] to consider and report 'whether an equitable and workable scheme could be devised for providing compensation in the case of persons who, after employment for a substantial period in card rooms and certain dusty parts of cotton spinning mills, become or have become disabled by respiratory illness, as indicated in the Report of the Departmental Committee on dust in card rooms'. The Committee reported[6] that chronic bronchitis was less prevalent than formerly among card-room operators, thanks to dust extracting apparatus, but that fresh cases were still occurring.

A properly constituted Medical Board would in the case of an incapacitated applicant who had been not less than twenty years in this employment be able to decide whether the respiratory disease from which he was suffering was occupational in origin—viz. byssinosis.

---

[1] Dr. Middleton, ibid., p. 381.   [2] A. 1207, 1209, see also Dr. Fisher, A. 22, 331.
[3] Debates H.C., Feb. 2nd 1939, col. 370.   [4] Ibid., Aug. 1st 1939, col. 2189.
[5] The other members were Mr. P. N. Harvey, F.I.A., Mr. T. Hutson, Prof. G. R. Murray, M.D., F.R.C.P., and Mr. W. F. Wackrill, O.B.E.
[6] Home Office Report of the Departmental Committee on Compensation for Card Room Workers, 1939.

They considered it possible to bring it within the framework of the Workmen's Compensation Act, provided that the applicant had been employed in the cotton-blowing and/or card room for twenty years, and within the last twelve months was totally incapacitated by byssinosis. Only male workers were to be eligible.

For men at present employed who may hereafter become totally incapacitated by byssinosis they proposed machinery similar to that devised to deal with silicosis. For those who are already so disabled and have left the industry they proposed a separate *ad hoc* scheme. The total number of such cases was estimated at not over 200: the cost, at 10*s.* per head per week, plus administrative costs, at not over £7,000, and steadily diminishing. It would be met by an annual levy from each employer.

The Industrial Pulmonary Diseases Committee of the Medical Research Council is engaged upon a comprehensive investigation of pulmonary disease in South Wales coal-mines. The investigation aims at relating differences in clinical types of pulmonary diseases—with particular attention to 'certifiable' as opposed to 'non-certifiable' silicosis—to environmental conditions. It is pointed out that industrial dusts, and in particular the siliceous dust may cause more disability than is at present included in the official term "silicosis" '. This investigation of the scientific problem arising from the incidence of pulmonary disease among coal-miners began in 1936, and was estimated to cost about £5,000 a year, of which the Miners' Welfare Fund provides £1,000.[1]

Compensation for silicosis and asbestosis, which in many respects resembles silicosis, is payable under Special Schemes of Compensation, of which the Various Industries (Silicosis) Amendment Scheme, dated January 29th 1935, is the most recent. Compensation paid under these schemes is treated separately by the Home Office. The distribution of cases and compensation paid under the various schemes in 1937 is shown on page 86.

The preponderating incidence of silicosis in coal-mining is a new factor due to the coming into force of the Various Industries Schemes of 1931, 1934, and 1935. Figures for silicosis in coal-mining were first quoted separately in 1933, when the industry accounted for 28 out of 154 fatal cases and for 126 out of 448 new disablement cases. Compensation for new and continued cases of disablement, at £16,451, represented about one-quarter of the total amount paid.[2] Since 1933

---

[1] *Royal Commission on Workmen's Compensation*, 1939, *Evidence*, p. 10. Further: *Eighteenth Annual Report of the Industrial Health Research Board*, June 1938, pp. 35–8, and 56–7. Also *Labour*, April 1939, pp. 44–5.

[2] Cf. *Workmen's Compensation Statistics for 1933.* p. 12.

Silicosis and Asbestosis

	Fatal cases		Disablement cases		
	Number of cases	Amount paid	Number of cases continued from previous year	New cases	Amount paid
		£			£
Coal-mining Industry* . . .	85	21,344	674	338	83,451
Sandstone Industry Scheme . .	15	3,824	313	44	14,950
China and Earthenware Industry .	35	7,369	197	44	14,102
Refractories Industries Scheme .	6	1,377	265	5	11,230
Builders	16	3,746	95	25	7,441
Miscellaneous	32	8,300	128	43	11,436
Metal Industries	12	3,489	46	7	2,646
Total	201	£49,449	1,718	506	£145,256

* The following figures for 1938 are of interest (*Debates H.C.*, Feb. 2nd 1939, col. 388.):

Applications to the Medical Board for certificates under the Various Industries (Silicosis) Schemes from Coal-miners

	1938			1937		
	Total	South Wales	Anthracite Mines	Total	South Wales	Anthracite Mines
Disablement or suspension:						
Number of applications for certificates	821	622	301	643	471	230
Number of certificates granted	434	382	205	286	251	132
Number of certificates refused	387	240	96	357	220	98
Deaths:						
Number of applications for certificates	94	80	32	99	84	45
Number certified as due to the disease	59	46	18	72	63	35
Number of certificates refused	35	34	14	27	21	10

the figure has greatly increased and the compensation paid for silicosis cases in the coal-mining industry now amounted to more than half of the total sums paid under the schemes.

This development was not anticipated by experts. As recently as 1931 the late Prof. J. S. Haldane could find no evidence that any class of work in coal-mining was subject to risk from silicosis except under

very exceptional and preventible conditions.[1] He had actively promoted such measures by calling attention to the very great risk which
may occur among men driving roads through sandstone or other
highly siliceous rock, particularly where machine drills were used.
A section forbidding such work was inserted in the Mines Act of
1911 but, as he stated twenty years later the clause was ignored; so
also were the resultant deaths. As silicosis in coal-mining thus
appeared incidental rather than consequential to mining processes
the term 'silicosis' only recently found its way into current medical
parlance on the coal-fields.[2] Men sickened and died of it, but it was
not recognized as an industrial hazard. The question attracted considerable attention before the Royal Commission on Safety in Coal-
Mines of 1936. Mr. Ebenezer Edwards, cross-examining Dr. S. W.
Fisher, H.M. Medical Inspector of Mines, suggested that 'there must
be hundreds of cases where doctors refuse to certify a man suffering
from silicosis because of the difficulty of an ordinary medical practitioner. It often happens that there is nothing at all done either indicating that it is a case of silicosis or anything for the dependants. There
may be a post-mortem examination and the doctor performing the
post-mortem examination will not certify that it is silicosis, and it will
be only in exceptional cases where the facts are revealed by the Silicosis Medical Board, where you have got a Board that really understand the matter.'[3] The suggestion was not controverted. In view of
the uncertain position of medical views in the matter, Dr. S. W. Fisher
went so far as to mention the possibility of affixing a new name to such
dust disease in mines which, though leading to grave consequences,
cannot safely be called 'silicosis'.

Death from silicosis is, as Dr. T. David Jones once put it, 'a terrible
death, and one never to be forgotten'.[4] It is aggravated by the uncertain circumstances which attend the analysis and the possible results as
relating to compensation. The suffering worker or his surviving
relatives cannot understand that their financial plight may be due to the
medical inability to identify the disease with medico-legal accuracy.
'I do not think what it is called interests very much the men who are
suffering,' declared H.M. Medical Inspector of Mines before the
Safety Commission. He agreed that 'if there is no remedy, at least the
sufferers themselves and their dependants should receive compensation' and that 'there are a lot of sufferers in the industry who are not
getting justice' who should be brought within the compensation

[1] Cf. Haldane, *Silicosis and Coal Mining*, pp. 8–9, Inst. Mining Engineers, 1931 (reprint). [2] Cf. *Royal Commission on Safety in Coal-Mines, 1938, Evidence*, Q. and A. 22,527.
[3] Cf. *Report on Safety in Coal-Mines, Evidence*, Q. 22, 540.
[4] Cf. Haldane, loc. cit., p. 14.

scheme.[1] Six years earlier Prof. Haldane had argued that 'scheduling' might be an 'invitation to endless litigation and expense, in the midst of which any real case would probably be missed'.[2]

The accepted measures of prevention are: suppression of dust, mainly by keeping the surface of the material to be worked wet; exhaust ventilation; the provision of breathing apparatus; and initial and periodic medical examination of persons exposed to risk.[3] But progress along these lines is slow and remedies officially recommended and even ordered are reluctantly applied in practice. Even were it otherwise it would not affect the urgent need for measures of compensation for sufferers, particularly in England, where the system of accident and disease prevention have always been administered independently of compensation. One of the indirect consequences of this undesirable division of responsibility and medical uncertainty[4] is that a workman who complains of silicosis has to pay for medical examinations if the outcome is negative.[5] If the workman fails to obtain the certificate from the Regional Medical Officer, he may decide to proceed with his application for examination by the Medical Board, but in that case he will be required to deposit a fee based on the full cost of the examination, part of which will be refunded to him if the Medical Board issue a certificate and the liability of the employer has been established.[6] The International Conference on Silicosis in 1934 reported that:

Experience proves that for the purpose of compensation of silicosis it is essential to entrust the diagnosis and certification of silicosis only to medical men specially qualified for this work, who should be provided with the necessary equipment, especially with facilities for adequate radiological examination.

[1] Cf. *Report on Safety in Coal-Mines*, Q. and A. 22, 551.   [2] Cf. Haldane, loc. cit., p. 9.

[3] Cf. *Home Office Memorandum on Silicosis and Asbestosis*, 1935, pp. 6–8.

[4] Cf. for this, apart from the facts already mentioned, the *Report on Safety in Coal-Mines*, p. 844, para. 14. 'The peculiar incidence of the disease among workers in coal-mines has not yet been satisfactorily explained. It has been suggested that stone-dusting in mines might be the cause of the disease. In this connexion it is only necessary to point out that in proportion to numbers employed by far the greatest number of cases come from anthracite mines, where no stone dusting is done.' (Statement made by the Medical Inspector of Mines made on Nov. 2nd 1936.) It is in this connexion also interesting to note that, according to American experience, it is the opinion of several authorities that when a man reaches the age of 40 or 45 and has had a dust exposure of 15 or more years, and shows no incapacity, he is usually an asset and not a liability. There are manufacturers in the U.S.A. who in face of such dust-proof condition of men who have been long in their employ in occupations prone to silicosis have replaced young workers by much older employees accustomed to dusty occupations. Cf. *1935 Convention*, loc. cit., address by Dr. Robert Hunt on 'Pneumococciosis', p. 89.

[5] For particulars cf. *Fees payable for examinations and certifications by Medical Board*, as prescribed by the Silicosis and Asbestosis (Medical Fees) Regulations 1931 and 1934.

[6] Also *Home Office Memorandum*, pp. 10–11.

The application of this proposal to English conditions would, however, involve far-reaching changes in the administrative structure of workmen's compensation. It is certainly applicable to many other industrial injuries and diseases. We shall discuss it in greater detail at a later stage.

The problem of silicosis bears directly upon many other branches of Workmen's Compensation. Experience in regard thereto shows that even though an occupational disease is legally classified for compensation and liability purposes as equivalent to an 'accident', the proof of disease is by no means simple. Litigation is not excluded by scheduling the disease or drafting special schemes; as the late Sir Thomas Legge wrote:

Satisfaction with these schemes, as now framed, is tempered with some bewilderment at the complicated conditions under which they have to be operated, but under the present Workmen's Compensation Act that is unavoidable. Although nominally covering all recognized industries in which silicosis might reasonably occur, the limitation of application in the definition of processes in one and another scheme, the limit of time (three years) after cessation of work laid down, as debarring a workman from claiming for a malady which may not cause incapacity until ten years or more later—let alone the fees that have to be paid—are bound to cause difficulties from time to time. Thus the Various Industries Scheme is made to apply to 'mining and quarrying silica rock', and heavy costs may have to be incurred by the workman to satisfy the court that a rock such as mudstone, capable of producing silicosis, is 'sandstone' within the meaning of the term 'silica rock', although the 'getting of granite', which may contain much less free silica than mudstone, is included in the Scheme.[1]

Similar complaints have been brought forward lately by the Trade Union Congress, which has dealt very fully with the matter in its Memorandum to the Hetherington Commission. The complaint among others concerns the delays experienced before a disease may be scheduled, and papilloma of the bladder in chemical workers and bronchitis in card-room workers were mentioned in particular as examples of such delay. As a matter of reform it is recommended that a Committee consisting of medical men, lawyers, and representatives of industry should periodically revise the Schedules.[2]

The extension of the three years rule is under consideration by the Government; a draft order extending the three years limit to five years has been prepared, and is expected to cover 85 per cent. of the hard cases, but no remedy apparently has yet been envisaged for the unfor-

[1] Sir T. Legge, *Industrial Maladies*, ed. by Dr. S. A. Henry, M.D., Inspector of Factories, 1934, pp. 34-5.
[2] See § 72 (4) Mr. Mainwaring's Bill of 1936. *Hetherington Commission, Evidence*, pp. 428–36. As to lack of uniformity see § 188 of T.U.C. Memorandum, and Q. 5051–92.

tunate 15 per cent. remaining outside.[1] The problem of detecting the malady at an early date and of measures for checking its development at the onset are dealt with in Chapter XI. The question of periodical examinations entails many difficulties, not only in this country, but also in the U.S.A. where it has been much discussed of late.

The fact that pre-employment and periodic examinations of workers have sometimes been used oppressively has aroused opposition to such practices. There are, however, examples of legal and administrative protective measures which have led to a more favourable attitude of workers towards medical examinations. In Wisconsin a recent law provides for payment up to the sum of Dollars 3500, predicated on wage loss, if a workman is discharged on account of non-disabling silicosis.[2]

Apart from the particular problem of silicosis, much attention was devoted to the 'time limit' of scheduled diseases in the Home Office Memorandum to the Hetherington Commission.[3] The general conclusion reached was that twelve months should suffice. Yet the same document gave figures relating to skin cancer in mule spinners which pointed a very different moral. Of fifty-eight such cases reported in 1938 in each of eight cases the man had ceased to be a spinner for more than twelve months at the time of the supposed onset of the disease.[4] In the hands of a competent medical board difficulties of diagnosis need not, as the Memorandum appears to suggest, be an obstacle to compensation. Nor should we be deterred from making provision for such cases by their relative infrequency: that is an argument that leads nowhere and ignores the very basis of the Act and of British jurisprudence, viz. to provide a legal remedy for every wrong, however infrequent. The rarity, for example, of cases of jactitation of marriage did not deter our forefathers from making appropriate provision against it. We do not underrate the efforts made of recent years to extend our knowledge of the character of many industrial diseases with a view to certification as such in appropriate cases.[5] The difficulties of diagnosis are great: 'Even the most severe cases are liable to be confused with other maladies and mild infections (poisoning by turpentine, papilloma occurring in workers liable to mule spinner's cancer and other diseases of related type) present still greater difficulty.'[6]

The introduction of regional Medical Boards as an integral part of the administration of Workmen's Compensation would certainly

[1] *Debates H.C.*, April 20th 1939, cols. 489–91.
[2] U.S. Dept. of Labor, 'Medical Aid under Workmen's Compensation Laws', *Monthly Labor Review*, Jan. 1939, reprint p. 13.   [3] §§ 450–6.
[4] The interval between leaving employment and notification was $1\frac{1}{2}$, 2, 2, 5, 7, 8, 10, and 12 years.
[5] Cf. *Home Office Departmental Committee on Compensation for Industrial Diseases, First Report* 1932; *Second Report* 1933; *Third Report* 1936.   [6] Third Report, p. 7.

assist diagnosis and facilitate certification. The Ross Committee on byssinosis in card-room workers were satisfied that a properly constituted Medical Board would in the case of an applicant of about twenty years' employment history be able after considering all the evidence, clinical and historical, to decide not only whether the applicant was incapacitated by respiratory disease but whether it was occupational in origin.[1]

In this connexion we may recall that the representative of the Ministry of Health, in his evidence before the Hetherington Commission, explained that his Department did not offer advice to panel practitioners, as 'doctors might feel that guidance from Whitehall on the diagnosis or prognosis or etiology of disease was ordinarily unnecessary'. Doctors preferred to rely on the Medical Press rather than upon 'some paragraph in a circular issued from Whitehall'.[2] Too much significance should not perhaps be attached to this somewhat cynical view, though it finds some confirmation in the record of Stationery Office sales of official Reports and monographs of the Ministry of Health and of the Medical Research Council often of first class importance and of publishers of medical text-books. But it shows how great is the need for a better organized treatment of industrial disease. Medical Boards would more readily assimilate the latest results of research in those directions with which they are most closely concerned, and would find it easier to invoke the assistance of specialists.[3]

The main deduction that we draw from the facts set forth in this and preceding chapters is that without better administrative machinery than at present exists little further protection against either accident or disease can effectively be given by fresh legislation. The best expert scientific knowledge in many fields can only be made available and applied to practical affairs by centralizing the administration of the Compensation Acts and combining it with executive measures of accident prevention.

[1] *Home Office Report of Departmental Committee on Compensation for Card Room Workers*, 1939, p. 11.
[2] *Hetherington Commission*, Q. 1852–6.
[3] Cf. Mr. Spearing, *Hetherington Commission*, A. 1755–6, where the possible functions of a Medical Officer as acting under the 'Compensation Officer' in conjunction with a Medical Board is discussed.

PART II

COMPENSATION

Every artisan employed in the Royal Workshops receives a
certificate under the King's Seal, authenticated by the appropriate Minister. A most praiseworthy feature of the Royal
Workshops is that workmen are engaged for life. If they are
injured or sick their pay is not reduced: more wonderful still
—they are given, on request, free medical treatment by
the surgeons, and apothecaries of the Court.

CHARDIN, *Voyages*, Paris, 1811, vii. 332. [Of the Safavid
dynasty towards the end of the eighteenth century.]

CHAPTER V

GENERAL SCALE OF COMPENSATION

Justice . . . demands that the interests of the working classes should be carefully watched over by the administration, so that they who contribute so largely to the advantage of the community may themselves share in the benefits which they create—that of being housed, clothed, and bodily fit, and that they may find life less hard and more endurable. It follows that whatever shall appear to prove conducive to the well-being of those who work should obtain favourable consideration. There is no fear that solicitude of this kind will be harmful to any interest, it will be to the advantage of all; for it cannot be but good for the commonwealth to shield from misery those on whom it so largely depends for the things that it needs. It is shameful and inhuman to treat men as chattels to make money by, or to look upon them merely as so much muscle or physical strength.'   POPE LEO XIII, *Encyclical 'Rerum Novarum'*, 1891.

THE aspect of Workmen's Compensation of first concern to an injured workman or, in the event of his death, to his dependants, is the legal aspect. Is his accident, injury, or disease within the scope of the existing law, or not? Only the highest courts, which throw long shadows over a large proportion of serious cases from the moment of their occurrence, may be able finally to decide this issue, for there is no other body of civil or social legislation affecting the masses of the people in which the rights of the subject in any given case are more dubious. Upon this point we shall have more to say hereafter. For the moment we will assume that the legal position is clear and concentrate upon the economic and social aspect, viz. how far existing rates of compensation, even if received in full, are 'fair', and how nearly they approach to attainable levels of human needs and social welfare.

To begin with, the term Workmen's Compensation is in some degree misleading. For the pain of a serious injury there can, in the nature of things, be no full monetary 'compensation'. In all countries, and particularly in Britain, the accepted view is that any 'compensation' can only be partial, and in this country the principle that the workman's share should not exceed a maximum of half the wages he might have lost has been acted upon since 1897. In the case of fatal accidents, the Holman Gregory Committee observed that it had 'at all times' been accepted that industry should provide 'a fair, but not extravagant sum'.[1] Moreover, Mr. Guthrie, representing employers on that Committee, had recorded in a Minority Report that Parliament had always intended that the pecuniary loss should be shared between employers and the injured and that employers' liability should be 'moderate and

[1] Cf. *Holman Gregory Report*, pp. 39 and 43.

limited'.[1] He did not, however, say what meaning he attached to the words 'fair', 'extravagant', 'moderate' and 'limited', but, as noted by an earlier investigator,[2] in practice it 'is doubtful whether much more than a third of the financial burden resulting from industrial accidents is shifted on the employer's shoulders' and that 'no understanding of the discontent of the working class with the existing compensation system is possible unless it is realized that about two-thirds of the total money loss resulting from accidents . . . is still borne by injured workmen'.

Can money alone compensate an injured workman? The question is one to which much attention has been given of recent years. That existing monetary scales are inadequate is now generally agreed. But there is no general recognition of the need for other remedial or compensatory steps to make good so far as may be the loss incurred and the suffering endured by the rank and file of the industrial army upon whom in peace and war our welfare depends—the men who 'maintain the state of the world, for all their desire is in the work of their hands'.[3] The aim should be, and in many civilized countries is, to restore so far as possible the health of the injured worker—not on grounds of social justice and humanity only but of national expediency, for every healthy able-bodied person is potentially an asset and every invalid or semi-invalid a liability to society. This ideal is supplemented and extended in some countries by an even broader aim, transcending physical reintegration and restoration of health. The victims of accidents, compelled to abandon their livelihood or to seek an alternative vocation often suffer sociological as well as medical injuries. Restoration to physical health is not automatically followed by *soziale Gesundung*—social recovery. To ensure this is the broad aim of those who have set out to study and remedy the evils of occupational injury.[4]

We have then these three distinct forms of compensation for the injured workman:

1. Compensation in money and kindred benefits.
2. Restoration of health.
3. Social rehabilitation.

In this chapter we are concerned solely with the first point.

We have already discussed in our first volume the present scales for money compensation in their historical setting. We have also shown how far existing legislation has lagged, in this respect, behind the pro-

---

[1] Cf. *Holman Gregory Report*, p. 75.
[2] Cf. Joseph L. Cohen, *Social Insurance Unified*, 1924, p. 29.
[3] Cf. Ecclesiasticus xxxviii. 34.
[4] Cf. Prof. Dr. Victor von Weizsaecker, *Soziale Krankheit und soziale Gesundung*, Berlin, 1930.

posals made by the Holman Gregory Committee. Full details of the maximum and minimum payments in respect of injuries resulting in death, and of injuries resulting in total or partial disablement, will be found in vol. i, pp. 241–72.

We have already stigmatized as arbitrary and unintelligent the existing distribution of the burden between employer and employed. An unskilled man earning 35s. a week, a skilled man earning £6 a week, a bachelor living with his parents, and a married man with six dependants are all alike subject to a maximum payment of 30s. a week. This system penalizes the better-paid worker who has naturally and properly assumed certain financial responsibilities and accommodated his mode of livelihood to the higher rate of wages to which his skill entitles him. He may, for example, be buying his house by instalments. The higher proportional amount of cash benefit conceded to the low-paid workers is merely a partial and inadequate recognition of the well-known fact that in the lower scales of income half-pay entails a catastrophic and anti-social drop in the standard of living. A large proportion of men who have been seriously injured are in receipt of Public Assistance owing to the inadequacy of existing scales of compensation.

How far the amounts now payable for compensation are just and fair is necessarily a relative matter. The sums payable in Great Britain may usefully be compared with those enforced in other great industrial countries. As compensation is usually reckoned as a percentage of the normal earnings, such comparisons are valid so far as concerns weekly payments, but of less value so far as concerns lump-sum payments, owing to currency fluctuations, which enhance the apparent value of cash benefits payable at death in some countries. But statutory compensation in Great Britain consists in cash benefits only, whereas in foreign countries it comprises medical and other statutory benefits, which may greatly enhance the real value of compensation.

The following statement shows in tabular form, for a number of different countries:

1. The basic percentage of the compensation payment (i.e. half wages, two-thirds wages, &c.) in cases of total incapacity.

together with a list of those countries whose laws provide for the payment to the injured person of the cost of:

2. Medical benefit.
3. Medical and surgical appliances.
4. Rehabilitation service.

Provision for vocational rehabilitation, viz. the re-training of injured men and machinery for placing them in employment, exists only in certain provinces of Canada, in France, Germany, Estonia, and certain

States of the U.S.A. The provision of this most important social service will doubtless receive full attention at the hands of the Royal Commission now sitting (figures compiled mainly from I.L.O. Reports publ. 1936).

Country	I Per cent. of wages for total incapacity	II Whether medical benefit is paid	III Whether medical appliances are provided	IV Whether rehabilitation service is provided
Great Britain	50	...	...	...
Australia.	66⅔	£100	...	...
Belgium	66⅔	Yes	Yes	...
Bulgaria	100	Yes	Yes	...
Canada[1]	55–66⅔	Yes	Yes	Yes[1] ✓
Finland	66⅔	Yes	Yes	...
France	66⅔	Yes	...	Yes
Germany	66⅔	Yes	Yes	Yes ✓
India	50	...	...	...
Italy	50	...	...	...
Japan	Not comparable	Yes	...	...
Norway	60	Yes	...	...
Netherlands	70	Yes	...	...
Sweden	66⅔	Yes	Yes	...
Union of South Africa[2] . .	60	Yes	Yes	...
Russia	50–100	Yes	Yes	Yes ✓
U.S.A.[3]	40–66⅔	Yes	Yes	Yes[3] ✓
Argentina	Not comparable	Yes	...	...
Austria (former) . . .	66⅔	Yes	Yes	Yes
Brazil	Not comparable	Yes	...	...
Czechoslovakia . . .	66⅔	Yes	...	...
Denmark	75	Yes	Yes	Yes ✓
Estonia	50–66⅔	Yes	Yes	Yes ✓
Hungary.	50	Yes	Yes	...
Luxembourg	66⅔	Yes	Yes	...
New Zealand	66⅔	Yes	...	...
Poland	66⅔	Yes	...	...
Portugal	66⅔	Yes	...	...
Rumania.	66⅔	Yes	Yes	...
Switzerland	70	Yes	Yes	...

[1] The scales vary in the different Provinces. As to Rehabilitation, the Workmen's Compensation Board may take measures to aid in getting the injured workman back to work and to assist in lessening or removing any handicap resulting from injury. See p. 103.

[2] 50 per cent. under 2 years' service with one firm rising to 100 per cent. after 6 years' service with one firm.

[3] The system varies in the different States. The same applies to Rehabilitation; the most far-reaching provisions relating to rehabilitation are found in six States, the District of Columbia and the U.S. Longshoremen's and Harbor Workers' Compensation Acts.

The basic regulation of the amounts payable under Workmen's Compensation in different industrial countries[1] is as follows:

GERMANY

The sum of all amounts payable weekly to an injured man may not exceed two-thirds of his annual wages. Funeral benefit is fixed at one-fifth of the victim's annual wages, but not less than Rm. 50.[2] Benefits in case of incapacity due to accident are:

1. Free medical attendance, including hospital treatment.
2. Free vocational rehabilitation (retraining and placing).
3. A pension from the day of the accident* for the duration of the incapacity for work caused by the accident, and full pension in cases of total incapacity being again $66\frac{2}{3}$ per cent. of the annual wages. In case of partial incapacity a proportion of such pension is granted corresponding to the degree of incapacity, with specified additions in certain cases for each child.

* or, in case of persons insured against sickness, from the end of duration of sickness benefit (see also later, pp. 120 and 215 sqq.).

The basic principle of German Workmen's Compensation is the $66\frac{2}{3}$ per cent. cash benefit, and is so represented in all publications. This benefit, however, relates to cases of prolonged disability only, i.e. cases of complete or partial incapacity, where a pension is granted. Before this the injured is compensated as he would be under National Health (*Krankenversicherung*) only (see below). When such sickness benefit, paid either by the National Health authority or the *Berufsgenossenschaft* (where the injured is not under National Health) ceases, the rent or pension starts.

There is no 30s. limit in the German Law.

If the pension is not less than 50 per cent. of the full pension (full pension is paid in case of total incapacity) a bonus of 10 per cent. of the actual pension is payable for each child dependant on the pensioner under 15 years of age.

The pension is payable with $66\frac{2}{3}$ per cent. or respective proportions in case of partial disablement. This is an *obligation*, which *may* be met after the thirteenth week and *must* be met at latest with the twenty-seventh week of disablement.

Sickness benefit under National Health is 50 per cent. of the basic daily wage from the fourth day of sickness, for a period not exceeding twenty-six weeks from the beginning of the sickness; if the head of a

[1] For full details see I.L.O., *International Survey of Social Services 1933*, 2 vols., Geneva, 1936, vol. i, p. 315.
[2] For details as regards the relative cheapness of funerals in Germany, cf. Wilson and Levy, *Burial Reform*, 1938, pp. 85–6, 172 sqq., if the annual wages are £100–£120—a low average—the sum of £5–£6 is a substantial contribution to burial expenses.

household is treated in hospital, his family receives a home benefit equal to half the sickness pay. This is what the injured man should at first receive. The sickness benefit may, however, be increased by a fund to 60 per cent. of the basic wage and a family increment may be added, but the total may not exceed 75 per cent. of the basic wage. This at present is what generally happens.

As to the incidence of these payments: the worker, indeed, pays two-thirds of the contribution to National Health. But the *Berufsgenossenschaft* has, after the forty-fifth day of the happening of the injury, to refund all the costs of benefits (cash and otherwise) to the National Health authority, so that it is only for these forty-five days that the injured participate in the contribution. Moreover, paragraph 1505 of the *Reichsversicherungsordnung* requires the *Berufsgenossenschaft* to pay for all medical provisions or benefits granted over and above what the National Health authority is obliged to give, even within the first forty-five days, and lays special duties upon the *Berufsgenossenschaften*, where medical care and restoration make such benefits necessary.[1]

In Britain, where no medical benefit exists under Workmen's Compensation, the injured worker who goes under National Health pays one-third of the cost of medical treatment for the entire period of his sickness by injury or of his disablement.

FRANCE

1. *Benefits in case of Death:*
   (*a*) Life annuity to the spouse equal to 20 per cent. of the victim's basic wage.
   (*b*) Temporary provision, up to the age of 16 years, for children, fixed on a particular scale.
   (*c*) In the absence of claimants under (*a*) and (*b*) a life annuity to parents and a temporary pension up to the age of 16 years to dependent children of the victim of 10 per cent. of the basic wage for each, subject to an aggregate maximum of 30 per cent.

2. *Benefits in case of permanent incapacity:*
   (*a*) A life annuity equal to $66\frac{2}{3}$ per cent. of the annual basic wage in cases of total permanent incapacity.
   (*b*) In cases of partial permanent incapacity a life annuity equal to half the reduction in the basic wage resulting from incapacity.
   (*c*) In all cases, until the injury is healed, the cost of medical and hospital treatment.
   (*d*) Vocational re-training.

[1] *Unfallversicherung*, § 558 *b*.

3. *Benefits in case of temporary incapacity:*
   (*a*) Daily allowance equal to half the wage (workdays and public holidays) from the first day if the incapacity lasts more than ten days.
   (*b*) The cost of medical and hospital treatment.

UNITED STATES OF AMERICA

Workmen's Compensation Laws lack uniformity and amounts payable vary greatly in different States.

1. *Total incapacity.* Compensation takes generally the form of a weekly payment of from 50 to 66⅔ per cent of wages in different States. Of forty-six States of the Union which have enacted workmen's compensation laws (leaving only two States: Arkansas and Mississippi with no legislation on this subject) thirty-three States concede more than 50 per cent., indeed most of them 66⅔ per cent., though as a maximum. Wisconsin has a limit of 70 per cent. In several States the percentage increases according to the number of dependants. In five States, in addition to the usual cash compensation, subsistence allowances are payable to disabled persons undergoing vocational rehabilitation from a Special Compensation Fund.[1] In Nevada and Washington compensation for permanent total incapacity is increased by 30 and 25 dollars monthly respectively, where the disabled person requires constant attendance. In Wisconsin compensation may be increased or decreased by 15 per cent. when employers or employees are shown to have violated safety regulations. Treble compensation is payable in the case of illegally employed children or adolescents.

2. *Partial incapacity.* Conditions as regards money compensation are similar to those payable as above in respect of total incapacity, though the system is somewhat different. The laws of all the States except New Hampshire contain schedules specifying, as compensation for each of the principal mutilations and permanent losses of function, a number of weekly payments at the rate prescribed for total incapacity, the number of payments being proportionate to the severity of the injury. It is necessary to distinguish between System I: weekly payments for temporary, and sometimes non-scheduled, permanent partial incapacity, and System II: weekly payments during fixed periods for scheduled and sometimes non-scheduled partial incapacity.

3. *Death.* Here again arrangements vary widely. Compensation for death, where total dependants are left, may take the form of a pension varying from 15 to 66⅔ of the wages. Five State laws provide for lump-sum payments, and five others for compensation in the form

---

[1] Cf. also *Handbook of Labor Statistics*, 1936 edition, Washington, pp. 1125 sqq.

of a periodical payment varying not with the wages, but with the number and kinship of dependants.

It is noteworthy that in most States a maximum term and amount payable in compensation has been fixed. In the case of total incapacity the sum may be from 4,000 to 15,000 dollars, the maximum number of weeks from 100 to 400; in case of partial incapacity the maximum amount varies from 3,000 to 7,500 dollars and the number of weeks from 100 to over 400. In case of death the total maximum amount payable ranges from 3,500 to as much as 15,000 dollars in North Dakota. These are substantial sums, yet in the official *Handbook of Labor Statistics* we read:

It is obvious that the reduction of the workmen's income by one half or even one third leaves a large proportion of his loss uncompensated. The burden on the employer is restricted further (and transferred necessarily to the injured employee and his family), since the term payment is not fixed in most States by the period of disability but by an arbitrary maximum.[1]

This statement shows that the cash amount payable is not officially regarded as constituting by itself an adequate form of compensation to the injured workers or to their survivors and dependants, although, in contrast to the system in this country, medical benefits play a very important part in all systems of Workmen's Compensation in the U.S.A. All State Compensation laws provide for medical aid to the injured employees; in fourteen States no upper limit is placed upon the amount nor the time during which aid shall be rendered. Ten States limit the amount but not the time, while in the others there are various restrictions as to the cash equivalent of time of medical assistance rendered and the period over which it may be claimed. The total compensation paid in Great Britain in the seven industries with $7\frac{1}{2}$ million employees for which statistics are available is the equivalent for 1935 of about 32 million dollars. The Bureau of Labor Statistics of the U.S.A. estimate on the other hand that the total amount of compensation paid yearly is about 240 million dollars besides 72 million dollars for medical aid, which brings the total to 312 million dollars. This relates to an insured population of 20 million persons. Thus, on a generous estimate, the proportionate compensation paid in Great Britain is not more than one-third of that paid in U.S.A. (for about 20 million insured people in Great Britain the payment would represent at present rates about 100 million dollars). We seek to draw no definite conclusions from these figures for the greater risks at present inherent in American industry invalidate mathematical comparisons. While the

[1] Cf. *Handbook*, loc. cit., p. 1125.

312 million dollars in the U.S.A. were paid in respect of 2 million injuries, the British figure of £6·5 millions or approximately 32 million dollars related to 461,557 cases which is a proportionately much larger number, so that it would appear at first sight that a much smaller amount of compensation is payable on the average to an injured workman in Britain. But it would be equally wrong to ignore the apparent wide differences in the total payments made, though in accordance with scales which vary very widely from State to State.[1]

CANADA

The great industrial neighbour of the U.S.A. does not appear to have initiated Workmen's Compensation benefits so liberally as most States of U.S.A., and here also, except for Government employees, the responsibility rests with provincial legislatures. There are in existence in Canada two kinds of schemes, the so-called Collective Liability Schemes and the Individual Liability Schemes which we shall discuss later when dealing with administrative questions.

I. COLLECTIVE SCHEMES

A. *Benefits in Kind*

1. *Medical Benefits:* granted in all cases of disability, including those for which no cash benefit is payable. These include, in all provinces, medical and surgical treatment, nursing, and the supply of artificial members and apparatus. Dental treatment is given in Ontario. The provision of machines for rehabilitation exercises is explicitly enjoined in several provinces. Artificial limbs are even usually kept in repair for the first year of use.

2. *Rehabilitation:* A Workmen's Compensation Board may take measures to aid in getting workmen back to work and to remove or assist in removing any handicap resulting from injury.

B. *Cash Benefits*

1. *Death.*

The widow or invalid widower receives in most provinces monthly payments ranging from 30 to 40 dollars. In Ontario, Quebec, and Saskatchewan in addition a lump sum of 100 dollars is paid to the widow and, of course, a sum for burial expenses. There are further

[1] An interesting illustration and analysis of these differences is to be found in the *Bulletin of the U.S. Bureau of Labor Statistics*, no. 511, April 1930, 'Workmen's Insurance and Compensation Series', pp. 14–15. Here the New York rates are taken as a base equal to 1,000. The comparative benefit costs grouped here according to the various schedules in the different States go as much down as to 275 and overste the 1,000 base in a few cases, thus exhibiting very wide margins.

additions for children, but in two provinces the total amount of benefit payable is limited to 60–5 dollars a month. There are also elaborate provisions for orphans and dependants other than widow and children.

2. *Temporary incapacity.*

(*a*) *Total incapacity:* Compensation consists of weekly payments according to a percentage of the average earnings, which varies from 55 to 62⅔ per cent. There is, moreover, a minimum rate of compensation guaranteed in all provinces. Where the worker's average earnings are less than the minimum rate, an amount equal to total earnings is paid. The minimum rate reaches 12½ dollars in three provinces.

(*b*) *Partial incapacity:* A corresponding percentage of the difference between the average earnings before the accident and the average amount which the worker is able to earn in some suitable employment or business after the accident is paid.

(*c*) *Lump sums may be paid:* In Manitoba the consent of the worker is required.

3. *Permanent incapacity.*

(*a*) *Total incapacity:* The same as 2 (*a*) above.

(*b*) *Partial incapacity:* The same as 2 (*b*) above. In New Brunswick the maximum under this head is 2,500 dollars.

(*c*) *Invalidity without diminution of earnings:* In several Provinces the Board may grant compensation in cases where there is no substantial diminution of earnings, if the worker is seriously or permanently disfigured about the face or head or otherwise permanently injured.[1]

(*d*) *Commutation for lump sum:* In three Provinces, to be made upon application of the workman only.

II. INDIVIDUAL LIABILITY SCHEMES

Benefit conditions do not differ notably from those under the Collective system. In Alberta compensation for temporary incapacity drops to 50 per cent.

BELGIUM

A. *Benefits in kind.*

Persons injured as a result of an industrial accident are entitled to medical treatment and medicaments including the necessary artificial limbs and orthopaedic appliances.

---

[1] In contrast to this see a discussion on the matter before the Holman Gregory Committee, vol. i, p. 190.

B. *Benefits in case of incapacity.*

1. In case of temporary incapacity 50 per cent. of the average daily wage, but if temporary incapacity continues beyond four weeks the rate is increased from the twenty-ninth day after the accident to $66\frac{2}{3}$ per cent.

2. In case of permanent partial incapacity $66\frac{2}{3}$ per cent. of the loss of wage resulting from the accident.

3. In case of permanent total incapacity, pension equal to $66\frac{2}{3}$ per cent. of annual wage, with a limit fixed, however: in the case of seriously injured persons whose condition necessitates the regular assistance of another person, the pension may be increased up to 80 per cent. of the loss of wages.

C. *In the case of death, burial benefit and pension.*

The capital required to provide the widow's pension is equal to the present value at the time of death of a joint annuity based on two lives of respectively the same age as the deceased person and his survivor. This hypothetical annuity payable until death of one of the two persons, has to be equal to 30 per cent. of the wage of the deceased person. There are further regulations for other dependants and orphans.

HOLLAND

1. *Death.*

Apart from funeral benefit the pensions are the following: wife of deceased 30 per cent. of daily wage. If the widow remarries, she receives in commutation an amount equal to twice her yearly pension. Similar regulations exist if the wife was a breadwinner. There are further regulations in regard to other dependants; orphans, children and grandchildren draw the pension until they have completed their sixteenth year if the deceased was contributing to their maintenance. The total pension in the event of death may not exceed 60 per cent. of the wage.

2. *Temporary incapacity.*

(*a*) Medical attendance or corresponding compensation.

(*b*) Temporary cash benefit *equal to* 80 per cent. of the insured daily wage, payable from the day of the accident, after three days' waiting period, but not longer than forty-two days.

(*c*) Pension in case of total incapacity *equal to* 70 per cent of the daily wage, the sum being reduced proportionately in the case of partial incapacity.

(*d*) Direct medical attendance by the employer's medical service if approved by the State Insurance Bank Law of May 12th 1928.

(*e*) When, as a result of an accident an insured person remains an invalid requiring constant attendance, his pension may be increased for the duration of such invalidity to a sum not exceeding his full daily wage.

3. *Permanent incapacity*.

Pension granted is the same as temporary incapacity exceeding six weeks.

ITALY

Workmen's Compensation here is of a relatively recent date; it was inaugurated in 1904, and amended by several Acts, the last and most important being the Royal Decree of August 17th 1935 which came into force on July 1936. Cash payments were not higher than 50 per cent. of the wages drawn by the insured persons, so long as temporary incapacity lasts, while for permanent incapacity the compensation is equal to six times the annual basic wage. By the new law benefits in kind have been added. In case of death the total amount of compensation payable to survivors is equal to five times the annual basic wage. The widow receives a smaller percentage of cash benefit if there are parents or brothers or sisters left to whose living the deceased contributed. Owing to the particular conditions of the value of the lira and its unstable purchasing power, the basic wage fixed as an absolute standard can hardly offer satisfactory indication of the sufficiency of compensation; the same applies to the special regulations made for agricultural workers which are all based on lira scales. In general, the legal provision made in Italy appears to be meagre, but Italy has always been a poor country.

JAPAN

Here too Workmen's Compensation dates only from 1911, and it was not until January 1st 1932 that the scope of organized accident insurance was effectively extended. Of 19¾ millions employed persons in the last Census year (1930), about 5½ millions were engaged in manufacture, construction, and mining. Of these only about 2¾ millions were covered by Workmen's Compensation legislation.

1. *Death*.

Funeral benefit to not less than thirty days' wages; a lump sum of indemnity of not less than 360 times the basic daily wage payable to the survivors. This is on a lower scale than for any European country.

2. *In case of temporary incapacity.*

Medical treatment and absence allowance of 60 per cent. *of the daily wages.* In factories and mines the absence allowance can be reduced to 40 per cent. after the first 180 days.

3. *In case of permanent incapacity.*

A lump-sum indemnity varying with the degree of invalidity. For partial incapacity the compensation may not be less than forty times the daily wage under the Factory Act or the Mining Regulations, which recognize four degrees of invalidity, and twenty times that wage under the Workmen's Compensation Act which recognize fourteen degrees. There are also regulations relating to commutation into lump sums.

SWITZERLAND

Industrial Switzerland appears to be particularly liberal towards its injured workers, perhaps because legislation dates only from 1911. The cash benefits in the case of temporary incapacity disabling the worker from earning his living are a daily allowance equal to 80 per cent. *of his wages,* up to a maximum of 21 francs a day.[1] For permanent incapacity the amount of compensation varies with the degree of incapacity. Invalidity pensions are fixed at 70 per cent. *of the annual earnings* with a maximum of 6,000 francs. In case of the infirmity of the worker being such that he must have constant attendance and other special care, the pension may be increased, but may not exceed his total earnings. Apart from this a wide range of medical benefits is granted, including the provision and renewal of appliances. A widow's pension equals 30 per cent. of the annual average earnings of the deceased insured person.[2]

We have now reviewed the general scale of compensation of the principal industrial countries. The outcome does little to justify any degree of complacency. The scales of compensation in Britain are notably inferior to those of Germany, France, the U.S.A., Belgium, or Canada, as well as of countries of much smaller industrial importance. Britain, the oldest of industrial countries, is in this respect nearer the level of Italy, the latest entrant into the industrial field.

Workmen's Compensation in England, even if viewed solely from the angle of weekly benefits, does not bear comparison with the corresponding legislation abroad. The 50 per cent. basis on which

[1] As prices had remained unchanged we need not take into account that, until 1937, the gold franc did not correspond to the English shilling.

[2] As to some further arrangements regarding lump-sum settlements for light cases, &c., see later p. 132.

the general scale of the amount of compensation is based compares ill with the 66⅔ per cent in vogue elsewhere (we have expressly empha-sized the figures exceeding the 50 per cent. basis in different countries). The lack of adequate statutory medical benefits and the absence of systematic provision for modern methods of medical and social rehabilitation reduce the actual compensation to a scale far below the international standard. There are, as always, laudable exceptions: thus the L.M.S. Railway, in their workshops, viz. factories at Crewe, have their own Accident Hospital, with a resident medical officer and staff who, apart from dealing with accidents in the works, have evolved interesting and novel schemes for rehabilitation of disabled men, in-cluding a gymnasium and a workshop in which men can gradually get fit. Many colliery firms have arrangements whereby local doctors can be summoned to the colliery to attend cases of injury or illness. The Walkden Collieries near Manchester are constructing a clinical centre for massage and electrical treatment. In Scotland the Lanarkshire Medical Practitioners' Union, with the financial assistance of the Miners' Welfare Fund, have organized a system of clinics to give orthopaedic treatment for injuries and after-effects, and to deal with chronic rheumatic affections. The Miners' Welfare Fund also makes grants for the creation and maintenance of ambulance services in colliery areas, for the support of miners' convalescent homes, and to schemes for providing miners with medical treatment and appliances.[1] But all this only touches a tiny section of the working-class com-munity which is liable to injuries by accident or disease. Such private and quasi-charitable endeavours,[2] to which we shall have to revert later (Chapter XII, pp. 222 sqq.), are mainly, if not exclusively, connected with very large organizations and are beyond the reach of the average worker in England where, in the laconic phrase of the International Labour Office, 'Compensation consists in cash benefits only.'[3]

The injured workman in Britain is entitled by Statute only to such medical treatment as may be available to him under the rules laid down for the time being by the Approved Society of which he is a subscribing member, and subject to the limitations of the N.H.I. Acts. He may not even be entitled to any benefit at all for in certain categories of Approved Societies, notably those managed by commercial insurance

[1] Cf. PEP, *Report on the British Health Services*, Dec. 1937, pp. 85–6, and further, *Miners' Welfare Fund Report*, 1934, pp. 20–1.

[2] Cf. *Committee on Compulsory Insurance: Minutes of Evidence*, 1936, where the point was amply discussed; several witnesses emphasized that insurers rarely contribute to treat-ment necessary for the workmen's recovery. Cf. Q. 5929–30 and 5987–93.

[3] Cf. *International Survey*, loc. cit., p. 357.

offices, the rate of lapse is heavy.[1] Moreover, the societies which cannot provide additional benefits are frequently those whose members are most exposed to occupational risks,[2] as the current expenditure on cash benefits leaves no margin for surplus; thereby additional benefits are not obtainable just by those who would be most in want of them. Moreover, some 900,000 persons covered by the Workmen's Compensation Acts are not subject to compulsory insurance under the N.H.I. Acts. Of these probably 250,000 are voluntary contributors, leaving 650,000 wholly uninsured. Of these it is estimated that about 300,000 are not manual workers earning between £250 and £350 a year. The remainder are employed persons earning less than £250 who are exempt from insurance under the N.H.I. Acts by the terms of their employment.[3]

The position of English Workmen's Compensation is in this respect unique, and contrasts sharply with the latest recommendations made by the International Labour Office. After going carefully into the question of the minimum amount of benefit desirable as an international standard, the Office in the first place and subsequently the International Labour Conference came to the conclusion (in 1925) that in consideration of the fact that for definite rules concerning the minimum benefit necessary a two-thirds majority could not be found, any attempt to settle the matter had to take the form of a mere Recommendation. The Report[4] provided *inter alia* that in the case of permanent total incapacity a periodical payment equivalent to $66\frac{2}{3}$ per cent. of the workmen's annual earnings should be provided, and in case of temporary total incapacity a daily or weekly payment also equivalent to this percentage of the workmen's basic earnings as calculated for purposes of compensation should be granted. As to fatal accidents the Report emphasized that the national schemes 'contain an even greater variety of solutions than those relating to incapacity'. But the recommendation laid stress on the point that $66\frac{2}{3}$ per cent. of the deceased's annual earnings should form the basis for a general scale of compensation. Apart from this the Conference held that injured workmen should be entitled to medical aid and to such surgical and pharmaceutical aid as is recognized 'to be necessary in consequence of accidents, the cost of such aid to be borne by the employer, accident

[1] See *Report of Government Actuary on the 5th Valuation of Approved Societies.* Cf. also Royal Commission on National Health Insurance 1928, *Minority Report,* p. 310 and *Hetherington Commission,* p. 424.

[2] Cf. *Minority Report on National Health Insurance,* 1928, p. 310, and *Hetherington Commission,* p. 424.

[3] *Debates H.C.,* April 20th 1939.

[4] I.L.O., *The International Labour Organization and Social Insurance,* Geneva, 1936, pp. 33–4. There is no indication as to which countries would have withheld assent from the proposed rules. For negative British attitude cf. *Hetherington Commission,* p. 235.

insurance, or sickness and invalidity institutions'. The Conference also recommended the supply to the victims of industrial accidents, at the employer's or insurer's expense, of artificial limbs and surgical appliances, or a cash grant in lieu. Their recommendation covered a first issue and normal renewals. Vocational re-education also received strong support.[1] The Memorandum to the Hetherington Commission presented by the I.L.O. stressed the necessity of the provision for artificial limbs though it was recognized as an 'expensive aid'. It was stated that in general all the laws provide for the supply of artificial limbs but that the laws of Belgium, France, Germany, Italy, the Netherlands, Sweden, and Switzerland go even further by giving the right to the worker to have them repaired or renewed.[2] Under British law all these necessities have to be defrayed in general by the injured workman himself,[3] although his actual compensation is based upon a percentage of his ordinary earnings which lags far behind the standard already adopted by most industrial nations, and has no relation to the medical costs he must incur.

The following table shows in parallel columns the compensation admissible in the event of death or injury during peace-time training to

A. Auxiliary firemen.

B. Members of other A.R.P. services.[4]

C. Payments in respect of death or injury to workmen under the Workmen's Compensation Act of 1925.

The disparity at every point is very marked and may fairly be regarded as an indication of the need for increasing existing scales under the Workmen's Compensation Act of 1925.

We may appropriately conclude this chapter with some reference to the question of 'disfigurement'—a type of injury of great social importance though it forms a very small proportion of industrial injuries. We noted in our first volume (pp. 190–1) how superficially this matter was treated by the Holman Gregory Committee, who seemed almost to regard it as a subject for jesting.

Just treatment of this problem in Britain is hampered by the fact that, as the law stands, an injured workman can claim only for loss of earning power, not for indirect consequences of an injury, e.g. impaired prospects of marriage. In civil life even slight disfigurement gives rise to heavy damages. A scar 'which showed in cold weather' brought a girl £130 and £18 special damages in 1939.[5] Under the

[1] Cf. I.L.O., *The International Labour Organization*, &c., pp. 39–41.

[2] Cf. *Hetherington Commission*, p. 599.

[3] Mr. Baird told the Hetherington Commission that Insurance Companies do supply artificial limbs, but not 'the smaller forms of surgical appliances or dental appliances'. Cf. A. 2613. On the other hand, he admitted later (Q. 2656) that 'trusses' are *not* supplied by Insurance Companies.   [4] Cf. *Debates H.C.*, March 2nd 1939, cols. 1470–1.

[5] *The Daily Telegraph*, July 20th 1939.

	A	B	C
DEATH:			
Widow without dependent children	£700	£400	£200 or 3 years earnings up to max. £300
Widow with dependent child or children	£1,000	£600	£200 or 3 years earnings up to max. £300 plus a sum varying with father's wages and age of children not exceeding £225 for 6-months-old child, £150 for 5-year-old child, £75 for 10-year-old child, and so diminishing *pro rata* with maximum of £600
Injury:			
Total disablement	£3 a week for 26 weeks, thereafter 30s. for single, 40s. for married man with one dependent child, with additions for other dependent children up to max. of 49s.	...	£1. 10s. a week or 50 per cent. of average earnings, whichever is less: no allowance for wife or children
Partial disablement	Rates in proportion to degree of disablement	...	Ditto (§ 9 (1) (c) of Act of 1925)
Medical expenses	Free during initial period of disablement	...	Nil

disablement schedules of the Ministry of Pensions, however, 'severe' and 'very severe' facial disfigurement may entitle the sufferer to a disability pension of 80 or 100 per cent. respectively of the maximum. A man may have full use of his limbs, and yet receive a pension for disfigurement, not only on the ground of loss of 'amenities' but of earning capacity, for 'facial disfigurement . . . may disqualify a man for employment . . . In some cases it is enough to debar a man from certain trades, e.g. waiter, valet or butler.'[1]

Recent American legislation has taken a different road. Successive decisions in the New York courts, which broaden the basis of compensation so as to include 'any substantial physical impairment attributable to the injury, whether it immediately affects earning power or not' have been upheld. In the words of Mr. Marshall Dawson, it is now accepted that, in the hands of an alert administrator, benefit payments based 'upon any substantial impairment' should be used to

[1] Cf. *Hetherington Commission*, p. 393 and Q. 3718–23.

obtain such expert surgical and other treatment as will restore as completely as possible both function *and appearance*.[1] The same writer remarks that, where a man is disfigured, but is awarded compensation based solely upon an estimate of his impaired wage-earning capacity, he is regarded, for compensation purposes, 'as a robot or animated machine in need of repair for continued work, instead of a human being subject to serious impairments other than those registered in wage loss.'

This view commends itself to us as both just and expedient and of particular importance in the evaluation of injuries to or losses of one eye. The practice of awarding compensation for loss of earning power ought to be replaced here by compensation for the physical loss of the eye, which may include an element of payment in respect of the disfigurement entailed in certain cases.[2] Recommendations made by the T.U.C. to the Hetherington Commission include special compensation for disfigurement,[3] 'Regard should be had to the worker's prospects and appearance and to the loss suffered by inability to take part in games or social functions.' The departure from the principle of merely compensating loss of earning becomes evident. A case was cited where a workman, though physically perfectly fit, had to wear a shield over his face.

We have now considered the state of compensation in its general legislative aspects. We have described what is the maximum and minimum sum the British workman may get in compensation according to existing regulations and we have provided a factual background of provisions in foreign countries. It remains to analyse what such compensation may entail to the actual social life and economic conditions of an English working-class family.

---

[1] Marshall Dawson, 'Adequacy of Benefit Payments', *Monthly Labor Review*, Sept. 1938. The author is a member of the Bureau of Labor Statistics, U.S.A.

[2] On this point cf. *Convention (1936) of International Association of Industrial Accident Boards*, Washington, 1937, pp. 100 sqq.

[3] Cf. p. 416; cf. also Q. 3794 and A. 3920.

CHAPTER VI

COMPENSATION AND THE WORKMAN'S BUDGET

The burden which the workman is required to bear he cannot shift upon the shoulders of anyone else, but the employer may and no doubt will shift his burden upon the shoulders of the community, or if he has any difficulty in doing that will by reducing the wages of workmen compel them to bear part of it.

THE HON. SIR WILLIAM MEREDITH, Chief Justice of Ontario and *spiritus rector* of the Ontario Workmen's Compensation Act, *Final Report on Laws relating to the Liability of Employers*, Toronto, 1913, p. 15.

ADEQUACY of compensation has never been a guiding principle of British Workmen's Compensation Law. Payments thereunder have always been regarded, with some justification, as contributions wrung from employers, who collectively and individually insisted upon the 'principle' that the injured workmen should shoulder a part of the loss arising from circumstances which, in most cases, were wholly beyond their control. Workmen's organizations responded by insisting that employers should bear as large a proportion of the loss as possible in all cases of injury, however great the workman's negligence.

This principle still prevails all over the world but, elsewhere than in Britain, has been, in practice, greatly modified by higher scales of cash benefit (usually 66⅔ per cent. of normal pay) and by the institution of far-reaching provisions for physical and even economic rehabilitation.

The principles thus evolved which now govern the award of compensation to an injured workman contrast sharply with those adopted in cases of injury by accident other than occupational. Very large sums are constantly awarded, by agreement or after litigation, to parties who suffer even only partial incapacity by such accidents. In a case,[1] for instance, which came before the High Court of Justice recently, a boy run over by a motor-car received by agreement £4,000 plus £750 for special damages, such as hospital treatment and other charges. For similar injuries a workman would not get over £900 including all medical and legal expenses and then save in rare cases only if he was a member of a strong trade union,[2] or had succeeded in interesting a competent solicitor and getting leave to sue as a poor person. The boy in question was destined for the bar, one of many professions in which the loss of one leg would not be prejudicial to success. A workman with one leg is far more gravely handicapped, for Mutual and other Insurance offices may, and often do, object to his employment in any

[1] *Davis and Another* v. *Downing and Another, The Times*, Dec. 1st 1937.
[2] For such a case cf. *The Land Worker*, April 1937, p. 9.

I

capacity. The prejudice against maimed men in many capacities is almost instinctive and occupations in which a man with one leg or one arm does not permanently lose much of his earning capacity are comparatively few.

In the case of a film actress who lost several weeks of remunerative employment damages were assessed at £500; it was argued by her representative that, as film stars' professional lives were brief, the interruption to her work through the shock would shorten her artistic career. But it is never contended that an injured workman, forced by injury or occupational disease to absent himself from work for a long period, should be compensated because he had lost his skill by disuse, or had been similarly handicapped in the exercise of his trade or profession. Such possibilities are to-day beyond the scope of compensation. Not even disfigurement, proved to have damaged the professional earning capacity of an industrial worker, is admitted as a ground for compensation, though a film star successfully claimed £500 from her chauffeur at Common Law for an injury which was not in fact serious, though it proved that he had been the less negligent driver in respect of the collision of the two cars. Had the chauffeur been killed in some accident, his dependants could not have recovered from the film star, under the Workmen's Compensation Acts, more than £600[1].

It may be argued that the legislature never intended to recompense the workmen fully for injuries and damages incurred, and that Statute and Common Law respectively have no common ethical basis. Our business at this stage is to establish the fact that existing scales of compensation are grievously low. If a workman who has been earning 50s. a week can barely keep himself, much less a family in addition, on 25s. without recourse to the public purse or to charity, a man who has been earning £2 per week, and receives during total disablement 22s. 6d., is in no better case. His position may become desperate when medical expenses are heavy or when he is in need of medical appliances. The fact that some charitable societies, and some hospitals, will provide such things in some cases gratuitously on proof of poverty makes little difference. Self-respecting men in every walk of life dislike parading their troubles before the Lady Almoner or the P.A.C. Officer, and to our knowledge some Public Assistance officers rigidly refuse relief not only to men in receipt of weekly payments but to men who have a claim to such but have as yet received nothing. His rent and his general expenses for food and clothes remain the same. He must obtain credit or starve. The Stewart Committee held no meeting outside London, and called for no evidence on this subject from the C.O.S. or other competent organizations, except in connexion with

[1] Cf. an interesting article in *The Economist*, May 14th 1938, pp. 344–5.

lump-sum payments, with which we shall deal in our next chapter. They were content to note the view of the T.U.C. that a maximum rate of compensation of 30s. per week was 'utterly inadequate' for the maintenance of a workman with a family who has been accustomed to live at the rate of perhaps £3 or £4 per week,[1] and that 'the result of this diminution of his income is that he rapidly gets into debt'. The Stewart Committee, with the consent of the Home Secretary, for reasons which have not been explained, withheld from publication the evidence tendered to them upon this and other subjects, and we do not therefore know what, if any, data were adduced by the T.U.C. in support of their view.

Investigations[2] have shown that the budget of an average working-class family with an income of £3. 2s. per week, consisting of two adults and one child between 5 and 14 years of age may be summarized as follows:

	£	s.	d.	Per cent.
Average weekly income	3	2	0	...
Expenditure	2	16	8½	100
Housewife's weekly expenditure:				
Rent and rate		9	6	16·8
Fuel and light		4	4	7·6
Food	1	4	7½	43·5
Clothing		2	4	4·1
Cleaning		1	5	2·5
Education, medicine		...		...
Recreation, tobacco, misc. . . .		2	8½	4·8
Trade unions and clubs . . .		2	0	3·5
Total	2	6	11	82·8

Another investigation reveals that with an average weekly income of £5 a week over 44 per cent. is spent on food and about 17 per cent. on rent and rates.[3] How can a family suddenly faced with the necessity of satisfying their needs with 30s. a week instead of £3 or more, manage this without drastically reducing their outlay on food? The true position is often much worse, for most working-class families maintain more than one child. In the voluminous literature on the subject of national nutrition the position of the injured workman in regard to compensation and his budget is completely ignored. If unemployed, or in receipt of public relief, the statutory payments made to him take

[1] Cf. *Stewart Report*, p. 89.
[2] Cf. *Survey of the Merseyside*, Liverpool, 1934, and *Journal of the Royal Statistical Society*, part ix, 1928.
[3] Cf. also R. G. D. Allen and A. L. Bowley, *Family Expenditure*, 1935, pp. 49 and 51, who have corroborated the Merseyside inquiry in many points.

into account the number of his dependants, but not if he is injured. Ignorance of the principles and main features of nutrition may well be one of the great causes of deficiencies of nutrition[1]—and not only in Britain—but it is a waste of time to give advice on the subject to men and women who are deprived of the financial resources necessary to provide the requisite minimum. Such is the condition at any given moment of some hundreds of thousands of families. This state of affairs is most acute, apart from the size of the family, in the lower wage-earning categories. The man who only earns 30s. a week, receives 20s. compensation for total disablement. His position is no better than that of an injured man who earned 50s. a week and now gets 25s. The man with the former income of 30s. will probably have to spend just 12s., viz. 40 per cent., of his former budget on food, while the man with a former income of 50s., who spent 20s. on food, may now possibly, in reverting to the food expenditure of the low-paid class, spend a like sum on food. In such a case the lower-paid worker would be worse off, having to pay 12s. out of 25s., while the other is paying 12s. out of 30s. Thus, as the amount spent on food cannot be appreciably reduced, the lowest paid injured workers are proportionately worse off than the better paid, even if we take into consideration that the law provides for a slight proportional increase of compensation for disablement (total as well as partial, see vol. i, p. 242) where the amount of average weekly earnings fall below 30s. a week.

Dr. C. Norris, who combines the position of Barrister-at-Law with that of the Medical Officer of two important public institutions thus explains how the lack of medical benefit under Workmen's Compensation affects the budget of the injured worker:

In Great Britain, employers as such are not under any legal obligation to provide or pay for treatment, and such omission is very imperfectly filled by existing arrangements; a workman is not as a rule entitled to benefit[2] under the National Health Insurance provisions, if his disability is due to an industrial accident, and he usually has no other claim on public funds unless he becomes destitute—which happens fairly often in cases of prolonged disability. *Recovery is often retarded because the workman is unable to obtain sufficient food or to pay for treatment out of his compensation money.*[3]

The Holman Gregory Committee[4] were told of the case of a workman aged 30, who met with an accident by a spark or piece of iron

---

[1] Cf. *The Problem of Nutrition*, League of Nations, II. 'Economic and Financial', 1936, II. B. 3, p. 21 and *passim*.

[2] Viz. to benefits in cash. He is entitled to the services of the panel doctor and to such medicines (but as a rule nothing else) which he may prescribe. (Authors.)

[3] Donald C. Norris, 'Industrial Accidents' in *British Encyclopaedia of Medical Practice*, 1938, vol. vii, p. 129. Cf. also Note on p. 128.   [4] Cf. loc. cit., A. 9855.

piercing one of his eyes. He was partially incapacitated and likely to become totally blind. He had become an epileptic through the accident and had to remain for a long time in an institution. He had a wife and four children, and his wife was expecting another child when the accident happened. He received 21s. 11d. for nine months. His wife was unable to carry on the home, owing to the fact that during the early stage of his incapacity she had pawned or sold her house and any utensils she had, to try to buy food for her husband and children.

The result was, a short time previous to her confinement, it was the opinion of her friends and of her husband that she would be better in a workhouse. The position was aggravated by the fact that the insurance company had stopped the insurance money and the sum she was receiving from public assistance funds amounted now to 17s. 6d. a week. While the family was in the workhouse, the insurance company settled the case by giving the man a lump sum of £60.

The insufficiency of the 30s. maximum is no longer seriously disputed. When in November 1937 a Workmen's Compensation Bill was presented to Parliament by members of the Labour party, Mr. Higgs, M.P. (W. Birmingham, C.), though opposing the Bill as an employer, said:

... I say, here and now, that I do not think 30s. a week is enough.[1]

Another M.P. said:

The standard of living of an injured workman is inevitably lower, by reason of his injury alone. In the past two years I have had the handling of half-a-dozen cases in which the injured man did not get enough to pay the rent and to keep the family in health. I have watched the consequent gradual deterioration of mental and physical health.[2]

How the position of the injured worker as head of a family is affected by his financial circumstances is thus recorded in the Rehabilitation Report of 1939:

The reduction of family income to 30s. a week represents to the father of a family a harassing problem. Another cause of anxiety is the possibility of a still further reduction when he is found to be capable of what is termed light work. Dame Agnes Hunt writes: 'The patients are afraid of improving because they know that they will be marked as "able to do light work". Others will refuse

---

[1] *Debates H.C.*, Nov. 19th 1937.

[2] Mr. W. J. Stewart, M.P., said in the House of Commons on Dec. 9th 1938 that 520 persons in receipt of weekly payments under the W.C. Acts were getting supplementary allowances from P.A. Committees in Durham County at a cost to the rates of £21,000. Cf. also *Memorandum of the London Charity Organization Society to Interdept. Committee on Rehabilitation*, p. 16 : 'Many sufferers from accidents apply to Public Assistance Authorities ... to supplement weekly allowances paid them under the Workmen's Compensation Acts.'

further treatment because it might result in a smaller sum when the final award is made.'[1]

Hard cases may arise where a workman's claim under the Compensation Acts is open to dispute and, while receiving such medical benefit as the National Health Acts provide, he is receiving nothing under the Workmen's Compensation Acts. The extent to which Approved Societies exercise their statutory power to make advances to members under such conditions was discussed lengthily but inconclusively in evidence before the Holman Gregory Committee.[2] Although the legislation of 1918 had made it easier for Societies to recover advances,[3] it was made clear that whether advances were made or not depended on 'the benevolence of the Approved Society', and that the worker often had great difficulty in getting assistance from either quarter: his position was obscure and needed further clarification.[4] The N.H.I. Act, 1936, provides (§§ 51–4) that where an insured person is incapacitated by industrial injury or disease, entitling him to compensation or damages, sickness benefit is not payable unless the compensation or damages received are less than the benefit otherwise receivable, in which case the Society pays the difference.

The detailed relationships of Approved Societies and employers under Workmen's Compensation are complicated and may be misunderstood. The matter was fully discussed before the Hetherington Commission. The Home Office Memorandum stated that 'most' Societies pay benefit by way of advances pending settlement of compensation claim but others do not 'where public assistance is also being paid, by reason of difficulty of recovery'.[5] No figures were adduced in support of this statement, which is not borne out by the C.O.S. or our own limited experience. The word 'most' in such a context may have little actual basis. It is certain that injured workmen have very frequently to go to a Poor Law authority to keep them going pending the receipt of weekly payments,[6] or a reference to a Court of Justice. Even if 'only in about one case out of fifty it is necessary to supplement workmen's compensation by poor law relief,'[7] the hardship entailed, and the total number of cases is great, and this relates only to poor law relief, the ordinary form of supplementation being more often from the U.A.B., whose jurisdiction does not extend to totally incapacitated persons. (A workman entitled to benefit under the Unemployment

---

[1] *Final Report of the Interdept. Committee on the Rehabilitation of Persons injured by Accidents* (Delevingne Committee), 1939, p. 54.

[2] Ibid., Q. 6515 sqq., 8106, 8449.

[3] Ibid., Q. 21,493.   [4] Ibid., Q. 22,546.

[5] *Hetherington Commission, Evidence*, p. 173; see also p. 159, § 106.

[6] Ibid., Q. 1989 A.   [7] Ibid., Q. 1982 A.

Assistance Act cannot draw Poor Law relief.)[1] There are some un-pleasant features connected with the alternatives of 'getting compensa-tion' or of supplementing insufficient compensation through the U.A.B. Mr. Baird, of that Board, explained in evidence before the Hetherington Commission that a man may be seriously incapacitated by a permanent injury or long-term disablement. After a time some measure of recovery supervenes, though its value in the labour market may be doubtful. The insurance company serves a statutory notice for reduction of compensation on the ground that the injured man is fit for some light employment. Knowing that so soon as he is declared fit for light work he becomes entitled to unemployment benefit, the man accepts without demur a reduced weekly payment in respect of his partial incapacity, and forthwith applies for his contractual benefits from the U.A.B. or, if not entitled thereto, to the P.A.C. His income is then brought up to the statutory standard on the basis of the size of his family, &c. This practice, Mr. Baird added, was increasing. Workmen in such circumstances may well be reluctant to undertake the onerous and anxious task of pressing their justified claims.[2] The great discrepancy between the two scales of allowances inevitably tempts men to these unworthy shifts, which cannot be effectively pre-vented by any means short of a State-managed system of Workmen's Compensation. The fact that there is far less stigma attached to Poor Law relief than of old[3] is no excuse for the present state of affairs, for the Poor Law was not intended to deal with such cases. Delay in dealing with compensation claims was another matter of complaint. Approved Societies in Scotland allege that a period of not less than two months elapses before a claim in respect of silicosis or asbestosis is disposed of, that the fees are high, and that the workmen are required to travel long distances.[4] These facts show how grave are defects inherent in the present dilatory, ambiguous, and expensive system of administration. It might be tolerable if the Voluntary Hospitals could fill the gaps, but this seldom happens. An injured man can rarely be treated from first to last at one hospital. He may be dealt with in the Accident Ward of one hospital and be ejected within a week owing to the shortage of beds; after attending as an out-patient, in other hands, at that or another hospital, he may be admitted as an in-patient to another hospital and again discharged. The resultant neurosis may be ascribed to his financial condition; it is not less likely to be due to hours spent daily in waiting for attention as an out-patient and in the confusion of coun-sel he may have received from different medical attendants. The

---

[1] Cf. *Hetherington Commission*, Q. 1956–7.   [2] Ibid., Q. 2594–6.
[3] Cf. ibid., Q. 1990–1.
[4] Cf. *Memorandum of Department of Health for Scotland*, ibid., p. 173.

difficulties are increased by the great variation in cash benefits. In some Societies with a membership drawn largely from trades most liable to accidents they average 16s. a week for men. In a few Societies with a low industrial accident experience they reach 24s. a week. As members do not become entitled to Additional Cash Benefits for five full years after joining, and are not eligible for Additional non-cash benefits until three full years after joining, juvenile and adolescent members derive little or no advantage from § 51 of the N.H.I. Act.

No information is available as to the extent to which Approved Societies make supplementary payments to workmen in receipt of weekly payments under the Workmen's Compensation Act, but it is understood that the sums paid are inconsiderable. Nor do injured workmen derive adequate advantage from the Medical and Additional Benefits (Nos. 8–14) for, in practice, workmen most in need of them are generally members of Societies whose financial position is not strong enough to enable them to afford additional benefits and such forms of treatment as X-ray therapy, specialist treatment, &c. Dr. D. Stewart, M.O. of I.C.I. Metals Ltd. and Hon. Sec. of the Association of Industrial Medical Officers, notes that 'most' Approved Societies make advances when asked but are aware of 'a number of hard cases' which have hindered the recovery of injured men.[1] Under the German law the Approved Societies (*Krankenkassen*) under the National Health Scheme (*Krankenversicherung*) are obliged to grant all benefits, medical as well as their cash benefits, to the injured, so far as he is under National Health Insurance, for a period of forty-six days *on their own account*; from that day the Mutual Association (*Berufsgenossenschaft*) has to refund the benefits, while the obligation to grant them remains with the *Krankenkassen* for twenty-six weeks, if the *Berufsgenossenschaft* does not prefer, at an earlier date, itself to administer the matter. This greatly eases the position, which in Britain might entail further pecuniary disadvantage to the injured workman, a point which should not be overlooked in considering the impact of compensation upon the workman's budget.

The Rehabilitation Report of 1939 enumerated six different means by which an injured person may seek to get artificial limbs or other appliances if, as is generally the case, he is 'unable to bear the whole charge himself'. The Report noted that artificial legs, if regularly used, require periodical renewal. All these possibilities enumerated contain their 'ifs' and 'whens'. (*a*) Approved societies '*may* supply or contribute' *if* the funds are available; (*b*) '*many*' employers provide appliances,

[1] Dr. Donald Stewart, 'Rehabilitation of the Injured Workman with special reference to the Workmen's Compensation Act' (*The Lancet*, Jan. 21st 1939, p. 8). See also our Note on p. 128.

the cost is 'frequently' shared in equal moieties; it is 'exceptiona , for an injured workman, to be called to bear the cost of an artificial limb, or a surgical appliance. We question the accuracy of these statements which seem to be based upon information supplied by one side only. If such is the fact why should it be necessary to have recourse to (c) Hospital Contributory Associations, (d) Charitable Societies, (e) Local Authorities, and (f) Public Assistance Authorities.[1] The T.U.C. hold that the action of employers and insurers in this, as in other cognate matters, has been quite inadequate, and urged that the proposed Board should meet the cost of artificial limbs and orthopaedic and other appliances necessary to ensure the success of curative treatment or to alleviate the results of injury.[2]

The lowness of weekly payment has another important, though indirect, effect in the matter. When a bread-winner is getting into financial straits through the small amount of weekly payments, the danger of an unfair lump-sum settlement increases. If injured workmen 'keep on as long as possible' with the weekly payment, the insidious temptation to accept proposals for a lump-sum settlement grows stronger with the increasing distress resulting from the lowness of such payments.[3] In such cases, and they are very numerous, the insurance offices are in a strong position for 'bargaining' and on this ground alone, as well as on general social grounds, a low scale of weekly compensation payments should be opposed. The position of the injured workman is hard if he gets his legal due: it is harder still if, as is very frequently the case, he gets much less.

We are not concerned here with cases in which litigation ensues, or in which the employer or the insurance office contests the workman's claim for compensation, but merely with the ascertainment of his 'average weekly earnings'. Earnings are held to include not only payments in cash to the workman, but also anything given or supplied to the workman by way of remuneration, the cost of which can be valued in money, such as the use of a cottage for instance, or the use of a uniform. They are also held to include tips where they are a recognized source of income, but not expenses consequent upon the nature of his employment, e.g. allowances for expenses when away from home. 'Average weekly earnings' are reckoned on the earnings of the workman for the twelve months previous to the accident if he has been so long employed or, if not, for any less period during which he has been in continuous employment of the same employer and in the same grade of employment as when the accident took place. It is, however, specially

[1] *Rehabilitation Report*, 1939, pp. 132–3.
[2] *Hetherington Commission*, 1939, pp. 424–5.
[3] See p. 209 of vol. i, and later under 'Lump-Sum Settlements' in this volume.

provided in § 10 (ii) of the Act that when a man works at one time for one employer and at another time for another employer under 'concurrent contracts of service', the earnings under all these contracts shall be taken into account. The Act lays down that average weekly earnings 'shall be computed in such manner as is best calculated to give the rate per week at which the workman was being remunerated'.[1] But legal subtleties have led to much hardship. In the words of Mr. J. J. Davidson, M.P.: 'The lawyers come upon the scene and take into comparison his holidays and his illnesses on previous occasions, and his average weekly wage. A man earning £2. 10s. per week . . . receives, if successful, the handsome sum of £1. 2s. 6d. per week.' Mr. R. J. Taylor, M.P., declared on the same occasion that 'the lawyers had a lot of trouble in giving a definition on the question of average earnings'. He drew attention to the fact that if on account of bad trade or for some other reason men are working half time, their earnings taken over the period, average 25s. or 23s. a week, in respect of compensation.[2] In some cases an estimate is made in the light of the average weekly amounts earned during the twelve months previous to the accident by a workman employed on the same work in the same grade. This method of computing average weekly earnings is applicable in the case of casual workers, such as, for instance, dock labourers, or in cases where the workman has been so short a time in the employment in which the accident happened that the first method would be impracticable and unfair. In other cases the total of the workman's earnings over the period of his employment is divided by the number of weeks actually worked by him in that period. Here again the average may be subject to further adjustment if, for instance, the period of employment includes some weeks in which, as a normal and recognized incident of the employment, no work was done, as, for example, during the closing down of works for a 'wakes' week or a similar holiday. These cases may be considered as exceptions, as no such calculations will as a rule be necessary where the workman has been in receipt of a fixed weekly wage—yet the differentiations mentioned may be sufficient to lead to injustice to a workman who meets with an accident and suddenly has to face the fact that he will get considerably less than he would expect according to what the general scale of com-

[1] For further details cf. *Home Office Memorandum*, 1936, pp. 11–12 and Willis, loc. cit., pp. 300 sqq.

[2] Cf. *Debates H.C.*, Nov. 13th 1936. Cf. also *John Smith has an Accident*, loc. cit., p. 4: The first question is: 'What are John Smith's average weekly earnings? Not 'What did he get when he worked a full week?' Unemployment counts against the average, holidays likewise, and all other incidents of employment. He may get £2. 10s. a week when he is working full time, but his average may be £2. It may mean another lawsuit to settle what is the correct figure.

pensation would appear to him to be. The whole matter was amply discussed before the Holman Gregory Committee and many of the views and cases mentioned there still hold true. Mr. James Crinion, J.P., pointed out, for instance, that in the cotton industry there are so many holidays and stoppages due to shortage of material in departments, broken time for various causes, and to short time, that, though under normal conditions a man may be earning £2, his average may not exceed 30s. Such a man will probably and rightly consider his normal earnings not 30s. but £2 per week. Mr. Crinion urged that holiday time and broken time ought not to depress 'average' weekly earnings.[1] This suggestion appears to be the more equitable since that overtime is not generally included in average weekly earnings, as this is not regarded as a 'normal' week;[2] 'broken time'—including sickness, incidental stoppages, breakdowns—are reckoned in and tend to depress average weekly earnings while overtime which raises them is excluded.

Every new device to avoid the difficulties of schematic assessment of compensation leads to new difficulties. When Mr. Appleton, the Secretary of the General Federation of Trade Unions, was asked by the Holman Gregory Committee whether it would not be fairer to take 'the full four weeks' earnings immediately preceding the accident' as a basis for computation of the average earnings, instead of a twelve months' period, he objected on the ground that there are many cases where just the 'earnings for the first four weeks are very low', so that a workman being a new-comer to the workshop would be penalized by such an arrangement.[3] The difficulties are not merely technical. Close study of the subject reveals a much deeper background. Can any legislation based upon wages earned do justice to the different cases and conditions of injured or maimed workers and their dependants? The injured man with many children may be penalized relatively to a bachelor or a man with fewer dependants. The man who earns more may be expected to have some financial reserves to fall back on, but the existing law is based upon the biblical maxim 'to him that hath much shall be given'. No possible scheme is free from grave anomalies and injustices. If a standard of remuneration to an injured workman could be introduced, based upon a standard wage, it would, as Mr. Neal suggested to Mr. Appleton before the Holman Gregory Committee, exclude 'the man who was earning more than the standard wage by greater industry or greater skill, and exclude the man who was earning less'.[4] Yet it was stated before the Holman Gregory Committee that the majority of judges 'were against anything in the nature of a flat rate', although they recognized that it would get rid of disputes over

---

[1] Cf. *Holman Gregory Report*, Qq. 4151–6. [2] Cf. Ibid., Q. 11926.
[3] Cf. ibid., Q. 3782 sqq. [4] Cf. Q. 3786.

earnings. But the following clash of opinion was particularly interesting,[1] when Mr. Bannatyne was interrogating His Honour Judge Sir Edward Bray:

Mr. Bannatyne: As regards the manner of arriving at the compensation, in case of incapacity, is it not exceedingly difficult to adopt any other basis than the actual earnings of the workman, for this reason; one workman is getting, say £5 a week, and another is getting £2 a week; the standard of living in the houses must be substantially different. Must you not make the amount of compensation proportionate to the standard of comfort?

Sir Edward Bray: Personally I am not altogether disposed to see the necessity of it. If you say a certain sum is necessary to maintain a man himself if he is alone, or a man with a family, need it necessarily vary because in the one case he is only earning £2 a week and in another case he is earning £5 a week?

We fully share the judge's view. But for the fact that Workmen's Compensation in Britain is merely a partial and arbitrary recompense to an injured workman for his loss of earning power, distinctions of the kind existing would hardly be necessary. If, under another 'system', some sort of 'living-wage' compensation had been adopted, it would be hardly possible that such a considerable number of injured men would receive what can merely be called 'not enough to live on, and not enough to starve'. As things are to-day such a living-wage compensation may in a few cases exist as regards the best paid men. If it were to be adopted for the less efficient or the less paid class or grade of workers, it would attain 100 per cent. of their actual earnings. Injustice can only be avoided by adopting the principle that the injured workman has to be assisted to tide over the vicissitudes of this period by a living allowance adequate to his needs and those of his family while he is being physically cured and socially rehabilitated. In the absence of such arrangements careful thought should be given to the elimination of injustices arising from applying the principle of the actual-wage basis, i.e. the average weekly earnings, which so frequently entails unfairness to the injured worker and his family when applied as a basis for computation. The Holman Gregory Committee was urged to adopt the basis of standard-wages 'assessed in accordance with the average earnings for that occupation in that district',[2] or, as His Honour Judge B. Fossett Lock suggested by adopting as a basis 'the minimum standard rate whether prescribed by law or by the scales which are enforced by agreement'.[3] Such a plea, coming from the Bench, deserves close attention. Mr. Andrew Cairns Baird, a solicitor, representing the Scottish Conference of Friendly and Approved

---

[1] Cf. *Holman Gregory Report*, Q. 15034 and 15043.
[2] Cf. Mr. Appleton, *Holman Gregory Committee*, Q. 3784; cf. also Q. 2240 and 3039. Cf. further Q. 3907-19.   [3] Cf. ibid., Q. 65551.

Societies (with a membership of 350,000 persons), held that 'the basis of computing the earnings should be the standard weekly wage paid to the workman in the particular class of employment' adding 'The question of average weekly earnings has long been a vexed question.[1] Why the Holman Gregory Committee totally ignored this aspect of the problem which was placed before them by a crowd of witnesses is nowhere indicated in their report.

In Germany the principle of computation on the basis 'Standard district wage' was adopted from the outset. Compensation payments are based upon earnings during the last year of employment in the occupation in which the injury took place; if the person injured has not been employed for a full year in the occupation in which the injury took place the average annual earnings of workmen of the same class in the same or similar occupations are used as a basis of reckoning; if these earnings do not reach the average daily local wages of ordinary labourers, as fixed by high administrative authority for insurance against sickness, the latter amount shall be used as a basis for reckoning. Here, therefore, the principle of relying upon district or local rate levels of wages was adopted. In the U.S.A. the question of computation by wage standards has also played, particularly of late, an important part in discussions on Workmen's Compensation. As Walter F. Dodd points out, 'certain factors have influenced the effort to establish standards of compensation'.[2] These factors have been primarily:

(1) the loss of earning capacity by the injured worker,
(2) the economic need of the injured workman and his dependants,
(3) the incidental use of increased or reduced benefits to enforce compliance with safety regulations and with child labour and other laws.

In Washington and Wyoming fixed amounts of indemnity benefits are prescribed, regardless of the wage of the injured employee; a similar plan is adopted in Oregon for injuries resulting in other than temporary disabilities, and in Massachusetts and Wyoming for widows and dependant children in fatal cases. On the other hand, as with other matters concerning Workmen's Compensation in the U.S.A., provisions lack uniformity,[3] but the trend of expert opinion favours a full consideration of other standards of computation of average weekly earnings than the primitive method of merely taking into account what the earnings of the worker had actually been. The problem was fully investigated by Dr. Carl Hookstadt in a study of 1922 not yet forgotten

---

[1] Cf. ibid., Q. 8235.
[2] Cf. W. F. Dodd, *Administration of Workmen's Compensation*, New York, 1936, p. 624.
[3] Cf. ibid., p. 652.

by American administrative authorities,[1] and further pursued by a 'Special Committee on Average Weekly Wage Bases, with special consideration of the effect of widespread intermittent employment' in recent years.[2] The Report of this Committee emphasized that the problem was the more urgent as 'short-weeks' and 'staggered work plans' had increased during the trade depression. Mr. Hookstadt suggests that different methods be employed in computing average wages for temporary and permanent disability respectively. In the first case emphasis should be placed on *actual* earnings at the time of the injury. We ourselves, however, regard *standard* earnings as preferable, so long as the whole administration of Workmen's Compensation rests on its present basis.

The Labour party supported a Private Members' Bill of October 29th 1937 which would have replaced 'average' by 'normal' weekly earnings in the 'normal occupation of the workman',[3] wages being computed with due regard to what represents 'a fair and equitable remuneration for the normal working week in view of the nature of the employment and all the circumstances of the particular case'. This will only be possible under a new structure of Workmen's Compensation administration, failing which all such 'fair' decisions would probably be subject to litigation. Employers sometimes claim that it is unjust that an employer having employed a man for a few days, in which time he meets with an accident, should be responsible for compensation, as though the man had been in his employ for a long period. Under a system of comprehensive insurance, accidents which happen a few days after employment would not bear hardly on the party responsible for compensation; such cases are uncommon and have, in practice, no effect upon premiums paid.

At this stage we limit our discussion on the sufficiency of compensation, and its relation to working-class family budgets, to the position existing in regard to weekly payments. Of the two cases where, instead of a weekly payment, a capital sum may be due, viz. payment for injuries resulting in death and commutation of weekly payments into a lump-sum payment, the first, relating to a relatively small number of accidents or diseases, bears a close relation to the position which we have described as regards weekly payments. Compensation is, indeed, computed with respect to three years' earnings, subject to a maximum

[1] Carl Hookstadt, *Comparison of Workmen's Compensation Insurance and Administration*, U.S.A. Bureau of Labor Statistics Bulletin, no. 301, Washington, 1922.

[2] Cf. *Discussion of Industrial Accidents and Diseases*, U.S. Dept. of Labor, Washington, 1935, pp. 192 sqq.

[3] Cf. *Workmen's Compensation, A Bill to amend the law relating to Workmen's Compensation*, 1937, Section 3 (p. 5 of the Bill).

of £300, if the average earnings exceed £200. Here again the question of average weekly earnings presents difficulties similar to those just described.[1]

The following case shows how disadvantageously the question of 'earnings' may affect the lump sum paid to the survivors. One Gough, a collier, met with an accident and received 15s. 8d. a week compensation. He returned to light employment and received a reduced weekly payment of compensation accordingly. His light employment consisted of carrying batteries in the mine. While doing this he was killed by accident. The arbitrator found that Gough was not working as a collier, but in a separate grade of work, and based compensation payable on the average weekly sum paid for that work, although the dead man had an agreement with his employers that in the case of any incapacity to follow his light employment he should receive again the first sum, i.e. 15s. 8d. His surviving dependants were not allowed to claim a lump sum based on the higher scale of wages, although their condition was certainly as much affected by the accident which led to his death, as one which would have led to total incapacity.[2]

One further point here requires attention, viz. the extension of the Act to non-manual employees earning more than the present maximum of £350.[3]

Provision for a salary limit in such cases of £500 was made in Private Members' Bills, sponsored by the T.U.C., in 1933 and 1935 with a further provision enabling non-manual workers with salaries of over £500 to be included at their request within the scope of the Act. In July 1936 the National Federation of Professional Workers asked the Home Secretary to extend the Act to all non-manual workers irrespective of remuneration. It was suggested on this occasion that non-manual employees in the higher ranges of salary 'might be expected to insure themselves against accident'. The suggestion does not bear close examination, nor is it encouraged by the Inland Revenue Dept. which allows no rebate on such policies. The premium charged by commercial insurance offices to individuals would be almost prohibitive unless they were in a position to insure a very large number of individuals against the risk which can scarcely be actuarially estimated.

[1] By 'three years earnings' is meant the amount earned by the workman in the employment of the same employer during the three years immediately preceding the injury, or if the workman has been employed less than three years, a sum equal to 156 times his average weekly earnings in that employment.

[2] Cf. also Willis, pp. 216, 294, 297, and 299.

[3] The Home Office memorandum to the Hetherington Commission stated (Section H. 432–7) that there were in 1936 a number of non-manual employees earning up to £500 a year who were exposed to industrial risks, particularly in the chemical, engineering, and building industries, and in docks and shipyards.

The cost of collection would be relatively high. It is on all grounds preferable that such cases should be included in a general policy covering all employees in a firm, salaries in the higher grades being adjusted accordingly. In Germany all persons employed in certain industrial undertakings are insured against industrial injuries, irrespective of remuneration. This is the logical consequence of the system which makes the undertaking (*Betrieb*) and not the individual employee the basis of insurance.[1]

Improvements of weekly payments and a change in the principles now governing the computation of earnings and average weekly earnings would automatically influence the amount paid to surviving dependants in computation of lump-sum payments. We need not, therefore, discuss the matter separately. As to the sufficiency of the capital sum from a social angle, the position does not differ from that relating to lump sums, as generally paid in the case of weekly payments redeemed for a lump sum. We can, therefore, defer to our next chapter a critical analysis of what the present maximum payment of £600 in the case of death resulting from accident entails to the surviving family.

[1] §§ 537 sqq. of *Unfallversicherung*.

NOTE

THE insufficiency of medical benefits under N.H.I. has often been disputed. While dealing with the point again in later chapters we want to put on record the view of Sir Arthur Newsholme, *International Studies on the Relation between Private and Official Practice of Medicine*, 1931, vol. iii, pp. 142 sqq. This elaborate work compares conditions in Britain with that of many other countries and should be studied by all interested in the matter of health insurance conditions. Sir Arthur declares that, 'apart from the restricted and unequal extensions of medical benefit provided by those Approved Societies which possess available surplus funds—and not completely supplied even by these exceptional (!) societies—medical benefits under N.H.I. are incomplete' in four respects: (1) there is no provision for treatment in hospital, or, alternatively, treatment at home for serious operations or other conditions requiring expert medical service; (2) there is a lack of specialist diagnosis and treatment; (3) there is no provision for pathological and physical aids; (4) there is 'usually' no provision for nursing the sick. All these deficiencies have their bearing upon compensation payments and the worker's budget.

CHAPTER VII
LUMP-SUM SETTLEMENTS
A. SOCIAL DANGERS

When sickness comes, the suffering by poverty increases tenfold.

ALFRED MARSHALL, *Economics of Industry*, 1922, Introd.

THE alternative to weekly payments of Workmen's Compensation is, as we have shown, a lump sum awarded to or accepted by the injured person in final settlement of his claim. Such payments are much more frequent than is indicated by official statistics, which compare the number of cases thus settled with the total number of industrial accidents involving absence from work for over three days and show that 95·80 per cent. are settled without a lump-sum payment.[1] Yet of about £6½ millions paid as compensation in the seven industrial groups, a little over £2 millions, or about 32 per cent., was paid in the form of lump sums.[2]

These figures and, in particular, these percentages, mask the true role of lump-sum payments which are, for practical purposes, quite inapplicable to slight injuries of short duration. Over 67 per cent. of all cases of industrial accident, and over 49 per cent. of all cases of industrial disease last less than four weeks: about 60 and 42 per cent. respectively last less than three weeks; 95 and 85 per cent. less than thirteen weeks. Lump-sum settlements only assume importance in relation to injuries of long duration. Accident and disease cases terminated in which compensation had been paid for twenty-six weeks and over were only 1·75 and 11·29 per cent. respectively of the whole. Lump-sum payments were made in 1937 in 7,329 such cases as compared with 6,836 cases of accident of like duration[3] exclusive of cases terminated by payment of a lump sum.

The preponderance of lump-sum settlements as a method of discharging employer's liability in serious cases is thus clear: it is even more marked in cases of industrial disease.[4] These figures, moreover, relate only to the 7½ million workmen included in the seven industrial

---

[1] Of 408,367 cases terminated in 1937, 3·97 per cent. were settled by a lump-sum payment after, and 0·45 per cent. without previous weekly payment. *Statistics for 1937, Home Office*, 1939, p. 9.

[2] Ibid., p. 23, Table V.

[3] Excluding 1,832 accident cases terminated without previous weekly payments which may be assumed to have been trivial.

[4] 1,123 cases of industrial disease of twenty-six weeks' or more duration were ended in 1937 by payment of a lump sum, as compared with 1,212 cases terminated without such a payment.

groups: lump-sum settlements outside these groups are of no less importance.

We have already referred to the significance of this system, and the doubts it inspired in evidence before the Holman Gregory Committee. But it still prevails, and the legislative safeguards devised to protect the workman against unfair and insufficient lump-sum payments are still ineffective. Even the fact that unregistered agreements for lump sums do not relieve an employer of his liability to make weekly payments has not prevented employers from risking the non-registration of an agreement.[1] Unnamed witnesses before the Stewart Committee testified that unregistered lump-sum payments are much favoured.[2] But the Committee, which seems to have been unaware of the earlier evidence of Sir Edward Bray, did not recommend compulsory registration.

Workmen's Compensation in most foreign countries[3] prohibits lump-sum settlements: indeed, in this matter Britain stands almost alone. Though 'a few' workmen's compensation schemes provide for the payment of lump-sum compensation in cases of permanent incapacity, they are allowed only where earning capacity is not reduced by more than a fixed percentage.[4] There is general reluctance to admit the principles of commutation. In former Austria the law provided that, with the beneficiary's consent, a pension, which in the case of incapacity of between $16\frac{2}{3}$ and 25 per cent. is granted for a period of three years, may be replaced by a lump sum not exceeding three times the annual pensions. Pensions based on a higher degree of incapacity may be commuted only if the workman agrees and can show that the money will be used to advantage. In Germany the Insurance Institution may replace an incapacity pension by a sum equal to three times the yearly pension, provided that *the pension is not more than 10 per cent. of that payable for total incapacity*. It may also, with the beneficiary's consent, commute pensions *not exceeding 25 per cent. of the total incapacity pension* for a sum representing their capital value. Under the Legisla-

---

[1] Cf. Wilson and Levy, vol. i, pp. 205–6, 247–8; and *Holman Gregory Committee, Evidence*, A. 15037. Sir Edward Bray, then a County Court judge and Hon. Secretary of the Council of Judges of County Courts, emphasized that many employers refrained from an application to register solely in order to avoid the intervention of the judges.

[2] Cf. *Stewart Report*, p. 91. 'Under the terms of the Act, however, an agreement is not binding unless and until it has been registered, and if this is not done the employer is not exempt from liability to continue weekly payments. The witnesses referred to were not satisfied that this provision of the Act afforded an adequate safeguard against improper "settlements" . . .'

[3] Cf. *The Evaluation of Permanent Incapacity for Work in Social Insurance*, I.L.O., Geneva, 1937, pp. 226 sqq. This interesting Report will be quoted subsequently as *Evaluation Report*.   [4] Cf. ibid., p. 138.

tive Decree of December 8th 1931 the Insurance Institution is also authorized to commute the pension for a lump sum if it appears probable that the insured person's condition will not justify the award of a permanent incapacity pension. Regulations vary in the different States of the U.S.A., but lump-sum agreements are, generally speaking discouraged,[1] and are, in any case, subject to legal restrictions. Partial or total commutation requires the approval of the Board or Commission administering Workmen's Compensation law, or else of a Court.[2]

In 5 States the initiative must come from the injured or beneficiary, in New Hampshire from the employer, in 12 States from either party, and in them the parties must agree on the lump-sum payment before it may be approved. Often the lump-sum payment must appear to be to the best interest of one or both of the parties; in 7 Acts it must be to the best interest of the injured or beneficiary, in 13 to the best interest of both parties, while in 14 it must appear to be to the best interest of either party or, as it is usually stated, it must appear 'that it is to the best interest of the beneficiary or that it will avoid undue expense or hardship to either party'.

The great importance thus attributed to the interest of the injured or beneficiary and the restrictions laid upon the granting of lump-sum settlements are a prominent feature of Workmen's Compensation legislation in the U.S.A. Experts have doubts as to the expediency of lump-sum settlements:

It is comparatively easy to grant lump-sum payments, but to do so in the interests of justice to all parties is an intricate and baffling problem.[3]

While in England the whole question of lump-sum payments has been relegated to the background of public discussion—though the Stewart Committee devoted twenty-three pages to the subject—in the U.S.A. all sides of the problem have been cautiously investigated by the International Association of Industrial Accidents Boards and Commissions for some time and have provoked lively discussions. In the words of Dr. Hatch, of the New York Industrial Board, 'instalment compensation is, for sound reasons, the rule; lump-sum compensation is an exception, with the burden of proof of its justification

---

[1] Cf. Dr. L. W. Hatch in U.S.A. Bureau of Labor Statistics, *Bulletin 1511*, 1929, p. 169. The difference between instalment payments or pension is 'virtually that between an assured income and a speculative investment'.

[2] Cf. Dodd, loc. cit., p. 721, noted that there are 51 Acts in the U.S.A. which make provision for lump sums.

[3] Mr. R. M. Little, Director of the Rehabilitation Division of the N.Y. State Education Department. Cf. 1935 *Convention of the International Association of Industrial Accidents Boards, Bulletin No. 4*, Washington (U.S.A. Dept. of Labor), 1936, p. 150. Also 'Co-operation of Workmen's Compensation Administrations with Rehabilitation Agencies', U.S.A. Dept. of Labor, *Serial No. R. 345*, 1936, p. 10.

on its side'[1]—an attitude common to other European countries,[2] but in sharp contrast to that of the Stewart Committee[3] whose view, it may be noted, has not been endorsed by the official representatives of the Labour party in the House of Commons. The British employer, on the other hand, may discharge his liability after a relatively short time (six months) by paying a lump sum calculated sometimes with reference to the degree of incapacity and sometimes fixed independently without other limitations than those imposed by the legislature to safeguard the injured workman or his family. In the words of the *Evaluation Report*:[4]

[In Britain] . . . these matters are left to the discretion of the arbitrator who, so far as is known, is not bound by any legislative provision as to the amount required to redeem weekly payments or as to the receivability of a private agreement between the parties. Commutation need not necessarily be based on the actuarial value of payments, that is, on capitalisation of future earnings lost, or in other words, on a calculation of their present value. It may also rest on a common-sense business basis. *The procedure in Great Britain is, however, quite exceptional,* in most countries the economic loss and the degree of incapacity are measured by the difference between earnings before and after the worker was disabled.

This aspect of the lump-sum system has never received due attention in Britain and was ignored by the Stewart Committee. The Committee of 1904–6 was better informed on the subject, as the Memorandum on Foreign and Colonial Laws relating to Compensation for Injuries proves. Under British law, in case of permanent incapacity of an injured adult, the lump sum must suffice to purchase a Post Office annuity equal to *three-quarters* of the annual value of the weekly payments. The I.L.O., on the other hand, recommended that

where compensation is paid in a lump sum, the sum should not be less than *the capitalised value of the periodical payment.* . . .

The proposed scale of periodical payments is moreover substantially higher and more favourable to the workman than that at present in force in Britain.[5]

---

[1] Cf. *Proceedings of the Sixteenth Annual Meeting of the International Association, &c.,* April 1930. *Bulletin 511* of the U.S. Bureau of Labor Statistics, 1930, p. 167.

[2] In addition to the restrictions in the U.S.A., Germany, Austria, as described above, it may be mentioned that in Sweden lump-sum payments are allowed only at the beneficiary's request if the competent authority regards the measure as justified by special circumstances; this seems so seldom to happen that the latest Swedish publication on the matter does not even mention such payments. Cf. *Social Work and Legislation in Sweden,* Stockholm, 1938, p. 115. In Bulgaria, Norway, Rumania, and Switzerland lump-sum compensation is strictly limited to certain low degrees of incapacity, for instance, when incapacity exceeds 10 per cent., but not 20 per cent. Cf. *Evaluation Report,* pp. 131–3.

[3] Cf. *Stewart Report,* p. 112: 'Generally lump sums are used to advantage.'   [4] pp. 65–6.

[5] Cf. Recommendation No. 22 concerning the Minimum Scale of Workmen's Compensation in I.L.O., *International Labour Organization 1936,* p. 128.

Such is the British lump-sum system in the light of that of other industrial nations. What is the position if viewed from the angle of British experience and expediency alone?

The question may conveniently be considered under the following headings:

1. What are the advantages and disadvantages of lump-sum payments under the present system of Workmen's Compensation in England?

2. Are existing means of coping with the disadvantages and of protecting the beneficiaries against abuse sufficient and effective?

The present system of lump-sum payments is naturally favoured by insurance offices and, in the words of the *Holman Gregory Report*,[1] 'it must be recognized that lump-sum settlements are popular with workmen. In the words of one witness: You will do one of the most unpopular acts if you abolish lump sums.' How far this is still true deserves careful consideration. In a propagandist pamphlet *John Smith has an Accident*, clearly written by an expert, the abolition or restriction of lump-sum payments is not proposed, though their adequacy is questioned: the Labour party Bill of November 1936[2] retained them. A Workmen's Compensation Board thereunder would have had power to 'commute at any time the weekly payments payable to a workman or a dependant for a lump sum'.

A later Bill presented in October 1937 did not alter the law in regard to lump-sum payments, though Mr. Arthur Henderson voiced the views of his friends that 'the system of lump-sum payments should be terminated',[3] and that weekly payments ought to be universal. The problem is not materially changed, if, instead of a lump-sum payment, a commutation of weekly payments takes place; employers and insurance bodies might be even more anxious to scale down the weekly payments in order to avoid higher commutation payments: on the other hand, the 75 per cent. basis of calculation might strengthen the preference of employers for lump sums and the danger of reckless spending by the beneficiary would not be lessened. The Bill did not take a clear line in this matter, but there is reason to think that lump-sum payments are less in favour in Trade Union circles than formerly.

It is of course to the advantage of the seriously and permanently injured workman to have a capital sum at his disposal. He cannot ascertain the probable amount of his weekly benefit. He cannot foresee how far his changed circumstances will affect his household budget.

---

[1] Cf. p. 53.

[2] Cf. *Workmen's Compensation Bill*, Nov. 6th 1936, pp. 10–11.

[3] Cf. *Debates H.C.*, vol. 329, no. 19, col. 746.

He often fails to realize, till his doctor breaks it to him, that there is no medical benefit under Workmen's Compensation beyond that normally provided under the N.H.I. Acts, no free medical cure or treatment for recovery, no allowance for appliances. The prospect of a lump-sum payment makes these handicaps appear unimportant. It is significant that in § 12(3) of the Bill of October 1937 the Board was empowered to advance lump sums 'where in its opinion the interest or pressing need of the workman or dependant warrants it'. This aspect of lump-sum payments is generally overlooked[1] and the prospect of commencing an independent business overstressed. Assuming, for the moment, that the system commends itself to injured workmen, we must inquire whether it is defensible on economic and social grounds. A drowning man clutches at a straw; to an injured workman burdened with debt and terrified—the word is not too strong—by the receipt of judgement summonses and rent and rates demands under threat of eviction and distraint, a lump sum, however small, is 'popular' if only because it offers a temporary respite at the expense of the future. But this is no justification of the system,[2] which should be so recast as to relieve the injured man or his dependants from the necessity of using a capital sum, intended as compensation for loss of current earning capacity, to meet debts or medical expenses consequent upon the accident.

It is generally assumed that a lump sum may enable an injured person to take up work which will compensate him for the loss of his previous occupation in which he has spent his working life. In all such cases there should be deducted from this benefit the sum which the injured man had already spent on such purposes. In some instances little may have been spent; in others little may be left. In some cases, but not in others, the Miners' Welfare Commission, or the local hospital, or some charitable agency, may have provided free treatment.

There are undoubtedly cases, says the *Holman Gregory Report*, where, with the amount of capital which the lump sum provides, the injured workman or perhaps his wife is able to establish a business and, *although many cases have arisen where the money so invested has been lost*, we think that if a man or his wife has had some business training, they may very well, with the capital of the lump sum, obtain a higher income than they did before the accident.[3]

[1] Cf. Cohen, *Workmen's Compensation*, pp. 125–7.

[2] *The Insurance Mail* which generally takes the employer's point of view writes '. . . it is often in the best interests of the insured person to continue to receive the weekly payment rather than to agree to a lump-sum settlement', July 13th 1938, p. 512.

[3] Cf. *Holman Gregory Report*, p. 53. Cf. also *Evidence*, for instance that of Mr. J. Houghton, Secretary to the Scottish Union of Dock Labourers. Q. 332: 'As regards lump sums, is it your experience, generally speaking, that lump sums are made good use of by the working people or squandered?' A.: 'Generally speaking I would not say squandered,

The Committee, however, stopped short at suggesting the need for inquiries as to the existence or possibility of the requisite 'business training' and of the cases where a higher income had followed. The researches of the Charity Organization Society do not encourage optimism, and emphasize the perils of exploitation of recipients of lump sums, through their ignorance and the overestimate of 'chances'.

We have had [said Mr. J. Jones, M.P.] in our union members receiving £500, £600 or even £700 . . . but before very long the whole of that money has disappeared. Sometimes they have been inveigled into investing the lump sums in some business; there are numbers of 'sharps' about who are very clever at finding out when people have got sums of money like this, and in putting before them various suggestions as to how they can invest it. Sometimes they have gone into a public-house—in more senses than one—and they are very soon out of it, because the little bit of money they have received as a lump sum has been frittered away in speculations.[1]

The records of the Charity Organization Society include the case of a steward who got £350 for a foot injury. He tried a refreshment bar in the provinces; ten weeks later he had lost his all and was in receipt of Public Assistance. A factory worker, aged 18, lost his right arm in February 1933: at the age of 21 he received £625 and bought a business. A year later he applied for Poor Law Relief. Another man who had been 'on the Parish' received a smaller amount, £122, in February 1935 which he invested in a women's underwear business; in May 1935 he was back on relief. In the face of such cases, derived from practical daily life experience, it is not surprising that the Society makes a strong protest against lump-sum payment and, with the unbiased experience of more than two generations, alludes to the 'terrible lump-sum system'.[2] In a Memorandum submitted to the Interdepartmental Committee on Rehabilitation of Persons injured by Accidents[3] the Society explains at length the serious objections to

but I believe lump sums are given to people who sometimes have not the business capacity to bank it.' Q. 333: 'You think it ought to be brought under the control of the Court?' A.: 'I know several cases where the recipients have fallen between two stools. They thought they could run a little business and could not, and the money went. . . . I am totally in favour of the abolition of lump sums in the case of total incapacity of the workman.' This view conforms exactly to the attitude of foreign legislation as described above, where lump sum payments are restricted to cases of lesser injuries and made dependent upon the actual expected result of their utilization. Cf. also *Evidence* of the *Holman Gregory Committee*, Q. 477 and p. 472 of vol. ii.   [1] Cf. *Debates H.C.*, Nov. 19th 1937.

[2] Cf. 'The Workmen's Compensation Acts', *Charity Organization Quarterly*, July 1934, p. 112.

[3] The material utilized has been supplied in the main by thirty District Committees of the London C.O.S. and in frequent and close consultation with a number of kindred bodies in the U.K., and has been printed. Cf. in particular p. 12: 'Small Retail Business as Rehabilitation Plan'.

the investment of lump sums in small businesses. 'Very great personal gifts are required to succeed (as a small shopkeeper). Those having them make big successes out of small retail shops. The sufferer from an industrial accident knows nothing of this. It is improbable that he or she can develop these gifts.' American experience has been the same:

Lump sums naturally tend to uncertainty of benefit . . . under lump-sum payments all security for the future becomes dependent upon the claimant's ability to manage a capital investment . . . a thorough investigation of lump-sum proposals is imperative; . . . such an investigation must cover not only the claimant's general capacity for such a responsibility, but also the actual use to which the claimant proposes to put his lump sum because the average wage-earner has had neither training nor experience to fit him for such undertaking.[1]

A speaker of much experience told his audience:

We have had men go into the pool-room business, the chicken business, into the dairy business, into the filling-station business, and into every kind of business you can think of—agricultural pursuits, to buy a home, to buy a building, to travel, to buy tombstones, to pay for an operation, &c.—and we find that in over 90 per cent. of those cases the money has not accomplished the purpose which we expected it would accomplish.[2]

Recent inquiries into lump-sum settlements in the State of New York brought one investigator to the conclusion that among men receiving lump-sum settlements of 1,000 dollars or more, an aggregate of not less than 100,000 dollars is lost annually by injured workers in the State 'because they are paid lump sums rather than weekly instalments'. The loss would have appeared much greater if small settlements could also have been taken into account. Of a great number of workers interviewed only about one-fourth could be called 'moderately successful'.[3] The American courts have frequently expressed their disapproval of lump-sum settlements.[4] Mr. L. E. Worstell, Chairman of the Idaho Industrial Accident Board, said in 1929 that 'our experiences [of 112 cases] shows that in over 90 per cent. of these cases the money did the claimants absolutely no good. They lost it.'[5]

[1] Cf. Dr. L. W. Hatch, *Bulletin of Labor Statistics*, 1930, pp. 166 sqq. Cf. ibid., p. 171, Mr. R. Jarnegan of the N.Y. Rehabilitation Bureau: 'The fact that they have been granted lump-sum settlement, or had their compensation commuted to lump sums, and the fact that it had been dissipated, multiplied the rehabilitation problem. Frequently it compelled re-employment in stop-gap jobs, when the compensation moneys, if conserved, would have made possible a far more constructive programme.'   [2] Cf. ibid., p. 195.

[3] Cf. 'Lump Sum Settlements in Workmen's Compensation in New York', *Monthly Labor Review* of *the Bureau of Labor Statistics*, U.S. Dept. of Labor, December 1936.

[4] Cf. W. F. Dodd, 1930, loc. cit., p. 723. He quotes many cases in which a lump-sum settlement was followed by entire loss of money.

[5] Cf. *U.S.A. Bureau of Labor Statistics Bulletin No. 511 (192)*, p. 195, and Dodd, pp. 727 sqq.

To the German administrative authorities the difference in their and our systems of lump-sum payments was always evident.

The system of social insurance against accidents and infirmity would fail in its object had not the method of pensions been preferred. Only in this way it is possible to provide adequately against need and to secure to people of small means, during loss of earning capacity caused by accidents or infirmity, a care which cannot be sacrificed owing to improvident conduct or misfortune, as may easily happen where compensation takes the form—*so largely favoured by private insurance*—of lump-sum payment.[1]

This is one of several problems which await official investigation in Britain. The Stewart Committee's terms of reference required them to inquire into 'the extent to which the workman derives the full benefit of the compensation when paid in a lump sum'. What little was said in the matter was mainly a summary of unpublished evidence.

Many witnesses referred to cases in which a workman may fail to receive the full benefit of compensation paid by lump sum through some action of his own: and we have had a considerable body of evidence on this aspect of the matter. We have been informed of cases in which the workman is alleged to have squandered the money in reckless indulgence, or in gross extravagance of various kinds: of cases in which he lost his money, in whole or in part, in rash enterprises, such as the purchase of small shops, or of businesses of which he had no knowledge; and again of cases in which the benefit of a lump sum was enjoyed mainly or wholly by persons other than the injured workman. Most of the witnesses who gave evidence had knowledge of cases of this character but they were generally of opinion that such cases were relatively few and tending to become fewer. It was generally recognized that there was a definite public interest in the wise use of capital sums paid as compensation to an injured workman since there was always the risk that if the money were lost or wasted the man and his family might become chargeable to the funds. Cases were cited in evidence where it was maintained that this had in fact occurred. Nevertheless it was apparent that there were wide differences of opinion as to what could and should be done to prevent such waste or loss.[2]

The Committee mentioned that two 'extreme' views were advanced. One apparently was to abolish lump sums altogether with some exceptions (i.e. those which are automatically paid and controlled by the court); the other was to leave things as they are. The Committee sought a middle course. It recommended, for instance, that the Registrar should see the man in all cases.[3] It noted that 'altogether inadequate sums have been offered' and suggested that something

[1] Cf. *Das Reichversicherungsamt und die deutsche Arbeiterversicherung* (Festschrift), 1910, p. 88. Also for a merely descriptive discussion of the matter cf. W. H. Dawson, *Social Insurance in Germany*, 1912, pp. 102 sqq.

[2] Cf. *Stewart Report*, pp. 97–8.   [3] Cf. loc. cit., p. 102.

should be done to assist the injured workman in the 'process of bargaining', but took for granted that this was not necessary where the workman had 'competent advice from the solicitor or otherwise', whilst recognizing that there 'are large numbers who have not the advantage of such advice'. The Committee, therefore, suggested that the Registrar should see the workman in every case, and record no agreement without full inquiry and a recent medical report insisting, in any case of doubt, on examination and report by the Medical Referee. They were, on the other hand, averse from any radical departure from the existing system. Their verdict was: 'Lump sums are generally used to advantage. Cases of misuse occur but the evidence is that misuse is not extensive.' The evidence was neither published nor summarized. We prefer to rely upon the considered judgement of the Charity Organization Society,[1] which accords with our own experience:

Lump sum settlements dislocate the victim's social habits and mental outlook, and those of his family; tempt him into a ruinous entry into business, in which he is not qualified to succeed; engender resentment inimical to the preservation of social solidarity, and induce victims to prolong their incapacity by an allurement not shared by weekly allowances payable under the Act.

The *Stewart Report* does not indicate how far 'the great body of evidence in the matter' which favoured 'some course of action between' the extremes was mainly that of employers or insurance offices, nor does it disclose the Committee's reasons for assuming that the evil is diminishing; such has not been the experience of the C.O.S. or, so far as we know, of any other competent body. The Committee could not deny that injured workmen are induced by 'bargaining' to accept insufficient lump-sum payments and to accept improvident settlements, that the money is often wasted, to the detriment of the injured man and his family, and that the prospects of lump sums being utilized in a profitable business are doubtful. Other countries have accepted such evidence as a sufficient ground to reject lump sums in favour of weekly payments. The Committee cited the 'testimony of most' of the witnesses as proving that lump-sum settlements were 'generally popular', but such questions cannot be settled by counting heads with no regard to experience or financial interest.

In the case of nystagmus the Stewart Committee described employers as looking upon the lump-sum settlement as not merely settling an individual claim in respect of a 'particular' attack but 'as buying the miner out of the industry altogether'. This statement, which was made in the part of the *Report* dealing with nystagmus, was not, however, alluded to in a subsequent discussion on lump sums in general.[2]

[1] Cf. *Charity Organization Quarterly*, July 1934, p. 105.
[2] Cf. *Stewart Report*, p. 42.

A partially disabled workman may well believe himself better able to find a new job when he has 'commuted' his weekly compensation payments.

When they [the prospective employers] knew that he was on compensation they would not accept the responsibility and would not give him work. The lad returned home. He could not get work, and he said to the people at the training centre: 'If I commute my claim will you recommend me for work?' They said, 'Of course, if you are not receiving compensation you will have a better chance.'[1]

Such cases throw light on the motives which may, in present circumstances, induce workmen and employers to seek a lump-sum settlement. When dealing with the 'security' aspect of Accident Insurance in England we shall see that difficulties connected with the actuarial assessment of the risk involved in weekly payments also make lump-sum settlements advantageous to insurance offices.[2] But we believe that this motive for supporting lump sums is less important than the second, viz. to facilitate 'bargaining' for a cheap settlement. We have shown elsewhere (vol. i, p. 153) how successful employers or insurance offices have been in that respect, particularly where the workman has no union or competent solicitor behind him, and where, for whatever reason, the Registrar has not played an active part. The difficulty of securing a fair settlement by lump-sum payment is often great in rural areas, partly because few farm workers are trade unionists, partly because they find it difficult to obtain advice. Moreover, many small rural employers are uninsured. It is certainly not accidental that lump-sum settlements prevail only where private insurance predominates, as in Britain and Denmark.[3]

A State Insurance office would doubtless take the view that the workman should, in the first instance, be restored to health so as not to be a burden on the community and that a capital payment should only be sought as a last resort. Such a consideration, however, cannot influence the private employer, either individually or, collectively, as a member of a mutual indemnity association, nor an insurance company. It is not therefore surprising that witnesses speaking before the Stewart Committee 'on behalf of the National Confederation of Employers' Organisations . . . were of opinion that no material change of any kind was called for', though some witnesses held that economic distress, resulting from the low rate of compensation and the heavy expenses for medical treatment, predisposed men to accept a lump

[1] Cf. Mr. Whiteley, M.P., *Debates H.C.*, Nov. 18th 1938.
[2] Cf. also *Cassel Report*, pp. 38–40.
[3] Of total payments of compensation in Denmark 55 per cent. was in the form of lump sums for total incapacity. *International Survey of Social Services*, 1936, vol. ii, pp. 128–30. *Evaluation Report*, p. 226.

sum in settlement of a claim and that employers or insurance offices are
ready to pay the fees of the claimant's solicitors if they can thus secure
a lump-sum settlement.[1]

'It was said [apparently by witnesses speaking for the B.M.A.] that
the position was made worse in some cases by persons calling on the
injured man in hospital within a few days—or even hours—of an
accident and implanting in the man's mind the idea of an early lump-
sum settlement.' The spokesmen of insurance offices denied that they
countenanced 'lump-sum touting'. The Committee accepted their
assurance: but did not question the veracity of the witnesses who spoke
of the practice, which is well known to exist, nor did they, apparently,
make inquiries from hospital staffs. No insurance office will agree
that their agents are encouraged or even allowed to employ undesirable
'high pressure' methods of business. But pressure for increase is the
mainstay of insurance businesses and offices will not repudiate policies
so obtained.[2]

The findings of the Holman Gregory and Stewart Committees,[3] the
Stewart Report, and the experience of the C.O.S. as to the methods
habitually used by insurance offices in negotiating lump-sum settlements, were confirmed in evidence before the Hetherington Commission by Mr. T. A. E. Spearing who, as Hon. Secretary of the Association
of Approved Societies, could speak from long first-hand experience of
many cases. He told the Commission[4] of 'cases where the first offer
was £35, settlement £60; first offer £35, settlement £250; first offer
£150, settlement £300 and so on'. He offered to submit a list of such
cases which, of course, figure in Home Office Reports as 'uncontested'.[5]
His Association was opposed to lump-sum settlements which were
almost always disadvantageous to the recipient.[6] Lump sums were
'popular' only because injured workmen were anxious to discharge
their accumulated liabilities. There were cases where a lump-sum
settlement was advantageous to the injured workman, but they were
few.[7] The evidence of the T.U.C. before the Hetherington Commission further amplifies our opinion. 'On the whole', so declared Mr.
Russell-Jones, 'we feel safer with weekly payments'.[8] 'We think, on the
whole, that the lump sum is a bait', said another representative of the
Congress.[9] Yet, as we shall see subsequently, the Memorandum of

---

[1] Cf. *Stewart Report*, pp. 89–90 and 99.

[2] Wilson and Levy, *Industrial Assurance*, 1937, Chap. XIII, 'Business Getting'.

[3] Vol. i, pp. 208–11.   [4] Q. 1764 A.

[5] One of the Royal Commissioners, Mr. J. S. Boyd, in cross-examining Mr. Spearing
took precisely the same line as Mr. Guthrie in 1920. Cf. vol. i, pp. 183–7 and *passim*.

[6] Q. 1769 A.   [7] Q. 1686 A.   [8] Q. 3921 A.
[9] A. 3937.

the Congress did not fully bring out the necessary conclusions to be drawn from such overwhelming experiences, but rather left a backdoor open to at least lump-sum settlements by commutation.

The question of lump-sum settlements has also an important bearing on considerations of a more public character. It is in the interest of the State that a system of compensation should not have the effect of retarding the re-entry of the recipients into productive occupation. The *Stewart Report* noted that some witnesses, including those who spoke on behalf of the B.M.A., referred to the practice of lump-sum settlement by agreement as creating an undesirable atmosphere inasmuch as it tended to make the workman concentrate on the idea of obtaining the largest possible lump sum rather than on recovering his full capacity. It was said that one result of lump-sum touting was the unwillingness of some men to attempt light work until a lump-sum payment had been definitely agreed upon. It was suggested by such witnesses that rehabilitation centres were needed to promote the recovery of industrial capacity, the men to remain on full weekly compensation until certified to have recovered as far as they were likely to do so, and that there should be no suggestion of any lump-sum payment until stability had been reached. The *Report* noted that in some cases the parties responsible for paying compensation 'trouble themselves little about the injured man's condition or any measures for its improvement'.[1] The Committee might have dwelt upon this point a little further: for it summarizes in a single phrase the greatest defect of the whole English system of Workmen's Compensation, which stamps the injury as a private liability which can be discharged by a single payment whereas, under a system of State administration, coupled with measures and institutions of rehabilitation, there is a strong inducement to promote the re-entry into industry of the injured workman. The insurance company or private indemnity association is concerned like the small employer only to pay what he must. This is particularly the case in Britain where there is no legislative provision for the restoration to health and re-entry into employment of the injured persons. Some large employers can and do provide orthopaedic treatment and suitable employment for injured members of their own staff, but it is not—as in the U.S.A.—financially to their advantage to do so. Only when some higher aim is pursued, as is the case with State or semi-State institutions, can the ideal of restoring the working capacity of the injured man prevail. Under the present system of lump-sum payments the interest of the employer is diverted from the incentive to find suitable work for the man which, if no lump sum existed, would be 'the only means by which he could reduce his

[1] Cf. *Stewart Report*, pp. 89–91.

liability to pay compensation'. 'More than one witness suggested that if lump-sum payments were abolished the persons liable to pay compensation would focus their attention on measures to restore the workman's capacity, and that would be a great improvement on the present position.' (*Stewart Report.*)

But there was also another view diametrically opposed to this attitude. It was suggested that lump-sum settlements should be encouraged and promptly made without waiting for the stabilization of the disablement, as the best means of terminating a neurosis. The Holman Gregory Committee had already hinted that the acceptance of a lump-sum settlement might sometimes make the injured man more inclined to resume work and might put a term to mental anxiety and brooding.[1] On the other hand, the Ministry of Pensions told the Stewart Committee that lump-sum settlements of war-disablements had not proved successful, *particularly in cases of neurosis and neurasthenia.*[2]

This conclusion was not lightly reached. Dr. W. A. Brend, for many years neurologist to the Ministry of Pensions, states that Sir John Collie, the first Chief Medical Officer to that Ministry, at first favoured lump-sum gratuities in lieu of pensions to soldiers discharged whilst still suffering from functional nervous disorders. 'The therapeutic effect of this procedure was, however, found to be small and the policy was soon abandoned.' Dr. Brend himself holds that 'prompt recovery from an apparently hysterical symptom after payment of compensation should always be regarded with suspicion'. Dr. Shirley Smith, moreover, recently declared that

contrary to frequent assertions, little if any benefit accrues in these cases from the conclusion of litigation.[3]

Our task at this point is not to argue whether or how industrial neurosis should be treated. Our concern is to ascertain how far lump-sum settlements now tend to increase the danger of neurotic aggravations of an existing injury. The part played by 'malingering' in this connexion is not of importance. We base this view upon the evidence and conclusions of the *Holman Gregory Report*, and upon very recent statements by high authorities—Dr. D. C. Norris, who only found three cases of malingering among some 15,000 examined, and Dr. W. McAdam Eccles.[4] Dr. Norris declared:

It might be thought that the practice of examining claimants would disclose a great deal of the seamy side of human nature, and that one would often have to deal

---

[1] Cf. *Holman Gregory Report*, p. 53. Also A. 15200. Judge Bray: 'There is no doubt that once the thing is settled by the payment of a lump sum the man gets better.'

[2] Cf. *Stewart Report*, p. 91.   [3] Cf. Brend, loc. cit., p. 34. Also *B.M.J.*, Aug. 6th 1938.

[4] Cf. *Holman Gregory Report*, pp. 42–3; Dr. D. C. Norris, *The Nervous Element in Accident Claims*, 1932, p. 35.

with malingering and other forms of fraud. Such cases are, in fact, quite uncommon, and an allegation that a patient is a malingerer often reflects more
unfavourably on the doctor than on the patient, and means no more than that the
examination of a difficult patient was carried out with insufficient care. . . .[1]

In exceptional cases a workman may simulate illness as a means to get
compensation, lump-sum or weekly payments. It is for the medical
examiner to get behind these tricks and to detect them; how this is done
has been well described by the late Sir John Collie in his work on the
medical aspects of Workmen's Compensation.[2]

What interests us here is not the possibility of fraud, but of a mental
attitude or psycho-physical condition connected with the anticipation
of compensation which affects, for good or evil, the processes of restoration and rehabilitation of the injured worker. The line between this
state of mind and 'malingering' may sometimes be narrow and may not
be with the cognizance of the injured man himself; but such a state of
neurosis is notoriously one of the common manifestations of the effect
upon health of an injury. This type of neurosis is not confined to cases
where lump-sum payments are to be expected, nor is its severity always
in proportion to the length of time that such settlement is delayed,
although such is the case.[3]

Compensation neurosis is not unknown in countries which have not
accepted the system of lump-sum settlements. In Germany it is called
Rentenneurose or *Sozialneurose* (rent-neurosis or benefit-neurosis or
social-neurosis).[4] In fact, an extensive literature has grown up round
this condition.[5] In the U.S.A. the term applied is 'desire neurosis',

---

[1] Presidential Address to the Hunterian Society, 1937, entitled *Some Medical Problems
in Accident Insurance*, Reprint, p. 19. Cf. also Dr. W. A. Brend, *Traumatic Mental Disorders in Courts of Law*, 1938, p. 47: 'Malingering, in my experience, has been rare,
whether I have been dealing with serving soldiers or ex-service men or workmen. Occasionally I have seen the deliberate exaggeration of a real symptom, but even that is not
common.'   [2] Cf. Collie, loc. cit., pp. 25 and 31 sqq.: 'Methods of exposing Fraud.'

[3] Cf. W. McAdam Eccles, *The Causes of Prolonged Disability after Industrial Accidents*.
Address before the Insurance Institute of London, Nov. 12th 1934: '. . . disability is not
lessened in its length of time, because there is a "lump sum" coming in the not far distance.'
The same in America: 'The elimination of traumatic neurosis enters into this picture . . . and
the longer you delay his settlement, the worse he becomes and quite frequently settlement is
the best cure.' Cf. Mr. A. Johannsen, Member of the Industrial Commission of Chicago
before 1935 meeting of the *Convention of the International Association of Industrial
Accidents Boards, &c.* U.S.A. Dept. of Labor, 1936, p. 163.

[4] Cf. Viktor von Weizsaecker, *Soziale Krankheit und soziale Gesundung*, Berlin, 1930, pp.
30 sqq.: 'Entstehungs- und Verschwindebedingungen der Sozialneurose.' The book is out of
print. It is, however, to be found in the library of the London School of Economics. Cf. also
Prof. Ludolf von Krehl, 'Neurosen' in *Ärztliche Mitteilungen für Baden*, 1931, no. 15, p. 251.

[5] Cf. Dr. Erwin Liek, *Die Schäden der sozialen Versicherung*, München, 1927. A book
sharply attacking social insurance so far as it leads to retarding of recovery by the mental
attitude of the worker.

viz. desire for compensation. It is skilfully distinguished from traumatic neurosis resulting from fright or other circumstances directly connected with the injury, and from neuroses due to mental conflicts and unexplained complexes.[1] 'There is no injury, however slight', writes Dr. Norris, 'which may not be followed, in a susceptible subject, by the gravest disability as a result of perverted mentality.'[2] The Stewart Committee[3] considered both mild neuroses and those arising in injured workmen who were already of a neurotic disposition. In such cases the question is whether a lump-sum settlement or a weekly payment is best calculated to prevent or overcome desire neurosis. It may well be that the very fact of a possible lump-sum settlement may be the primary and predisposing cause of neurotic disturbance. It is undoubtedly from this angle that the influences are most vigorously brought to bear upon injured workmen.

Compensation officials have been known to approve lump-sum payments because they thought of it as ordinary insurance and also because it was a quick way to dispose of claims and expedite administration. Insurance companies have frequently encouraged lump-sum payments because this method closed the business, reduced reserves, and was less costly. Employers at times have favoured lump-sum settlements. Physicians for some claimants have advocated lump-sum payments on therapeutic grounds. Lawyers have pressed for lump-sum payments for their clients that they might receive lucrative fees. Runners and pseudo-friends have done their part to help claimants get money in lump-sum payments in order that they might share in the awards. Real estate men and others in the commercial field have advocated lump-sum payments in order that they might sell estate or something else, or collect debts. Politicians have used their influence to secure lump-sum payments to please their constituents. In short, an injured worker who has a considerable amount of compensation to be paid him will have a lot of friends and advisers to persuade him that if he can get the money at once he will be much better off than if he receives it in bi-weekly payments.[4]

An injured man, exposed to such suggestions, may well become obsessed with the idea that his present state of health and his prospective ability to earn allow no other solution than a substantial capital payment. A weekly compensation will never be so tempting as a lump-sum payment. The ideal will always remain: the return to normal work and the restoration, thereby, of a normal occupational life. The weekly payment does not so 'dislocate' the victim's social outlook and is therefore not liable to create those intense desire complexes which the lump-sum settlement creates. This should be

[1] Cf. H. H. Kessler, *Accidental Injuries*, New York, 1932, p. 543 and *passim* as to New Jersey.

[2] Cf. Dr. Norris, *The Nervous Element in Accident Claims*, 1932, p. 48.

[3] Cf. loc. cit., p. 91.

[4] Mr. R. M. Little, Director of the Rehabilitation Division of the New York State Education Department. Cf. *1935 Convention*, pp. 151–2.

recognized even if due consideration is paid to the existence of *Renten-neurosis* as well as 'lump-sum' neurosis.

It is sometimes argued that a lump-sum payment, being definite and final, has a beneficial effect upon the workman's mind: this, of course, mainly relates to cases of partial disablement. We agree with Mr. Carl Norcross of the New York Rehabilitation Division that 'it is the settlement of the case, the ending of the litigation, which is the important factor', but not that 'the therapy, if any, comes from the closure and not from the particular manner in which the money is paid'.[1] If the injured workman knows definitely from the beginning of his mishap that he may expect a weekly payment, fixed by an impartial authority, viz. one not adverse to his own interests, but not likely to be greatly influenced by any particular attitude of his own, this will discourage neurotic development; whereas anticipation of a capital disbursement, dependent upon 'bargaining', may encourage it. British insurance offices believe that lump-sum settlements are cheaper than fixed weekly payments in that they offer greater possibilities for 'bargaining'. If so the lump-sum payments—to the extent that they include an inherent element of uncertainty—must be more disturbing and lump-sum neurosis must be more pronounced than rent-neurosis. This contrast would be even greater where the continuance of weekly settlements is ensured by administrative control.

The argument that lump-sum payment entails a quick settlement raises another objection. It all depends *how* and *when* the settlement or the commutation takes place. It all depends on how far a prolongation of proceedings and the whole pressure put upon the victim have undermined his state of mind and given rise to serious nervous trouble. We constantly hear about such effects in respect of lump-sum litigation. Why not in respect of weekly payments? The B.M.A. declares in its *Report on Fractures*:[2]

The 'lump-sum' form of compensation is responsible for much prolongation of disability. . . . .The worker is in an unaccustomed atmosphere, created by an insurance company, his trade union, his approved society, his employer, the medical officers employed by these bodies, his own medical practitioner, and perhaps a relieving officer. There is evidence that 'touts' from solicitors actually wait on 'accident cases' to promote profitable litigation. It is small wonder that, until the compensation claim is settled, the worker's attention is focused on his financial prospects rather than on his restoration to full activity.[3]

---

[1] Cf. Dodd, loc. cit., p. 730.

[2] Cf. B.M.A., *Report of Committee on Fractures*, 1935, p. 30.

[3] Cf. also Dr. Norris in his latest publication, 'Industrial Accidents', in the *British Encyclopaedia of Medical Practice*, 1938, p. 134, 'Neurosis in relation to Injury': 'The prognosis in these cases depends largely on the length of time which elapses before a settlement, and is adversely affected by repeated medical examinations and especially by litigation.'

The Charity Organization Society takes the same view:[1]

Hamlet enumerated 'the law's delays' amongst the reasons which make men desire to take their own lives. No one who has accompanied the victim of an accident through all the stages of procedure following it would call in question Shakespeare's insight. A brisk, courageous, competent man will retain his courage through the long-drawn miseries of operations, dressings, and convalescence. He leaves hospital, as he entered it, a reliable weekly wage-earner, a good husband, and a good citizen. But he has been gradually expending his reserves of moral capital. His powers of endurance have been sapped: he has been cut off from social intercourse almost as effectively as though he had been in gaol.

'A wise physician, skilled our wounds to heal', wrote Homer, 'is more than armies to the public weal'. If at the end of his convalescence a competent psychiatrist with a good equipment for remedial exercises could take him in hand, this useful citizen would be saved to his industry and country. In the few instances where such facilities are available the positive results in the great majority of cases are most gratifying.[2] But, alas, *at this point commences 'the long-drawn-out struggle' for the lump sum*. By the time it is over, the high-spirited, honourable citizen who lost his leg two or three or four years before is often a moral wreck, scarcely recognizable and often shunned by his old friends. Much has been attempted, and something has been done to expedite these legal proceedings, but much remains to be done. The danger of these psychological disasters of which, declares the Charity Organization Society, we have been too frequently witnesses, is real: we respectfully commend it to the consideration of experts.

It is often claimed, and it is often true, that the getting of a lump sum in final settlement has an invigorating if not a 'healing' effect upon the injured man's mind and thereby upon his corporal welfare. But there is also the other side, recently stressed by the late Sir John Collie, who had a wide practical knowledge of the matter. He wrote in 1935:[3]

Many such men anticipate a 'lump-sum' settlement, and, until that is received incapacity may extend over months and even years, during which time the idleness involved makes them more and more unfit for laborious work. The enforced idleness makes them both physically and mentally unfit for the work to which

[1] Cf. *Charity Organization Quarterly*, July 1934, p. 105.
[2] We shall have to deal with this at a later stage when Rehabilitation is under discussion and not, as here, merely the influence of lump sums on recovery; but the C.O.S. is right in drawing attention to the difficulties in the matter. Cf. also Dr. Norris, *Industrial Accidents*, p. 134: 'Psychological treatment is, generally speaking, expensive and difficult to obtain, so that it is seldom available for the injured workman.'   [3] Cf. Collie, loc. cit., p. 86.

they have been accustomed, and has the effect of producing a vicious circle entailing much misery both on the men themselves and on those who are dependent on them.

This aspect of the matter must be balanced against the claim that lump-sum settlements tend to accelerate recovery. They may do so some times, but may retard it at others.[1]

Vocal British medical opinion has sometimes displayed a preference for lump-sum settlements; thus Dr. Archibald M'Kendrick in a valuable address before the Insurance Society of Edinburgh in 1937 claimed that while it took years to overcome certain injuries in Germany, where only weekly payments exist as a rule, 'in Switzerland, where lump-sum compensation is paid just after the accident', the injured have 'not only, after some weeks, been able to earn full wages, but after twelve months have become habituated to their loss'.[2] But Switzerland does not in fact pay compensation by lump sums only. On the contrary: a daily allowance is first paid, accompanied by curative treatment, which does not exist in Britain. If no appreciable improvement supervenes, this is replaced by either a fixed monthly pension or a monthly pension of gradually diminishing amount. A lump sum is awarded only where it is considered that payment in this form will bring about entire recovery; the sum is not large: it is equal to the present value of a fixed or decreasing pension for not more than three years. Moreover, incapacity is evaluated in Switzerland by the Accidents Service of the National Accident Insurance Fund and the decisions are given in its name.[3] This is quite a different thing from the British lump-sum settlement, and comparisons not having regard to these material differences are irrelevant, though under certain conditions where an increase in earning capacity by adaptation and habituation might be expected, small payments in regard to minor injuries may play a useful part.

We are well aware that medical experts regard a final settlement as one of the best ways of overcoming industrial neuroses, but we cannot agree with Dr. R. D. Gillespie, who suggests that 'the settlement should be made as soon as possible, whether for a lump sum or an annual payment'.[4] The doctor's ambition to see the workmen removed

---

[1] Our view in this matter is shared by Dr. D. Stewart: 'In some cases lump-sum payments have the effect of producing rapid cure, especially with minor injuries ... in other cases the holding-up of lump-sum settlements produces a *mental imbalance.*' He also draws attention to the frequent mismanagement of lump sums in his experience. Cf. Donald Stewart, loc. cit., p. 9.

[2] Cf. Archibald M'Kendrick, *Medical Reports*, Reprint of a lecture given before the Insurance Society of Edinburgh, Feb. 9th 1937.

[3] Cf. *Evaluation Report*, 1937, pp. 163, 235.

[4] Cf. 'Industrial Dermatitis and the Workmen's Compensation Act', *British Journal of Dermatology*, 1937, pp. 422 sqq.

as early as possible from any risk of neuroses is comprehensible, but it should not blind his eyes to the latent dangers of such settlements. Dr. Gillespie himself mentioned a case: 'I have known a workman do no work for two years after receiving a lump sum . . . £400 was a fortune to him and lasted two or more years.' Would he consider this an ideal solution? We have, moreover, been assured, both orally and in writing, that doctors in general are acutely aware of their inability to follow up more than a very few of the cases that come before them or under their care. In the words of a very experienced medical referee: 'I deal with cases in my consulting-room: I keep full records. I spare no pains to reach a just conclusion, but I seldom hear of a case again; the man may get better, he may die in hospital, or commit suicide, but I shall probably never know.'

The Stewart Committee was satisfied that the system of 'lump-sum settlement is generally popular with both employers and employees', and urged its retention. The various statements which we have quoted in criticism of lump-sum payments in connexion with the recovery of the injured person, make no mention of weekly payments or settlements for weekly payments. Yet, the Stewart Committee found no proof that lump-sum settlements retarded recovery 'in any considerable body of cases'.[1] In the text of its findings the Committee[2] asserted that 'cases . . . vary so much individually that it is, in our view, quite impossible to express an opinion in any general terms as to the effect of existing provisions and practice in promoting or retarding recovery'. This statement directly contradicts the highly authoritative writers just quoted, who are in no doubt that the expectation of a lump-sum settlement frequently and indisputably retards recovery.

Dissenting from the *Stewart Report* we are led inescapably to the following conclusions:

1. The term 'popularity' is ill-advised. On the part of employers—apart from the secondary motive of getting rid of a continuous obligation—the preference for lump sums is prompted by the hope of arriving at a cheap settlement, disadvantageous to the workman and inconsistent with the spirit of Workmen's Compensation legislation. On the part of the workman lump sums are preferred in most cases as a means of escape from acute financial embarrassment, the immediate effect of the injury.

2. Where the motive to accept a lump-sum settlement is prompted by the idea of acquiring an independent means of earning money, such hope is very seldom realized. The workman who has settled for a lump sum is in many cases and for various reasons likely to lose his money, already diminished by deductions for various expenses. Before long he

[1] Cf. *Stewart Report*, p. 112.   [2] Cf. ibid., p. 102.

is as badly off as before: he will then become a public burden. The success of a few cannot be accepted as a reason for encouraging or permitting others to incur this risk.

3. While it should be the aim of Workmen's Compensation to promote recovery of the injured and his reinstatement into work, lump-sum settlements have an opposite tendency. The employer's attention is diverted from securing other work for the injured man so long as his concern is that of getting rid of the obligation by a final settlement. The injured man himself is bent upon a lump-sum settlement, and not upon his rehabilitation. The longer the time taken to achieve a settlement, the greater the susceptibility to industrial neurosis. This neurosis, however, is much more typical of lump-sum settlement than of weekly payment. It is, in fact, an addition to the nation's ill health due to the system of Workmen's Compensation.

For all these reasons lump-sum settlement, whether by agreement or by commutation, should be abolished. In doing so Britain would only follow the example of leading industrial countries. The commutation of small pensions for the corresponding capital amount may be accepted, provided that the injured person is capable of making judicious use of the sum he receives and retains the right to claim compensation for any aggravation of his loss.[1] Under the German accident insurance legislation a special permit may be granted by the Ministry of Labour to provide a lump-sum payment for the injured man for the purpose of acquiring landed property; elaborate safeguards, however, exist to secure the proper and profitable management of such property, and the age for such permits is limited to $21-55$.[2] Where the injured person has acquired a neurosis which for the time being precludes return to work, the New Jersey system might advantageously be copied. Here, if the injured worker fails to get over his neurosis within the allotted time, he is granted compensation by a lump sum equal to one year's earnings, being one-tenth of the amount he would receive for total permanent disability. The measure might be commended as an exception to the *general* principle which, however, should prevail in all serious cases[3] and should preclude the payment of lump sums as now practised. The T.U.C. Memorandum to the Hetherington Commission took a firm stand against lump sums so that it will be difficult in future to argue that 'workers' favour them:

[1] Cf. also *Evaluation Report*, 1937, p. 136: 'Since commutation is an exception to the general rule, by which compensation should, in principle, take the form of a pension, the exception should be limited to comparatively slight losses.'

[2] An ordinance of Feb. 10th 1938 requires Accident Insurance Administrations to see that in such cases 'there is a useful application of the money'. Cf. *Reichsversicherungsordnung*, vol. iii, para. 618*a*, and *Commentary*, pp. 180-3.

[3] Cf. also Dr. Norris, *Nervous Element*, &c., p. 47.

We recommend that, except in the case of the lump sums payable for disfigurement, no lump sum should be payable except by way of commutation of weekly payments awarded by the Board.[1]

The expediency of the last proviso is very doubtful. Lump sums by way of commutation seem to us as dangerous as any other form. Whether and how the 'Board' would apply the necessary brake—in particular in cases where, as the Memorandum proposes, the worker himself makes the application—is doubtful.[2]

[1] p. 417.
[2] See Q. 3921–30. The discretion proposed to be vested in the Board appears to us unduly heavy.

CHAPTER VIII

LUMP-SUM SETTLEMENTS

B. THE ADMINISTRATIVE SIDE

Few who consider dispassionately the facts of social history will be disposed to deny that the exploitation of the weak by the powerful organized for the purpose of economic gain, buttressed by imposing systems of law, and resounding rhetoric, has been a permanent feature in the life of most communities that the world has seen.

PROF. R. H. TAWNEY, *Religion and the Rise of Capitalism*.

LEGISLATIVE recognition in Britain of the fundamental defects and latent evils of lump-sum payments finds full expression in the elaborate 'safeguards' provided against the abuses touched on in our previous chapters.

How far are these safeguards adequate? This question has been dealt with in the U.S.A. in an exhaustive inquiry covering the whole field of Workmen's Compensation, running to 850 pages, made by W. F. Dodd for the Legal Research Committee of the Commonwealth Fund, a body composed of leading members of the American legal profession and distinguished representatives of the law faculties of prominent Universities. No even remotely comparable investigation has hitherto been made in Britain.

Lump sums are payable:

1. From the onset of disability, partial or total. This possibility was exploited by employers (see vol. i, *passim*) so long as it was believed that the prescribed legal safeguards were not applicable to such agreements, a belief which the highest courts have dispelled[1]. An agreement whereby the workman gives up his right to a weekly payment under the Act is void; the only way by which an employer, apart from a certified scheme, can avoid future liability under the Act is by recording the agreement.

2. In redemption or commutation of weekly payments[2] the employer has a right under § 13 of the Act, when weekly payments have

---

[1] Cf. Willis, loc. cit., pp. 433–4.

[2] The distinction between these categories of lump-sum payment is important. It is well brought out in the statistics dealing with schemes adopted by the workmen of the Crown in Admiralty, War Office and Air Ministry Establishments. A distinction is here made between Hurt Pay, Payment of Compensation after cessation of Hurt Pay in cases of continued incapacity or, where no Hurt Pay issued, Payment of Compensation in fatal cases, and Payment of Lump Sums in redemption of weekly payments. The first and second amounts were £13,958 and £50,587 in 1935, the next £5,114 and lump sums under these special schemes only £525. Cf. *Report of Chief Registrar of Friendly Societies*, 1937, Part I,

continued not less than six months, to redeem them for a lump sum, provided that

(a) if an adult workman's incapacity is permanent, the lump sum must suffice to purchase a Post Office Annuity for the work- man equal to three-quarters of the annual value of the weekly payments, and

(b) where incapacity is not permanent the sum necessary to redeem the weekly payment is determined by arbitration in the event of disagreement,[1] for, under § 13 (a)

nothing shall be construed as preventing agreements being made for the redemption of a weekly payment by a lump sum.

But for this proviso optional agreements between injured workers and employers for lump-sum settlements would be illegal.[2]

3. Lump sums play a part in composition agreements, viz. where the defendant disputes his liability to pay compensation, but under § 24 of the Act makes a 'composition' agreement whereby acceptance of a lump sum debars any further claim.

The Stewart Committee regarded itself as 'directly concerned' only with 'cases involving the redemption of weekly payments *by agreement*[3] for lump sums'.

This limitation was the consequence of its terms of reference, which were restricted to lump-sum settlements *by agreement*. The Committee was thus precluded from considering the broader issues. Yet lump-sum settlements have played (see pp. 116–17, vol. i) an important part in settlements where no weekly payment was made at all. The Holman Gregory Committee, in Part VIII of their *Report*, emphasized the importance of both categories of lump-sum payments, and witnesses urged that every settlement should be registered. The Stewart Com- mittee side-tracked the proposal with the following comment:

199. It seems to us possible that the cases which these witnesses had in mind were not in fact agreements for the settlement of claims by lump-sum payments within the meaning of the Acts. It has emerged from the evidence of several witnesses that even in cases of minor incapacity there is apt to be created some resistance to the idea of return to work; and in such cases payment of a small sum

p. 8. When the present form in which Workmen's Compensation Statistics are presented to Parliament is reconsidered, this difference should be borne in mind.

[1] Cf. Willis, loc. cit., p. 348.

[2] We omit here contracting-out schemes which, as shown in vol. i, have played an im- portant role in history, but ceased to do so when the Act required such settlements to be in no case less favourable to the workpeople than the provisions of the Act itself. In 1936 there were only eleven schemes in operation and not more than 44,788 were involved. Cf. *Report of Chief Registrar of Friendly Societies*, loc. cit., p. 7.

[3] Cf. *Stewart Report*, p. 85.

by way of gratuity often has the effect of breaking down the resistance. We see no reason why this should not continue, it being understood of course, that in the absence of registration, an employer making such payment is not relieved of future liability under the Acts.

Not knowing the names of the witnesses or the precise tenor of their evidence it is difficult to offer constructive comment, but we see no point in distinguishing between lump sums and payments 'by way of gratuity', a term which implies absence of any legal obligation. Whatever the reason for 'resistance', the payment is made because the injured man claims compensation on the ground that he is still incapacitated. It seems to us unwise and incorrect to describe as a 'gratuity' a sum paid in order to discharge a liability and incidentally, perhaps, to avoid registration. The Committee should have scrutinized the economic and social details surrounding such cases and not have restricted itself to the legal aspect of the matter.

In this connexion the evidence by Mr. Charles Squire, a County Court registrar, before the Hetherington Commission was extremely illuminating and an ample proof of the mistaken view of the Stewart Committee in the matter. Mr. Squire, while stating that the view of his colleagues was in general that 'the present method of coming before the Registrar was on the whole a satisfactory one', told the Commission, on the other hand, that he had 'a large list' of cases where the settlements had been increased after coming before the registrar, in some cases from £70 to £200. Later in his evidence he stated that in his opinion 'there are a good many small agreements for say £20, £25, or £30 which are never registered'.[1] This being so, who will know whether these so-called 'small sums' do not represent in many cases instances where, if brought before the registrar, the sum would have been increased to £100 or more? Mr. Squire himself mentioned a case where an insurance man said to the injured worker, 'Here is £20, we are going to treat you generously' while 'he ought to have had £200 which was eventually paid'. No better contradiction could be supplied to the above-quoted opinion of the *Stewart Report*![2]

The same observation applies to the treatment of composition agreements (see pp. 248–50, vol. i.) by the Stewart Committee, which 'understood that "Composition Agreements" under § 24 of the Act represent only a small proportion of all the lump-sum settlements recorded in the Courts'. The Committee noted that such agreements,

---

[1] Cf. *Hetherington Commission*, A. 5786 and 5872–5.

[2] Cf. also *Hetherington Commission, Memorandum presented by the Mineworkers' Federation of Great Britain*, §§ 94 sqq. It is on the very ground of the conditions described above that the Memorandum declares: '. . . in the majority of cases lump-sum settlements are of no advantage to the workman.'

made when an employer disputes his liability but nevertheless declares his willingness to settle for a lump sum, were, according to 'most' witnesses, 'most convenient and satisfactory'. We do not know what opinion was expressed by other witnesses, but the Committee upheld composition agreements, which are not binding unless recorded by the court upon evidence that the amount is adequate, having regard to the question as to whether or not liability under the Act is doubtful.[1] The returns of 1937 show 588 registered agreements where the employer, while disputing liability, agreed to compromise by the payment of a lump sum.[2] The registrar or the judge is here confronted by the same problems as arise in regard to any other agreement presented for registration.

The question of lump-sum payment by composition agreement does not, however, end here: such agreements may be in avoidance of a more adequate settlement; liability may be disputed to start with in order to compel a lump-sum settlement. If the matter is not brought before the registrar or court, the agreement differs in no way from any other lump-sum settlement where liability is undisputed. Here lies the danger. The Holman Gregory Committee took a great deal of evidence on composition agreements[3] which the Stewart Committee might with advantage have studied, showing that though lump-sum composition settlements are a small proportion of those recorded in the courts, their importance is not thereby diminished. What matters is that they are *not* recorded.

Here is a dilemma: if a composition settlement is entered into to avoid the cost of expert evidence, &c., it must be approved by some arbitrator, registrar, or judge, who is entitled, if not obliged, to go into details in order to satisfy himself as to its propriety. To do this is to stultify the whole purpose of the agreement. But if it is not done, the danger of unfair settlements by composition agreements remains.[4]

---

[1] Cf. § 25(4) of the Act, second paragraph.

[2] Cf. *Workmen's Compensation Statistics for 1937*, 1939, p. 14.

[3] Cf. Index, vol. i, p. 472, under Lump Sums, 'in cases where no weekly payment has been made'.

[4] Cf. *Holman Gregory Committee, Evidence*, Q. and A. 8496: Q. (Mr. Guthrie): '. . . my point is where the workman has a very doubtful case; there is a remote chance that he may succeed in getting £100; he may get nothing; the employer feel he has a fairly strong case and will probably get off without any liability, or he takes the risk of paying £100. If both parties, knowing the shaky position compromise in order to avoid going into Court, do I understand you would compel them to go to Court with the risk that the case might be brought up for review and thorough investigation?' A. (Mr. Thomas Neal, J.P., on behalf of the National Conference of Industrial Assurance Approved Societies): 'I do not see any other way of preventing improper lump-sum settlements.' The position was further discussed with His Honour Judge Ruegg. Mr. Neal, interrogating the judge, contended: 'You go to the Judge who may ultimately have this case to try, and *you have to damn your own*

His Honour Judge Ruegg, in the course of a lively cross-examination by members of the Holman Gregory Committee, explained that he generally relied in such cases on the advice given by a solicitor to the claimant:

I know all the gentlemen who practise before me, and I trust them, and that almost settles the question—'If you have had his advice, and he thinks it best for you, I shall pass the settlement'.[1]

It was pointed out to him that the solicitor might exaggerate the risks run by his client. Insurance companies 'can always command . . . the best legal . . . assistance to maintain their case in any dispute'.[2] The workman's legal advisers may be less competent: they may also be influenced by the knowledge that their client cannot afford to pay for independent medical or other testimony, for adjournments, &c. The insurance office instructs solicitors and counsel who specialize in this particular corner of the legal labyrinth: the workman's solicitor and barrister, unless instructed by a trade union, must often be men of less experience. The judge may overestimate their competence and the workman might lose a good case.[3] (An arbitrator cannot award a lump sum except in redemption of weekly payments.)[4] As His Honour Judge Ruegg observed to the Holman Gregory Committee, 'the Judge will not even say, in a case where he thinks it proper: "I think you ought to bring the case forward", but simply: "I cannot approve this settlement." '[5]

From whatever side this difficult problem is examined, the conclusion emerges that composition agreements deserve closer examination than has yet been accorded. The *Stewart Report* quoted witnesses as emphasizing that in this type of case a man got something who, had the case been contested, might have received nothing. But what of cases where a man is persuaded to settle for much less than might have been awarded? Is not a settlement which gives the worker more than

---

case before the very Judge who may have to try it.' Cf. Q. 10431. This ridiculous position might indeed supervene if a composition agreement is brought before a judge who may decide that the worker is entitled to compensation while the latter is expected to show that his claim is rather ill founded!

[1] Cf. *Holman Gregory Report*, A. 10433.

[2] Cf. PEP, *British Health Services 1937*, pp. 76–7.

[3] The practice mentioned by Judge Ruegg appears to be general; His Honour Judge Sir Edward Bray also mentioned it before the Holman Gregory Committee. Cf. A. 15225: '. . . I am quite certain that no Judge would ever interfere in a case of that kind. If he saw that the workman was well advised in the matter, and had considered it, and desired to take £20, no Judge would interfere.' He further said that the judge, though having power to interfere, would 'never interfere after seeing the parties'. A. 15222.

[4] Cf. Willis, loc. cit., p. 252.

[5] Cf. A. 10434,

his due as objectionable in the eyes of the law as the reverse? We agree with His Honour Judge Sir Edward Bray's dictum in 1919:[1]

I would be glad to see any provision to except cases of that kind, but I do not see the possibility of doing it.

Under the present system of Workmen's Compensation in Britain there seems to be indeed no way out of this difficulty except to forbid lump-sum payments by composition agreements altogether. Composition agreements may be useful in cases of civil liability, where problems of lesser importance are at stake and where neither party is under pressure to accept the agreement, in which case any attempt to arrive at a 'fair' composition agreement entails arbitration on lines which may differ little from litigation, and may seldom benefit the injured person. Such legislation is but another attempt to retain the practice of 'bargaining'.

Do the safeguards which the Stewart Committee regard as sufficient to justify lump-sum settlements really protect the worker? To get a clear view of the present administrative requirements for lump-sum settlements under §§ 23, 24, and 25 of the Act, it is necessary to consult the County Court Rules which prescribe the requisite procedure. Rule 51 requires the registrar to make the necessary inquiries. The registrar, and the judge, if the matter is referred to him, has power under Rules 43–51:

1. To require either party to the agreement to furnish him, orally or in writing, with all necessary information.

2. To require any parties to the agreement to attend before him.

3. To require a Report as to the workman's condition to be obtained from a medical referee, when the information on the subject is insufficient or conflicting.

4. To refuse registration of the Memorandum if either party fails to comply with any of the foregoing requirements, and to refer the matter to the Judge, for such order as he may think proper in the circumstances.

5. To refuse registration if the medical referee's Report shows that the prospects of the workman's recovery from incapacity cannot then be approximately determined.

6. To require the solicitor of the workman or his dependants to submit his bill of costs to him if the costs disclosed in the agreement appear excessive and to tax the same.

7. To award costs in respect of the application for registration of any such agreement where there is a hearing or a Report from a medical referee is obtained.[2]

Of these seven powers the first five relate primarily to our present

[1] Cf. *Holman Gregory Report*, A. 15225.   [2] Cf. also Willis, loc. cit., p. 438.

purpose. The law has done its best to create a framework within which lump sums could be justly settled. On paper the system appears adequate; yet we know that defects exist, and that a Royal Commission has been set up to consider the matter afresh. A great gulf intervenes between the procedure envisaged by the legislator and the realities of daily life.

The Stewart Committee seem, like the Holman Gregory Committee and its *Report*, to have been bent on detecting certain deficiencies and to propose remedies within the existing legal framework without exposing the basic difficulties. The existing 'medical machinery' was judged as 'generally' well designed, the substitution of medical boards for the medical referee was rejected as 'not necessary' and lump-sum payments were defended as 'popular'. Their *Report* reveals, nevertheless, certain aspects of lump-sum settlements which we must here record.

It notes[1] that the main advantages of registration of agreements lie less in the fact that the Memorandum is enforceable than in the inquiries which could, or should, be made by the registrar before registration.

We have had a lot of evidence as to what is actually done at present in England and as to what, in the opinion of the witnesses, should be done in this matter. Broadly the result is that while there are Registrars in England who make the most careful inquiries, there are others who fall short of what is necessary; and the result is a lack of uniformity in practice.

Coming from such a source this is a grave criticism which must be carefully borne in mind when the statistics of rejected Memoranda are considered.

The T.U.C. Memorandum to the Hetherington Commission states bluntly[2] that 'Although many (!) Registrars have discharged their functions well, we consider that on the whole their supervision has proved inadequate'.

Dr. John Foster recently stated before the Section of Ophthalmology of the Royal Society of Medicine that 'many registrars' will no longer agree to a settlement for loss of one eye until they have the assurance of a consultant that there is no risk of sympathetic ophthalmia (see also Chapter III, p. 50).[3] This is a laudable practice. But such matters should not be left to the discretion of registrars. In 1937 there were 1044 cases where the registrar refused to record the Memorandum at first presented, but subsequently recorded it without reference to the judge after the original amount had been increased. In 313 cases he referred the matter to the judge and in 139 of these cases the

[1] Cf. *Stewart Report*, p. 92. [2] Cf. p. 417, § 47.
[3] *Roy. Soc. Med. Proc.*, vol. xxxi, 1938, p. 862.

Memorandum was recorded after the sum originally agreed had been increased.[1]

These figures illustrate the latent danger of inequitable agreements which never come before the registrar. The number of cases in which increased benefit was insisted on is disquieting. Mr. Cassels, K.C., a Scottish Member, speaking in a debate on Workmen's Compensation in the Commons, declared: 'My experience of these settlements has taught me that, unless there are objections from the workman's trade union, the settlement goes through.' He mentioned a case of a man who lost the fourth finger of his right hand above the knuckle. Being in financial straits he 'settled' for £17. 10s. although he had a neuroma on the site of his original amputation.[2] In Scotland the sheriff-clerk seldom feels called upon either to see the injured man or to make more extensive inquiries than the law requires. The Stewart Committee were told that it was unusual to submit a medical report, and that even when a report was furnished the wording might fail to disclose the gravity of the case. In some areas but not in others the sheriff-clerk makes it a practice to see the injured man and to call for a recent medical report. In such circumstances, where the workman has no solicitor and no union behind him, his position is unenviable and there are 'large numbers of workmen in this position'. A registrar can do little without seeing and questioning the workman in each case and without having before him a full memorandum of the facts together with a recent medical report. The Committee therefore recommended:

1. that the registrar should invariably see the workman and record no agreement without full inquiry and a recent medical report; and

2. that in any cases of doubt the registrar should insist on examination and report by the medical referee.

Is a solution possible on these lines? We doubt it. We prefer the testimony of those witnesses who thought the inquiries necessary to safeguard the workman against improvident lump-sum settlements would involve work which few registrars could conveniently undertake and for which not all were fitted. We are attracted by the idea of an Advisory Committee for each court, empowered to go into the

[1] Cf. *Workmen's Compensation Statistics for 1937*, 1939, p. 14. The relative figures for 1936 were 257 and 112.

[2] Cf. *Debates H.C.*, Nov. 19th 1937, Col. 798. The fact was restated in strong terms before the Hetherington Commission in the Memorandum of the Executive of the Scottish Association of Friendly and Approved Societies (p. 305): the sheriff-clerk 'rarely challenges the adequacy of a lump-sum settlement unless facts are disclosed in the Memorandum lodged which makes the inadequacy very patent to him'. Cf. also Mr. Baird's evidence, ibid., Q. 2689–94.

whole of the facts of a case in which lump-sum settlement is proposed, and to advise the registrar as to the general suitability of the case for lump-sum settlement and as to what the amount of any lump sum should be. In the event of the adoption of a system, at least in the principal industries and trades, of administering Workmen's Compensation through joint councils or associations (analogous to *Berufsgenossenschaften*) on which both employers and workmen are represented, their decisions might be final, subject only to ratification or registration by the registrar, and to an appeal to the County Court judge.

The Stewart Committee rejected this recommendation, though it was sponsored by the B.M.A. and the T.U.C., and proposed to add to the already heavy responsibilities of registrars, i.e. that any lump sum over £100 should be paid through the court for the purpose of affording the registrar an opportunity to advise the workman as to use. We should be glad to see lump-sum payment forbidden, where no beneficial purpose can be demonstrated, but doubt the wisdom of making the registrar a commercial adviser to the injured man. Not all workmen will listen to his advice, and those who do will, in the event of failure, feel that they have a just grievance against the courts. Such a procedure places too much responsibility on the registrar. There are, moreover, in practice, limits to his utility in this field of social service:

> . . . the Registrar is given no guidance as to the manner in which he is to satisfy himself that the amount fixed by the agreement is in fact adequate. Each Registrar is free to adopt his own standard in the matter, subject only to his right to refer to the Judge in case of doubt. We have had little evidence as to the methods by which agreements are in fact judged: but witnesses have informed us that in their experience there is very considerable variation and inequality in assessment.

Many witnesses deemed variations inevitable so long as each registrar was left to exercise his own discretion as to what constitutes an adequate sum in any individual case.[1] The registrar *must* record the Memorandum unless it appears to him that the agreement ought not to be registered by reason of inadequacy of the agreed sum or because agreement has been reached by fraud, undue influence, or other improper means. The registrar's duty is therefore mainly negative—to say yes or no—not to make positive suggestions, still less decisions. In flagrant cases of unfair settlements the registrar probably has little difficulty in coming to a conclusion. But an agreement refused by one court may be lodged at another, without disclosure of that fact. A case was brought by the Home Office to the notice of the Stewart Committee where the workman was urged with this object to acquire temporary residence in the jurisdiction of a different County Court

---

[1] Cf. *Stewart Report*, p. 95.

district;[1] it is of importance primarily in showing that the variation in the practice of different courts is well known and can be turned to advantage. This has some bearing on the suggestion made by a solicitor with large experience of Workmen's Compensation cases that cases should be concentrated in a few courts in the interests of uniformity.[2]

In face of these criticisms the proposals of the Stewart Committee appear jejune and inadequate. The recommendation (see above, p. 158) made seems unlikely to change the situation materially. If the registrar is required, at long last, to see the injured workman, will he be able *ipso facto* to decide as to the adequacy of the lump sum and the expediency, in the man's best interest, of a settlement which he may himself, perhaps short-sightedly, desire? The main concern of the registrar or the court must always be the statement of the medical referee and the solicitor, who may be no match for the other side and may not be inclined[3] to weigh fully the relative advantages of weekly payments and a lump sum.

Then there is the report of the medical referee. The present medical procedure was unfavourably criticized before the Stewart Committee. 'There is a strong feeling against an individual Medical Referee having the power to give a conclusive decision'[4] and 'a somewhat widespread distrust in certain areas which arises from the fact that some Referees frequently appear in Courts as expert witnesses for a particular side in districts adjoining their own'. These quotations suffice, at this point in our narrative, to show how difficult it is for the registrar or, at a later stage, the judge, to rely entirely on the medical referee. The Stewart Committee proposed certain further safeguards, the enlargement of panels of referees by the inclusion of more specialists, and the establishment of Medical Appeal Tribunals acting under 'rules designed to secure the reputation of the Referee for impartiality'. These words are themselves a condemnation of the present system. In the words of Mr. Marshall Dawson of the U.S.A. Bureau of Labor Statistics:

Controversial medical testimony is an outstanding example of 'hang-overs' from court proceedings grafted upon compensation practice by legislatures and administrators acquainted with court methods but less familiar with the more scientific

[1] Cf. *Stewart Report*, p. 104. Such a case was heard at Maidstone County Court by Judge Clements who described the conduct of the insurance company concerned as reprehensible: he hoped it was 'a solitary instance', but 'had his doubts about it'. Cf. *Debates H.C.*, July 26th 1937, col. 2678.

[2] Cf. also *Stewart Report*, p. 95: 'Many witnesses gave evidence concerning the wide variation in assessments which occurs under present conditions—variation which the witnesses deemed inevitable so long as each Registrar was left to exercise his own discretion as to the sum which would be adequate in individual cases.'

[3] Cf. vol. i, pp. 209–10, and *Stewart Report*, pp. 97 and 105 for overcharging by solicitors.   [4] Cf. p. 110.

method of inquiry, and the care needed by injured persons. A drastic reform a this point awaits the public recognition . . . that workmen's compensation administration is a new professional speciality and not a revamping of the accustomed phases of law practice.[1]

'The proper use of authority', said Lord Wright recently, 'is a difficult art';[2] it may sometimes be too difficult, but no effort at improvement is too great in a matter which so vitally affects the life and social health of the worker,[3] even if it should entail the complete reorganization of administrative procedure, under special bodies of arbitration.

We conclude that, apart from all objections to lump-sum settlements, existing safeguards are inadequate and would be little bettered by the proposals made by the Stewart Committee. The administration lacks uniformity, and in some cases goodwill. The injured workman's position is uncertain and liable to be influenced by accidental factors. The value of composition agreements is dubious. The insurance offices have an immense advantage at every point over the injured workmen in all court proceedings. The worker's legal and medical advice, fortuitously secured, must almost always be inferior to the insurance company's standing counsel, regular solicitor, and salaried medical adviser. However carefully the law may be administered, it may fail to do justice to the injured man and his family and the future prospects and security of his life. The present legal and administrative safeguards do not offer the necessary protection to a worker anxious, or driven by economic need, to bargain for a lump-sum settlement. Even were such safeguards theoretically sufficient, the actual administrative practice does not afford that modicum of protection to the worker which the law was designed to assure him.

We conclude by a reference to the policy adopted by the Ministry of Pensions whose arrangements for disbursing sums due to dependants,

[1] Cf. 'Claims Administration in Workmen's Compensation', *Monthly Labor Review*, June 1938, Serial No. 734, p. 17.

[2] Cf. The Rt. Hon. Lord Wright, *Law Quarterly Review*, April 1938, p. 190.

[3] An interesting discussion of this point is found in the evidence before the Holman Gregory Committee of Mr. George Henry Pooley F.R.C.S., L.R.C.P., who was, apart from his academic position, a medical referee and assessor in three County Court Areas. Cf. Q. 20045 sqq. He emphasized that in his opinion 'the Judge's opinion on matters of medicine is about as good as a medical man's knowledge of law, which, after all, is very small'. He further emphasized that 'the medical man, even though he is a general practitioner, understands (if called to decide about the evidence of two other general practitioners) what these two medical men mean in their evidence better than the actual legal intellect, to put it quite candidly. He can see through the medical evidence better than the Judge, although his intelligence might not be as great.' Cf. regarding this point also ibid., the views of Judge Ruegg, Q. 10223–8, 10481–7; and of Sir Edward Bray 15019–27, and other parts of his evidence.

M

and to disabled persons, are based on principles which contrast sharply with those embodied in the Workmen's Compensation Act.[1] An Assistant Secretary of the Ministry told the Hetherington Commission that the primary object of the Ministry was 'to make a man as fit again as possible. Medical treatment comes before pension.'[2] Lump-sum payments were only given on this condition. The Ministry was required to make lump-sum grants whenever disablement was less than 20 per cent.; 'or where it is considered more in the interests of the soldier, a gratuity or final weekly allowance may be granted in place of any pension'.[3] Commutation of pensions is permissible:

1. To assist in purchasing a house.
2. For the purpose of starting (or extending) a business.
3. For emigration.

Of these alternatives the second bears the closest resemblance to our subject. Applications are closely investigated and disallowed unless the applicant can satisfy the Ministry that he has a definite project in view, that it would be to his 'distinct and permanent advantage' to surrender part of his weekly pension in exchange for a lump sum, and that refusal would entail great hardship. The applicant has to state the nature of the business, his experience, if any, whether he is starting a new business or taking over an old one and, if so, in what circumstances. Such a system corresponds closely to our conception of the precautions necessary in the case of injured workmen who may be entitled to receive any sum in excess of £100. How these restrictions work in practice is demonstrated by the fact that of 44,992 applications made between 1921 and 1938 only 2,530, or 5·6 per cent., were granted. In 1938 there were 1,351 applications to the Ministry[4] of which all but 56 were refused! We have no reason to think that the same system applied to Workmen's Compensation cases would lead to a different result. A Test Inquiry was made in 1935 in regard to fifty-eight grants made in 1928 and 1929 to assist applicants in carrying on businesses, including such occupations as general dealers, boot repairers, grocers, nurserymen, insurance agents (men who bought 'Insurance Books'),[5] &c. It transpired that twenty-five pensioners

---

[1] Cf. also Brend, loc. cit., p. 34.

[2] Mr. C. H. Glover, cf. A. 3438. Cf. also *Memorandum*: 'The Ministry's first care is to restore the disabled man's physical capacity as much as possible by means of treatment.' Ibid., p. 380.

[3] Royal Warrant on Pensions, Article 1 (2). The total of such grant may not exceed £200.

[4] In addition there were many hundreds of inquiries at local offices of the Ministry which, owing to the stringent regulations, were not followed by a formal application.

[5] See for this Wilson and Levy, *Industrial Assurance*, 1937, pp. 66–7, 229, 242–3.

were probably still in business; twenty-three had probably suffered total or partial loss; ten could not be traced. In spite of all safeguards, there were probably fewer successes than failures. The evidence showed that 'the lump sum was not, generally speaking, well used; the pension was of greater value to the man'.[1] The witness in making this statement did not disagree when pressed to say whether lump sums were not 'popular', but added that they were not regarded 'with favour' by the officials of the British Legion. Lump sums had not prevented neurasthenia: 'they always came back after a lump sum and wanted more.'[2] This evidence amply confirms the conclusions, previously presented to the Commissioners, of the present writers.[3]

[1] Mr. Glover, Ministry of Pensions. Cf. A. 3520.
[2] Cf. A. 3524-5.
[3] Cf. *Paper 9. Memorandum* by Sir A. Wilson and Prof. Hermann Levy, §§ 11–16.

NOTE

WHEN our chapters on lump-sum settlements were in print, a number of Memoranda were submitted to the Royal Commission on Workmen's Compensation which confirmed the view which we have tried to present in this and in our former volume. The following passages may be quoted: Central Council for the Care of Cripples, Royal Commission, p. 1243: 'Lump sums are not a rational nor a good form of settlement.' British Medical Association, after dealing with the writings of Dr. Norcross (see our quotation of his work and of the American investigation on pp. 136 and 145): 'The Association believes that if a similar investigation were undertaken in this country the results would be very much the same.' Cf. Royal Commission, Evidence, p. 1224. This remark relates to the experiences of lump-sum wastage in the U.S.A. Memorandum of Evidence by the Haldane Society, ibid., p. 1256: 'The inequality of position which exists between the workman and his employer in the matter of lump-sum settlements is not, in our view, capable of remedy by any modification in the terms of section 23, or by increasing the powers of the Courts.' Memorandum of Evidence by Mr. W. H. Thompson, solicitor, ibid., p. 1004: 'The real vice of the lump-sum system is the method by which the settlements are so often obtained.' Sharp criticism of lump-sum payments was also expressed in the Memorandum submitted by Dame Georgina Buller, D.B.E., J.P., see Evidence, p. 1154.

CHAPTER IX

WEEKLY PAYMENTS AND INCAPACITY SCHEDULES

Take care of him; and whatsoever thou spendest more, when I come again, I will repay thee.

Luke x. 35.

WE have already noted the important part played by the lump-sum settlement in the British, as opposed to most other, systems of Workmen's Compensation,[1] and we have shown that it is most frequently applied to cases of serious injury resulting in partial or complete disability. Comparatively few men who receive lump sums return to the particular occupation in which they were engaged at the time of the injury.

For less serious injuries, and in most cases of industrial disease not likely to cause permanent disablement, e.g. dermatitis and chrome ulceration, i.e. for 95 per cent. of all cases, the statutory method of weekly payments predominates. From the point of view of the work and life of the highly skilled and unskilled workman alike the weekly payment is of supreme importance. It differs from the 'sick pay' he draws from his 'club', viz. an Approved Society under the N.H.I. Acts, only to the extent that he receives it from another source, and that it is calculated on a different basis. He may have received it in respect of a trifling and temporary disablement, or in respect of a grave injury: in either case the social significance of these payments is great, particularly because they are made not by 'the club', which still retains, as its name shows, the faint tradition of mutual self-help, nor by the employer, whose relations with his workmen are, in the vast majority of cases, based upon confidence and mutual respect, but by a third party, the insurance office, represented by a man who is a complete stranger, but endowed with statutory authority to negotiate a settlement.

Whereas Compensation in 1937 was paid in 488,865 cases (compared with 362,043 in 1932), so the number of applications for arbitration was only 749 for weekly payments and 716 for lump sums, which seems small.[2] Of 28,888 memoranda registered in County Courts only

[1] The I.L.O. *Evaluation Report*, p. 226, declares: 'A few workmen's compensation schemes provide for the payment of compensation in the form of a lump sum in all cases of permanent incapacity.' The British methods in this matter have not been reviewed in particular by the *Report*, as apparently they were considered as rather the exception, an omission which can be understood as the *Report* was mainly concerned with the International aspect of the matter.

[2] *Workmen's Compensation Statistics 1937*, pp. 28 sqq.

1,384 related to weekly payments, and of 390,300 cases of accident settled without a lump-sum payment during the year almost 265,000 cases had lasted less than 4 weeks, and another 107,000 between 4 and 13 weeks. As the necessity for administrative interference generally arises with regard to cases of much longer duration, any attempt to express these and other figures in comparative form is bound to be misleading. What we have to consider is how far the assessment of weekly payments works smoothly in present circumstances, bearing in mind the fact that many cases are never the subject of legal discussion.

We have already shown in Chapter VI that great hardships may follow upon certain interpretations of, for instance, the term 'average weekly earnings'. This chapter is a pioneer attempt to examine this question in the light of general principles of evaluation of weekly payments as applied in other leading industrial countries.

The economic loss entailed by disablement is normally represented by the consequent reduction in the workman's wages, and the universal starting-point of the evaluation of weekly payments for received injuries has naturally been, in principle, the difference between the wages which the workman is capable of earning after what is called the 'consolidation' or stabilization of his injury and the wages earned before the injury was sustained. The principle is clear enough, but its application is by no means free from difficulty. The I.L.O. has done much to clarify the issues involved and we do not hesitate to follow their analysis and to accept most of their conclusions.[1] Their *Evaluation Report* shows that lump-sum procedure in Great Britain is inconsistent with the principle that economic loss and the degree of incapacity should in general be measured by the difference between pre- and post-disablement earnings. Redemption of weekly payments by a lump sum, whether by agreement or under compulsion, avoids the necessity for a definite evaluation on the basis of reduced earning capacity. The agreement may not take this into consideration at all, for commutation need not be based on the actuarial value of payments, viz. on the capitalized value of loss of future earnings. Moreover, compensation is, in general, assumed to be the recognition of a permanent disability. Where, however, doubt exists as to whether incapacity within the meaning of the Act is permanent, there is no rational basis for determining the amount necessary to redeem weekly payments, which must, in consequence, be fixed by agreement between the parties or the arbitrator.[2] In such cases, therefore, lump-sum payments do not

---

[1] Cf. *Evaluation Report*, pp. 65 sqq.

[2] Cf. Willis, loc. cit., p. 347: 'The great difficulty is as to the meaning of the word permanent.'

offer any escape from the difficulties of assessing the difference between pre- and post-disablement earnings. While the British procedure in regard to such settlements may diminish the difficulties of the calculation of weekly payments, this fact is not the main reason for their existence nor does it in any way mitigate their social disadvantages. Even in regard to lump-sum settlements the great difficulty is to discover a just rule for calculation of pre- and post-disablement earnings.[1]

The basis may be:

(a) observed earnings, or
(b) estimated earnings, or
(c) the earnings of an ordinary worker of the same grade in similar circumstances and in the same region.

Under (a) there are again two possible categories: (1) actual individual wages over a period prior to incapacity, subject to adjustment in order to take account of unemployment or economic and monetary fluctuations which may have affected it; and (2) actual wages received when the incapacity is evaluated. In both cases the presumed individual wage has to be distinguished as being the amount which the injured person should probably be able to earn; here again many other factors are involved, notably the difficulty of finding fresh employment.[2]

The British system of Workmen's Compensation is based mainly on the first of these categories, i.e. the 'observed' wage; incapacity is primarily evaluated by a comparison of pre- and post-disablement earnings. This system is also in force in the Canadian (Ontario) and New South Wales schemes. But the second possibility, of an incapacity evaluated by comparing the presumed individual wage with the actual individual wage over a period prior to incapacity, also plays its part in the British system, although not as in the systems of Australia, Canada, former Czechoslovakia, Denmark, France, Germany, Hungary, Poland, Switzerland, and Yugoslavia. It is a secondary factor in

---

[1] Cf. Willis, loc. cit., pp. 347–8: 'Put in other words, the phrase "incapacity is permanent" means not that the physical injury is permanent, but that in all reasonable probability the weekly payments to which the man is entitled will never alter.' The following difference is of importance: 'In reviewing weekly payments under Section II of the Act the arbitrator must only deal with existing facts and must not prophesy or speculate as to the workman's future condition. But in redeeming under Section 13 he is bound to speculate. He must not rest content with finding that the weekly payment which has been continued for six months is at the moment the proper sum. He must start with the assumption that the existing weekly payment is proper; but he must go further and ascertain as best he can whether that payment is likely to be proper during the rest of the man's life.' The matter should not be overlooked when lump-sum settlements are analysed with regard to evaluation of weekly payments.

[2] For a full analysis cf. *Evaluation Report*, pp. 66 sqq.

the British scheme, but of major importance in other countries. It plays a part in Britain only when there is found to be a reduction in earnings, and when actual earnings after disablement do not fairly represent the worker's remaining earning capacity.[1] British legislation originally empowered the arbitrator to award such part of the difference between pre- and post-accident earnings as he might think proper in the circumstances; this provision has been repealed and the compensation is now determined[2] by mathematical calculation, with due regard to any payment, allowance or benefit which the workman may receive from his employer during the period of incapacity.

There are two sets of cases to be considered:

(*a*) Cases in which the maximum weekly payment for total incapacity (i.e. 50 per cent. of the average weekly earnings before the accident subject to a maximum of 30*s*.) would have amounted to 25*s*. a week or upwards, viz. all cases where pre-accident earnings were 50*s*. or upwards. In these cases the compensation is to be half the difference between average pre-disablement earnings and the average weekly amount which the workman is earning or able to earn in some suitable employment or business after the injury (§ 9 (3) (i)).

(*b*) Cases in which the maximum weekly payment for total incapacity, together with any additions under the Act would have amounted to less than 25*s*., viz. all those in which average pre-disablement earnings were less than 50*s*.

From all this emerges the fact that, under the British system, both actual and presumed earnings after the injury must be taken into consideration. This arrangement has given rise to many serious difficulties, and experts like W. Addington Willis, even when refraining from animadversions on the existing state of the law, feel compelled to criticize the interpretation of the phrases 'able to earn', 'ability to earn', and other terms contained in § 9 of the Act.[3] The *Report* of the I.L.O. mentions significantly that in Australia and Canada the part played by the reduction in earnings in evaluating incapacity is less important than in Great Britain owing to the use of disability schedules showing either the amount of compensation payable for each injury listed, or the

---

[1] Cf. ibid., p. 82. Also Willis, loc. cit., p. 271: 'If the workman is not earning anything, or if it be alleged that he is able to earn more than in fact he is doing, the arbitrator must consider what, if anything, the workman is able to earn in some suitable employment or business.' Cf. also pp. 347–8 as quoted on p. 166.

[2] Cf. § 9 (1–4) of the Act of 1925.

[3] Cf. Willis, loc. cit., p. 269: 'More light has been thrown on the question, *but without definitely disposing of it*, by a case in the House of Lords in 1930.' Further, p. 273: 'There still remains the vexed question', &c. Further, p. 275: 'Many border-line cases have resulted in decisions which are difficult to reconcile.'

percentage of incapacity to be fixed, even when the injuries do not appear to have seriously affected earning capacity.

The absence of such schedules in Britain complicates the task of the arbitrator in fixing the weekly compensation where, if the employer can prove that the physical condition of the workman does not prevent him from doing ordinary light work, the arbitrator must forthwith estimate the amount the man might so earn. The *Evaluation Report* reaches the following important conclusions;[1] two essential conditions must be fulfilled before the difference in earnings can be used to measure incapacity:

(a) the worker's wages before disablement must afford 'reliable' indication of his past earning capacity and also of what it would have been at present and in future, and

(b) his wages after the injury must be truly representative of what he is likely to earn after 'consolidation'.

'In many cases' records the *Evaluation Report*, 'these two requirements are far from being satisfied.' On the one hand, the question arises whether before the accident the workman was really earning what he usually earned or might hope to earn in normal circumstances, e.g. after completing his training. On the other hand, until the workman has been reabsorbed into industry or has secured employment, his pay-envelope, or his failure to earn, is no reliable indication of his capacity or incapacity to earn. In spite of the apparent simplicity of this method, which probably tempted British legislators to adopt it, it may be a source of injustice to the injured workman, and the *Report* rightly concludes that 'reference to the difference in the worker's actual earnings is, in the main, *a theoretical standard for evaluating incapacity*'. English arbitrators are obliged, and find it hard, to decide whether an injured worker, who has partially recovered and does not find employment, is the victim of his partial incapacity or of the state of the labour market.

We have seen[2] how far § 9 of the Act of 1925 was amended in this respect by the amending Act of 1931 which aimed at doing justice to the workman who could not find employment owing to the condition of the labour market. This Act, which provided that, under certain conditions, partial incapacity should be treated as total incapacity, was to some extent frustrated by decisions of the lower courts[3] that the words 'but for the continuing effect of injury' had reference only to the physical condition of the workman, so that failure to obtain employment was not a 'continuing effect' if, owing to the condition of trade,

---

[1] Cf. *Evaluation Report*, p. 81.   [2] Cf. vol. i, pp. 257–8.

[3] Altered since 1938 by a decision of the House of Lords, see vol. i, p. 258.

there was no demand for the type of work in which he was engaged before the accident.[1] The same difficulty arises in respect of workmen who, being partially disabled, may find only employment inferior to what they could find, even in their partially incapacitated state, if the labour market conditions were different.

We have a case where the judge, after personal inspection of the works, decided that, had the employers not been obliged to dismiss a great number of workers, the injured man would have been given his former work.[2] In another case Lord Hailsham declared that

if a man is prevented by injury from following his pre-accident occupation and is compelled to adopt a less remunerative occupation it is a little difficult to see why the resultant loss of earnings is not occasioned by his injury, even though the lower wage which he earns in his new employment results in part from the economic conditions prevailing in that employment whether they be reflected in a reduction of pay or a reduction in the hours of work.

The difficulties are evident, and every attempt to indemnify the injured worker against the real loss he has suffered serves to increase them. It is bound to be difficult to decide whether the reduced earning capacity of a workman after an injury is due solely to his partial incapacity or to extraneous economic circumstances or to both causes, and in what respective proportions. The employer who gives him new work might be compelled by economic reasons to pay him less or to shorten hours, whereas his former employer might have been able to give him much better wages had his post not been filled since. Such possibilities are innumerable. The *Evaluation Report* (p. 76) mentions cases in which the injured person is not sufficiently trained to earn full wages in his new calling, or not fully restored to health. In the eyes of the law his case is settled and cannot be reopened, though his condition has not been stabilized. These factors may, by affecting the continuity of his earnings, reduce them to a figure much below that indicated by the contents of his pay envelope during the first few weeks after his assumed 'recovery'. In assessing a war injury the Ministry of Pensions compares a man with a normal man of his own age and, for certain types of injury, awards a definite percentage of the total pension. Under the Workmen's Compensation Act a man is compensated for 'loss of earning power', a difference well stressed by Dr. Brend,[3] whose experience is wide. The conflicting legal views manifested themselves very clearly when Lord Hailsham declared in a case that 'the proposition of law is that where a man is actually earning wages, the compensation to which he is entitled is to be assessed by reference

---

[1] Cf. *Barstow* v. *Ingham Collieries Ltd.*, [1934] A.C. 304. Also Willis, loc. cit., p. 259.
[2] Cf. *Neary* v. *Boby*, [1932] B.W.C. 357. Also Willis, loc. cit., p. 270.
[3] Cf. Brend, loc. cit., p. 59.

to the normal earnings under normal market conditions in that employment, and not by reference to his actual earnings in the conditions prevailing at the time'. This view was, however, rejected by Lord Atkin, who pointed to the difficulties, numerous and varied, to be met in attempting to ascertain a 'normal standard'.

These difficulties are not in reality insuperable. They have indeed been successfully met under such Workmen's Compensation schemes as have adopted the last method of assessing weekly payments to be discussed here, viz. with reference to the average normal wage of a normal worker in the same occupational category in similar circumstances. The *Evaluation Report* of the I.L.O. stresses the fact that such a system becomes necessary because the presumed individual wage of a period prior to the incapacity can only yield a correct result if this figure truly represents the normal or usual earning capacity of the worker. This principle is even more applicable to the British system of comparing mainly—though not exclusively—pre- and post-disablement earnings. The *Evaluation Report* declares that:

the body responsible for evaluating incapacity must, where the actual individual wage prior to incapacity does not represent the normal earning capacity which the worker concerned would probably have acquired or retained if he had not been disabled, choose another basis of comparison. *This basis may be the usual wage of a normal worker in the same circumstances as those in which the disabled person found himself prior to his incapacity, or in the same circumstances as those in which he would have found himself after his occupational training had been completed.*

This method was first applied in the German invalidity insurance scheme,[1] which provided that basic earnings shall be the amount usually earned in the same district by a physically and mentally sound person of the same kind with similar training; it is embodied in the invalidity insurance laws of Belgium, Chile, Denmark, France (Alsace-Lorraine), Hungary, Italy, Luxemburg, the Netherlands, Poland, and Rumania and is implicit in French law. This method allows the probable degree of incapacity to be evaluated independently of any exceptional circumstances which may have affected the worker's earnings before he was disabled.[2] An arbitrator who attempts to do full justice

---

[1] Cf. Section 1254 of the Federal Insurance Code. It was also embodied in the invalidity laws of former Austria and Czechoslovakia.

[2] In Germany § 563 of the *Gewerbe-Unfallversicherung* decrees that the last *Jahresarbeitsverdienst*, i.e. the last year's earnings as resulting from any kind of labour, shall be the measure for the fixation of the pension. The fixation of this wage-rate, however, *is closely linked up with the German Mutual Indemnity Associations*: these average wage-rates are fixed for the various kinds of workers within the scope of the *Berufsgenossenschaften* according to their earnings during one year; the insured workers may be divided into 'groups'; in fixing the compensation (*Rente*) the wage-rates as represented by the collective wage-agreements (*Tarifverträge*) shall be taken into consideration. The fixation of the compensation

to the parties by attempting to assess future earning possibilities or by comparing pre- and post-disablement earnings finds himself drawn into a labyrinth of hypothetical questions. It seems preferable by far to replace these 'objective' items by the assumption of a certain normal wage which the injured man could have earned before his disablement, to contrast it with the wage he might expect to earn after partial disablement, and to fix the amount accordingly.

It may be contended that collective wage agreements are indispensable. British Workmen's Compensation legislation indeed envisages this method where under the *Rules for Determining Earnings* regard may be paid in certain cases to the average weekly amount which during the twelve months previous to the accident was being earned by a person of the same grade employed at the same work by the same employer or, if there is no such person so employed, by a person in the same grade employed in the same class of employment in the same district.[1] But this only relates to 'earnings' or 'average weekly earnings' and not to the evaluation of compensation, of which the calculation of such earnings is only one part. This point, however, was covered by the Private Bill, sponsored by the Labour party in October 1937, which not only varied the wording of § 10 of the Act of 1925 as regards the computation of earnings but proposed to insert the following important proviso:

If, however, the workman at the time of his accident was temporarily employed on work other than that on which he was normally employed then in assessing the normal weekly earnings regard shall be had to the normal occupation of the workman.

The Bill proposed to relate weekly earnings strictly to 'normal weekly earnings', i.e. the sum earned by the workman in a week during which he was continually employed for the full number of hours, and of working days, usually and normally worked in the industry or employment in which he was engaged. Mr. Arthur Henderson, K.C., M.P., thus explained this clause:[2]

We propose as the basis the normal weekly earnings of the workman in his regular industry, in a normal week, a normal number of days and a normal number of hours in each normal day.

The novelty of this proposal is evident. In drawing a sharp line between actual wage conditions in an individual case, so frequently adverse to the injured workman's cause, and presumed 'normal' wage-earning conditions it sought to achieve a measure of standardization

must also refer to the local districts. Cf. *Die Reichsversicherungsordnung mit Anmerkungen*, vol. iii, 1930, pp. 136–9.

[1] Cf. § 10 (1) of the Act of 1925.   [2] Cf. *Debates H.C.*, Nov. 19th 1937, col. 748.

in assessing compensation. This method may well prove fairer and more satisfactory than the present system.

This question was dealt with at some length in the Home Office Memorandum placed before the Hetherington Commission,[1] which mentioned repeated representations that the present basis 'operates hardly where industry is depressed'. It recognized that in such circumstances it might be unfair to the workman to calculate compensation on the basis of 'actual' earnings though 'average earnings' for the previous twelve months, calculated in accordance with the Act, would not be reduced by periods of unemployment.

The Memorandum made no attempt to deal with cases in which the workman might be prejudiced by the present system of assessing his incapacity (Q. 216–17) consequent upon acceptance after the accident of 'light work' employment wholly unlike his previous job. Nor did it examine cases where advantage might befall a workman, whose wages immediately before the accident were abnormally high.[2] 'Slack-time' is, however, more important than either of these contingencies. It was touched on in the following terms:

> Q. 2236: Two men are employed by a certain employer, they are injured and their compensation is 30*s*. These two men have agreed, since the works are on short time, that instead of one of them being discharged, they shall work one week on and one week off. What effect has that on the compensation?
> A. (*Mr. G. R. A. Buckland*): So long as there is no break in the employment the effect is to reduce the man's earnings by half and to reduce the compensation.

This statement should be read in the light of a recent case[3] in which, under a 'spread-over' system, miners in a colliery agreed to suspend the 'custom of seniority' whereby, in general, junior men were the first to be stood off when employment was slack. The employers claimed that the effect of this voluntary agreement was to reduce proportionately the average earnings during the previous twelve months of all concerned and, in particular, of an injured workman suffering from silicosis. The Court of Appeal upheld this view, whilst noting that it involved 'some hardship upon the applicant'.[4]

The Home Office Memorandum opposed the assessment of compensation upon normal earnings in normal times suggesting (§§ 443–9) that:

if instead of basing compensation on the actual average earnings of the particular workman over a period, it is to be based on what he might have earned in different circumstances . . . a great deal of guess work would be introduced, litigation would

---

[1] *Home Office Memorandum*, §§ 439 sqq. [2] Cf. also *Evaluation Report*, p. 76.
[3] Cf. Butterworth, 1938, pp. 448 sqq.
[4] *Morgan* v. *Tareni Colliery Coy.* [1938]. Butterworth, pp. 448 sqq.

tend to be much more frequent, and the Courts would have greater difficulty in assessing compensation.

A workman might belong to an industry in which short-time work was prevalent: he might be a dock-labourer, where daily or half-daily engagements prevail, or a piece-worker. The *Evaluation Report* of the I.L.O., which has shown that a 'theoretical' standard of assessing earnings according to certain presumed or presumable earnings was generally accepted in most industrial countries, was barely alluded to. The Home Office Memorandum ignored the statement at p. 77 that the worker's presumed wage when his incapacity is evaluated is used for purposes of comparison in all invalidity insurance and workmen's compensation schemes, although in some of the latter, e.g. in Australia (New South Wales), Canada (Ontario) and Great Britain reference is made to presumed earnings only when actual wages do not appear to afford an adequate measure of real earning power.

The *Evaluation Report*, moreover, noted (p. 81) that the British system involved two conditions:

(1) that the worker's wages before disablement must afford a reliable indication to his earning capacity in the past and also to what it would have been at present and for the future; and

(2) his wages after the accident must be truly representative of what he is likely to earn once his injuries have healed;

and remarked, as stated before, that 'in many cases these two requirements are far from being satisfied'.

This informed comment on the British system of assessing earnings in the light of the normal practice in most important industrial countries found no place in the Home Office Memorandum, the writer of which was content to invite reference to the 'conclusions' of the *Report* without drawing attention to the passages we have quoted.[1] He did not, however, resolve the doubts of the Commission as to the justice of the present system, nor satisfy them that no alternative system could be devised.[2]

It is unlikely in practice that any difficulty would be experienced in this country but for the interposition between the employer and the workman of a third party, viz. the insurance carrier. It is safe to say that, in nine cases out of ten, representatives of masters and men would agree within a few minutes, in any given case, on a figure representing normal earnings. Wages in the principal industries in Great Britain are paid according to schedules agreed upon from time to time between employers and trade unions: a great number of smaller industries are

[1] Buckland, Q. 2152, 2155 A. Cf. also *Evaluation Report*, p. 66: 'The procedure in Great Britain is quite exceptional.'   [2] Q. 2226–9.

covered by trade boards. In every factory figures, computed as a matter of routine, are available showing average earnings on piece work of men and women, boys and girls, in every department, month by month. Indeed the Home Office Memorandum (§ 449) noted such a possibility and adumbrated the establishment of a Special Authority to administer the system. One Commissioner, Mr. Bannatyne of the Home Office, adduced (Q. 2229) the existence in County Durham of a Joint Committee of Coal Owners' and Miners' representatives which could handle such matters. There is, however, in our view no need to create special machinery. So far as it does not already exist, the services of the Ministry of Labour's representatives in every part of Britain could be utilized to fill the gap.

The T.U.C. Memorandum to the Hetherington Commission dealt very fully with this matter. It called attention to the 'gross injustice' of the present system;[1] in specially prepared tables the hardship arising from the computation of average weekly earnings under the present law was fully illustrated[2]; and some characteristic cases of hardship were given. The tables show that the injured worker in many cases gets 30–50 per cent. less in weekly compensation payments than would correspond to his 'normal weekly earnings'. In one case a worker whose normal weekly earnings would have been £3. 5s. got 12s. 1d.!

The difficulties of arriving at a just evaluation of incapacity in regard to the future earning chances of the injured early led to another means of measurement based upon certain criteria derived from the physical state of the injured workman, viz. 'Disability Schedules'. By computing incapacity not on the basis of presumed future earnings or of actual post-injury earnings but on that of the actual physical incapacity of the worker, so far as it affects his general earning capacity, legislation in various countries has attempted to prescribe definite standards of general application to the evaluation of incapacity. The *Holman Gregory Report* drew attention to them with a view to further investigation by the proposed Workmen's Compensation Commissioner.[3] Since then they have been widely adopted abroad and several types of disability schedules may now be distinguished. The first step was merely to draw up, by scientific methods and with medical assistance, some rough standard of incapacity. In course of time the schedules became more complete; forms of incapacity were more carefully differentiated, and modified by reference to the influence of age and occupation on the consequences of the injury and disability. Such schedules differ also in their enforceability, some being compulsory and others optional. Following mainly the classification of the

[1] Cf. p. 415.   [2] Cf. p. 438.
[3] Cf. *Holman Gregory Report*, p. 44.

I.L.O.[1] these schedules may be distinguished with their respective features and advantages:

A. *Incapacity Schedules taking no account of Age and Occupation*

Schedules which do not take account of age and occupation usually consist of a list of injuries with a percentage of incapacity entered opposite each. In some cases no percentage is fixed, the schedule merely giving the amount of compensation due or the length of time for which it is payable. Some such schedules give simply the percentages of capacity; others give the total amount of compensation due as well as the duration of payments. The first-named class of schedules is the most frequent. It is found in the administration of Workmen's Compensation in Argentina, Canada, Chile, Costa Rica, France, Germany, India, Italy, Mexico, and the Union of South Africa. The second class—giving the total amount of compensation and duration of payments—is to be found in Australia, the U.S.A., and Japan. In New South Wales a system of disability schedules is linked up with lump-sum payments, the schedule applying to injured workmen suffering from specified injuries who choose compensation in the form of a lump sum, giving the amount of the final indemnity for each injury. In the U.S.A. the system varies greatly in different States. The matter has been frequently discussed since 1921[2] before the International Association of Industrial Accidents Boards and Commissions —but little progress has yet been made towards unification.[3] The amount of detail in the lists also varies widely in the different international schedules. The schedules in current use in Germany and France cover several hundred injuries. In California the schedule is a paper-bound book, 9 in. × 12½ in., containing 70 pages. The list of occupations comprises 1,050 items arranged in alphabetical order. It has been computed that this elaboration contains about 13 million possible combinations of ratings which have been carefully computed and made readily understandable by a person of sufficient diligence and intelligence to plan a cross-country journey in Britain with the aid of *Bradshaw*.[4] Even in a country so little industrialized as Brazil the

---

[1] Cf. *Evaluation Report*, pp. 88 sqq.

[2] Cf. Bureau of Labor Statistics, Washington, 1923, Bulletin no. 333, pp. 72 sqq.

[3] Dodd, loc. cit., p. 633, writes in 1936: '. . . the permanent disability schedules remain as unscientific as ever, and change has come only through the pressure upon legislative bodies and without systematic effort of improvement.' Dodd gives particular instances of the absolute lack of uniformity and the great variations in the legislation of the different States of the U.S.A. He calls attention to the fact that permanent partial disability constitutes the most serious problem with respect to standardization of compensation. See pp. 630–2 and 640.

[4] Cf. *Holman Gregory Report*, p. 44, and *Evaluation Report*, p. 104.

disability schedule includes as many as 966 items. Apart from this the different injuries have to be specified according to the part of the body affected: arm, leg, face, neck, spine, chest, abdomen, &c. As already mentioned this list covers several hundred injuries in Germany and France, it comprises about 240 in Mexico and 100 in Japan, but only some 15–40 in other countries including South Africa, India, Italy, Spain, Argentina, and Canada.

B. *Incapacity Schedules taking account of Age and Occupation*

These are the more progressive type of disability schedules as developed in several countries which have attempted to mitigate disadvantages arising out of the somewhat rigid working of the first method. As the economic consequences of injuries vary with the age and the previous occupation of the disabled workman, an attempt is here made to draw up schedules giving, for selected injuries, a series of incapacity percentages graduated according to the workman's age and occupation at the moment of disablement. These schedules are based primarily on observation, i.e. on evidence obtained as to the reduction in wages normally resulting from each of the injuries in the case of workers of different ages and occupations. Exceptional circumstances are carefully taken into account and the data corrected accordingly. Owing to the large number of individual cases to be observed, the multiplicity of the observations to be made, and the length of time that must elapse before any generally applicable conclusion can be drawn, the difficulty of correcting data obtained when not sufficiently representative and, in general, the scope and detail of the investigation necessary in order to take account of age and former occupation in establishing invalidity schedules, attempts to draw up schedules of this type have hitherto been few.[1] Outstanding examples are those in force in California and Brazil.

It is also important to distinguish between binding schedules and guide schedules. The latter are meant to be merely optional. If the schedule is binding, the description of the injuries entails the compulsory recognition of a given percentage of incapacity, at least where a single percentage is given for each injury. But even here a certain latitude is necessary. Even where the injury is well defined—amputation of the leg above the knee, for instance—a binding schedule may well leave a margin for the personal factors likely to influence the reabsorption of the injured workman into industry. Where this is the case certain maximum and minimum limits of the general schedule only may be made binding, while a varying degree of elasticity may

---

[1] Cf. *Evaluation Report*, p. 103.

be left to the evaluating authority. We give here a condensed list
of the elaborations of disability schedules in some of the important
industrial nations (Binding Schedules marked 'B'; Guide Schedules
marked 'G'):

Incapacity Percentages Applicable to Certain Injuries

Typical Injuries

	Loss of left arm at shoulder or between shoulder and elbow	Loss of right hand	Loss of thumb involving meta-carpal bone	Loss of foot	Loss of one eye	Deafness of one ear
France (G) .	66–70	66⅔	25	40	33½	10
Germany (G) .	75–80	60	25	35	25	10–15
Former Czecho-slovakia (G)	70	75	40	40	33⅓	15–25
U.S.A. (B):						
New Jersey .	50	38	15	31	25	10
U.S.A. (B):						
Wisconsin .	50	33	10	25	20	5
Japan (B) .	66⅔	55	27	55	33⅓	27
Canada (G) .	65–70	37½	9 (minim.)	30	18	3
Sweden (G) .	70	60	30	40	25	10

Although this list is only a random extract from an elaborate and
complex tabulation of each of these nations, it serves to reveal the great
divergences in the existing system of evaluation by disability schedules.
This may be due to differing circumstances such as the general conception of the necessities of Workmen's Compensation, the particular
features of industrial development, &c. It is, however, noteworthy
that in those neighbouring countries with high and almost similar
industrial structure such as France and Germany, the schedule shows
a remarkable likeness; it may be assumed that, under similar conditions, compensation schedules tend to develop on uniform lines. In
both countries the schedule was originally drawn up as a 'private'
schedule.

We give here as an example of the possible specialization of disability
the following enumeration of hand injuries taken from private guidance schedules in Germany:[1] the calculations are based upon the
experience gathered from the decisions of the Federal Insurance
Office (*Reichsversicherungsamt*) subject to an explicit warning against
any attempt to apply them rigidly and without discrimination. On the

[1] Cf. also Ickert-Weichsel, *Grundriß der sozialen Medizin*, Leipzig, 1932, pp. 265 sqq.

N

contrary each case should—in spite of the guiding schedule—be examined on its merits. The schedule[1] runs as follows:

Hand Injuries (Germany)

	Right	Left
Finger, whole or at joint	0–10	0
Index finger	0–10	0
Index and one other finger	25–30	20
Two fingers other than index	20–30	20
Index and two other fingers	40	30
Three fingers other than index	$33\frac{1}{3}$	30
All four fingers	50	40
Thumb at distal joint.	0–15	0–10
Thumb between distal and proximal joints . . .	10–20	10
Whole thumb	20–30	15
Thumb with metacarpal bone	$25–33\frac{1}{3}$	20–5
Thumb and one finger	35–45	30
Thumb and two fingers	45–50	40
Thumb and three fingers	50–5	45
Thumb and all four fingers	60	50
Hand	$66\frac{2}{3}$	50

The disability schedule of Japan, which, in contrast to the German one, is binding in character, enumerates 100 disabilities. In the case of a disability not mentioned in the schedule the evaluation is made by analogy, the disability being compared to the one most closely resembling it in the schedule. This detail is not uninteresting as it is likely to show—as does the German example—that the application of the disability schedule principle is not necessarily one of strict rigidity but much more one of relative guidance. The schedules in Japan are arranged into what is called fourteen 'degrees of incapacity' which relate to the above-mentioned number of disabilities. The compensation varies with these degrees, beginning with a compensation due 540 times the basic daily wage and ending with twenty times the basic daily wage. For instance, the loss of both legs above the knee is compensated by a sum equal to 540 times the basic daily wage, while the loss of the use of the little finger is compensated by a sum which is twenty times the basic daily wage. These scales represent minimum scales only and, in cases of temporary incapacity, medical treatment and an absence allowance of 60 per cent. of the daily wages is granted. Yet the absolute figure of compensation appears to be low in comparison with European measurement, though the system of evaluation deserves earnest consideration.

There can be no doubt that the system of disability schedules has its advantages as well as its disadvantages. The I.L.O. has given careful attention to both sides.[2]

[1] See *Evaluation Report*, p. 308.   [2] Cf. ibid., pp. 346–7.

In favour of the system it may be urged that:

1. The use of a schedule makes it possible to obtain throughout a country uniform evaluations for identical injuries or disabilities (when mentioned in the schedule).
2. The work of the bodies responsible for the evaluation can be done more easily and quickly and disputes tend to be fewer.
3. These advantages are particularly important in countries with little experience of evaluating incapacity and without experts in this field, especially those with undeveloped means of communication so that cases of appeal necessarily involve long delays and costly journeys. Hence the elaboration of such schedules in countries of relatively small industrial development, where such schedules are more the outcome of geographical necessity than of a spirit of social progress. Yet the older industrial nations may have something to learn from them.

The disadvantages of the schedules clearly relate to their automatic character which in many cases may be against the workman's interest. Where the schedule is not binding the danger of litigation is not averted; on the other hand, the binding schedule, leaving age and occupation out of account, as the *Evaluation Report* suggests, does not 'allow of taking individual factors into account that play a part of capital importance in determining loss of earning capacity, in particular, the worker's age and previous occupation'. On the whole, the I.L.O. appears to view the more elementary form of disability schedules with disfavour, so far as they do not take into account age and occupation and do not allow wide discretion in application. On the other hand, age and occupation are taken into account only in Brazil and California. The *Evaluation Report* concludes that the use of such schedules cannot be recommended unless

(*a*) they are not binding;
(*b*) they are constantly revised in the light of experimental observation of an increasing number of individual cases.

If this is the case one might argue that the very object of such schedules, i.e. to standardize evaluation methods and administration, would be handicapped by a number of rules which would tend to deprive the schedules of their authority. Yet the fact that the principal industrial nations, except Britain have, in some guise or other, adopted such systems and are developing them on scientific lines[1] should not be

---

[1] Cf. for an interesting summary of methods and principles of rating eye-disabilities in the U.S.A.: *1936 Convention of International Association of Industrial Accidents Boards, U.S. Dept. of Labor, Bulletin No. 10*, Washington, 1937, pp. 99–110. Particular attention is

overlooked. It is to be regretted that even in such valuable contributions to Workmen's Compensation as those by the late Sir John Collie disability schedules are not treated, although it is to be supposed that their medical aspects would have interested him. The suggestion, made by the Holman Gregory Committee eighteen years ago, that the whole question should be made the subject of detailed investigation has not found any response, and no report on it has been prepared by the Medical Research Council. The matter is not merely one of compensation method but one which should be of great interest to the medical profession, for the medical considerations are the very basis of disability schedules, and the tables cannot be prepared without much detailed medical experience and pathological knowledge. The German table which we have quoted before is taken from the well-known work of Ickert-Weichsel on Social Medicine,[1] a fact which shows the interest which the problem has aroused in German medical circles. In France books relating to the evaluation methods here described have emanated from medical writers and publishers.[2] Important contributions to the elaboration of schedules relating to eye disabilities have been made of late in the U.S.A. by Dr. William H. Mehl, Dr. Walter L. Small, and others, while the American Medical Association has played no little part in the matter.[3]

Disability schedules are clearly not an ideal solution: as has been said of Admiralty Instructions, they are 'a guide to the wise, and a law to the foolish'. They need constant revision and, even if full weight is given to age and occupation, must often fail to do justice to the fact that even injuries or infirmities bearing identical names may have very different economic and sociological effects, a fact which has not escaped the attention of the I.L.O.[4] But these difficulties and disadvantages should not be allowed to discourage preliminary action in Britain to devise disability schedules for purposes of guidance in the light of the experience of other countries. The Ministry of Pensions has made use of elaborate schedules of disability which could be usefully studied and applied if such system should be introduced into this country.[5] Such

drawn to the work of the American Medical Association which has compiled the respective tables and given 'a great deal of thought' to it.

[1] Cf. Ickert-Weichsel, *Grundriß der Sozialen Medizin*, Leipzig, 1932, pp. 384 sqq.

[2] Cf. E. Forgue and E. Jeanbrau, *Guide Pratique du Médecin dans les Accidents du Travail*, Librairie de l'Académie de Médecine, 1924. Also Léon Imbert, C. Oddo, and P. Chavernack, *Guide pour l'Évaluation des Incapacités*, Librairie de l'Académie de Médecine, Paris, 1923.

[3] Cf. *1936 Convention*, &c., U.S. Dept. of Labor, Bulletin No. 10, Washington, 1937, pp. 99–133. As to Medical Association see p. 122 in particular.

[4] Cf. *Evaluation Report*, p. 348.

[5] Cf. *Hetherington Commission*, pp. 393–6; also Mr. Glover's evidence, Q. 3649–52.

schedules would serve to discourage inadequate offers and acceptances of inadequate lump-sum settlements by indicating a rough minimum sum which an injured workman might reasonably claim and expect in justice to receive. This point has not been dealt with in the *Evaluation Report* as lump-sum settlements are peculiar to this country. Such schedules might be of substantial value to judges and registrars, arbitrators, and others concerned with the administration of Work-men's Compensation. Accustomed as they are to be guided by pre-viously decided cases, whilst careful to note any and every circumstance which distinguishes one case from another, they might be expected to welcome a careful compilation of decided cases relating to disability and, eventually, a schedule based thereon.[1]

[1] Cf. also an interesting article by Earl D. McBride on 'Disability Evaluation' in *The American Journal of Surgery*, December 1938, pp. 840–4.

NOTE

ATTENTION may be called to the Disability Schedules drawn up by the Ministry of Pensions for Major Disablements (Specific Injuries and Diseases). There are nine ordinary grades of war pension which are calculated in tenths of a maximum of 100 per cent., beginning at 20 per cent. and going up to 100 per cent., and three sub-grades in the less than 20 per cent. classification. See *Hetherington Commission*, p. 382; for text of Schedules, pp. 393–4. The evaluation takes into account the degree of loss of general working capacity with reference to the *normal healthy man of the same age*.

CHAPTER X

REVIEW OF WEEKLY PAYMENTS

Who shall decide, when Doctors disagree
And soundest Casuists doubt, like you and me?

POPE, *Moral Essays*, iii.

THOUGH we have shown the social dangers of lump-sum payments, and the inherent defects of the existing system of weekly
payments, our study of methods of compensation is not as yet complete.
Both forms of payment are based upon certain physical assumptions.
The physical condition of the workman after, or the sums he could
earn before and after, the injury dictated the initial amount of his compensation. We have still to consider cases where either the employer,
or the workman, appears to be justified in asking for a variation of the
compensation payments. The employer may hold that it is time to
reduce or to stop the payments altogether on the ground that the
man's health is better. The injured workman may ask for an increase
of weekly payment on the ground that his disablement has increased.
Such claims for a '*review of weekly payments*' form a tangle of difficult
issues—perhaps the most complex within the whole structure of
Workmen's Compensation.

We have already discussed[1] how far the Act of 1925 alleviated the
hardships from which injured workmen formerly suffered. Uncertainty
as to the condition of the injured man may at any moment give rise to
litigation, from either side, which may be without medical or legal
justification and which may give rise to hardship and injustice. The
Evaluation Report describes how different industrial countries deal with
this matter, but does not dwell upon the harm done by a mischievous
use of the powers given. Sir John Collie regarded the procedure on
review or termination of weekly payments primarily as a means to
enable employers to protect themselves against unjustified claims:

Assuming that liability to pay weekly compensation under the Act has been
accepted by the employer or determined by the Court, the employer, as has been
stated previously, is frequently confronted with difficulty in securing the workman's return to work. The loss of the work habit, due perhaps in the first instance
to compulsory abstention from work, is only one of the factors giving rise to the
difficulty of getting the workman to return to work.

Another may possibly be found in the fact that, in many cases, contributions
from clubs and other sources, which become payable in consequence of the injury,

[1] Vol. i, pp. 243–4.

together with the weekly compensation, approximate to, or exceed, the income received whilst at work. There is little inducement to resume work so long as such benefits can be obtained. The Act, therefore, gives the right to either party to apply to the Court for a revision of weekly payments.[1]

This typically one-sided explanation of the necessity for a review, which may, indeed, well be demanded by the injured man himself on the advice of his medical attendant,[2] is based upon a misconception of the nature and causes of 'malingering', the prevalence of which has been denied by successive Parliamentary Committees.[3] In a recent treatise Dr. Norris again emphasizes the point, noting that

(1) inefficient treatment,
(2) inadequate compensation, and
(3) mistaken advice

may in each case produce a neurosis wholly unrelated to 'malingering'.[4] This considered verdict should be set against the popular view that injured workmen often malinger in order to prevent a proper review of weekly payments.

Before entering upon a discussion of general principles we will deal at some length with a recent case which, though admittedly exceptional, throws light upon the subject. A glazier in Liverpool fell 24 feet from a ladder, receiving severe injuries to the spine and sacrum. A year later his doctor made a Report to the man's employers at their request. It gave many details about the injured man's deteriorated state of health, body, and mind, and concluded that the injured man was at that time only fit for sedentary or semi-sedentary light work. This Report was sent on to the employer's insurers who wrote a letter to the workman's solicitor saying that he had made considerable progress towards recovery and that it was advisable that he should be given light work as it would give him occupation and tend to make him fit. Thereupon the employers through their insurers offered the workman employment in their stores in Birmingham consisting 'of a certain amount of clerical work and also sorting small parts and handing them out if he desired' at £2 a week plus a sum for costs of removal and travelling expenses, as the new place of his work would have been 100 miles away from his domicile. This offer was refused. The employers then applied for review of the weekly payment on the ground

---

[1] Cf. Collie, loc. cit., p. 88.
[2] Cf. *Evaluation Report*, p. 205, where the point is well considered.
[3] Cf. vol. i, pp. 13, 185–6.
[4] Cf. Dr. Norris, 'Malingering', *British Encyclopaedia of Medical Practice*, vol. viii, 1938, pp. 357–8.

that the workman was able to earn £2 a week. The County Court judge found that the workman had no earning capacity in the open market (viz. he was, within the meaning of the authorities, an 'odd lot'[1]) but that the offer of work was suitable. He therefore found for the employers. The workman appealed.

The Court of Appeal dealt with the matter from two points of view, inquiring

(1) whether the offer of employment was in the circumstances, genuine, and
(2) bearing in mind the distance from the workman's home of the employment offered, whether it was suitable employment for a workman in such condition.

As regards the letter that the company had written to the solicitor of the workman, Slesser L.J. declared:

There is no object in using hard words. It is sufficient to say that that letter is a complete misrepresentation, a deliberate misrepresentation, in my opinion, being a letter written by persons versed in this class of work (*sic!*) of what the doctor said. So far from the doctor saying their client had made considerable recovery, he said that apart from a freer movement his injuries were the same and had reached a stage where not much further improvement could be expected; and as regards the right foot he said it was worse. In the light of that letter, it is not surprising to find later on, when the question comes before the Courts for review, that the insurance company resolved not to allow Mr. Thompson [the solicitor of the workman] to have a copy of that report; it would immediately disclose the false nature of their letter.

The judge then inquired whether the offer was 'genuine'. Sir Stafford Cripps, K.C., on behalf of the workman, had already pointed out that the offer had been made 'under the cover of a false statement', that the place of employment was remote from the man's domicile, and the amount offered 'out of all proportion to the services a man in his physical condition could be expected to render'. Slesser L.J. declared that these matters were for the consideration of the County Court judge whose task it was to decide whether it was 'a genuine offer of a contractual relation between the parties, or an offer of something charitable or possibly worse'. He went on to discuss whether the offer, 'being personal to the man, is made in regard to a district so remote from that in which he is habitually working that it cannot be taken to be a reasonable offer at all'. Romer L.J. agreeing, spoke of the 'somewhat sinister circumstances in which the offer was made'. The appeal was allowed[2] and the matter sent to another County Court judge for new trial, at which the employers' application for review was dismissed.

---

[1] Cf. vol. i, p. 190.
[2] Butterworth's *Workmen's Compensation Cases*, vol. xxx, 1938, pp. 145 sqq.

The case presents some exceptional features, but is typical of many which never reach the courts, and of some that do.

The present system [writes Dr. Brend] has created a class of what may perhaps best be termed professional medical witnesses, who appear constantly in the Courts, some of them regularly acting for insurance companies representing employers, and some regularly appearing for organizations representing workmen. These witnesses have a sound knowledge of their work and at the same time are highly skilled in presenting a particular aspect of a case which may exercise much influence on a lay court.[1]

It matters little whether or not such cases occur frequently. What matters is that such a case could happen at all. The workman in question was lucky; he had secured the services of a firm of solicitors very well known for their experience in this branch of law, which was able to induce very eminent Counsel to accept a brief. What would have happened had he stood alone? These questions are hardly considered by those who view the right of review as a safeguard for employers. Could such a case occur where the right of 'review' is exercised by a quasi-official body such as the *Berufsgenossenschaften* in Germany, or in Switzerland, where the National Accident Insurance Fund is the only authorized insurance carrier permitted to institute a review.[2]

A similar case is that of *Birch Brothers Ltd.* v. *Brown*, decided in the workman's favour by the House of Lords on June 11th 1931. The workman, a van driver and wheelwright, lost his eye as the result of an accident, and was capable of working as a wheelwright only at reduced wages. He was first awarded compensation for partial incapacity, then full compensation for total incapacity. The employer's doctor later reported that the sight of his right eye was deteriorating because of a cataract, not associated with the accident, and that he would soon become totally blind. The employer's insurers offered the workman a job in their town office as a cleaner at £3 a week. The man, being practically blind, refused the job. The employers then applied for a review with the object of reducing his compensation on the ground that his refusal of a suitable offer of work was due to a disease of the other eye, which had never been affected by the accident. A County Court reduced compensation to 1s. 8d. a week; the case was then taken to the Court of Appeal and thence to the House of Lords, where Lord Atkin said:

The Judge has found that it was a *bona fide* offer. So far as he finds that there was a vacancy for a cleaner at the insurance company's office and that they would

[1] Cf. Brend, loc. cit., p. 93. Cf. also ibid., p. 63, for rather bitter remarks on the subject.
[2] Cf. W. Lauber, *Praxis des sozialen Unfallversicherungsrechts der Schweiz*, Bern, 1928, *passim*.

have employed a one-eyed man there is evidence to support it. But it is also beyond question that the offer was one which the insurance company knew the workman could not accept, or accepting, could not fulfil, and that the rate of wage offered was not a wage rate at all, but a weekly payment determined by the insurance company's liability, designed, if refused, to destroy the liability to them of 30s. per week, which was, in fact, the market rate for the job.

Lord Atkin further noted the 'remarkable anomaly' that 'a man with the full sight of one eye may be totally incapacitated but when he becomes completely blind he may revert to partial incapacity'.

The question of 'light work' which runs through the whole history of Workmen's Compensation,[1] comes here again into the picture. Can the man do light work, and if so of what kind? Will he be able to get it or will he end his working career in the 'odd lot' category? The point was illustrated by a recent appeal case.[2] A haulage man (under 21) had sustained an injury which had healed but caused pain if he walked far. After paying compensation for total incapacity for seven months the employers applied for review. The County Court judge found the man capable of unskilled 'light work'—'such as gardening work of not too arduous a nature'—and, assuming an earning capacity of two-thirds of the ordinary remuneration of an unskilled labourer, reduced his compensation to 3s. 11d. a week. The Court of Appeal allowed the workman's appeal and remitted the case to the County Court judge to decide whether the man was or was not an 'odd lot'. Slesser L.J. doubted whether the special employment indicated by the County Court judge was available and also whether it was within his capacity:

The doctor for the employers says that this man can do gardener's work and that it would be admirable for him, and thinks him fit to be engaged in all forms of light work where the ground is level. It does not seem to me necessarily consistent with doing gardener's work . . . these are difficulties which I do not see that the learned County Court Judge has resolved.

It appears to us to be risky, from the point of view of the injured and partially disabled man, to single out certain occupations, e.g. gardening, as particularly 'healthy'. Recent statistics point the other way. The Occupational Mortality Tables, for instance, show that while per 100,000 living the mortality of farmers and agricultural labourers in the age-group 25–35 years is 250 and 268, that of gardeners is 349.[3] What may be an excellent occupation for one liable to lung trouble

---

[1] Cf. vol. i, p. 206.
[2] Cf. *Acton Hall Colliery Co.* v. *Barker*. See Butterworth's *Cases*, vol. xxx, 1938, pp. 89 sqq.
[3] Cf. *Occupational Mortality*, loc. cit., 1938, p. 78.

may be harmful for a rheumatic subject. Spinal arthritis is common 'among labourers, gardeners and those who work with a bent back' and there are 'painful muscular conditions among those who wield shovels or brooms'.[1] The right leg of the man in question had been bowed outward and backward, he walked with a limp and with his right foot somewhat inverted. Was gardening 'of not too arduous a nature', and if available, desirable in the man's interests? In such matters medical opinions frequently conflict. In a recent discussion relating to eye injuries one ophthalmologist, replying to another who had declared 'the occupation of a blacksmith as suitable' for a one-eyed man, declared flatly that 'all work which calls for rapid judgement of distance was unsuitable', and especially that of a blacksmith, and drew attention to the fact that a man who has lost his eye in a factory is more liable to lose the other than is a man with two to lose one.[2] In this as in many other matters opinions expressed by medical men are often tacitly assumed to be those of experts but are not, in fact, based upon experience, 'expertise', or upon a scientific examination of accumulated evidence. Little is known upon the subject and those who know most are not always called as witnesses or available as such.

A firm of solicitors in a Memorandum to the Hetherington Commission declared: 'No one has yet been able to define "Light Work".' And, as has been done more than once, a man walking about on crutches can be certified as fit for 'light work'.[3]

A lecture on 'The One-Eyed Worker in Industry'[4] by Mr. Joseph Minton of the Royal Eye Hospital not only reveals the difficulty of such cases, but also shows the value of scientific experience and research work of the trained specialist. Mr. Minton states that a large number of engineering firms send the one-eyed worker back to his old job of grinding, turning, or drilling almost invariably with success; given the opportunity, and time to adjust themselves, injured workmen of all ages find themselves able to perform their old jobs satisfactorily In other trades, as Mr. Minton shows, conditions are different. The one-eyed workman who cannot revert to his original job is placed in a position of great difficulty. In such cases, says Mr. Minton, the 'right opportunity' must be found and 'careful rehabilitation' is essential, if only in order to overcome the injured man's fear in regard to the limitation of his field of vision and to help him in visual readaptation. For such measures there is at present no legal or financial

---

[1] Cf. Dr. M. B. Bray (Senior Physician British Red Cross Clinic for Rheumatism), *The Treatment of Rheumatism*, Chadwick Lecture 1930, p. 17.

[2] Cf. *Proceedings of the Royal Society of Medicine*, Jan. 14th 1938, vol. xxxi, p. 865.

[3] Cf. *Hetherington Commission*, p. 704.

[4] Cf. J. Minton, *The One-Eyed Worker in Industry*, 1939 (reprint).

provision, the responsibility of employers or insurance offices being discharged by lump-sum payments.[1] Mr. Minton notes that many employers refuse to reinstate men who have lost an eye. He cites the case of a large firm employing 45,000 work-people who insist upon eye-sight tests for all employees and now refuse to employ one-eyed men. A special inquiry made among twenty-seven industrial firms revealed great diversity of procedure. The one-eyed workman can, if properly looked after, generally earn his old wages at his old job but he seldom gets the chance to do so.

Most one-eyed men are greatly handicapped in the labour market because of the added financial risk to which the new employer is exposed in cases of injury to the workmen's remaining good eye and the total incapacity resulting therefrom. In some countries this handicap is avoided by a system whereunder the 'added risk' involved is centrally borne, and does not fall on the last employer. Meanwhile, Mr. Minton urges that the workman should register a Declaration of Liability[2] in all cases of serious injury to, or the loss of, one eye. We doubt, however, whether under the present system it will be possible to follow Mr. Minton's suggestion that the workman should 'return to work, leaving, if necessary, the settlement of his claim to a later date'. It would be both practicable and desirable under alternative systems which we shall discuss later. As things stand at present one-eyed men tend to drift into ill-paid occupations. Mr. Minton is satisfied that 'the deformity caused by the absence of an eye, or the presence of an artificial eye, constitutes the greatest physical handicap in finding employment'. In these circumstances there is clearly a case for compensating eye injuries on some other basis than loss of earning capacity, and for adopting most careful measures of rehabilitation.

These cases, which might be multiplied a hundredfold, show where the difficulties for the injured man may lie. They would be lessened if the review of weekly payments was deferred until he had actually found new work suitable to his partial disablement. This would entail amendment of § 12(3) of the Workmen's Compensation Act; it may appear unfair to burden employers with full weekly payments for disablement where a workman 'might' on his own initiative be able to secure work of some kind according to his partial recovery. On the other hand, great injustice is caused to the workman who may theoretically be capable of working, but is unable in practice to find work adapted to his lowered working capacity. In the case just quoted[3] the

---

[1] Cf. also J. Minton, 'Eye Injuries in Industry', in *Industrial Welfare*, 1939, vol. xxi, no. 249.

[2] Mr. Minton urges that this procedure should be simplified not only in ophthalmological cases but in general.   [3] See p. 186.

County Court judge was satisfied that 'there is, in fact, no light work market offering him any reasonable prospect of obtaining such work with any degree of continuity'. How great then was the injustice to the workman, not from the point of view of the present law as it is, but from that of dire social necessity, when the weekly compensation was reduced to 3s. 11d. The difficulty would be less if there existed in Britain, as in Germany, a statutory body of experts[1] charged with the duty of 'placing' injured men in industry, conversant with the physical as well as the economic possibilities of each case, i.e. working capacity and state of the labour market. The German insurance law expressly empowers *Berufsgenossenschaften* to restore men to full compensation in cases where the 'injured man has been workless without his own fault'; they may do this for a certain period and renew it.[2] In Britain, on the other hand, where a man has been found fit for light work, but has been unable to find employment, the reduced rate only is accorded to him,[3] though it is now for the employer to prove that the workman has *not* taken all the reasonable steps.[4] The possibility of placing upon existing Employment Exchanges the exclusive responsibility for placing partially disabled men should be borne in mind. 'Looking for work', in the literal sense, is a hopeless task, particularly now that workmen tend to live on housing estates twelve miles or more distant from possible employment.

We endorse the proposal made by the T.U.C. before the Hetherington Commission that before reassessing compensation on the basis of partial, instead of total, incapacity, the administrative authority should be satisfied that suitable light work is available in the employment in which the worker was injured or in some other employment suitable to the worker.[5] It should be, however, quite evident, and the point has not been overlooked by the Memorandum, that such duty could hardly be discharged under the existing system, but would require an entirely different machinery of administration.

The whole question of review of weekly payments is closely linked up with the question of medical evidence; here the administrative

---

[1] *Berufsfürsorge*, viz. 'help for getting work'.

[2] Cf. *Reichsversicherungsordnung*, § 562.

[3] Cf. for many examples: *Durham Miners' Association: Report of Proceedings of the Arbitration Committee Meetings*, Durham, 1938, p. 15: 'No suitable light work being available, Stocks now claims full compensation. Awarded compensation at the reduced rate of 10s. per week.' Cf. also ibid., pp. 16, 18, 20, 22. In our vol. i (see pp. 257–8) we have called attention to the progress made in the matter as regards the employee's interest by the decision of the House of Lords in 1938 in the case of *Ingham* v. *Barstow*.

[4] Experience unfortunately shows that employers and insurance officers are very adept in securing the requisite proofs. Cf. also for an interesting case touching on these matters that of *Palmer* v. *Watts, Watts & Co.*, Butterworth, *Cases*, vol. xxx, 1938, pp. 120 sqq.

[5] *Hetherington Commission*, p. 417, § 52.

problem differs little from that which presents itself in respect of other aspects of Workmen's Compensation connected with medical evidence (in the matter of lump-sum settlements for instance, or the conditions of 'incapacity' in general). The statutory ground for review is an alleged change in the workman's physical condition, and this change is in general a matter to be decided upon medical evidence. It is here that the greatest difficulties arise and that possibilities of deception and injustice are latent. In a recent case[1] the solicitors for the employers remarked that 'a workman may go before a medical referee who finds nothing to be wrong and as a consequence his compensation may be ended for all time, although it is subsequently established that he was still suffering from a disease which may ultimately prevent him from working altogether'. This seems not unfamiliar to those dealing with such matters legally, for the solicitors in question remarked 'that may frequently happen'. There had been no application for a declaration of liability made; and as Green M.R. observed, it might have been doubtful whether such a declaration would have been made as this requires a foundation of fact, which, in turn, involves a decision upon an issue of fact, viz. whether or not the disease is likely, in the future, to lead to a decrease of earning capacity. The case is typical of many recorded cases which demonstrate the injustice which may flow from a prognosis which is not borne out by subsequent events.[2] In a recent lecture[3] Dr. R. Fortescue Fox, an authority on rheumatism, declared that 'in later life local strains and injuries are very commonly followed by osteo-arthritis'. Dressmaking, typewriting, laundry work, and charing often tend to develop in women an arthritis in overwrought joints. The injured and 'healed' worker who never expected these and other remote effects of his injury may thus be greatly disappointed by accepting what was considered 'light' and 'suitable' work for him when his weekly payment was reviewed.

Insurance offices, and employers, naturally adduce medical evidence that the workman would soon regain his capacity if he would only make a start; doctors and laymen alike take the view that 'where there's a will there's a way'. They know how easily a man or woman may become bedridden by mere atrophy of the muscles consequent upon lack of will-power. They recognize the significance, in certain cases, of the converse process of faith-healing and the importance of instilling in the patient a feeling of self-confidence and desire for recovery.

They are aware that the return to the discipline of early rising and

---

[1] Cf. Court of Appeal, *Blades* v. *Wool Exchange and General Investments Ltd.*, Nov. 3rd 1937.   [2] Cf., for example, Butterworth, *Cases*, vol. xxx, 1938, pp. 395 sqq.
[3] Cf. Dr. R. Fortescue Fox, *Arthritis in Women*, 1936, p. 19.

long hours of labour at a task which is, in itself, unattractive or distasteful, becomes more difficult the longer it is deferred and that even physically fit men lose the desire to work as well as their ability to do so if they are long absent from work. There is for a short period a sense of release—a feeling of holiday freedom; anxiety and depression set in, followed by a certain loss of mental equilibrium, which is finally stabilized at a new and debased level, in which neither hope nor fear for the future plays a part. A medical officer has noted[1] that the principal effects of prolonged unemployment upon health are 'a subtle undermining of the constitution through lack of physical exertion, the absence of physical stimuli, insufficiently varied diet, and worry'. 'Men often "go to pieces" when long unemployed and become chronically neurasthenic.' Again, 'higher allowances alone will solve very few problems, but low allowances certainly create problems of the kind that we can least afford to create'.[2] It is true that, as noted by Sir John Collie, contributions from clubs and other sources which become payable in consequence of the injury may, together with the weekly compensation, for a brief period approximate to the income received whilst at work. In very rare cases, when the wage earned is very low, the total sums received may exceed it for a brief period. It is true that in such cases there is little inducement to resume work.

The true remedy here lies in intelligent administration of workmen's compensation funds and 'sick clubs' by bodies on which the men themselves, as subscribers, are fully represented. It is the universal experience of firms with contracting-out schemes,[3] and of the smaller Approved Societies, in which the 'friendly' element has not been overlaid, that wage-earning members of local committees are quick to recognize abuse of funds and better able than anyone else to stimulate recipients of sick benefit to make an effort to resume work.

But action on these lines may entail serious injustice unless it is based upon careful and complete diagnosis. The following case is typical of many.

A dock labourer, employed by the Cunard Steamship Company, was totally incapacitated for fourteen months, during which time he received compensation at the rate of 26s. a week. At the end of this period his employers obtained a medical certificate to the effect that the workman had lost the power of gripping with his left hand but would regain this power at work. 'I am satisfied', declared the doctor in his certificate, 'that he could do quite heavy work'. The employers thereupon reduced the weekly payment to 10s. a week on the ground that the incapacity was only partial. Three months later the workman filed

---

[1] Cf. *Men Without Work*, A Report made to the Pilgrim Trust, 1938, p. 137.
[2] Ibid, p. 133. [3] Vol. i, App. I.

a request for arbitration, claiming total incapacity. The employers called the certifying doctor who again declared that the injured man 'could now do full work, but with discomfort, for a fortnight, and with some discomfort for six or eight months, after which it would go. . . . He ought to do full work. He will soon get over the discomfort, but at first he will tire very easily.' Accepting this diagnosis the County Court judge held that the workman had completely recovered and refused an award of compensation. The Court of Appeal reversed the decision on the ground that there was no evidence of complete recovery. Lord Hanworth M.R. said: 'The evidence shows that capacity for work was not the same as that of an ordinary healthy man' and that 'the learned Judge went in advance of what the man could do'. Two years later, in 1935, when the workman was re-examined by specialists and X-ray photographs were taken, it was discovered that he had been more seriously injured than had been apparent two years previously, five fresh fractures being disclosed.[1] The injured man being still incapacitated, applied for a new trial to the County Court judge who refused it on the ground that, with reasonable diligence, the new evidence could have been available at the original hearing; the responsibility for the inadequate presentation of the case rested on the workman and his advisers. The injured man appealed, but the House of Lords held that the County Court judge had rightly exercised his discretion in refusing to grant a new trial. In dismissing the appeal, Scott L.J. said: 'One cannot help feeling sorry for the workman, but it is essential that litigants, plaintiffs and applicants, should not have two bites at a cherry. If unfortunately he [the workman] is wrongly advised [by his doctor] that is no ground for asking a new trial.' Blanesburgh L.J. said: 'There was some evidence upon which the learned Judge could find, as he did, that incapacity from every relevant point of view had ceased. And if so, then whatever might have been my own view, the award must stand; for it is of the first importance that the finality of an arbitrator's findings of fact in cases under this Act should be jealously maintained.'[2]

That the law, as here stated, contrasts sharply with justice, is plain from the facts, and from the expressions of sympathy of the judges. Such cases are bound to occur so long as the forecast by a doctor ranks

[1] The case should prove of great interest to men of the medical profession and referees in particular as casting doubt upon the contention of Dr. M'Kendrick (loc. cit., p. 12) that diagnosis can always be correct, while prognosis is a 'different matter'. It is doubtful whether prognosis based upon diagnosis should play a decisive and final part in Workmen's Compensation.

[2] For particulars of *Moore* v. *Cunard S.S. Co.* and *Cunard S.S. Co.* v. *Moore* : see Butterworth, *Cases*, vol. xxviii, 1936, pp. 162 sqq. and 469 sqq. Also I.L.O., *Legal Decisions on Labour Law*, Geneva, 1937, pp. 74–5; Willis, loc. cit., p. 232.

in this branch of law as a 'fact' upon which a final legal decision can be based. The B.M.A. *Report on Fractures* (1934) shows that such cases are not uncommon. Had the injured man been treated at a special Fracture Clinic or been required to attend a rehabilitation centre, the true nature of his injury would probably have been ascertained in good time, to the benefit of both parties and in the interests of justice. In the apparent absence of such facilities, even in Liverpool, a city famous for the pioneer orthopaedic work of Sir Robert Jones, the true facts were only brought to light by chance, and too late to serve the ends of justice. Under German law[1] a case can only be reviewed if the change in the physical condition is *wesentlich*, viz. of a fundamental character and in no way fluctuating or uncertain. German administrative practice has further stressed that the change must be plainly existent; a probable future amelioration is no sufficient cause for review.

This case is one of many which we could adduce in support of our thesis that the right of review of weekly payments on either side requires, in justice to both sides, fundamental changes in the structure and administration of Workmen's Compensation. It also exemplifies the relative helplessness of the injured man even when, as in this case, he was presumably a member of an important trade union. He finds it difficult to obtain competent and impartial medical advice; and has scarcely less difficulty, unless he belongs to a strong trade union, in obtaining the best legal aid. *The Insurance Mail*[2] was recently asked how a 'labourer in a quarry' who had lost his eye and was having difficulties in recovering damages could get assistance, as his legal advisers 'seemed unable to get a settlement'. The reply was: 'Consult a firm of solicitors who specialize in Workmen's Compensation Claims.' As well recommend a workman suffering from dermatitis to consult a London specialist as the only way to remedy injustice resulting from the diagnosis of inexpert medical referees.[3] Mr. Bowden, giving evidence before the Hetherington Commission for the T.U.C., explained the difficulties arising when a union wishes to confront the doctor of the insurance company, who generally engage a 'doctor of high standing' with another authoritative specialist. 'It is no good putting up a panel doctor against a specialist.' One has to 'produce a doctor of equal standing'. He mentioned a case relating to dermatitis where the union decided to 'have a patch test made of that particular man to find the effect of crude oil on his skin'. There was no doctor to do this in the locality and the man had to be sent to Bristol. The

---

[1] *Reichsversicherungsordnung*, vol. iii, Berlin, 1930, pp. 164–5.
[2] Cf. *Insurance Mail*, May 11th 1938.
[3] Cf. *British Journal of Dermatology*, 1937, pp. 428–9.

specialist asked £10 for appearing at Penzance.[1] A firm of solicitors with a twenty years' experience of Workmen's Compensation practice stated in a Memorandum to the Hetherington Commission that in the north-east district specialists invariably charge a minimum of 10 guineas up to 15 guineas per case. 'The employers call two and sometimes three of these gentlemen and the workman has to follow suit, if he is to have a chance of success.'[2]

The Stewart Committee noted that:

Cases occur from time to time in which the injury sustained may give rise to much more serious consequences than can possibly be ascertained at the time of the accident or, indeed, for some considerable time afterwards. . . . Serious lesions might not be demonstrable until years after the workman's claim for compensation had been settled and, in such a case, where liability had been terminated by decision of the Court or the medical authority, the workman might find himself, although completely incapacitated, without any right of claiming further compensation.[3]

This is also the view of Dr. Brend:[4]

The chief difficulty which occurs in these cases arises not from any fault in the Workmen's Compensation Act, but from general social conditions and from the operation of the Acts. The papers generally reach the Medical Referee much better documented from the point of view of the employer than from that of the workman. The employer's side of the case is usually set forth very fully in a medical report *which has been made by a specialist of standing*, but although these reports are generally very fair they cannot be regarded as necessarily free from bias. The workman may have no medical statement to support his case, or he may have a few brief lines from his panel doctor.

This statement fully explains the situation. The law does not protect the injured man against errors of his medical or legal advisers. That such errors should sometimes occur is inevitable; but it does not follow that the whole burden should be borne by the injured person and that there should be no means of reopening his case. The late Sir Thomas Legge held strongly that some industrial maladies 'may not cause incapacity until ten or more years'.[5] This should be borne in mind when the matter of review arises.

Apart from any major changes in the structure of the existing system, §§ 29 and 30 of the Workmen's Compensation Act, whereunder

[1] Cf. *Hetherington Commission*, Q. 4880–1.

[2] Cf. ibid., p. 705, also Q. 6754–5.

[3] Cf. *Stewart Report*, pp. 82–3. An interesting case where a man developed epilepsy by an injury to his head was mentioned by Mr. Quin before the Hetherington Commission (A. 4051); the Report from the employer's doctor was rejected by another medical officer 'who definitely stated that in his opinion it was a condition arising out of the accident'.

[4] Cf. Brend, loc. cit., p. 82. Dr. Brend is Gold Medallist in State Medicine, University of London; Barrister-at-Law; Lecturer in Forensic Medicine, Charing Cross Hospital.

[5] Cf. Legge, loc. cit., p. 34.

acceptance of one payment under award precludes a workman from appeal, urgently require amendment. They were in the Act of 1906; and have been the subject of many judicial decisions. Their weaknesses have long been apparent and very recently several Lords Justices of the Court of Appeal have expressed in strong language their regret at being bound by decisions based thereon, though the law cannot be regarded as finally settled as the House of Lords have not yet come to a decision. Acceptance of one weekly payment under an award precludes a man from appealing on the ground that the award is inadequate.[1]

The *Evaluation Report* of the I.L.O. has something of importance to say as regards the English procedure in the review of weekly payments. It notes that in Germany and in the Scandinavian countries there must be a 'substantial' or 'material' change in the condition of the injured man. The British Act also recognizes that the restarting of work should not mean casual employment or temporary employment,[2] but this safeguard seems in practice to afford little protection to the worker. The *Evaluation Report* stresses that the recovery of the worker must be really lasting and notes that § 12 of the British Workmen's Compensation Act provides that the resumption of work should be taken as a proof of permanent readaptation.

Although, generally speaking, it may be regarded as reasonable to allow review in the event of successful readaptation to another occupation, due caution should be observed when the claim for review is based solely on this ground. Although the worker may have acquired new abilities, his infirmity remains, and it is probable that sooner or later a conjunction of unfavourable circumstances will throw him back into the ranks of the disabled. . . .

From the medico-legal standpoint it is not desirable to introduce by law or regulation a general or absolute limit for the period of review, to be applied to all cases.[3]

The *Evaluation Report* thus follows Sir Thomas Legge's views. But it also suggests that the bodies responsible for evaluating incapacity should have the right, in individual cases, to decide that the evaluation may be no longer subject to review when they have satisfied themselves that the incapacity is permanent. The beneficiary, however, should have a right of appeal against any such decision.[4] This would prevent injustices such as occurred in the case of *Moore* v. *Cunard S.S. Co.*, detailed above. The *Evaluation Report* also notes that under the German system the 'competent authority' frequently does not consider it necessary to have recourse to a medical examination in certain cases where the

---

[1] Cf. *Lissenden* v. *C. A. V. Bosch Ltd.*, *The Times*, Dec. 8th 1938.
[2] Cf. Willis, loc. cit., p. 333.
[3] Cf. *Evaluation Report*, pp. 209–10.   [4] Cf. ibid., p. 360.

question is at stake whether habituation has resulted in reducing incapacity, and is content to base its findings on 'general experience'. Such a procedure has much to commend it, on grounds of economy as well as justice, if the tribunal enjoys the confidence of the injured person and is empowered to administer the law with due regard to social and economic aspects of each case, without debarring the injured person from appealing if a further deterioration in his physical condition should supervene. But this would entail fundamental changes in the existing system of Workmen's Compensation.

PART III

RESTORATION TO HEALTH AND REHABILITATION

The objects of treatment in a case of industrial injury should be to carry out all necessary surgical and medical measures so as to secure the repair of the damaged part as quickly and as completely as possible, and then to do what may be necessary to replace the workman in remunerative employment—at his former job if possible or, if the nature of the injury does not permit of this, in some other appropriate occupation, for which he may first have to be trained.   DONALD C. NORRIS.

CHAPTER XI

RESTORATION TO HEALTH

'Granted the maze, the unwieldiness, the overlap, the uneconomy, the lack of integration of our Health Services as they at present exist, we should remember certain facts in connexion with them which should go to hearten us a little, and help us to endure all the criticism—healthy, well-meant, and largely justified.'—LORD HORDER.

WE have already dwelt upon the importance of the medical aspect of Workmen's Compensation. It is a dominant but incalculable factor in the Law Courts, where medical witnesses under cross-examination give reasons for their diagnosis and prognosis, and the weight of medical evidence tends to be found on the side which pays best. Where capacity for work is the issue, medical evidence is generally decisive. With these legal aspects of the medical problem of restoration to health of an injured person we are not here concerned; the problem before us is yet wider, viz. the active role of the State, or of *ad hoc* agencies, in restoring health to injured workmen.[1] Our task is to show how far 'recovery', as we shall hereafter term it, should play its part within the framework of Workmen's Compensation.

The British legislature has not yet even considered extending Compensation law to include provision for treatment. The law merely requires that the injured workman should receive some financial recompense. The idea that cash payments should be a secondary factor and restoration of the workman to health and occupational fitness the primary consideration, has not until recently been seriously considered by Trade Unions or by students of the subject.[2] This attitude of mind to-day finds few defenders.

Apart from the restricted and unequal extensions of medical benefit provided by those Approved Societies which possess available surplus funds—and not

---

[1] The State on its own behalf, or autonomous agencies acting on behalf of the State, the workman, and the employer, where such exist, may bring to public notice the latest fruits of science and pathology, or develop existing and create new institutions in which they can be applied. In this treatise, the scope of which is social and economic, we cannot enter the sphere of purely medical discussion.

[2] Cf. Sir Arnold Wilson, M.P., *Debates H.C.*, Nov. 19th 1937, col. 771: 'The primary basis of Workmen's Compensation should be rehabilitation. We should say to the workman, "Our first job is to make you fit again, and make you fit we will if by any means we can, before we discuss compensation. Treatment for your injury which will restore you to the category of regular wage-earners will be followed by training in a new job and, finally, by placement in suitable employment." '

completely supplied even by these exceptional societies—medical benefits under National Health Insurance are incomplete in certain serious respects.[1]

The Poor Law Act of 1930 requires local authorities to relieve the indigent poor who for any reason are incapable of work, but not all can, and some perhaps cannot, properly perform this statutory duty. 'What Glasgow can do is one thing, what Caithness can do is another.'[2]

In this respect the British system stands almost alone, for all great industrial countries, and many others, have long ago done something, often much, to connect medical care with compensation. In Germany, as we have seen, free medical attendance, including hospital treatment, has from the outset been provided to injured persons under the Workmen's Compensation Insurance Law, as now also in the U.S.A., where medical, surgical, and hospital treatment and medicine are provided in all States, though in a few cases the workman pays a small part of the cost.

In Canada conditions are not quite uniform, but in all cases of disability, including those for which no cash benefit is payable, medical benefits are granted, comprising full medical and surgical treatment, nursing, and the supply of artificial limbs and apparatus. Dental treatment is given in Ontario; medicines in Alberta, British Columbia, Manitoba, and Quebec. Artificial limbs, &c., are in all provinces kept in repair, usually for one year. In Nova Scotia, however, medical benefits are limited to thirty days.

In Australia conditions vary. Employees of the Commonwealth receive the cost of reasonably necessary medical, surgical, and hospital treatment not exceeding £100. In N.S. Wales the cost of medical treatment, hospital treatment, or ambulance services, including the supply of artificial limbs, &c., medical and surgical supplies or curative apparatus is included in the benefits, subject to maximum limits. All States have made far-reaching regulations for medical benefits in the case of such industrial diseases as lead poisoning and silicosis. In Queensland, S. Australia, Tasmania, and Victoria no benefits in kind are given; in Western Australia medical benefits are included up to a certain sum.

The Union of South Africa has introduced medical benefits by the Workmen's Compensation Act, 1934, § 55 (1), including the supply and repair of artificial limbs and apparatus, to a maximum of £100.

In France free medical and hospital treatment for injured workmen

---

[1] Cf. Newsholme, loc. cit., p. 142 and Norris, *Industrial Accidents*, p. 129. Dr. Norris states that the facilities for rehabilitation 'are extremely defective in Great Britain'.

[2] Mr. J. N. Beckett, Asst. Sec. Ministry of Health, *Hetherington Commission*, Q. 2003–4 A.

is compulsory, as also in Belgium persons, where injured as the result of industrial accidents, are entitled to medicaments and medical treatment including artificial limbs and orthopaedic appliances. In Japan medical treatment is included in benefits: in cases of permanent incapacity an injured person may receive medical treatment for three years under Factory or Mining Rules or for one year under the Workmen's Compensation Act, after which the employer can redeem his liability by a lump-sum payment.[1]

The U.S.S.R. is the only country in which an injured workman is offered medical services at the entire charge of the State.[2] Medical benefit, preventive and curative, is administered by the Commissariats of Public Health of the Federal Republics, which are required to organize a medical service for the whole population including insured persons, persons incapable of working, pensioned workers, and their families. The law requires every available form of medical benefit (attendance by physicians and surgeons, special orthopaedic treatment, artificial limbs, &c., hospital treatment, preventive measures in sanatoria, &c.) to be granted free of charge, the cost being met in part from social insurance funds. Some sanatoria and most 'homes of rest' belong to the equivalent in the U.S.S.R. of trade unions. Workers and salaried employees sent to sanatoria and health resorts receive cash benefit for temporary incapacity during the treatment and the journey.[3] We have no information as to how these schemes work in practice or how far they exist on paper only.

In Poland all victims of industrial accidents are entitled to the necessary medical and surgical treatment and drugs, the cost being at first borne by sick benefit societies and later by accident insurance institutions. In Switzerland benefits in kind are extensive, comprising medical attendance and drugs, the provision and renewal of appliances, any nursing needed, and free transport if required; so also in Denmark, where insurance institutions supply dressings, artificial limbs, spectacles, invalid chairs, and other appliances necessary to ensure successful medical treatment and to diminish the effect of accidents or increase capacity of work. Special additional treatment, such as physiotherapeutical treatment, is provided.[4]

It is not our task here to consider these measures of medical assistance towards recovery from the point of view of 'benefit'; we have already done so (cf. p. 97 sqq.) when discussing the problem of benefits under Workmen's Compensation in general, and have noted how disadvantageous British Workmen's Compensation law must appear to

---

[1] Cf. for these details I.L.O., *International Survey of Social Services*, vol. i *passim*, Geneva, 1936. [2] Cf. Norris, loc. cit., p. 129.

[3] Cf. *International Survey*, vol. 1, p. 631. [4] Cf. ibid., vol. ii, *passim*.

the impartial student. Apart, however, from economic and social aspects, there is another important factor to be considered. Effective medical treatment may greatly expedite recovery and thus diminish the cash cost of compensation. This is the question which here concerns us. It is bad enough for the injured workman and his family that he should be left to bear the financial burden of his recovery (apart from medical benefits to which he may be entitled under National Health Insurance[1]) where medical benefit under Workmen's Compensation is lacking. His position is worse still when he cannot obtain proper medical treatment. Many insured persons are subscribing members of Hospital Savings Associations, but this is no guarantee of proper medical treatment. 'It is clearly desirable', writes Dr. Norris,

that in every case [of industrial injury] treatment should be planned as a whole from the beginning, and should be carried out under the uninterrupted control of a surgeon who has special experience in industrial practice, and who is familiar with the physical requirements of industry, aided by such specialists as may be required.

He deprecates the lack of such planning and notes that 'as a rule' there is little or no continuity of control, the patient being left to find his way from one institution to another or from one to another independent doctor in the same institution, as from the wards to the massage department. A recent B.M.A. publication stresses the same fact:

The individual passes from local authority to voluntary body, from consulting room to clinic or hospital, from private to official doctor and often back again, to obtain from many unrelated agencies a service which could be more efficiently provided as one co-ordinated whole.[2]

This criticism applies even where State assistance in the matter of medical treatment exists; the lack of medical co-ordination, and of correct and efficient treatment is still more pronounced where, as in the case of Workmen's Compensation, the injured man is normally left to his own penurious devices. The need for such co-ordination is now widely accepted even in Britain. One witness before the Hetherington Commission suggested that a Compensation Officer, acting in conjunction with a Medical Board, would, as a matter of course, arrange for an early examination of the injured workman by a Medical Officer. As in analogous cases under the Regional Medical Service of the Ministry of Health, the examining doctor would be supplied with such information on the case as the panel doctor and the industrial

---

[1] The income limit for National Health Insurance is £250; that of the Workmen's Compensation Act (for non-manual workers) £350.

[2] Cf. *A General Medical Service for the Nation*, B.M.A., April 1938, p. 7. Cf. also an interesting little pamphlet by F. M. Doughty, *The Legacy of a Fracture*, published by F. M. Doughty, 34 Fentiman Road, London, S.W. 8, 1937.

medical officer, if any, possessed.[1] The Medical Card kept for all
patients under the Health Insurance Acts would, *if properly maintained*,
serve a useful purpose in this connexion.[2]

Of recent years doctors have stressed the importance of continuity
of treatment. To some extent it can be secured by better organization,
but it is not reasonable to expect that it can be achieved wholly through
the agency of existing voluntary hospitals. Special institutions such as
the Astley-Ainslie Institution of Edinburgh will be necessary in large
industrial centres.[3]

Recovery proper is achieved in two stages:

(1) preliminary, including first aid; and
(2) final.

The last-named consists in the occupational or vocational rehabilitation
of the injured or diseased—and embraces the restoration of the patient
to his position as a useful member of society.

First aid. The *Holman Gregory Report* emphasized the importance
of first aid in preventing trivial injuries from developing into serious
cases, and in mitigating the effects of serious accidents, thus expediting
return to work.[4] The Chief Inspector stated lately that in the larger
factories the standard of first aid is slowly improving.[5] The Mines
Commission has also made recommendations on this subject which
have been accepted in principle. Particular attention was drawn to

[1] Cf. *Hetherington Commission*, Q. 1754–6. Such procedure resembles the medical
organization of compensation treatment by the German *Berufsgenossenschaften* who employ an 'interim' doctor—see further below, p. 215. See also Memorandum of the T.U.C.,
§ 64. 3 for a similar proposal.   [2] Ibid., Q. 1842–4.

[3] For latest discussion of the matter by medical men: Dr. A. W. Sheen, 'The Return to
Work of the Injured Colliery Workman', *B.M.J.* (*Supplement*), Mar. 26th 1938, pp. 153
sqq., in particular his recommendations as to 'industrial accident hospitals'. The importance
of continuity of treatment is implicit in Dr. Henry H. Jordan's *Orthopaedic Appliances*, New
York, 1939. He urges that the surgeon ought to be familiar with the technique of manufacture and the character of materials used in orthopaedic appliances. Treatment should be
undertaken by a single specialist and continued until the injured person returns to work.
Cf. pp. vii and 7. Cf. also Sir Morton Smart, in the *Journal of the Royal Institute of Public
Health and Hygiene*, July 1939.

[4] Cf. *Report*, p. 50. The Act of 1923 included important enactments as regards first-aid
and ambulance facilities (§ 29), particularly as to the provision and maintenance of first-aid
boxes and cupboards. Under the Factories Act, 1937, first-aid requirements must be
available whether or not mechanical power is used: a first-aid box or cupboard of a prescribed standard is required for each factory and more than one if over 150 persons are
employed at a time; each box must be in charge of a responsible person, whose name must
be posted in each workroom for which the box is provided and who must always be readily
available. If more than 50 persons are employed in a factory every such person must be
trained in first-aid treatment under § 45 of the Factories Act, 1937. If, however, there
is an ambulance room at the factory the Chief Inspector may grant exemption from the
requirements.   [5] Cf. *Report for 1936*, p. 57.

Dr. S. W. Fisher's statement that at one of the German mines he visited every man employed was being trained in first aid, while at another every employee was given a small booklet containing elementary instruction in first aid. These observations by a visiting Englishman remind us of those made almost a hundred years ago by Tremenheere (cf. our vol. i, pp. 22–8) who also tried to impress upon his countrymen the value of German industrial safety provisions. The Mines Commission also proposed the compulsory appointment of a qualified doctor to exercise general supervision over collieries, and to advise the owner in relation thereto. The Commission added that it would be an excellent thing if arrangements could be made for the same doctor to attend to all cases of injury requiring medical attention before the injured man is sent away from the mine.[1]

Employers increasingly recognize the value of ambulance rooms and trained attendants, and local National Safety First Association competitions help to stimulate general interest in first aid. While, however, there is no evidence of bad results due to the neglect of treatment for major accidents, minor injuries are neglected, and are apt to become septic, necessitating absence from work for more than three days.[2] This natural tendency to neglect minor injuries can only be overcome by steady pressure. It is well in this connexion to remember that liability to sepsis is in general in inverse proportion to physical health. The Chief Inspector notes that only large establishments can afford whole-time medical officers, but urges that in the grouping of smaller works for the purpose, each firm should contribute *pro rata*.[3] The Miners' Welfare Fund already maintains ambulances, and some colliery companies and a few large concerns own their ambulances.[4]

A cognate problem confronts us in the treatment of industrial disease. In the case of an accident, the fact of injury—though not its exact nature—is usually evident and the task of first aid is to apply remedial measures, however rudimentary. The existence or onset of industrial disease is difficult to discover or is reported too late. Fractures,

---

[1] Cf. *Rayal Commission on Safety in Mines, Report*, 1938, pp. 444 sqq. Also Dr. Norris, *Industrial Accidents*, 1938, p. 129: 'treatment should be planned as a whole from the beginning'.

[2] Cf. *Report of Chief Inspector of Factories for 1937*, p. 71.

[3] Several German Mutual Indemnity Associations have created and administer first-aid and ambulance stations. There are five such ambulatoria in Berlin, one in Hanover, all serving the purpose of particular associations, and one in Bremen created by several associations in common. These institutions, however, also cover other medical treatment apart from first aid.

[4] Cf. PEP, *British Health Services 1937*, p. 265. The allocations made up to the end of 1934 for ambulance services by the Miners' Welfare Fund amounted to £120,927. Cf. *Miners' Welfare Fund Report 1937*, p. 21.

fresh wounds, and other injuries by accidents cannot be concealed nor can treatment be postponed. In the case of industrial disease the onset may be slow and almost painless, and 'first aid' may not seem urgent.

In regard to nystagmus, for example, the Medical Research Council reported in 1932 that

In spite of the belief that the 'neurotic' patient is too ready to talk about his symptoms, it must be emphasized that many symptoms are withheld for fear of ridicule, and these very symptoms are the ones that matter most. A man with claustrophobia[1] or severe fear of the dark, for example, is incapacitated by it from working down the pit, but will rarely tell of it unless he feels sure that it will be granted as much validity as his bodily pains, his headaches and insomnia.

Stress is often laid on psychological factors in the treatment of this disease and regret expressed that the first symptoms are frequently concealed.[2] This tendency is aggravated in cases of nystagmus, by several exceptional factors. The disorder in many cases never reaches the stage of causing even temporary incapacity for work underground, so it is hard for the sufferer himself to find out at an early stage whether his *malaise* is or is likely to prove a serious malady. His condition may be merely 'nystagmic' but eligible for compensation. Yet such a case might develop, while fear of losing employment underground or anywhere else—once they have obtained a certificate of disablement—deters workmen from giving early expression to their fears.[3] Diagnosis is difficult and requires examination not only by an ophthalmologist but also, in view of possible concomitant neurosis, by a physician.[4] Such developments should be recognized and contentious procedure avoided as far as possible.

The Stewart Committee recommended the replacement of Referees by Medical Boards which would supervise every case continuously and thus 'reassure workmen as to the true nature of the disease'. Such 'first-aid' measures, applied from the outset, would go far to secure better and more efficient recovery.

The same applies to other diseases. Lead poisoning may be contracted in many ways which are 'unfortunately not always realized in time'. The number of notified cases of chrome ulceration has recently increased because notification was made immediately after diagnosis. Much is done to provide early detection and early treatment of cancer of the scrotum and bladder, but the importance of early treatment of

---

[1] Cf. also Brend, loc. cit., p. 43.

[2] Cf. *Third Report of the Miners' Nystagmus Committee*, Medical Research Council, 1932, pp. 12–14.

[3] Cf. *Stewart Report*, pp. 3, 4, 17, and 21. A witness mentioned this as one of the reasons for the recent fall in the number of certificates issued in Scotland.

[4] Cf. ibid., p. 108.

minor injuries in order to ward off dermatitis is still not sufficiently understood.[1]

The early treatment of silicosis and other dust diseases, leading to phthisis and other maladies, presents many difficulties. Viewed as an industrial 'injury', the disability caused by silicosis is, in the majority of cases, not stationary but develops erratically and, in general, gradually. The significance of silicosis in early stages is, as was pointed out before the Silicosis Conference at Johannesburg in 1930 'not what it is at the moment but what it may become'.[2] The average expectation of life of an early case of the disease when first notified is about fourteen years, with a wide variation above and below the average.

In the early stages, in which disability is either absent or not serious, the real problem is less medical than economic—viz. that of securing alternative employment. Only at a later stage does it become one of permanent disability.[3] Early detection is here particularly urgent, and has been stressed by medical authorities, who have not, however, inquired whether and, if so, why the workman himself ignores the onset of the disease. Neither the Johannesburg Conference of 1930, nor the I.L.O. Report on Workmen's Compensation for Silicosis of 1937, dealt with this aspect of the matter. Prof. J. S. Haldane urged that no diagnosis of silicosis was complete 'without the knowledge of the man's history'.[4] Such a record should explain why the workman did not seek relief at the early stage of the malady. Was it ignorance, or fear of losing his job, or anxiety lest loss of his regular work—and a low rate of compensation—would bring ruin to him and his home? Or was it the fear that his claim might be rejected or might lead to fruitless litigation? Or was it a manifestation of that form of courage which Sir Philip Sidney called 'the confidence of men unwonted to be overcome', the indomitable spirit of optimism which animates the vast majority of mankind?

[1] Cf. Report of Chief Inspector of Factories for 1937, pp. 55, 57–8, and 66. 'The importance of treatment of minor injuries as a preventive of dermatitis is still not sufficiently appreciated. A woman aged 49 employed on a bottle-washing tank containing weak alkali scratched her leg on a packing case and the drip from her oilskin apron entered the wound. She did not seek first-aid treatment. Four days later the superficial injury was healed but dermatitis made its appearance a few weeks later on the site of the injury.' Further instances are given on pp. 67 sqq.

[2] Cf. I.L.O., Silicosis, Geneva, 1930, p. 25.

[3] Cf. ibid., p. 689. 'The ante-primary stage of silicosis is not associated with any apparent impairment of the capacity for work.' 'The primary stage of silicosis is associated with some impairment of the capacity for work although the impairment is not of a serious and permanent nature. In the great majority of instances the reduced capacity for work is not admitted by the man himself; he is usually, to all appearances, in vigorous health.'

[4] Cf. Silicosis and Coal Mining. The Institution of Mining Engineers. Excerpt from the Transactions, vol. lxxx, part 5. Reprint 1931.

The importance of early treatment of silicosis and asbestosis is accepted, though the Mines Commission left it to the Industrial Pulmonary Committee of the Medical Research Council to make recommendations.[1] Representatives of colliery managers and workmen opposed a general system of medical examination, except for young persons engaged in mines, as in factories. Such examinations would only partly fall under 'first aid', but might help to explain why, in many cases, 'first aid' has been shunned. Apart from the question of general medical examinations of miners—which is largely a matter of 'accident prevention'—little if any inquiry has been made as to why men are so unwilling to invoke medical assistance at the early stages of a disease, though this tendency is far commoner, and its medical effects more injurious, than 'malingering' which medical authorities, already quoted, agree in regarding as very infrequent.[2]

The detection and treatment of industrial disease in its earliest stages can be promoted by legislation. Workers in certain processes must be examined medically when first employed, and at intervals thereafter.[3] Periodical examinations at the works enable incipient cases of silicosis and asbestosis to be detected; if the workman is then refused, or voluntarily abandons, further employment in a dusty process, further development of the disease may be arrested.[4]

No progress has yet been made in applying this principle to nystagmus, one of the most formidable of industrial diseases. The Stewart Committee and the B.M.A. have reached divergent conclusions, which we here summarize:

A. *Recommendations of Stewart Committee*

1. The Medical Board should have power in certain circumstances to declare men under 30 to be unsuitable for further employment at

---

[1] Cf *Report on Safety in Coal Mines*, 1938, pp. 468–9.

[2] An interesting table taken from a Swedish source showing the effect of early treatment of rheumatism on the process of recovery was given by Dr. R. Fortescue Fox in a recent lecture. It showed that restoration of normal or reduced ability to work within five years after 'cure' resulted in 79 per cent. of cases, if the treatment was begun within one year after the first symptoms occurred, in 56 per cent. of cases after a period of 1–3 years, and in only 50 per cent. of cases where treatment was begun after a period of more than 3 years. The importance of treatment at initial stages cannot be overestimated. Cf. Fox, loc. cit., 1936, p. 34.

[3] Cf. *Silicosis and Asbestosis (Medical Arrangements) Scheme*, 1931, §§ 12 and 13 as amended by the Scheme of 1934. The requirements apply to the processes in the Refractories, Sandstone, and Pottery industries which are set out in the Schedule to the Scheme of 1934; as regards asbestosis these periodical examinations are obligatory for workmen employed in the process of breaking, crushing, disintegrating, opening, or grinding asbestos, and in the mixing of asbestos textiles and insulating mattresses.

[4] Cf. also Memorandum of the Home Office, *Silicosis and Asbestosis*, 1935, pp. 9 and 13.

the coal face; in the case of older men found to be unsuitable for work at the coal face they should be advised against continuing such work.

2. For men who may elect to leave industry, facilities should be available at the training or instructional centres maintained by the Ministry of Labour.

B. *Recommendations of B.M.A.*

Cases examined by the Medical Board should be classified as follows:

1. Wholly incapacitated but likely eventually to resume their previous work.	Such cases should be re-examined at intervals with a view to an early return to work. A man should not remain idle for more than six months.
2. Wholly incapacitated and unsuitable for further employment in the industry.	Such cases should include those fit for training at vocational centres, and those who are too old, i.e. over 50. Rehabilitation centres should be established.
3. Partially incapacitated.	Surface work should be found for these. Cases should be re-examined at intervals. Periods of light surface work should be given.
4. Not incapacitated.	These cases should return to work underground but not immediately to the coal face. In the event of a relapse they should be certified.

The *Stewart Report*[1] did not accept these recommendations. While 'unable to disregard this volume of medical testimony' they declared that 'in view of the information before us that by no means all work underground is performed under conditions capable of giving rise to miner's nystagmus . . . some less drastic measure than that suggested should suffice'.

Reference should be made in this connexion to the Workmen's Compensation Acts (1925–34) Amendment Bill,[2] which was strongly opposed by nearly all miners' representatives, and withdrawn on Nov. 11th 1938. It would have replaced a single referee by two men, sitting as a Board, but their powers under § 7 (1) would have been mainly advisory. Their task would have been to examine workmen, to issue certificates in relation to claims for compensation, to supervise workmen entitled to compensation, and to arrange for periodical medical examinations. They were further to give advice with respect

[1] Cf. p. 35. Cf. also *Transactions of the Ophthalmological Society*, vol. lix, 1939, pp. 749 sqq.

[2] It was a Private Member's Bill, though drafted with the assistance of the Home Office.

to nystagmus and as to suitable employment for any workmen examined by them. Provision for medical rehabilitation, to which the
B.M.A. attached such importance, found no place in the Bill, which
was primarily concerned with the payment of compensation to, and not
the rehabilitation of, the workman, although rehabilitation by provision
of work is recognized to be of outstanding importance in cases of
nystagmus. We do not underestimate the difficulties of the problem.
The question whether 'recovery' has taken place or whether a legacy
of 'susceptibility' remains is one upon which experienced ophthalmic
surgeons and practitioners differ profoundly.[1]

This fact should not, however, deter us from devising measures for
early treatment. The reliability of medical examinations might be usefully estimated on the lines recently adopted by the *Examination of
Examinations* made by Sir Philip Hartog under the auspices of the
Carnegie Trust. A large and representative sample of cases of
nystagmus might be dealt with by several ophthalmic surgeons of
experience, each acting independently of the other, and their reports
correlated. Apart from this a fresh statistical examination might be
made of as many cases of nystagmus as possible. A fresh analysis by
age, by occupation, working conditions, temperature, depth, &c., by
the length of time worked, with due reference to general health, might
produce important results. In any event, however, it is certain that
effective rehabilitation, including provision for finding suitable employment, must precede any serious attempt to tackle this most intractable problem.

In considering existing arrangements for recovery, in the proper
sense of the word, of injured workmen, i.e. after first-aid treatment and
apart from first-stage measures, we must recall that the *Holman
Gregory Report*[2] recommended that, apart from such medical benefits
as may be available under the National Health Insurance Scheme,
injured workmen should be able to command the services of expert
physicians and surgeons, hydro-therapeutic treatment and other kinds
of treatment, not requiring residence of the patient in the hospital or in
another residential institution, and other aids to 'recovery'. The
Committee suggested that a comprehensive scheme on these lines
should be worked out under the guidance of the Workmen's Compensation Commissioner. By refusing to appoint such an official, the
Government of the day seem effectively to have prevented progress on
such lines. As things stand, recovery is often retarded because the

---

[1] Cf. *Stewart Report*, loc. cit., p. 109. Cf. also for a full description: *Report of the Committee on the Diagnosis and Certification of Miners' Nystagmus*, B.M.A., London, 1936,
passim.

[2] See our vol. i, pp. 196–7.

workman is unable . . . to pay for treatment out of his compensation money.[1]

The surgeon responsible for the primary treatment and the early remedial stages is unable to secure for his patient a full restoration of working capacity, mainly because the limit of his hospital facilities has been reached.[2]

An important step towards finding a remedy for these deficiencies was taken when, on July 26th 1933, the Council of the B.M.A. appointed a Committee 'to consider the existing arrangements for the treatment of fractures and other associated injuries of the limbs and to make recommendations for possible improvement therefor'.[3] The Committee estimated that the proportion of fractures to total injuries varies for the different industries between 1·5 per cent. in the case of mines and quarries to 5 per cent. in the case of railways. In the heavy industries the percentage goes up to 8–10[4], though most of the injuries in question are trivial, while the proportion of fractures to major injuries is 'very high'. It also notes that as fractures constitute the more serious of industrial accidents, the cost of compensation represents a much higher proportionate percentage of the total cost. We, too, have found that comparisons of general percentages are often misleading and that only the differential grouping of injuries according to the periods of disability involved is of any practical value. The Report, however, shows conclusively that among industrial injuries fractures are of outstanding importance and require particular attention.

The main results of the Committee's inquiry were disquieting. It had carefully investigated the fracture services of the large hospitals in this country; the replies recorded to their questionnaire showed that 'in the majority of cases there is no efficient organization'.[5] Fracture cases were admitted to the general wards, in charge of surgeons who rarely had at their disposal the experienced technical assistance required. The actual care of the fractures often devolved upon a house-surgeon 'who lacks the knowledge and experience required for their adequate treatment'. Lack of unity of treatment is repeatedly stressed:

As a rule, on leaving the ward, the patient is referred to a massage department under the charge of a different officer, who has taken no share in the earlier treatment. Union of the fracture is thus the signal for a complete break in the

---

[1] Dr. Norris, *Industrial Accidents*, p. 129.

[2] Evidence of the Joint Committee of the T.U.C. and the B.M.A. to the Delevingne Committee. This evidence was not printed.

[3] Cf. *Report of the Committee on Fractures*, B.M.A., Feb. 1935. The Committee did not deal exclusively with fractures coming under the Workmen's Compensation Statute, but also with road accidents; but the former played by far the most important part in the Report.   [4] Cf. ibid., p. 7.   [5] Cf. ibid., pp. 13 sqq.

continuity of treatment; those responsible for the initial treatment do not know the end-results of their cases; and those who see the end-results do not know how the cases were treated in the early stages. There is no one individual to follow the case from start to finish and to feel pride or disappointment in the final result.

These remarks relate only to the medical or pathological side of the picture. The effect upon the injured workman of the mistaken treatment of a fracture is illustrated by the case of *Moore* v. *Cunard S.S. Co.* (p. 192). In a recent case before the Court of Appeal a man was stated to have been treated after a relatively slight accident for what his doctor and the injured man himself believed to be a strained cartilage due to the accident. Later on it became evident that he was suffering from a tubercular knee-joint. The employers did not succeed with their appeal against the workman's claim based on his failure to make a claim within six months, but the case once more clearly showed how litigation may arise from a mistaken diagnosis which, in turn, may be the result of the lack of examination by what the B.M.A. calls 'experienced technical assistance'.[1] No one, in any country, is immune from the possible consequences of incorrect diagnosis or treatment of injuries. Mistakes are bound to occur from time to time: the aim of the State should be to ensure that, in cases within the scope of Workmen's Compensation, the best expert treatment should be available.[2] It is of even greater importance to a manual than to a non-manual worker; the psychological effect of an injury upon a man with small educational resources, whose horizon is limited by his craft, is far greater than upon men of education and talent.

The B.M.A. Committee, which sat under the Chairmanship of H. S. Souttar, M.D., F.R.C.S., noted that incapacity remains permanently in only a small fraction of cases—1 per cent. of 276 cases statistically recorded—where patients are treated in organized clinics; the risk of permanent disablement is far greater—37 per cent. out of the same number—where patients are not so treated. Incapacity lasted three times longer in unorganized than in organized clinics. If the 276 cases had been treated in well-organized clinics their incapacity period would have conformed to the average; the aggregate period of incapacity would have been 4,440 weeks against 13,206 weeks. Weekly compensation payments would have been about £7,000 instead of about £20,000 (both figures exclude lump sums payable in

---

[1] Cf. *Fitchett* v. *C. D. Holmes Ltd.*, Butterworth's *Cases*, 1938, pp. 289 sqq.

[2] Complaints were made before the Hetherington Commission that it frequently happens that injuries on ships are not entered in the log, so that if an injury or disease later on takes an unexpected development for the worse the position of the claimant becomes difficult. It was proposed to have a record of issues from the ship's medicine chest, cf. A. 4518.

the cases of permanent disablement). The Committee further estimated that inappropriate treatment had cost the injured workmen £22,000 in wages, through delay in restoration of regular wage-earning capacity. These figures are some indication of the vast aggregate waste, private and national, of time, money, and physical stamina involved by the existing lack of system.

The Committee mentions a company which arranged for its patients to be treated by an organized fracture service, with the result that the average period of incapacity for wrist fractures was reduced from 23 to 5 weeks and, despite special expenses for travelling and treatment, the cost per case was reduced from £117 to £19. These figures should suffice to convince employers that 'there is money in' the application of medical science and skill to their 'hands'.

It is depressing to learn that 'in most hospitals the organization and continuity of success' in regard to fracture service 'are almost entirely lacking'. One of the most effectively organized fracture clinics in Europe is Boehler's famous Austrian Clinic. It consists of a hospital of 120 beds, with operating theatres, X-ray department, laboratory, lecture rooms, and out-patient department, staffed by six whole-time qualified assistants. It is entirely supported by insurance companies, who have found that, thanks to the shortness of invalidity and completeness of recovery, it has saved them money. The B.M.A. are rightly envious of the achievements of this institution.[1]

In the U.S.A. fracture cases in workmen are becoming increasingly serious, and the American College of Surgeons has formed a Committee on Traumatic Surgery to improve matters. This body deals among other things with the following subjects: type of surgeons in traumatic work, noting the development of clinics operated by insurers, such as the large clinic in Boston equipped with all modern facilities; study of the failure of insurance companies to retain good surgeons, which 'is remedied in large part, but at times retarded by, "free choice" ' of physicians; recommendations relating to improving consulting services; increasing scope of Compensation Acts; use of proper hospitals and proper use of hospitals; education of medical profession in compensation work. The American College of Surgeons recommends that all hospitals treating traumatic cases be approved by the College. The doctor should be experienced in traumatic surgery, accurate records must be kept, and the end-results made available for study.[2]

In February 1937 the Interdepartmental Committee on Rehabilitation of Persons injured by Accidents, under the Chairmanship of Sir

[1] Cf. *Report on Fractures*, pp. 18–19.
[2] Cf. *1934 Convention of the International Association of Industrial Accident Boards, Bulletin No. 2*, U.S.A. Dept. of Labor, 1935, p. 147; also pp. 152 sqq.

Malcolm Delevingne, submitted, after sitting for over two years, an *Interim Report* which largely adopted the views sponsored by the B.M.A. whose *Report on Fractures* was mentioned in its terms of reference. The Delevingne Report drew attention to the 'growing dissatisfaction' with the results obtained under the current system of treatment of fractures. The question of the provision of fracture clinics, as outlined by the B.M.A., had been under consideration, by hospital and other authorities, employers and their organizations and, in particular, by a conference held on that subject at Manchester in October 1936 by the General Federation of Trade Unions and a Joint Committee appointed by the T.U.C. and the B.M.A. The process of forming fracture clinics had already begun, and others had been planned or were under consideration.

The Committee endorsed most of the medical recommendations made by the B.M.A. and called particular attention to the question of the remuneration of the surgeon-in-charge. It is not the custom for the visiting staff of a hospital to receive remuneration for their services; but as the surgeon-in-charge of a fracture clinic organized on the lines proposed in their Report would have to undertake much more onerous duties than those usually falling to a visiting surgeon, and would probably be compelled to give up other remunerative work for this purpose, the Delevingne Committee thought it desirable that he should be paid for his services; otherwise it might be difficult to secure the man best qualified for the work. 'As it has been put bluntly, "there is no money in fractures", so far as practice outside the hospital is concerned'[1]—a depressing dictum.

The treatment of fractures, and of industrial accidents in particular, is one of medical treatment as well as of organization. The medical aspects were effectively dealt with in the Delevingne *Interim Report* and a 'model scheme' has been drafted which offers all necessary requirements;[2] only action is required. The Committee, however, had little to say with regard to organization in its *Interim Report*, though it suggested that groups of employers or workers who were thinking of establishing fracture clinics should put themselves in touch with the Committee, which would take the opportunity of 'consultation with the authorities and others interested in any areas which desire it and of considering and discussing with them any difficulties which they may experience in working out the application of the scheme'.

Neither the Delevingne nor the Souttar Committees have hitherto touched the economic and organizing side of the fracture problem. Questions of administration are discussed in the latest publication of

[1] Cf. *Interim Report on the Rehabilitation of Persons injured by Accidents,* 1937, p. 9.
[2] Cf. ibid., Appendixes I–IV, pp. 16 sqq.

the B.M.A.,[1] but Workmen's Compensation is not particularly mentioned, though the improved clinical service would presumably be available to injured workmen, if insured under the N.H.I. Act. The peculiar position of persons covered by the Workmen's Compensation Act is not referred to.

The reference in the *Interim Report* to 'groups of employers or workers' suggests that the Committees may have had in view some system of contracting out such as is provided for under § 31 of the Act of 1925, but we doubt whether such groups can be formed without an entire alteration in our system of Workmen's Compensation. The difficulties were discussed before the Holman Gregory Committee. Mr. R. R. Bannatyne of the Home Office doubted whether, in Britain, 'miscellaneous occupations, in which neither masters nor men are organized, and in which the frontiers of the trade are ill defined, could become entities for this purpose'.[2] The advantages of the German system, which links up the activities of the Mutual Indemnity Associations, was not questioned, but it was recognized that these bodies (see vol. i, pp. 157–8) have no counterpart in Britain, and the limited success of Whitley Councils does not encourage hopes of action on these lines, though it may be possible to set up Regional Fracture Committees on which masters and men are represented.[3]

In Britain, where neither employers nor insurance institutions have a direct financial interest in the complete speedy recovery of the worker, the possibility of linking Workmen's Compensation law and medical recovery has scarcely been studied. The B.M.A. *Report on Fractures*[4] records the following verdict, which deserves to be remembered:

The Workmen's Compensation Acts, although designed to protect the workman, have in many cases played a powerful part in prolonging his disability, in delaying his return to work, and, on occasion, in converting him into a permanent invalid.

On the subject of the relationship between the German National Health Scheme and Accident Insurance it is to be noted that unless the *Berufsgenossenschaft* objects the injured man is treated by the medical

[1] Cf. *A General Medical Service for the Nation*, 1938, pp. 41 sqq.

[2] Cf. *Holman Gregory Report*, vol. i, *Evidence*, Q. 859–61.

[3] In the U.S.A. for the past fifteen years the American College of Surgeons through its Committees on Fractures has conducted an educational programme among surgeons to promote better care of fractures. The influence and work of this committee have been extended through the appointment of regional fracture committees throughout the country, which co-operate with the central committee. These efforts are undoubtedly aiding greatly to reduce the tremendous social and economic loss which results from the 1,000,000–1,500,000 fractures which are estimated to occur annually in the U.S.A. Cf. *Medical Service in Industry and Workmen's Compensation Laws*, American College of Surgeons, Chicago, 1938, p. 19.   [4] Cf. loc. cit., p. 27.

institutions under National Health; the 'Approved Societies' have to bear the cost until the forty-fifth day of the malady. From that day onwards the *Berufsgenossenschaft* has to refund the costs to the *Krankenkasse*: from the fourteenth week onwards the *Berufsgenossenschaft* may, and from the twenty-seventh week must, grant a *Rente*, i.e. a continuous weekly payment.[1] The National Health institutions must grant medical as well as sickness benefit to injured workmen; it is the duty of the *Krankenkassen* to provide for the medical care of the injured, but their expenditure on that account is limited to the above period. The tendency has been to entrust the *Berufsgenossenschaften* with specific responsibility for certain 'recovery' services, as is shown by the institution of several specialized types of physicians connected with the early stages of injury treatment, such as the *Durchgangsarzt* and the *Beratungsfacharzt* (forwarding doctor and consulting specialist). These are chosen at the request of *Berufsgenossenschaften* to give advice before the treatment by the practitioner.[2]

Medical benefit was, as the reader knows, from the outset an integral part of German Workmen's Compensation law.[3] It has since received the constant attention of the legislators and plays an important part in the framework of the present *Gewerbe-Unfall-Versicherung*.[4] The law declares that medical treatment 'should by all suitable (*geeigneten*) means remedy the disturbance of health, bodily damage, and occupational incapacity created by the accident', and prevent aggravation of the worker's condition. Medical treatment embraces treatment by the doctor, the supply of medicine, &c., provision of artificial limbs, orthopaedic and other facilities 'necessary to secure the success of medical treatment and to alleviate the effects of the injury'. This part of the law is set forth in great detail. Thus, for instance, the insured person may not be asked to contribute to an additional cost of an appliance, e.g. the cost of an expensive surgical boot made to order. The range of what is considered as 'facilities' is very wide and covers almost everything, from artificial eyes to false teeth, invalid chairs, and even wigs. Special regulations provide for extramural treatment of patients elsewhere than in institutions. Nurses (male and female) and facilities for home treatment are provided free of charge 'wherever the taking over of assistance and attendance cannot fairly be expected from the family of the injured in conse-

[1] Cf. *Reichsversicherungsordnung*, München, 1938, Book V. *Relations of Insurance Carriers to Each Other*, paras. 1501 sqq., also paras. 559 and 559 c.

[2] See also later when the administration of medical treatment will be discussed.

[3] By § 5 of the first Act, from July 6th 1884.

[4] Cf. *Reichsversicherungsordnung mit Anmerkungen*, edited by members of the Imperial Insurance Office, Bd. III: *Unfallversicherung* (*Drittes Buch der Reichsversicherungsordnung*), Berlin, 1930, pp. 115 sqq.

quence of illness, number of children or any other important reason'. The *Berufsgenossenschaft* also has discretion, if the injured man agrees, to allow the treatment to be given in his home, and can include in medical treatment free fares to and free treatment in a nursing-home or sanatorium (*Heilanstalt*).

These developments illustrate the tendency to entrust medical treatment of the injured man from the outset to *Berufsgenossenschaften* and, if possible, to avoid recourse to the National Health institutions (*Krankenkassen*). This is the underlying idea of an ordinance of June 19th 1936,[1] which aims at enabling the insurance carriers to initiate the medical treatment by *Berufsgenossenschaften* (*berufsgenossenschaftliche Krankenbehandlung*) 'to ensure that from the very beginning medical treatment (*Eingriff*) which, in general, exercises a decisive influence on further developments, is made by a specialist (*Facharzt*), if need be in hospital, and only in an emergency by the general practitioner'. The same ordinance emphasizes that the *Berufsgenossenschaft* should be in a position to devise treatment adapted to particular industrial injuries:

All such cases should be detected and, if possible, be given medical treatment from the beginning under the *Berufsgenossenschaften* (*berufsgenossenschaftliche Heilverfahren*), in which it appears likely that the *Berufsgenossenschaft* is capable of offering a more effective method of bringing about recovery with a view to the quicker and more complete restoration of earning capacity.

The *Berufsgenossenschaften*, by the same ordinance, are entitled to inform the *Krankenkasse* (i.e. the German Approved Society) in respect of what injuries *berufsgenossenschaftliche Krankenbehandlung*, i.e. medical treatment under a Mutual Indemnity Association's care, appears to be desirable. The *Krankenkassen* are also to be kept informed of doctors who are particularly expert in the treatment of certain industrial injuries and of the most suitable hospitals for the purpose, and immediately to hand over injured men suffering from certain fractures to a suitable hospital.[2] The amended German Workmen's Compensation law applies the principle that a co-ordinated treatment should be attempted from the outset so as to make the treatment a 'unified whole', avoiding the 'confusion' which may be the result of 'duplication'.[3] It is clear that the matter is as much one of well-planned organization as one of medico-technical skill.

How to reshape the existing provisions of Workmen's Compensation in Britain with due regard to existing National Health provisions

[1] Cf. *Die Neuregelung der Beziehungen zwischen den Trägern der Krankenversicherung und der Unfallversicherung*, official text, Berlin, 1936, pp. 16 sqq.

[2] See para. 6 of the Ordinance of June 19th 1936.

[3] Cf. *Report on Fractures*, p. 20: 'Co-ordination of the successive stages of treatment, which should be closely related as integral parts of a unified whole, is essential.'

is now engaging the attention of the Hetherington Commission. It is to be hoped that they will not underrate the German system, whereunder *Berufsgenossenschaften* also effectively assist recovery from industrial injuries and diseases by collecting valuable specialized experience and by preparing and administering schemes for particular trades.

Attention has been drawn in recent American publications to 'the importance of well-organized and fully qualified medical services in preventing loss to employers and undue suffering to and disability of injured workmen'. This observation is specifically based upon current industrial accident statistics in Europe. Prof. Alfred Manes, a former expert on German Social Insurance, claims that, in Holland, 95 per cent. of all industrial accidents involve absence from work for less than six weeks. (The corresponding figure for Britain cannot be stated with precision but is probably about $72\frac{1}{2}$ per cent.)[1] This favourable figure is attributed by Prof. Manes to the fact that, in the Netherlands, even trivial accidents receive prompt and skilled treatment.[2]

Dr. Hans Boywindt some time ago thus summarized the medical aims of the *Berufsgenossenschaften*: 'Our Association will always keep in mind that its noblest task must be to bring to perfection medical treatment and medical welfare by a complete *early treatment* through all Mutual Indemnity Associations.'[3] It does not, however, follow that these Associations should themselves provide hospitals, sanatoria, &c. It may be more convenient to make use of existing facilities— State, semi-State, or even private—than to initiate a fresh service, and, in fact, few special hospitals have been started by the *Berufsgenossen-schaften.*[4] But these institutions play a very small part in the system of medical treatment. Their whole expenditure in 1936 was less than 500,000 RM.[5] What matters is that *Berufsgenossenschaften* now exercise a decisive influence upon the medical treatment of injured work-men, combining co-ordination of treatment with highly specialized and expert treatment of injuries, in the various industries including agriculture.

---

[1] See table at foot of p. 310, Wilson and Levy, loc. cit., vol. i.

[2] Cf. *Monthly Labor Review*, Jan. 1939, reprint, Washington, 1939, pp. 17–18. Also Manes, *Monthly Labor Review*, 1938, p. 435.

[3] Cf. Dr. Hans Boywindt (legal representative of the *Vereinigung berufsgenossenschaft-licher Verwaltungen für Groß-Berlin und Provinz Brandenburg* [Association of the Administrative Bodies of Mutual Indemnity Associations of Berlin and the Province of Brandenburg]), *Die Berufsgenossenschaften der Neuzeit*, Berlin, 1921, p. 11.

[4] These consist, so far as hospitals are concerned, of some institutions formed by the (mining) *Knappschafts-Berufsgenossenschaft*, which owns four such hospitals, one each in Bochum and Gelsenkirchen-Bür. and two in Halle, and by the *Nordöstliche Eisen- und Stahlberufsgenossenschaft* (iron and steel trade) in Berlin, together with six ambulatoria and similar institutions.

[5] Cf. *Amtliche Nachrichten für Reichsversicherung*, Dec. 25th 1937, no. 12, p. 463.

The possibility of such developments in Britain has not yet been considered by any official body although the possibilities of 'group'-organization is noted in the B.M.A. Report on a State Medical Service. In Germany, as stated in Dr. Boywindt's treatise,[1] employers are anxious to ensure that specially skilled craftsmen should, if injured, be able to regain full working capacity, and regard complete medical recovery as second in importance only to accident-prevention. Here lies the real difference between the British[2] and German systems for, in Britain, few insurance-carrier offices are concerned and none are required to do more than discharge their statutory obligation to an injured person by means of a 'negotiated' and economical lump-sum settlement.

In other words, the German system of Workmen's Compensation, and that of most great industrial countries, turns upon the bodily welfare of the injured workman, his restoration to full health and working capacity. The British system conceives of his injury as an 'accident' for which the employer, if his liability is legally established, must pay a certain sum in cash—the sole nexus between master and man.

This profound difference in outlook is no less evident in the next phase of the process of social restoration of the injured man, which we shall attempt to treat in the succeeding chapter.

[1] Cf. loc. cit., p. 9.

[2] Vivid testimony to the incompleteness of the existing system of medical benefit under the N.H.I. Acts and of the consequences to injured workmen of the omission from the Workmen's Compensation Act of any provision for medical treatment is to be found in the Annual Reports of the Royal Surgical Aid Society (in charge since 1938 of the work of the London Spectacle Mission).

The following is mentioned in their Report for 1938 (p. 23) as a 'typical case':

'F.E., aged 30, a miner, lost his arm in a colliery accident. Supplied with an artificial arm and hand he writes: Words fail to express my gratitude to you all. You can realize *after 15 years with only an arm stump* what a valuable asset this arm and hand is to me. *Already I am able to do many jobs that were impossible before.* It has altered my outlook on life, and gives me a brighter vision for the future.'

NOTE

THE arrangements of medical care provided under the German law were admirably presented to the Royal Commission in the Memorandum of Evidence of the I.L.O., see pp. 606–8.

In section 65, however, the 'specialist' provided by the existing arrangements is referred to as 'medical adviser'. This might lead to some misunderstanding. The German term is definitely *Beratungsfacharzt*. *Fach* always refers to specialists, and the doctor in question, indeed, is an advising specialist. It is gratifying that the Central Council for the Care of Cripples in their Memorandum expressly refers to these arrangements, see *Minutes of Evidence*, p. 1243, 'as proper medical attention to special cases' provided under the German law.

CHAPTER XII

REHABILITATION

Felicitas in eo consistit quod homo suum esse conservare potest.   SPINOZA.

Human happiness consists in man's power to preserve his own personality.

Cash-payment is not the sole relation of human beings; we think . . . that it absolves and liquidates all engagements of man. 'My starving workmen?' answers the rich mill-owner: 'Did I not hire them fairly in the market? Did I not pay them, to the last six-pence, the sum covenanted for? What have I to do with them more?' . . . When Cain . . . killed Abel, and was questioned: 'Where is thy brother?' he too made answer, 'Am I my brother's keeper?' Did I not pay his wages, the thing he has merited from me?

                                                CARLYLE, *Past and Present*, 1843.

THE 'recovery' of an injured person involves, and implies, much more than the healing of wounds, the union of broken bones, the restoration of muscular power, and the apparent disappearance of any specific disorder of the nervous system. His condition may be patho-logically normal; he may be anxious to resume work, and confident of his capacity to do so without fear of consequences and without pain. 'For the bulk of patients attending the fracture clinics of hospitals—children, housewives, and sedentary workers—the ordinary use of the limbs is sufficient and special provision is not necessary.'[1] This is certainly true of most minor injuries. But it must be remembered that under the Workmen's Compensation Acts there were in 1937 about 26,000 cases of accident and 3,500 cases of industrial disease which had lasted one year and over, and had not been terminated;[2] and over 7,000 cases of industrial accident and 1,100 cases of industrial disease in which lump sums were paid after the injury had lasted twenty-six weeks and over.[3] These are only a proportion of the total number of serious accidents, but collectively they would suffice to keep several large hospitals fully occupied. In some cases, the social consequences to the injured person have been calamitous; in almost all cases serious.

Two distinct meanings attach to the term 'rehabilitation'. To Dr. Norris it is

the fitting of the injured person, after his injuries have healed, for remunerative employment.[4]

---

[1] Cf. *Report on Fractures*, B.M.A., 1935, p. 24.

[2] i.e. exclusive of cases settled by lump-sum payments.

[3] Cf. *Compensation Statistics for 1937*, pp. 22–3.

[4] Cf. Norris, *Industrial Accidents*, 1938, p. 129. The T.U.C. Memorandum to the Hetherington Commission adopted this distinction; and urged that 'treatment' should comprise: (1) an initial stage of medical treatment, (2) 'a subsequent stage of treatment for

The *Interim Report on Rehabilitation*[1] defines the term as

the process of reconditioning which will be required in certain cases after clinical treatment, in order to obtain full restoration of working capacity.

According to the B.M.A. it is

the stage between the completion of a course of massage and exercises in a massage department and the point when the stresses and strains of heavy work can be undertaken.[2]

This definition appears to us to be very appropriate for particular purposes, and we use it in this sense throughout this chapter.

It is essential that our minds should be clear upon this point. Medical treatment of a fracture, e.g. by physiotherapy, baking, massage, electrical treatment, and remedial exercises may be necessary stages on the road of medical recovery, but are distinct from the process of so reconditioning the injured man that he may regain his full capacity to resume work. This must of necessity assume many forms. In the case of nystagmus, for instance, the possibility of securing a complete change of occupation or at least of work above ground is of outstanding importance, and the choice of a particular medical treatment to regain capacity for work is a secondary matter.[3] The object of rehabilitation in this case is to accustom the injured worker to the performance of work and, at the same time, to prevent serious psychoneurosis which would perpetuate his incapacity. In some cases 'work' must be considered as the best means of 'rehabilitation'; in others medical recovery or the end of actual sickness must be followed by specific treatment.

Recent investigations have disclosed great difficulties in the case of tuberculosis, and something like a deadlock has been reached. 'The tuberculous person must work in order to live, but the pressure of work endangers his life.'[4] A tuberculous adult possesses a certain earning capacity which is essential for his well-being, and is an economic asset to the State and to himself. To deprive him of it is cruel; to enable him to develop it is the highest form of philanthropy. It is not principally a matter of 'placing' in suitable employment but of providing special opportunities for work in organized settlements where employment is combined with treatment, and the exercise of skill is

---

the period intervening between the termination of purely medical treatment and the recovery of full capacity for the stresses and strains of heavy work'. Cf. loc. cit., p. 424 (§ 119).

[1] p. 8.   [2] Cf. *A General Medical Service*, B.M.A., p. 40.

[3] Cf. *Stewart Report*, p. 108: 'Work plays a large part in the cure of the disease.' 'Remedial work' is urged for workmen 'when they are fit for it'.

[4] Cf. E. Brieger, *After-care and Rehabilitation, Principles and Practice* (International Union against Tuberculosis). Reprint from *British Journal of Tuberculosis*, vol. xxxi, no. 4, 1937, pp. 77, 130–1, and *passim*.

not accompanied by the pressure of highly organized industry. An industrial plant, set up under hygienic conditions and fully mechanized, can in some cases be staffed almost wholly with tuberculous patients.

The process of rehabilitation may include efforts to find suitable employment for the individual workman when he has recovered from his injury. Dodd distinguishes 'vocational rehabilitation' including vocational guidance, vocational training, and 'placement' from 'physical rehabilitation'. In the last-named term he includes not only 'the greatest possible restoration of function in the disabled parts through surgical and medical treatment, but also the provision and instruction in the use of artificial appliances, and the training of other members of the body to take over new compensating functions. It may also include psychiatric treatment.'[1] While the supply of artificial appliances is, properly speaking, an integral part of medical treatment, it should be distinguished from those aspects of rehabilitation which primarily concern physicians and surgeons, and from those which relate to the economic and social welfare of the worker.

'Rehabilitation provides a series of aids and services to persons who are physically and vocationally handicapped. . . . These services involve specialized case-work technique of advisement, placement, and supervision, and may include physical restoration, guidance, vocational training, placement, job adjustment, placement or establishment of the individual in business.'[2] The processes of rehabilitation include, in fact, a number of distinct services and processes which cannot, like the treatment of a fracture, be conducted under one roof, though they should be under centralized control. Of this there is, at present, almost no sign. In the words of a well-known colliery surgeon:

Neither small nor large hospitals are rehabilitation centres. There is often delay in admission, and discharge is almost invariably hastened because of a long 'waiting list'. Patients partly recovered return to their homes where adequate methods of treatment necessary for restoration to full health are no longer available. The 'company's masseur' is a poor substitute for a well-equipped physiotherapeutic department. Disabilities drag on; time is lost. There are aching heads or injured arms, for with either of these the patient can walk. There are complications, early or late, which should not occur. Afflictions become permanent when they should not. Circumstances, not the doctor, prevent the best results and the speediest recovery.[3]

It is unfortunately true that not even a beginning has been made towards the systematic provision of physical or occupational rehabilitation.

---

[1] Cf. Dodd, loc. cit., pp. 714–15.

[2] Cf. *1935 Convention of the International Association of Industrial Accident Boards*, Washington, 1936, p. 101. Mr. Mark M. Walter, Director of the Bureau of Rehabilitation of Pennsylvania: *Rehabilitation in Workmen's Compensation Administration*.

[3] Dr. A. W. Sheen, in *British Medical Journal (Supplement)*, March 26th 1938, pp. 153 sqq.

This is not surprising, seeing that the elementary processes of medical recovery have no place in our Workmen's Compensation legislation. A start has indeed been made by private enterprise on charitable lines and by some Mutual Indemnity Associations on a small scale.[1] The *Interim Report* of the Delevingne Committee does not mention such efforts, and its 'survey of the present position' is inadequate. There is for example a Council for the Promotion of Occupational Industries among the Physically Handicapped, founded in 1934, which is doing useful work so far as its limited means permit. The Cripples' Training College, opened at Leatherhead in 1935, provides, at a cost of 35*s*. per head per week, board, lodging, and training in several industries, including those of cook, gardener, clerk, handyman, and acetylene welder. The last-named occupation has been found to be suitable for one-armed men. The Central Council for the Care of Cripples, founded in 1919, co-ordinates work on behalf of the disabled. Lord Roberts Memorial Workshops, where disabled ex-Service men were taught trades, have almost disappeared, but they inspired in 1919 the first Rehabilitation Law of the State of New Jersey, U.S.A., whereunder treatment, training, and placement in industry were available to all State citizens. In 1920 the Federal Government passed a similar Act, setting up a Federal Board of Vocational Education; since then forty-four States of the U.S.A. have made similar provision for crippled citizens.[2] 'A prophet is not without honour save in his own country.' Lord Roberts Memorial Workshops have found no imitators in this country, but inspired effective legislation and organization—in a foreign country! We may also here mention the courageous efforts of Enham and Papworth Village Settlements, and of Preston Hall, the aim of which is to help by their factories and fields workers who are unaided in the 'industrial battle of life'.[3]

In France the *Ligue pour la Réadaptation du Physique Diminué* endeavoured, before the economic crisis, to employ ex-patients of sana-

[1] Cf. *The British Health Services*, PEP, 1937, p. 77: 'In some cases the Mutual Indemnity Associations, since they are not run for profit, are more interested in encouraging . . . treatment for injured workmen.' But Mutual Indemnity Associations are as much concerned to discharge the liabilities of their members as cheaply as possible, as are Insurance offices in respect of the liabilities of their clients.

[2] Cf. Dr. Norris, *The Effects of Injuries upon Earning Capacity*. Address before the Insurance Institute of London, 20 Jan. 1936, reprint, pp. 11–12.

[3] Papworth Village Settlement forms a complete unit with a hospital for advanced cases, sanatorium suitable for this form of treatment, and the Village with its hostels and houses, Workshops and Recreation Hall. Preston Hall Sanatorium and Colony was remodelled on the lines of Papworth and the training was reorganized on industrial lines. Cf. Brieger, loc. cit., pp. 118, 121–2, and *passim*. There is also a Rehabilitation Clinic at the Albert Dock Hospital (Mr. H. E. Griffiths) which deserves attention.

toria as *mi-temps* workers in industry. The wage deficiency was made good by the *Assurance Sociale*. But the system was not entirely satisfactory, though it is proof of a serious attempt to tackle the problem. Not all workers took their work seriously; some failed to occupy their leisure on lines calculated to hasten reconvalescence. For this reason it is now intended to create special after-care workshops for non-stabilized cases, and at the same time to place the adults in hostels.

In Germany the *Reichsversicherungsamt* has introduced measures to provide temporary financial assistance, 'to be diminished as health is regained, for the tuberculous patient who, on completion of sanatoria treatment, still needs special consideration; he will be thus enabled to resume his vocation step by step until he can do full-time work'.[1]

British attempts, however, are but rare exceptions to the rule. The injured workman has no legal claim to rehabilitation, physical or social, e.g. in regard to placement in remunerative employment. We have once more to look, if we want to see what can be done by Statute, to the German example which, whatever its imperfections, is a comprehensive and systematic effort to cope with the matter.[2] Rehabilitation of injured workers was from the outset regarded as the primary objective, and as of transcendent importance. In a paper read by the President of the Imperial Insurance Office (*Reichsversicherungsamt*), Herr Bielefeldt, and prepared for the St. Louis Exhibition in 1904, we read:

A Trade Association (*Berufsgenossenschaft*) that reduces the pensions, after having granted a thorough treatment for cure, and has hereby given the injured health and capacity, has done far more from the political and economic point of view than the most liberal Trade Association that grants recompense for the consequence of accidents, and does not trouble much about the removal of these consequences.[3]

This spirit is still active in Germany to-day, as the essay of Dr. Victor v. Weizsaecker amply proves.[4] The objective is not the 'medical' recovery but 'social' recovery in the widest sense. In Britain the conception of *soziale Gesundung* is not to be found, nor has the phrase

---

[1] Cf. Brieger, p. 70. Also *Reichsarbeitsblatt*, 1930, Heft 33, iv, p. 324: *Nachfürsorge bei Lungenkranken*. Brieger considers the ideal solution for temporary sheltered employment the 'creation of after-care workshops and colonies in connection with existing sanatoria'.

[2] Medical benefit was a feature of the original German Workmen's Compensation law of July 6th 1884, and was extended by the later law of June 30th 1900.

[3] Cf. *Dept¹. Committee on Workmen's Compensation*, vol. iii, 1905, pp. 21–2 and 42.

[4] Cf. *Soziale Krankheit und soziale Gesundung*, pp. 49 sqq. Other writings of Weizsaecker on the subject are to be found in: *Veröffentlichungen der Berliner Medizinischen Wochenschrift*, 1937, p. 736. Ibid., 1931, reprint nos. 39 and 40. Further in *Amtliche Mitteilungen für Baden*, 1931, no. 15; also *Zentralblatt für Psychotherapie*, Bd. viii, H. 5, Sonderabdruck, N.D.

a current equivalent in English as yet. While *Gesundheit* may be translated by 'health', *Gesundung* implies the process of restoration of health. To give reality and expression in Britain to the term 'social restoration' (including health and occupation) would be a worthy object for a great new voluntary association.

Experienced German medical experts hold that 'rehabilitation' is the most effective means of combating industrial neurosis so far as it is directed towards compensation. *Rentenneurose*, as we have already pointed out, is a common feature of German Compensation experience; the term is so well known that it has found its way into popular books on family medicine.[1] The existence of such 'compensation-neurosis' ought not to be taken as an argument in favour of lump sums, though it may be contended that neurosis is not restricted to any particular system of payment. The expectation of a higher weekly payment, or any payment at all, may of course lead to the same psychological consequences as the desire for a lump sum, and though such neurosis may disappear after settlement for a lump sum, the long process of bargaining or litigation attendant upon such settlement makes the development of neurosis as or even more likely than in the case of a definite weekly payment which, in general, is seldom contested.

The great interest which German medical men take in the question of industrial neurosis in connexion with Workmen's Compensation has a wider and deeper background, namely, the conviction that *rehabilitation or social restoration is of primary and cash compensation of only secondary importance*. Carlyle's words, 'Cash-payment is not the sole relation of human beings', have, in the words of Rudyard Kipling, 'come to life, and walk up and down in the hearts of men'. In the words of Dr. von Weizsaecker, a Professor in the Medical Faculty of the University of Heidelberg,

Adequate relief for the social distress of the injured can never be sought in a provision of cash, but must consist in a relaxation of the psychological depression with a restoration of an adequate opportunity for work—it must not consist in a mere compensation for the reduced working capacity by money. Instead of looking at the social-neurotic insufficiency from the angle of a provision of weekly payments, we must provide an opportunity for transmutation, we must provide as a means of equalization some opportunity for work and not a rent. . . .

'The usual procedure to-day', continues Weizsaecker, 'is centred around an analysis of and evidence as to the nature of the illness of the insured and its causes', whereas, in his view, the primary question should be the capacity of the injured man for work. He holds it to be impossible to ascertain the working capacity of the injured man merely

[1] Cf. Knaur's *Gesundheitslexikon*, edited by Dr. J. Loebel, 1930, p. 339, under *Rentenkrankheit*.

by taking as a basis his *Krankheits*-status, i.e. the degree of his illness from a purely medical viewpoint. He is not satisfied with the German medical procedure.[1] What would be his verdict on the British system, which makes provision neither for rehabilitation nor for medical recovery, the injured workman being liable for the cost of after-treatment, trusses, and other artificial appliances and substitutes? Dr. Weizsaecker's views are shared by another German authority, Prof. Rhode, the medical director of one of the *Sonderstationen* (*Oberhausen*) for the treatment and social rehabilitation of severely injured persons.

Surgical measures are not decisive factors in the later processes of occupational rehabilitation. They only create the anatomic conditions for them and prepare the ground for the cure of the disturbances consequent upon the accident. After-treatment is of decisive importance. It should be part of a continuous process, concurrently with the procedure of operation. . . . A man who has recovered, but whose capacity for work is impaired, must not have to rely upon his weekly payments, nor should his prospects in life be restricted to the prospect of employment, as an act of charity, as a porter, subordinate clerk, or messenger. He must be reconditioned for industry and be able himself to undertake physical labour. If this is not provided for during after-treatment by getting information about the usual work of the injured man, by investigating the possibilities of his reintroduction into the working process by the application of particular appliances, by discussing the matter with the works management and, in the case of bodily impairment, by instituting the readaptation of the injured man to the new work—the man so injured returns into work as an unskilled worker and probably falls into a lower social stratum.[2]

This passage is typical of the broad social outlook of the German medical profession, and displays a determination not to shirk the trouble connected with the necessary inquiries into single cases and their individual needs. Such views are now widely held by many British medical men. Thus Dr. Norris writes:

Merely to pay money to a man affords no guarantee that he will get these three things—treatment for his disability, training in an appropriate job, if he is unable to resume his former work, placement in remunerative employment—or any of them. More often than not he has but little idea how to apply the money so as to restore his earning capacity as early and as fully as possible; and present arrangements in this country are wholly inadequate for this purpose, almost everything being left to chance, or to the initiative of the injured person. The consequence is that disability is needlessly prolonged and a vast amount of money wasted, to say nothing of the wastage in human life and happiness.[3]

The B.M.A. takes the same line. It regrets that the present Workmen's Compensation Acts 'contain no provision for the rehabilitation

---

[1] Cf. Weizsaecker, loc. cit., pp. 49–50 and *passim*.
[2] Cf. *Die Berufsgenossenschaft*, April 1938, p. 99.
[3] Cf. Norris, *Effects of Injuries upon Earning Capacity*, 1936, reprint, pp. 10–11.

of the man after injury and place no liability upon him to prove that he has sought and obtained efficient treatment', and holds that these Acts, although designed to protect the workman, tend in many cases to prolong his disability, delaying his return to work and, on occasion, converting him into a permanent invalid. No stronger language could be used.[1] It is clear that there is a strong body of informed opinion against establishing a new 'Rehabilitation Department', to take over control of cases which have passed through the hospital wards, and then through the massage department, thus entailing yet another break in continuity of treatment. For the time being it may be necessary to have 'Rehabilitation Centres' equipped to deal with other people's failures or with persons requiring special training, but the work of rehabilitation should be planned as soon as the case comes under treatment, and carried out without interruption or change of supervision, as soon as other methods of treatment have been used at the appropriate stage. Dr. Howard E. Collier, when head of the Department of Industrial Hygiene and Medicine, Birmingham University, took a similar view:

To treat industrial workers as if their illnesses were *either* physical *or* psychological is unsound and unscientific. Physical, personal, and social factors constitute an aetiological complex, which determines industrial disease.

He strongly urges more consideration of 'mental' factors in respect of injured workers 'if our treatment of them is to be efficient', a point of particular importance when the stage of rehabilitation has been reached.[2]

While German medical authorities still press for administrative improvements, German legislation of the last fifteen years has prepared the ground for a wide application of after-treatment, training, and rehabilitation.[3] Both medical treatment and vocational rehabilitation are designed:

1. To remove the disturbance of health or the bodily injury and the incapacity for work as caused by the accident, and to prevent a change for the worse; and
2. To restore the capacity of the injured man to resume his former occupation or, where this is not possible, to help him to find new employment.

[1] Cf. *Report on Fractures*, B.M.A., p. 27.

[2] Cf. Howard E. Collier, 'The Mental Manifestations of Some Industrial Illnesses', *Occupational Psychology*, 1939, vol. xiii, no. 2, pp. 95–6.

[3] The two outstanding enactments in regard to vocational rehabilitation (training and placing), of which the general term is *Berufsfürsorge*, are the Second Law concerning Alterations in Accident Insurance of July 14th 1925 (see paras. 558 sqq.) and an ordinance relating to Medical Treatment and Vocational Rehabilitation of Nov. 14th 1928. For full text of both enactments, cf. *Reichsversicherungsordnung*, loc. cit.

This paragraph already contains a wide conception of rehabilitation. Yet it does no more than state the general framework and the object in view. The details of vocational rehabilitation are further explained in a later section (paragraph 558 *f*):

Vocational rehabilitation embraces:

1. Vocational training with a view of regaining or increasing earning capacity, in so far as the injured person has been seriously handicapped in the performance of his professional work or any other employment which might be in fairness offered to him including, if need be, training for a new profession.
2. Assistance to get employment.

These important amendments were further complemented by the later Ordinance, dated Nov. 14th 1928, of which the following is a short extract:

Vocational rehabilitation may be given for one year; and for a further period if the injured person is suitable and keen to benefit therefrom.

The insurance carrier (almost always the appropriate *Berufsgenossenschaft*) must grant to the injured man and his dependants the expenses of maintenance during training subject to a means test. Assistance to get new employment must be given where

(*a*) the injured man is obliged to leave his employment owing to the injury;
(*b*) if he becomes unemployed for other reasons, while the securing of new employment is made difficult by the injury, provided that he has not given up his employment without sufficient reason or that he has not lost it by any serious fault on his part.

Vocational training should be preceded by consultations with the departments concerned with vocational or occupational guidance (*Berufs- und Arbeits-Beratung*). If such guidance is carried out by the insurance carriers themselves, other departments officially concerned with the matter of guidance may delegate responsibility to experts connected with the occupations in question, as also representatives of public assistance bodies.

The insurance carrier may also provide an allowance for such workers as have regained by training the necessary ability and accepted work again, but are not yet able to earn full wages (*Anlernezuschuß* = 'allowance for learning period'), and may also provide payment for tools if needed (*Arbeits-Ausrüstung*).

The insurance carrier is entitled himself to carry out the process of rehabilitation, but may delegate his responsibility to the *Haupt-Fürsorgestelle*, i.e. the principal body concerned with public assistance.

It must be explained here that public assistance in Germany is administered by the State, through State and District Public Assistance Unions (*Fürsorgeverbände*). It is for the State to decide what organizations are to act as such, and to define their responsibilities. For more specialized duties, including the care for seriously disabled persons (assistance by provision of employment for seriously disabled), State and provincial authorities usually act as public assistance institutions.

The reabsorption into industry of partially disabled workmen is thus effected jointly by the *Berufsgenossenschaft* and *Hauptfürsorgestelle* (the principal public assistance office). Every employer employing twenty persons or more must[1] employ a certain proportion of seriously disabled persons (average minimum 2 per cent.), who enjoy legal protection against arbitrary dismissal—a fact of interest in respect of complaints in Britain that employers sometimes employ injured men temporarily in light occupations in order to get the compensation payments reduced, and soon afterwards dismiss them.

Wherever vocational rehabilitation is undertaken by the Mutuals themselves[2] they are required by law to try to find occupation for the injured 'within the works for which they are the insurance carriers'. Any dispute between the injured person and the Mutual Indemnity Association is settled by the President of the *Oberversicherungsamt* (the Provincial Department of State Insurance). In the case both of medical treatment and of vocational rehabilitation, it is expressly ordered that 'insurance carriers have to provide for all measures and institutions' whereby the most speedy and effective medical treatment, and so far as necessary specialized medical care, may be ensured. Where such institutions are in existence Mutuals should refrain from starting others on their own account.[3]

Though medical authorities in Britain have for some time past recognized the necessity for vocational rehabilitation, no systematic attempt has yet been made to meet this need as a medical service. The *Interim Report on Rehabilitation* urges the creation of a network of 'fracture services', organized and conducted on certain principles laid down by the Committee. But these principles, and the 'model' scheme itself, deal only with the medical and clinical aspects involved. The aim of the Committee is, indeed, to 'secure the utmost possible restoration of working capacity', but the economic and administrative problems involved are not even mentioned in this Report, nor any suggestions made as to how to bring such hospitals within the orbit of a working arrangement with the social services; nor as to how far those injured by industrial accidents should be able to benefit by

[1] Under the Public Assistance Order of Feb. 13th 1924 and other administrative regulations.

[2] These of course have to refund the Public Assistance bodies for their expenses in the matter.

[3] This proviso probably explains the relatively small number of hospitals and sanatoria independently owned and maintained by the *Berufsgenossenschaften*.

specialized hospital treatment where National Health legislation does not provide for free additional medical and rehabilitation treatment, the provision of appliances, &c. The German example shows how elaborate such arrangements must be. Better provision for medical treatment, e.g. fracture clinics, will avail little unless it synchronizes with measures devised to restore the injured man's capacity as a productive unit in the society of which he is an integral part.

The Stewart Committee's recommendations for the treatment of nystagmus are more comprehensive. The Committee proposed:

(a) that the whole of an employer's liability in respect of this disease should be covered by insurance;

(b) that the Coal Mines Act, 1934, should be amended to make it compulsory to insure against liability arising out of nystagmus from the commencement of the disablement;

(c) that insurance rates or levies should be on such a basis as to prevent the cost of second or subsequent attacks being wholly debited to the claims record of the individual employer, and such cost should be pooled as far as possible.[1]

In framing these proposals and explaining them under the heading of 'Insurance' the Committee was well aware that vocational rehabilitation was closely connected with the administration of Workmen's Compensation, and endorsed the view of the Medical Research Council that 'practical treatment of the disease from an administrative point of view should consist in the elimination of a hopeless dependence on compensation by the provision of work'. Thus the proposed compulsory insurance, together with the formation of a single fund or pool for the entire coal-mining industry, would mean that the risk arising out of the re-employment of a nystagmic miner would be borne by the fund without increased liability to the individual employer. Such a statutory arrangement would be much more effective than private arrangements, such as exist in the South and West Yorkshire districts and provide 'light' work for the nystagmic miner as the best way to restore his physical and occupational capacity. Where such arrangements exist, 'if a man fails to secure employment, the failure will not be due to the fact that he has suffered from miner's nystagmus, but solely to the state of the labour market. In short, his position will no longer be the result of the Compensation Law.'[2] The proposal for compulsory insurance coupled with one or more nystagmus funds shows clearly that, where rehabilitation is boldly approached, compulsory insurance administered by Mutual Associations under statutory obligations and through a common fund is inevitable. The proposals of the Stewart Committee, indeed, approach closely to the German system.

[1] Cf. *Stewart Report*, pp. 43 and 109, and para. 97.   [2] Cf. ibid., p. 30.

It may be asked whether, if these recommendations are accepted, it would not be well to bring the administration of this matter of vocational rehabilitation under the care of Mutual Indemnity Associations subject to the supervision and guidance of a Department of State. In the matter of nystagmus, however, the problem of vocational rehabilitation is relatively simple, as the main remedy and 'treatment' is not clinical but the provision of suitable work.

Apart from Germany and the U.S.A., which have their own Vocational Rehabilitation laws,[1] some other industrial nations, e.g. France and Canada, have accepted the principle of vocational training as an integral part of Workmen's Compensation. The I.L.O. has also dealt with the question; the delegates to the International Labour Conference in 1935 were unanimous in recognizing its importance. But differences arose when a Draft Convention was attempted. Some delegates pointed out that if the employer or the insurer had to bear the cost of vocational re-education, the purpose of which was to reduce the extent of the injury, he should be entitled to claim that the result of vocational re-education, and the increased earning capacity to which it gives rise, should be taken into account when the degree of incapacity is determined and the final compensation or pension fixed. This, in the opinion of the Report of the I.L.O., would have the serious disadvantage of leaving the rights of the injured persons in suspense, perhaps for several years, and would be regarded by workmen with suspicion as an attempt to reduce the amount of their cash benefit.[2] No agreement was reached.

The B.M.A. views on rehabilitation are lucidly set forth in a memorandum which notes that, apart from clinical treatment, the provision of light work is of paramount importance, but also emphasizes that this provision presents

almost insuperable obstacles in present industrial conditions. . . . Unless and until the injured workman is able to perform the full and complete work of his usual job his chances of employment are small. These chances, however, are greater if he is employed in a large workshop, and especially so if his employer (or the representative of his employer) makes some effort to provide light jobs for the disabled man. The workman otherwise not only finds it difficult to obtain suitable employment, but is actually afraid to take up work that might prove too much for him and lead later to his discharge in favour of a man more physically fit, there being no dearth of substitutes in the present state of the labour market.

The injured man, wishing to go back to work, vainly explores all possible openings.[3] Thus he may apply for employment to a Local

[1] Cf. Dodd, loc. cit., pp. 716–18.
[2] Cf. *International Labour Organization*, Geneva, 1936, pp. 40–1.
[3] Evidence of C.O.S. before Delevingne Committee.

Authority, only to be informed that the Disablement and Pension Fund of the Council is so constituted that the Council cannot employ men with any perceptible physical disability and that the terms of their insurance policy with a Mutual Association further preclude his employment. If he should try to obtain employment in a light industry, he is told a similar story. In a case heard in the County Court at Bury before His Honour Judge Crosthwaite on April 24th 1939 the applicant, on oath, provided a list of one hundred employers to whom he had vainly applied for work during the forty weeks that had elapsed since he was declared to be fit for light work, during the whole of which period he was on the books of the Employment Exchange.

The B.M.A. suggests the establishment of rehabilitation centres.[1] The same view was expressed by Sir Geoffrey Peto, Chairman of the Executive Committee of the Central Council for the Care of Cripples, in *The Times* on September 1st 1937. He suggests a combined effort 'by all concerned', employers, trade unions, and mutual indemnity bodies. The same idea is explained in the same issue by Major-General Sir Cecil Pereira, Chairman of the Executive Committee of the Cripples' Training College at Leatherhead.

A good practical example of what can be done in practice comes from the U.S.A. All the different kinds of work done in the Ford Works were surveyed and analysed. The analysis showed that there were 7,882 kinds of work, of which 949 (12 per cent.) were classified as heavy, requiring men of first-class physique; moderate strength was required for 3,338 jobs (43 per cent.), while 3,595 jobs (45 per cent.) required very little physical effort and could have been done by girls or older children. It was considered that 670 of these jobs could be done by legless men, 2,637 by one-legged men, 2 by armless men, 715 by one-armed men, and 10 by blind men. At the time of the survey there were actually 9,563 physically defective employees in the factory, including about a thousand suffering from tuberculosis, 253 nearly blind in one eye, 3 totally blind, 234 with one foot or one leg amputated, 123 with crippled or amputated arms, forearms, or hands, and 60 epileptics. Commenting on these facts the head of the firm emphasized that 'no one applying for work is refused on account of his physical condition'. And he further added: 'We do not prefer cripples—but we have demonstrated that they can earn full wages.'[2]

Experience in other countries is not less encouraging. After the mechanization of the German Railway Shops at Dessau it was possible to employ hitherto unemployable tuberculous ex-patients of sanatoria. In Russia, according to Brieger,[3] the earning capacity of tuberculous

---

[1] Cf. *Hetherington Commission*, pp. 446–7.
[2] Cited by Dr. Norris, *Effects of Injuries*, &c., pp. 7–8.　　　　[3] Loc. cit., p. 75.

persons has been widely utilized in normal industry through careful adaptation, part-time work, separate dining and rest rooms, special diet, &c. It is stated that at one Russian mine 90 per cent. of the tuberculous mechanical workers are 50 per cent. more efficient than the average healthy worker in the same department, whereas among healthy miners only 60 per cent. had more than 100 per cent. efficiency; but we do not know with what form of tuberculosis these facts are concerned or whether they include 'active' cases. Nor should such bold statistical statements carry undue weight, when based upon results in a single mine in which it is most unlikely that 100 tuberculous persons were employed.

Several American firms have taken steps to provide organized treatment for industrial neuroses 'in such a way that the injured person works at something so soon as he is able to work at anything at all'. The formation of 'Rehabilitation Workshops' was recently particularly commended by Dr. R. D. Gillespie,[1] and the C.O.S. are satisfied that 'the services of the handicapped are often valuable'.[2] The Joint Conference of the Invalid Children's Aid Association and the Central Council for the Care of Cripples, held on November 7th and 8th 1935,[3] displayed great interest in the same point. Mr. John W. Cox, of the National Institute of Industrial Psychology, lays particular stress on the advantages of 'training' as contrasted with 'uninstructed repetition' and suggests the replacement of the current crude procedure by a short course of systematic training in the general principles underlying manual control. The results of certain experiments in that direction made by the Institute should be carefully considered in any future rehabilitation scheme.[4] Dr. Gillespie expresses his surprise that

insurance companies do not conduct an extensive inquiry into the question of compensation for injury and sickness resulting from it, or is it that they do not realize the existence of the problem? Or does it affect so small a proportion of insured people that it is not worth while worrying about for them? Or—let us whisper it darkly—is it that they have no real desire that the position should be improved? . . . They often drag on in the most unsatisfactory way, and it is often useless to hope for a cure till a final settlement of compensation has been made.[5]

Disfigurement. Apart from the necessity of some cash-compensation[6] the problem of rehabilitation is also of importance. Expert medical

---

[1] Cf. *Journal of British Dermatology*, 1937, pp. 426–7.

[2] Cf. *Memorandum*, loc. cit., p. 28.

[3] Cf. *Report of Joint Conference*, &c., of the said bodies, pp. 80–4 and 102–3. Again Dr. Norris made valuable suggestions.

[4] Cf. John W. Cox, 'Some Experiments on Formal Training in the Acquisition of Skill', *The British Journal of Psychology*, vol. xxiv, part i, July 1933. Also Brieger, loc. cit., pp. 130–3.   [5] Cf. Gillespie, loc. cit., p. 426.

[6] Cf. Wilson and Levy, vol. i, pp. 190–1; vol. ii, pp. 111–12.

care may restore functions but leave the disfigurement unaffected. Rehabilitation of appearance is generally costly, but may greatly facilitate re-employment. Future British legislation might well provide benefit. Care should be taken that where disfigurement can be diminished by medical treatment it should be at the expense of the insurance carrier before the injury is assessed for compensation. This would prevent the offer of or acceptance by the workman of a lump-sum payment inclusive of compensation for disfigurement.[1]

In the U.S.A. the attempts to procure light work for the blind have made considerable strides. Mr. Joseph F. Clunk, himself blind, first persuaded steel mills to try a few blind men on pipe-threading and testing machines. They made good, holding their own with the sighted men around them. It is widely believed in the U.S.A. that any modernized factory can use blind people;[2] Clunk and others have shown by practical demonstration under factory conditions that there are some 275 occupations in which blind persons can compete equally with sighted workmen, even without getting special treatment.[3] Among such operations are: weighing, assembling, and stacking parts, running metal working machines, stuffing of cushions and assembling carburettors in automobile factories. In Britain, however, where the question of light work is likely to be greatly influenced by the weight of authority adduced by insurance companies and their expert advisers, extensive employment of cripples may be used as an argument for the reduction of lump-sum payments. The matter is different where collective bodies and committees or State institutions, which are not primarily interested in the reduction of payments, have the last word. They are far more likely to reach an objective judgement on general scientific experience and advice.

How, then, can the necessary machinery be created? Little can be expected from the individual employer. Some large firms in this

[1] Cf. *Adequacy of Benefit Payments under Workmen's Compensation.* Reprint of an article by Marshall Dawson in the *Monthly Labor Review* of Sept. 1938, p. 7.

[2] Cf. M. A. Rose, 'A blind worker in every factory,' in *The Reader's Digest,* January 1938, pp. 93 sqq.

[3] An interesting little pamphlet has been issued under the title of *The blind citizen can, will, and must work* by the Westphälischer Blinden-Arbeitsfürsorge-Verein in Dortmund. Several groups of occupations are enumerated, and the specific tasks to be given to the blind within these groups are given in detail. The groups are: Mining (subsidiary occupations); several heavy and small industries in the iron and steel group, the textile industry, the tobacco industry, the manufacture of sweets, the soap industry, the leather and shoe industries; business occupations of all kinds, e.g. packing, sorting, cleaning, &c.; in hospitals and nursing homes (massage); in pianoforte factories and shops (tuners); in churches and cemeteries; in schools and educational institutions; in offices. Prof. Dr. Graf of the Institute for the Physiology of Labour in Dortmund-Münster has undertaken to make a preliminary examination of blind persons with a view to assessing their capacity for various tasks.

country, to their credit, do contrive to retain nearly all injured work-men in remunerative employment and, when the number is not large, the task is not one of great difficulty. Such firms do not advertise what they have done, nor pool their experience. The great majority of medium-sized and small employers cannot afford to maintain a rehabi-litation service and have little scope for the employment of disabled workmen who have not been fully reconditioned. It is in such cases that the need for a rehabilitation service is greatest. It is only possible under a system of mutual insurance, compulsory and comprehensive, where the employer is not seriously handicapped if the re-employment of a partially incapacitated man proves unsuccessful after a fair trial. On the other hand, a mutual and co-operative association, acting under some sort of State control, would more readily assume responsibility. for retaining skilled workers within the sphere of its trade. That, as the name implies, is the object of '*Berufsgenossenschaften—mutual care* associations for well-defined occupations.[1] This, the administrative and organizational side of vocational rehabilitation, ought to be given particular attention in coming legislation.

The need for specialized rehabilitation schemes ought not to be overlooked. The Trades Union Congress in its Memorandum to the Hetherington Commission appears to have solely concerned itself with rehabilitation in regard to fractures, which are of outstanding importance.[2] But other injuries and diseases also require rehabilitation services. This should not be ignored. For the treatment of fractures less specialized 'industrial' knowledge and experience is perhaps needed than for other 'industrial' injuries involving loss of a limb or eye or hand or leg. In such cases rehabilitation services for well-defined occupations,

---

[1] A particularly interesting account of Vocational Treatment in the *Reichsunfallver-sicherung* was given by Dr. Walther Johst on Dec. 10th 1937. Cf. *Die Berufsgenossenschaft, 1. April Heft,* 1938, pp. 83 sqq. Dr. Johst referred to the continuous effort of the *Berufs-genossenschaften* to 'improve the medical treatment from year to year in consideration of the fact that good medical treatment also means vocational provision'. He emphasized that in the *Sonderstationen zur Heil- und Berufsfürsorge*—special institutions for medical treatment and vocational care for the seriously injured—a planned treatment of recovery has been inaugurated with a view to the future re-employment of the injured in some occupation. He mentions the many discussions about single cases with local mayors, with gild-masters, former teachers of the injured, and also his wife. 'Every case must be treated individually.' He also mentions that particular attention is paid to the intellectual faculties of the injured. There are further special courses for elderly workers, for whom the learning of a new trade is out of the question. There is also provision for the settlement of injured people on small plots of land. The administration of one of the *Berufsgenossenschaften* has itself given em-ployment to seven one-armed workers, after they had received the necessary training, three have been taken over as typists, one as a telephonist, and one as a clerk-assistant. Dr. Johst is himself General Manager of the Rhenish-Westphalian Association of *Berufsgenossenschaften*.

[2] *Hetherington Commission,* pp. 445 sqq., App. D.

assisted by the experience of men conversant with the particular conditions of such occupations, might be of vital importance, and the creation of such bodies, committees, or boards represented not only by doctors, but also by industrialists and workers of the particular groups and branches of occupation, might be imperative. The Rehabilitation Report of 1939 has not taken the point up, but deals almost exclusively with fractures where 'industrial' injury as a particular feature does not arise. More research into the possibilities of rehabilitation, paying due regard to the great variety of industrial injuries, by accident as well as disease, is urgently needed.[1] As regards miners, a very instructive article by Dr. E. A. Nicoll, Surgeon-in-Charge, Mansfield Hospital Fracture Clinic and Surgeon to the Miners' Rehabilitation Centre, Berry Hill Hall, in News Letter (Central Council for the Care of Cripples) October 1940 on 'The Rehabilitation of Injured Miners' deserves particular attention. Dr. Nicoll writes: 'A great deal of the success in rehabilitating severe injuries depends on treating each case as an entirely individual problem.'

[1] Cf. for instance as regards dermatitis the instructive article by A. L. Leigh Silver in Journal of the Royal Army Medical Corps, July-December 1938, pp. 87 sqq.; for the rehabilitation of the tuberculosis worker: E. L. Sandiland in the Journal of the Royal Institute of Public Health and Hygiene, vol. i, 1938, pp. 46 sqq.; for occupational rehabilitation of the worker recovering from silicosis and asbestosis, see Lanza, loc. cit., p. 56.

PART IV

THE ADMINISTRATION OF WORKMEN'S COMPENSATION

THE LEGAL SIDE

THE MEDICAL SIDE

THE ECONOMIC AND SOCIAL SIDE

CHAPTER XIII

THE LEGAL SIDE: EMPLOYERS' LIABILITY, WORKMEN'S COMPENSATION, AND COMMON EMPLOYMENT

Mr. asquith (later lord oxford and asquith) Feb. 20 1893: '. . . a "contract" had been "invented"—for it can only be described as an invention—an implied contract on the part of the workman to take upon himself all the risks of the employment, and among those risks the negligence of the fellow servants.'

UNDER the heading 'Administration', with which this part of our work deals, we attempt to examine, in the light of past experience, certain apparently unrelated problems involved in any reform of Workmen's Compensation Law. Administration is more than the conscientious execution of statutory provisions. It includes the selection of skilled legal and medical experts for regional or central executive duty, and the provision of appropriate equipment and office accommodation, with the necessary financial backing and clerical staff. Administration, in this sense, has three separate aspects, which we shall attempt to discuss:

1. Legal.
2. Medical.
3. Social and economic organization.

The present tripartite system, based upon the concurrent existence of Common Law, Employers' Liability, and Workmen's Compensation, was critically examined in a Home Office Memorandum presented to the Hetherington Commission.[1] As Mr. J. A. Lillie, K.C., put it, 'an action under the Employers' Liability Act is really an action at Common Law with certain defences of the employer cut out . . . . It is scarcely worth while to sue under the Employers' Liability Act alone; in fact they [injured workmen] never do.'[2] A workman who has been unsuccessful under Common Law and Employers' Liability retains his right, within a certain time-limit, to claim compensation, subject to the deduction of costs previously incurred.[3] Nor does receipt of compensation money deprive him of his Common Law rights, unless acceptance is held to constitute 'definite election',[4] but recourse is

[1] Cf. *Hetherington Commission, Minutes of Evidence*, pp. 97 sqq.
[2] Cf. ibid., A. 715.
[3] Cf. § 29 of the Act.
[4] Cf. *Hetherington Commission*, Q. 378–9. Also Willis, loc. cit., pp. 457–8.

rarely had to the Employers' Liability Act, which is now seldom invoked.[1]

We must, however, be cautious in making deductions from this fact. How far is the number of actions taken under the Act a measure of its utility, seeing that there may be many cases in which workmen make a claim under the Employers' Liability Act which are not and cannot be disputed?[2] Comparisons between disputed and undisputed cases should be regarded with like caution. The law may deter litigants, but is also the basis of any settlement; it is the injured workman's charter though it may fail to protect him if he is ignorant of his rights or lacks reliable legal advice.[3]

After making all allowances, however, the significance of Common Law and Employers' Liability remains small. Yet both are frequently mentioned in the Commons, and the abolition of the defence of Common Employment is constantly discussed in Socialist publications[4] for, were it wiped out, the scope and application of Employers' Liability would be widened. The Labour Party are opposed to 'the Common Law principle of liability under the Employers' Liability Act'.[5] They maintain that Workmen's Compensation was enacted by Parliament in addition to, and not in substitution of, existing rights or remedies, and that the defence of Common Employment is what Lord Justice Nevill called 'a purely arbitrary and artificial rule founded neither upon principle nor, prior to 1837, upon authority—a mere excrescence upon the Common Law, devised apparently for the purpose of exempting a particular class from an otherwise universal liability'.[6] The Labour

---

[1] Cf. *Workmen's Compensation Statistics for 1937*, pp. 30–1. Also Wilson and Levy, vol. i, pp. 48 sqq. 'The total number of cases under this Act taken into court in the whole of Great Britain was only 32 in 1937 (against 48 in 1936) and the total amount of damages awarded was not more than £3,179 (including cases where money was paid into court and taken out in settlement).'

[2] Cf. *Hetherington Commission*, Q. 716–17.

[3] For this reason Mr. Davie, from the Home Office, pointed out that in his opinion the Employers' Liability Act might be used even more in the future than in the past. Cf. ibid., A. 718.

[4] Cf. *Labour*, May 1938: Frank Stillwell, *The Doctrine of Common Employment*. The indifference of the leading daily, weekly, and monthly papers to the subject, even when the Hetherington Commission was sitting, contrasts strongly with the prominence given to the subject by 'labour' journals. This is perhaps the reason why few employers, even of very large numbers of workmen, know what the rates of workmen's compensation are. It is enough for them that they are insured against the risk.

[5] Cf. Attorney-General, *Debates H.C.*, March 11th 1938, cols. 2275 sqq.

[6] The defence of Common Employment is severely criticized by Professor W. A. Robson in *The Modern Law Review* of December 1937, p. 225: 'The time has clearly come when the doctrine of common employment should be abolished. It is, as Lord Wright observed, based on a principle which has little regard to reality or to modern ideas of economics or industrial conditions.' See also J. Unger, ibid., June 1938, p. 48.

Party hold that a workman should not, in a case of proved negligence by a responsible employer, be treated worse than a stranger. They point out that whereas under Employers' Liability legislation the amount of compensation that may be recovered is limited to the sum total of three years earnings in the said employment (inclusive of any payments in kind, such as food and clothes), an injured workman often receives at Common Law ten times as much as the maximum sum payable under Workmen's Compensation. Is it just, they ask, to deprive him of his right at Common Law on the ground that a fellow workman was at fault? There are many industrial workers to whom neither the Employers' Liability Act nor the Workmen's Compensation Act applies, the former only assisting manual workers and the latter non-manual workers whose annual earnings do not exceed £350: upon them the defence of Common Employment falls very heavily. The Home Secretary recently suggested that such persons might be expected to insure themselves against industrial risks, but the premiums asked are exceedingly high and, unlike life policies, are subject to no income-tax rebate.

Those who still wish to retain the defence of Common Employment do not deny that it is, in the words of the late Lord Oxford and Asquith, a judge-made invention, 'a fantastic distinction between the position of workmen and third persons as regards the liability of the employer',[1] but they hold that the issue to-day is not one only of legal logic. Legislation in all great industrial countries has long sought to make *ad hoc* provision for the victims of industrial injuries, which recur with such statistical regularity that any attempt to assess negligence or non-negligence on the part of the worker must be ruled out. 'Negligence is always a difficult thing to prove, except in most palpable cases',[2] hence the decision to deal with industrial injuries by *ad hoc* legislation, at fixed rates of compensation, covering 'good' and 'bad' cases and 'just' and 'unjust' claims alike, including a few cases in which the demonstrable negligence of the employer might lead at Common Law to an award of damages on a much higher scale. It may seem unjust that a workman should have at Common Law no remedy against his employer for an injury caused by the carelessness of a fellow workman, but it is almost as unreasonable to hold an employer of thousands of men personally responsible at Common Law for the wilful and inexcusable carelessness of individual employees. That is why Workmen's Compensation legislation has disregarded the factor of negligence in favour of the principle that every injury was to be compensated on a statutory basis regardless of the employer's personal responsibility.

[1] See also vol. i, pp. 57–63.
[2] Attorney-General, *Debates H.C.*, March 11th 1938.

Whether these payments are adequate, and whether restoration of earning capacity should be included is another matter.

'Negligence' as a legal factor having been eliminated, it is important to prevent its reintroduction in the courts in a fresh guise. The view of negligence embodied in § 1 of the Workmen's Compensation Act should in our opinion be maintained with the utmost strictness. Any attempt to distinguish between lesser and greater carelessness, sensible or foolish acting would create afresh the very difficulties which the Workmen's Compensation Act was designed to remove.

In theory it might seem desirable to distinguish between industrial injuries caused:

(a) by the workman's negligence;
(b) by the employer's negligence; or
(c) by some other and unavoidable cause.

Some official British statistics (relating to accidents of young workers) make such distinctions, viz. accidents for which the firm was responsible, accidents for which the young worker was responsible, and accidents for which no blame attached to anyone.[1] The validity of such classifications is, however, limited.

It may be argued, on the other hand, that the disregard, under Workmen's Compensation legislation, of any question of responsibility may tend to discourage employers from doing more to diminish accidents than is required of them under the Factory Acts. Though these are already stringent, the danger of negligence on the part of the employer may be increased if his insurance premium indemnifies him against the consequences of some laxity in accident prevention, and there are very large numbers of persons within the scope of the Act employed upon non-factory premises. Employers united in some kind of mutual association may feel greater responsibility. In Germany, where all employers belong to *Berufsgenossenschaften*, the law requires them to bear the full cost of compensation where it has been judicially proved that they 'have caused the accident by intent or by negligence through lack of the attention obligatory upon them in view of their official position, profession or trade'.[2] An employer guilty of such neglect has to recompense the Mutual Indemnity Association for all expenditure incurred. Neglect of obligations imposed by Statute, or by Regulations made by the Mutuals which administer industrial accident prevention, thus deprives him of the protection he enjoys through insurance.

In Britain the occupier (or since 1938 the owner) of a factory may

---

[1] Cf. Chief Inspector of Factories, *Report for 1937*, 1938, p. 43.
[2] Cf. *Gewerbe-Unfallversicherung*, loc. cit., para. 903.

incur fines. But the maximum of £100 is much less than the probable cost of indemnifying an injured workman or a dead hand's dependants. What would be the position of a British industrial employer if on proof of negligence, he might be deprived of any protection under his insurance policy, and be further required to refund to the insurance company or to his Mutual Association all expenses incurred by them on behalf of an injured person? The Holman Gregory Committee were told that insurance offices desired to prevent claims and sometimes sent inspectors to establishments where accidents were of frequent occurrence,[1] but Sir Alexander Gibb took the view that an employer was little concerned to prevent accidents because 'if he is paying 100s. per cent. it does not matter to him how many accidents he has'.[2] It was repeatedly stated before the Committee that the interest of insurance offices in reducing the incidence of industrial accidents was limited to keeping premiums low. An inspector of a Mutual Association stated that they could repudiate liability if an accident arose through the negligence of a member firm but had never done so.[3] An insurance office in such circumstances might be reluctant to give an employer notice, particularly if he was a valued client in other branches of business, e.g. fire risks or pension schemes. On the other hand insurance offices might refuse the risk if it showed a loss on their books.[4] In neither case is fear of heavy losses as real an incentive to the employer as if he were obliged to belong to a trade association which, in the event of his proved negligence or default, would be responsible to pay compensation to the workman and to recoup themselves from his pocket.

Accident prevention can be effectively promoted only by bodies, such as Mutual Associations, in close touch with a particular industry, and not by insurance companies in general. The late Mr. W. A. Appleton, C.B.E., then Secretary of the General Federation of Trade Unions, told the Holman Gregory Committee that the 'technical knowledge' of insurance companies in these matters was small; he often had to tell the insurance company what was wrong, and ask them to act if the employer failed to do so. He wanted 'something more efficient than the present system' and suggested some form of 'trade control' which would inculcate *esprit de corps* among employers.[5] It is very generally believed that the standard of safety is highest in general in those great companies which carry their own insurance.

There is in British Workmen's Compensation little or no inducement to the insured employer to diminish risks. Insurance offices are

[1] Cf. *Holman Gregory Report*, Q. 17565.   [2] Cf. ibid., A. 1829.
[3] Cf. ibid., Q. 21041 sqq.   [4] Cf. ibid., Q. and A. 15895.
[5] Cf. ibid, Q. 3665–74.

unlikely to refuse liability and lack the technical knowledge to prevent accidents or to assess blame. There is little or no 'merit-rating' (see later). The only effective deterrent is the risk of an action at Common Law or under Employers' Liability instead of under Workmen's Compensation and even here the insured employer is covered. The existence and the maintenance of this legal recourse is thus a necessary corollary of the imperfect condition of Workmen's Compensation in Britain.

But the problem may also be viewed from another angle. The retention of the defence of Common Employment is sometimes criticized on the ground that the injured workmen, for whom Workmen's Compensation has been devised, should not also have the option of claiming under Common Law or Employers' Liability if negligence of the employer is alleged.

Actions for damages at Common Law, both in the U.K. and U.S.A.,[1] in regard to industrial injuries, are, and have always been, dilatory, costly, uncertain, and calculated to arouse sharp antagonisms between the master and man. The legal difficulties inherent in Employers' Liability cases where claims under Workmen's Compensation may arise are illustrated by four actions brought in a County Court by four widows under the provisions of the Fatal Accidents Acts.[2] Each widow claimed on her behalf, but not on behalf of any other dependant. At the same time four applications for arbitration were made on behalf of the four respective sets of children for compensation as dependants under the Workmen's Compensation Act. The action went to the Court of Appeal which sent it back to the County Court judge.[3] In another case, recently reported, a widow had deliberately refrained, on legal advice, from claiming under the Workmen's Compensation Act, because it was considered that she had an unanswerable claim under the Fatal Accidents Act. Her legal advisers unfortunately failed to discover the right defendant. She had sued a number of contractors engaged on the building where her husband met with death, but not the party that might have been liable, viz. the Fulham Borough Council. The judge said he would have assessed damages at £2,500 if she had established liability. In dismissing the widow's claim Lord Justice Goddard remarked: 'I deeply regret the position which results —a position disastrous in the extreme for a much injured woman.'[4] To

---

[1] Cf. Dodd, loc. cit., pp. 19–25.

[2] Lord Campbell's Act, see vol. i, p. 30, and the Employers' Liability Act, 1880.

[3] Cf. *Avery, Harris, Bonner, and Watson* v. *L.N.E.R.*, Butterworth's *Cases*, 1938, pp. 204 sqq.

[4] Cf. *The Daily Telegraph*, Oct. 27th 1938. The decision in this case was reversed on appeal on a technical point.

what abstruse complications it may lead when the defence of Common Employment is used by employers to avoid liability became very evident in *Radcliffe* v. *Ribble Motor Services*. The driver of a motor omnibus was killed by the driver of another omnibus who happened to be a fellow employee. The firm denied liability. The House of Lords held that the action of the driver who caused the death of his fellow employee was an independent operation. Lord Atkin in a considered judgement noted that 'at the present time the doctrine of common employment is looked at askance by judges and text-book writers. There are none to praise and very few to love. But it is too well established to be overthrown by judicial decision.' On the other hand, he held that there was no connexion between the driving of the one car and that of the other: 'for the purpose of the doctrine, the risk of injury in the streets by a vehicle driven by a fellow servant is not one of "the natural risks and perils incident to the performance of his service".' The appeal of the widow was allowed, and she was awarded £1,579 plus £500 for loss of her husband's expectation of life.[1] This decision established 'community of risk' as a necessary element in common employment.[2]

By widening the scope of Common Law and Employers' Liability the risk of litigation is increased. A better course would be so to increase the scales of compensation and the opportunities of rehabilitation that injured workers should have no inducement to have recourse to other and less certain legal remedies. In several States of the U.S.A. compensation is awarded on a higher scale if the injury was occasioned by the wilful neglect of statutory safeguards by an employer. Some States also impose a corresponding penalty upon a workman whose injury is due to a breach of regulations by reducing the compensation payment.[3] Recent American writers offer no opinion as to the practical effect of such measures, which are unlikely to commend themselves to British courts, employers, or employees. It seems to us that masters and men, both individually and collectively, should have a more direct interest than at present in the prevention of accidents and of industrial disease. If accident prevention can be pursued as an integral part of a revised system of Workmen's Compensation, the present anomalous competition between Common Law, Employers' Liability, and Workmen's Compensation as parallel and alternative remedies would

[1] Cf. *The Times*, Feb. 24th 1939.

[2] The case was quoted by the Master of the Rolls in the Court of Appeal case *Metcalfe* v. *London Passenger Transport Board*—a very similar case to *Radcliffe* v. *Ribble Motor Services*. The widow in this case got £3,715. Cf. *The Times*, April 28th 1939.

[3] Cf. Dodd, loc. cit., p. 704. Also *Handbook of Labor Statistics*, Washington, 1936, p. 1127, note 32.

disappear by mere desuetude. The defence of Common Employment would retain little significance, and the whole system of compensation for industrial injury would constitute a single and uniform system of legal administration, under a scheme of collective compulsory insurance.

This appears to be the view of the Home Office whose representative, Mr. R. A. Buckland, observed that 'if the workmen's compensation provisions were very greatly improved there would be a revived tendency not to resort to civil actions which are often speculative and costly, when they can get pretty good benefits under the Workmen's Compensation Acts'.[1] The Home Office Memorandum was noncommittal as to the probable effect of the abolition of the defence of Common Employment though it noted that its scope had of late years been narrowed by decisions in the House of Lords, and that the further development of industry into larger units involved increased risk to individuals from the carelessness of those with whom they were in common employment.[2] This was before the House of Lords had decided, in *Radcliffe* v. *Ribble Motor Services*, that 'community of risk' was a necessary element in 'common employment'. That judgement is likely further to reduce the number of cases in which it can be pleaded with success. Men in one part of a pit may be held not to be in common employment with those on the surface: men in one part of a factory may be held to have no community of risk with those in another. The judgement is a good example of the manner in which the House of Lords can apply ancient principles to new conditions consistently alike with law and with justice.

[1] Q. 720 A. The same view was expressed by Mr. Russell Jones speaking for the T.U.C. before the Hetherington Commission (cf. A. 4975 and 4942–8, and also pp. 449–50).

[2] Cf. *Hetherington Commission*, p. 108. Cf. also Christopher Saunders, 'A Backward Area in Social Legislation', in *Toynbee Outlook*, May 1939, pp. 10–13.

CHAPTER XIV

THE LEGAL SIDE: METHODS AND DEFICIENCIES OF ADMINISTRATION

A. THE INTERNATIONAL BACKGROUND

Hurt not the servant that worketh faithfully, nor the hired man that giveth thee his life.

Ecclesiasticus vii. 22–3.

THE legal aspects of the administration of Workmen's Compensation have been a constantly recurring theme in preceding chapters.
The frequency and severity of accidents depends in part on administration, and is often of overriding importance in the recording of
claims, the conclusion of settlements, in the evaluation of incapacity
and benefits under the Act, in reviews of weekly payments, in the
fixing of lump-sum payments, &c. We have hitherto been concerned
primarily with the existing system of administration and its effects upon
the actual working of Workmen's Compensation, and have not yet
analysed it, nor commented upon its deficiencies. The results of our
researches in this imperfectly explored field are set forth in this and
subsequent chapters.

The British system of Workmen's Compensation cannot be
adequately discussed without some reference to other systems whose
characteristics were scarcely understood when the Holman Gregory
Committee was sitting.[1]

Foreign systems fall broadly speaking into three main categories:

1. *Court Administration.* This is the British system and of some
States of the U.S.A. Though it does not produce uniform results, it
has 'developed a fairly adequate plan of compensation for a homo-
geneous body of workmen'.[2] Complete uniformity is neither possible
nor perhaps desirable; the growth of medical science is slow; new
forms of diagnosis and treatment take time to establish themselves.
Judges and registrars, like other men, may reach different conclusions
upon identical premises in successive decades. The system of Court
Administration is not exclusively judicial. 'No action at law can be
brought to obtain the compensation recoverable under the Act, but in
place thereof is substituted a kind of quasi-legal arbitration, placed in
the hands sometimes of laymen and sometimes of lawyers, regulated

---

[1] The American investigation referred to exhaustively in our vol. i, pp. 157–8, remains
an exception and has, as we have seen, not been of practical influence upon British legislation. [2] Cf. Dodd, loc. cit., p. 98.

in county courts, or before an arbitrator appointed by a county court judge, by rules framed under the Act.'[1]

2. *The Commission System*. This prevails in the U.S.A. where the Court Administration system has been retained in full vigour in a few States only.[2] There are, however, great differences between the systems in force in the several States.[3] The jurisdiction of the courts is not entirely excluded. Commissions comprising Industrial Accident Boards, Industrial Boards, or other administrative agencies responsible for the supervision of Compensation Laws,[4] often make preliminary authoritative and technical investigations which may be accepted by the courts as a basis for their decisions.[5] The system, however, admittedly differs widely from that of Court Administration.

3. *Administration by State Institutions*.[6] This system is usually asso-ciated with the existence of a State Insurance Fund or some similar institution. It was originally devised, and has grown up, in Germany, but *Berufsgenossenschaften* have nothing in common with existing British Mutual Indemnity Associations of employers, which are 'private' bodies of employers for mutual protection, whilst the former are *Körperschaften des öffentlichen Rechts*—bodies with legal person-ality but without the attributes of a State department. Membership is compulsory for employers in the respective trades or industries.

[1] Cf. Ruegg and Stanes, *The Workmen's Compensation Act 1906*. 1922.

[2] Alabama, Alaska, Louisiana, New Hampshire, New Mexico, Tennessee, and Wyo-ming. Cf. *Claims Administration in Workmen's Compensation*, U.S. Dept. of Labor, reprint from *Monthly Labor Review*, Washington, June 1938, p. 10.

[3] Cf. Dodd, loc. cit., pp. 100–16: 'Although the assertion that many States adopted the commission form of administration is generally accurate, the patterns into which this type of administration fell in the different States were almost as diverse as the employments included or the benefits granted under several laws.'

[4] Cf. *Handbook of Labor Statistics*, Washington, 1936, p. 1132.

[5] Cf. Dodd, loc. cit., p. 114, where the 'compensation problem in a typical State' is mentioned: an 'appeal to a trial court or to an intermediate court of review, with the issues in most cases heard by the court on the basis of the record made in the administrative review' by one of the Boards; a further judicial review may be made by the highest State court, 'also based on the record made in the hearing before the "administrative" body'.

[6] The I.L.O. *Evaluation Report*, 1937, speaks of 'Social Insurance Institutions' in con-trast to 'ordinary law courts' and 'special tribunals or special assessment committees', cf. loc. cit., p. 361. The term appears to us somewhat vague; Workmen's Compensation, wherever regulated by law, is a social service and the bodies entrusted with the carrying out of such law appear as 'social institutions'; thus the bodies mentioned under (2) may be so classified, whether they are Boards, Committees, Commissions, &c. What matters under (3), however, is that a special administrative and executive body is created which has official authority and powers. In our opinion this very important point has not been brought out clearly in the I.L.O. *Evaluation Report*. We therefore prefer to say 'Administration by State Institutions', drawing a clear line between these and Court Administration on the one hand, and Commission Administration on the other, which does not or must not represent centralized and specialized State administration.

Such associations have the power to regulate their procedure and, to some extent, the obligations of their members, as well as to form regional branches with full administrative powers[1] such as appertain to authorized cartels. Member firms are bound to obey the regulations and by-laws of their respective associations, which are subject to official scrutiny and approval. The *Berufsgenossenschaft* is the executive nucleus of the system of Workmen's Compensation, subject to control and inspection by the local and regional insurance offices (*Versicherungsämter* and *Oberversicherungsämter*) and the Imperial Insurance Office in Berlin.[2] These offices do not merely arbitrate or decide disputes, although appeal and recourse (*Berufung* and *Rekurs*) are among their functions.[3] They also have to adjudicate upon many administrative questions, and deal with the *Berufsgenossenschaften*. As these are quasi-official bodies, the other offices being State institutions, the whole administrative organization of Workmen's Compensation in Germany may fairly be described as one of State Administration.

The systems in force in France and Sweden and in Victoria stand midway between the Commission System and that of State Administration. The supervision of Workmen's Compensation is here entrusted to a State Institution; employers can choose between insuring with private institutions or with employers' mutual associations under official supervision and control.[4]

These three alternative methods of administering Workmen's Compensation have roots in history and are not fortuitous. The British system was designed to reduce to a minimum the prospect of bureaucratic intervention which British employers of the Manchester School regarded with alarm. There was no provision for compulsory insurance, or for an accident fund. As Oliver Goldsmith wrote a century earlier,[5] they clung, as employers of labour, to

> That independence Britons prize too high
> Keeps man from man and breaks the social tie.

County Courts, in which most actions under the Employers' Liability Act, 1880, were brought, had been set up only in 1846 under

[1] Cf. for details *Reichsversicherungsordnung*, vol. iii, sections 649 sqq.; *Verfassung der Berufsgenossenschaften*, pp. 276 sqq.

[2] The intervention of the Imperial Insurance Office was, until 1935, limited to areas or cases in which the State Insurance Offices (*Landesversicherungsämter*) did not exercise the final authority normally vested in them.

[3] Cf. *Reichsversicherungsordnung*, ed. 1938 (edited by Dr. Eichelsbacher), paras. 1675 sqq. and 1699 sqq.

[4] Cf. *International Survey of Social Services*, 1936, pp. 221 and 573. Also *Social Work and Legislation in Sweden*, The Royal Social Board, Stockholm, 1938, p. 113.

[5] *The Deserted Village*.

'An Act for the Recovery of Small Debts and Demands', with a limit of jurisdiction in actions for debt of £20, increased in 1850 to £50 and in 1905 to £100. They were already heavily burdened and loath to extend their administrative responsibilities. Insurance carriers were private companies or associations of private people against whose insolvency the injured workman was in no way safeguarded. Judicial administration under the Acts of 1897 and 1906 remained with the County Courts whose powers were gradually extended in deference to repeated representations by County Court judges to the Lord Chancellor, and to public opinion. The Holman Gregory Committee in 1920 wished to create a Workmen's Compensation Commissioner who would have been assisted by District Commissioners who, in their turn, would have been in close touch with employers and workmen as advisers and conciliators, and would have dealt with disputed cases 'with less formality and, consequently, less delay and expense than exist to-day'.[1] The proposal was shelved.

In making this suggestion which Court Administration would have supplemented by some sort of Commission Administration, the Holman Gregory Committee drew particular attention to the work and methods of American Accident Boards. The U.S.A. were familiar both with the British and German systems.[2] They rejected the former, and only partly adopted the latter, which inspired the Ohio State Insurance Fund, and encouraged a tendency to limit the functions of the courts and extend those of administrative bodies.[3] Constitutional difficulties made it impossible to initiate a nation-wide system of Workmen's Compensation in the U.S.A.,[4] although 'the desirability of an administrative agency charged specifically with the supervision of the compensation laws is recognized by all but seven States'.[5] Yet all is not well in Ohio where 'a cumbersome and costly procedure of "rehearings" prefatory to court appeals' is fastened upon the compensation agency and 'attorneys in Ohio are active in securing business from compensation "claimants" '.[6] This shows the fundamental difference between Commission and State Administration. The nearest approach to federal co-ordination and co-operation is the International (sc. interfederal) Association of Industrial Accident

---

[1] Cf. *Holman Gregory Report*, p. 58.   [2] See vol. i, pp. 156–8 and 194–5.
[3] Cf. Dodd, loc. cit., pp. 353–4 and *passim*.
[4] The failure of the States to accept Federal Legislation was and still is much lamented. It has been emphasized recently as one of the reasons for the incompleteness of rehabilitation opportunities. Cf. *Monthly Labor Review*, Feb. 1936, reprint, Washington, 1936, p. 3. Cf. also Marshall Dawson, 'Coverage Limitations of Workmen's Compensation Laws', ibid., June 1939, p. 1270. For further complaints see ibid., pp. 1280–1.
[5] Cf. *Handbook*, 1936, p. 1132.
[6] Cf. *Monthly Labour Review*, June 1938, reprint, p. 15.

Boards and Commissions, dating from 1914, whose activities mainly take the form of investigation and discussion, though it has, incidentally, made important contributions to Rehabilitation.[1] Another nation-wide institution, dating from 1915, is the National Council on Compensation Insurance, which limits itself to the technical aspects of rate-making; it has been sharply criticized. These institutions are proof of a desire for greater uniformity which may one day find expression in a reorganization of Workmen's Compensation on national lines. Meanwhile Workmen's Compensation is administered by almost as many institutions as there are States, mainly upon Commission lines[2] designed to limit or reduce the powers of ordinary courts.

In this connexion the following citations from recent American literature may be of interest. In June 1938 the U.S. Department of Labor called attention to the advantages of the Ontario Act, drafted by Sir William Ralph Meredith, Chief Justice of Ontario, after an exhaustive study of Workmen's Compensation systems in Europe and in America. His guiding principle was 'to get rid of the nuisance of litigation' and 'to have swift justice meted out to a great body of men', even though some mistakes might be made. He was shocked by some English cases in which workmen failed to recover, though the court decisions might be legally unimpeachable. The workman seemed to him to be at a disadvantage in a court of law. Some mistakes are inevitable under any system of procedure, but Sir William Meredith was convinced that those made by an expert board with final administrative authority would be fewer than those made by the courts.[3] The U.S.A. Department of Labor in this connexion uses the term 'complete emancipation from court interference or control' which had enabled the Workmen's Compensation authority to 'develop its own routine' and 'virtually has no problem with procedure'.[4] As Mr. C. M. Knowles told the Holman Gregory Committee: '. . . they [in Canada] seem to be turning definitely away from the British Acts and following . . . the American form of Workmen's Compensation

[1] Cf. Dodd, p. 715.

[2] Cf. ibid., pp. 825–6 and 581 for criticism of the 'National Council'.

[3] Cf. *Monthly Labor Review*, June 1938, *Claims Administration* reprint, pp. 2–3.

[4] The 'Ontario' system, however, should not be confounded with State Administration. The machinery created for the settlement of claims is not identical with a government department administering the whole complex system of Workmen's Compensation; on the contrary, in Ontario large employers are made individually liable to pay their accident costs, but the compensation is paid through the Provincial Workmen's Compensation Board at the same rates as under the collective liability schemes, while the Workmen's Compensation Board has jurisdiction to determine matters affecting workmen employed by employers who are individually liable. Cf. *International Survey*, I.L.O., 1936, pp. 146 and 150.

legislation'.[1] The main incentive in the U.S.A. for 'turning away' from the Court System was the experience of its failures.

In the United States [writes Dodd in 1936][2] court administration has failed, not because of the inefficiency in the courts, but because the judicial machinery is not, and cannot be, adapted to the new problem of administration presented by Workmen's Compensation . . . [which] presents many problems of continuous supervision for which the Courts are ill adapted. Judicial machinery designed for the settlement of private controversies cannot . . . meet the entirely different needs of an efficient system of Workmen's Compensation.

Finally, the U.S. Department of Labor writes in June 1938:[3]

No constructive contribution to the theory and practice of compensation claim settlements has been made by any American jurisdiction under Court administration. On the contrary, the merit of the systems displacing court administration may, as a rule, be gauged by the relative completeness of their departure from court attitudes and practices.[4]

This explains why in the U.S.A. administration of Workmen's Compensation has departed from the British 'model' of administration. The Home Office told the Hetherington Commission that the British system of Workmen's Compensation 'was widely copied in other parts of the Empire, in the U.S.A. and elsewhere'.[5] Our investigations show that the U.S.A. have, in fact, been inspired from the beginning by the conception of State or semi-State administration. Workmen's Compensation was first introduced in Washington (1911), where insurance is compulsory with an exclusive State Fund.[6] Ohio, with its compulsory State Insurance Fund, followed in the same year. To-day there are 18 general State Fund Insurance systems of which 7 are either monopolistic or semi-monopolistic, while 11 compete with private or self-insurance. In the monopolistic group Ohio permits self-insurance, whereas West Virginia permits self-insurance by employers who can in turn protect themselves through insurance companies. The stringent requirements for self-insurance in West Virginia, however, have caused most industrial organizations to subscribe to the State Fund.[7] Sixteen States have compulsory insurance.

---

[1] Cf. *Holman Gregory Report*, Q. 1049.

[2] Cf. loc. cit., pp. 98–9.   [3] Cf. loc. cit., p. 11.

[4] Cf. also Marshall Dawson, 'Problems of Workmen's Compensation Legislation', in *Labor Information Bulletin*, vol. iii, no. 1, of Jan. 1936, p. 6: 'When a worker is injured he ceases to earn his wages and needs compensation badly. Injured workers cannot afford delay, the expense, the waste of time, or the uncertainty involved in court trials. Court procedure as a means of Workmen's Compensation administration has, therefore, been discarded in all but six States of the Union.'   [5] *Memorandum*, § A i. 4.

[6] It was attacked at first as an experiment in State Socialism. Cf. Dodd, loc. cit., p. 35. Also R. H. Blanchard, *Workmen's Compensation in the United States*, Geneva, 1926, *passim*.   [7] Cf. *Medical Service in Industry*, &c., loc. cit., p. 43.

Most States have provided a Commission or Board to administer and supervise the compensation laws and claims; six States, and Alaska, are lacking in this respect. If ever there was an attempt (which we doubt) to copy the British system, the present trend appears to be in the opposite direction.

American experts on Workmen's Compensation administration are leaning more and more towards Board administration, as preferable to the former system of Court administration.

The evils that attended the court system, with its delays, its contingent fees for lawyers, the substitution in many cases of compromise settlements [see for this point our observations on pp. 153–4], often woefully inadequate, and the reliance upon technical rules of evidence to defeat otherwise meritorious claims, reacted powerfully to bring about a new era in the field of compensation for industrial injuries ... boards, acting in a quasi-judicial capacity, are usually not bound to apply technical rules of evidence or procedure. In many States their fact-finding power is final. Through their operations attorneys are not necessary in any but the exceptional case. The effort seems to have been successful to establish a method of adjudication that is informal, non-technical, summary and speedy. The workman gets quickly what is his due and gets it all. He gets it when he most needs it, that is, while he is incapacitated. The trend of the moment towards injecting lawyers into compensation procedures, with the almost inevitable result of introducing technical and legal elements, is one to view without enthusiasm, if not with actual distrust.[1]

The British Dominions display somewhat similar legislative tendencies. In Canada collective liability prevails. There are also individual liability schemes for some large employers, but even in such cases compensation is paid in Ontario and Quebec through the Workmen's Compensation Board which has wide jurisdiction. There are 'accident funds' for different risk classes. The Union of South Africa, since 1934, has a Workmen's Compensation Commissioner with wide powers. In the Northern Territory of Australia there is an Insurance Institution approved by the Minister of the Interior. In New South Wales it is compulsory to insure with an insurance company licensed by the Workers' Compensation Commission; appeals lie to an 'Industrial Magistrate'. In Queensland the insurance is administered by a single inter-occupational institution, the State Insurance Office, which is managed by an official appointed by the Governor in Council, the Insurance Commissioner. In Victoria there is a State Insurance Office, apart from private insurance. Insurance is compulsory.

Alike in the U.S.A. and the Dominions the German State System of Administration has found no imitators, though the Ontario system in practice resembles it. The reason is not far to seek: these new

[1] Cf. Henry D. Sayer, Dep. Exec. Director, N.Y. Insurance Fund, *Amer. Journal of Surgery*, Dec. 1938, p. 499.

countries had no social institutions upon which they could build. They started on individualistic lines; their social institutions assumed that the interests of Master and Man could not be reconciled in any joint institution. The remnants of some gild institutions enabled Germany[1] to base Workmen's Compensation from the outset on a system of regional or occupational organizations which constituted a corporative liability of employers; it enabled the German Empire to build up within a short time a system of State Administration of Workmen's Compensation which many Americans who have at heart the progress of Workmen's Compensation administration in their own country regard with admiration.[2]

[1] Cf. vol. i, pp. 7–9.   [2] Cf. ibid., pp. 157–8.

CHAPTER XV

THE LEGAL SIDE: METHODS OF AND DEFICIENCIES IN ADMINISTRATION

B. THE PROBLEM IN BRITAIN

The necessity for having technical and practical competence that can be acquired only by long experience suggests the desirability of having special bodies dealing solely with social insurance questions.

I.L.O., *Report on Evaluation of Permanent Incapacity for Work and Social Insurance*, 1937.

THE official administration of Workmen's Compensation in Britain must in present circumstances be strictly limited in scope. There is no compulsory insurance, except in the coal-mining industry, and no Compensation Fund.[1] (Both necessitate, where they exist, important administrative duties.) There is no medical benefit for injured workmen, no systematic rehabilitation, and no machinery to facilitate the re-entry of injured workmen into their former or into a new occupation. The limit of official administration is set by existing legislation in which there is no place for Accident Boards or Commissions. The administration, such as it is, is conducted by commercial institutions, i.e. commercial companies, and mutual indemnity associations of employers or, more rarely, by committees of employers and men. This limitation of official functions is characteristic of the British system of Workmen's Compensation, which was deliberately designed to restrict the sphere of official initiative.

It follows that under present conditions official intervention relates primarily to the settlement of disputed claims[2] by the courts, though registrars play an increasingly important role in the registration of agreements, particularly for lump sums. Approved Societies sometimes take an interest in particular cases,[3] but have no administrative functions and cannot be regarded even as semi-official institutions for our purpose.

On the other hand the Court of Appeal, and the House of Lords, have had a great influence upon the administration and have evolved, in the last thirty years, a number of important principles relating to the application and interpretation of the existing Compensation Acts. Judge Ruegg told the Holman Gregory Committee:[4]

I so greatly prefer the decisions of the House of Lords to those of the Court of Appeal, that I should not in the least object to them all going to the House of

---

[1] Apart from special schemes.

[2] The Chief Registrar of Friendly Societies has moreover a well-defined duty of control in respect of contracting-out schemes under § 31 of the Act.

[3] Cf. Willis, loc. cit., p. 593. [4] Cf. *Holman Gregory Report*, A. 10248.

Lords, but I expect the House of Lords would object very strongly to having all appeals coming before them.

Our main concern is, therefore, the *Procedure for Determining Compensation and Settling Questions*, under which heading of the Act are grouped the following:[1]

Section:
§ 21. Procedure for settling questions.
§ 22. Varying awards.
§ 23. Registration of agreements, &c.
§ 25. Invalidity of unregistered agreements.
§ 26. Payment of Compensation into Court.
§ 27. Jurisdiction of county courts.
§ 28. Powers of Committees.

With the registration of agreements we have dealt elsewhere; of the other sections relating to the Court administration of Workmen's Compensation those which mainly concern us are the first and the last mentioned above.

Outstanding questions between the workman and his employer may be settled by agreement[2] or by arbitration. It is the latter which interests us here. Discussions on the subject of 'litigation' are often obscured by the reiterated assertion that the percentage of claims subject to litigation 'must have been quite small, certainly less than 2 per cent.'.[3] A member of the Hetherington Commission, Mr. Boyd, invoked the figure as evidence that 'the present scheme works very easily and smoothly'.[4] A competent witness[5] stigmatized the same figure as 'very gravely misleading'. The overwhelming majority of injuries to be compensated are trivial and could not conceivably be the subject of litigation. The fact that they are settled by 'agreement', i.e. without disagreement leading to an application to be filed with the Court,[6] does not justify a statistical comparison of such cases with cases of serious or partial disablement in which litigation necessarily and properly plays an important part. To use figures thus is to bring other official statistical interpretations under suspicion. While the total number of compensation cases, so far as statistics go, was 488,865 in 1937, cases of longer duration, i.e. terminated after weekly payments lasting thirteen weeks or over, were about 20,000 in the case of accident and 2,000 in case of industrial disease, while cases in which

---

[1] Cf. Willis, loc. cit., p. 412.   [2] Cf. *Workmen's Compensation Statistics for 1937*, p. 14.
[3] See also *Home Office Memorandum*, Hetherington Commission, p. 14, para. 104; for a discussion of the underlying fallacy see our vol. i, p. 312.
[4] Cf. *Hetherington Commission Evidence*, Q. 1825.
[5] Cf. ibid., Mr. Spearing, Q. 1825 A.
[6] See Mr. Buckland's evidence for this terminology, A. 26–7. See also Q. 2244–5.

lump-sum settlements were arrived at after twenty-six weeks were about 7,000 cases of accidents and 1,000 of injuries. It is within these groups that the possibility of and need for litigation lies. A full analysis of the figures would certainly show that the proportion of cases referred to the County and Appeal Courts varies with the serious-ness of the injury and therefore of the amount at stake: it is probable that six out of ten cases involving permanent disability are the subject of litigation. It is improbable that one case in ten thousand involving less than thirteen weeks disability is the subject of Court proceedings.

There is another point of equal importance which should not be overlooked. Under the present system compensation in serious cases is admittedly a matter of 'bargaining', in which the injured person is too often the weaker party and is, in many cases, compelled to accept less than his due, often in spite of the friendly efforts of registrars and sheriff substitutes. In such circumstances an agreement reached with-out litigation is not necessarily a genuinely agreed settlement, or pre-ferable to one reached after public hearing by a judge. Many cases, indeed, occur in which litigation would have been to the advantage of the injured workmen. It not infrequently happens that cases do not reach the courts because the injured party cannot afford, or is afraid, to resort thereto. The Ministry of Health told the Hetherington Commission of cases brought to their notice[1]

where an insured person, through fear of losing his employment, not only refuses himself to claim compensation, but also is reluctant that action should be taken by an Approved Society on his behalf.

To regard such cases as uncontested and to adduce them in proof of the 'smooth working' of Workmen's Compensation is disingenuous. 'From the moment', so declared Sir Walter Citrine, before the Hethering-ton Commission, 'a claim is put in, from that moment onwards the litigation starts. The company nearly always tries to limit its liabili-ties in the early letters that pass between the parties and costs are piled up right away, immediately.' This is long before, if at all, 'real liti-gation' starts.[2] It is true that, as Sir H. Hetherington remarked, taking 'litigation' in this sense widens its interpretation; but the narrow meaning of the legal term, i.e. restricting it to the mere legal procedure, has led to a dangerous underestimate of the actual expenses (not to speak of the anxiety and trouble) resulting in regard to almost any important claim through legal correspondence and the entry of the solicitor. We fully agree with Sir Walter Citrine when he expressed the view that 'litigation' starts long before the actual judicial proceedings.

We shall later see to what surprising results an investigation of un-

[1] pp. 158-9.　　　　　　　　　　[2] A. 4209 and 4214.

contested cases has led in the State of New York; we regret that no such investigation has ever been attempted in Britain.[1]

Arbitrations may relate to the liability to pay compensation, the amount of compensation, and the duration of its payments. There is also the question of compensation payable to partial dependants; their title and identity, and the review and redemption of weekly payments, to which we have already alluded (see Chapters IX and X). We mention them here merely from the viewpoint of the 'system' of administration as practised in Britain. An 'arbitration tribunal' may consist of:[2]

1. A representative Committee.
2. An agreed arbitrator.
3. The County Court judge.
4. An arbitrator appointed by the County Court judge.

The single arbitrator is practically never used. The Holman Gregory Committee had high hopes of the system of representative committees, which was stated to be working well in the coal-mining industry in County Durham.[3] These expectations have not been fulfilled. Though § 28 of the Act empowers the Secretary of State to confer, by order, on any committee representative of employers and workmen, all or any of the powers conferred by the Act exclusively on County Courts or judges of County Courts, only one such order appears to have been made, and that in 1907.[4] Such committees might have developed on the lines of *Berufsgenossenschaften* in Germany, to which the arrangements of certain large firms with contracting-out schemes under § 31 of the Act already approximate, but they have in fact not come to anything. The anxiety of the Holman Gregory Committee to encourage the Durham scheme was conditioned by the belief that 'such committees depend for their success on their voluntary character'.[5] After a lapse of twenty years it seems clear that, as voluntary organizations, they will never play an important part. Most claims are dealt with in County Courts.[6]

[1] There is a wide gulf of degrees between 'negotiations leading to an agreement' and negotiations culminating ultimately in litigation. The point is dealt with in para. 470 of the Home Office Memorandum to the Hetherington Commission. The question 'whether the present system involves an undue amount of negotiation' was left open by the Memorandum—to be decided by further evidence. The character and social aspect of such 'negotiation', however, was not analysed.

[2] Cf. *First Schedule of the Act, Arbitration*, &c., 1–3.

[3] Readers will find a full description of this Committee in the evidence of Mr. Robert Watson Cooper before the Holman Gregory Committee. Cf. Q. 5940 sqq. Cf. also *Report*, p. 57. Between 1913 and 1918 the number of cases dealt with by the Committee had increased from 366 to 531, while the number dealt with by the County Court had decreased from 53 to 13.

[4] Cf. Willis, loc. cit., p. 453.   [5] Cf. *Holman Gregory Report*, p. 57.

[6] Cf. *Memorandum on the Workmen's Compensation Acts, 1925–31*, 1936, p. 13.

The Holman Gregory Committee were satisfied that the County Courts were acceptable tribunals. This statement is as true now as it was then. In the words of the I.L.O.,[1] 'The ordinary courts offer every guarantee of impartiality and judicial competence'. Any criticism of Court Administration in these pages is directed not against judges or arbitrators but against a system which does not allow them sufficient judicial power to administer the Act. The maxim *ultra posse nemo obligatur* is not applicable only to the defendant. The *Holman Gregory Report* notes that 'the formality—which is a necessary and important feature of the administration of justice in the Law Courts—causes delay and considerable expense to the parties'.[2] This again is not a criticism of judges, but of the administration.

The Holman Gregory Committee, however, noted that it was commonly recognized that settlements that would be passed by one County Court judge or registrar would be rejected by another. The Committee proceeded, in this connexion, to explain why they recommended the appointment of a Workmen's Compensation Commissioner with a staff of District Commissioners. The Stewart Committee has, so far as concerns lump-sum settlements, adduced further evidence of lack of uniformity; though this is only one aspect of Court Administration, it is probably typical. In 1938, as in 1920, the evidence showed that 'different registrars may take wholly different views on the question of what are adequate amounts'. We have also heard of a practice, of unknown extent, whereby certain agreements which have been refused at one court are lodged with some other court.[3] The Stewart Committee did not attempt to analyse more closely the admitted lack of uniformity which gives rise to such practices. They emphasized that 'both employers and workmen prefer present methods as possessing the necessary degree of flexibility, and desire to retain their present freedom of bargaining', but did not criticize this 'desire', nor place against it the observations of the I.L.O. *Report on Evaluation* that[4]

liberty of contract does not exist. . . . 'Amicable' agreements between a weak claimant and a powerful employer tend to become leonine contracts. . . . Legislators in various countries have recognized the necessity for taking the evaluation of incapacity out of the hands of two unevenly matched parties.

The Stewart Committee regretted that 'no general rules designed to bring about a greater measure of uniformity' in administration could be attained,[5] but went no further, although 'many witnesses gave

[1] Cf. *Evaluation Report*, 1937, p. 362.   [2] Cf. loc. cit., p. 58.
[3] Cf. *Stewart Report*, p. 104 and *passim*.
[4] Cf. loc. cit., p. 242.   [5] Cf. loc. cit., p. 103.

evidence concerning the wide variations in assessments which occur under present conditions'—variations which witnesses held to be unavoidable so long as each registrar was left to exercise his own discretion as to the sum which would be adequate in individual cases. An experienced solicitor suggested that cases should be concentrated in a few courts. This proposal, as also the creation of a central authority to advise registrars, was negatived by the Committee.[1] The lack of general guidance is certainly felt. The late Sir John Collie declared that[2] 'a decision of a County Court Judge in one particular district may not be on the same lines as a decision in a similar case given by a judge in another district, although the facts and circumstances may be similar'. Dr. Brend notes[3] that the attitude of judges towards the employment of Medical Assessors lacks uniformity, though 'if a Judge does not consider Medical Assessors helpful, no useful purpose is likely to be served by calling one'. County Court decisions, moreover, are rarely officially reported, and what one County Court judge may decide does not of course bind another one in another County Court. Among other unfavourable features of Court Administration in Britain is the fact that the judge is often dependent upon authoritative and reliable evidence, particularly upon medical matters, and especially in evaluating partial incapacity, in the review of weekly payments, and of agreements to be recorded. We deal with this important question in our next chapter, and may here pass it by; in any event the medical problem does not appear to us to offer serious administrative difficulties for Court Administration. It remains to inquire whether a judge, with very many other judicial questions daily before him, can be expected to be so fully acquainted with the whole sphere of Workmen's Compensation as to be able to give adequate weight to economic and social considerations which are relevant to a legal decision. Some of the witnesses before the Stewart Committee thought that matters of evaluation (mainly respecting the recording of lump-sum settlements) might involve work which the registrar could not conveniently undertake; and suggested the creation of an Advisory Committee empowered to go into the whole of the facts of a case in which lump-sum settlement was proposed. Other witnesses suggested that a social worker should be attached to the court for this purpose.[4] These suggestions found little support.

'Agreements' are not restricted to lump-sum settlements but may and indeed should have much wider connotations (see Chapter VIII). The Home Office told the Hetherington Commission, for example, that 'many agreements are not, in fact, submitted for registration'.

[1] Cf. *Stewart Report*, pp. 95–6.   [2] Cf. Collie, loc. cit., p. 44.
[3] Cf. Brend, loc. cit., p. 75.   [4] Cf. *Stewart Report*, p. 93.

Although § 23 of the Act uses the word 'shall' the obligation 'is rather indefinite' and 'there is, in many cases, *no very strong incentive* to submitting an agreement to registration'. A recorded agreement is enforceable as a County Court judgement; but an unrecorded agreement can be pleaded in answer to a request of arbitration or as a defence in an action.[1] The point was only touched on in Mr. Buckland's evidence[2] but gained significance from his admission that 'if all these agreements were registered . . . an immense burden would be placed upon the Registrar'. We are thus faced with the fact that the Home Office regrets the absence of a strong incentive to register agreements,[3] but admits that the present machinery of administration by Registrars would be overtaxed if registration were universal. The irresistible conclusion is that either the law or the administration must be changed in order to secure to the injured worker his legal rights.

Few will now dissent from the view that the administration of Workmen's Compensation requires wide knowledge of industrial, technical, and social conditions, and that it demands specialized knowledge of a kind which a judge, who spends nine-tenths of his time, if not more, upon other matters, may find it difficult or impossible to acquire, for it cannot be learned from books. How many judges, for example, are or can be familiar with the well-established aspects of accident proneness adumbrated in our first chapters? Yet the outlook of the judge upon such matters may be decisive. The conflicting views of County Court judges, the Court of Appeal, and the House of Lords show the importance of the personal factor. Again, it is difficult for a judge to assess the conditions of the labour market in so-called 'odd lot' cases.[4] In the case *Blades* v. *Wool Exchange and General Investments Ltd.* the County Court judge used his local knowledge of employment conditions in order to fix the wages of a woman disabled by dermatitis from following her ordinary employment. His right to do so was questioned. Greene M.R. ruled that 'as a result of his experience' the trial judge had an accurate idea of the wages which would be earned by a person in the applicant's position; but, he added:[5]

If the case were concerned with a person earning a much higher wage in some skilled trade, it would be possible to understand the view that local knowledge or a general knowledge of affairs might not be sufficient to enable the judge to come to a finding of fact as to wages that could be earned.

[1] Cf. *Hetherington Commission*, p. 26.
[2] Cf. Q. 355–6.
[3] Cf. 'Strictly speaking every agreement should be sent to registration': Mr. Buckland, A. 355.
[4] Cf., for details, Willis, loc. cit., pp. 275–8.
[5] Cf. Butterworth, *Cases*, 1938, pp. 402–3.

This shows where expert knowledge might come in. The *Evaluation Report* of the I.L.O. also remarks:[1]

'The judges of the ordinary courts, who have numerous duties, cannot acquire all the necessary technical and practical knowledge for efficiently evaluating incapacity' and frequently 'lack a social outlook and are insufficiently acquainted with the social circumstances and parties', though 'these objections lose some of their validity if certain judges or sections of the ordinary courts can be required to specialize in social insurance cases and more especially in cases involving evaluation of incapacity', and if, in addition, 'the ordinary courts can always have recourse to experts for explanations on technical practical points'.

The *Evaluation Report* in its 'Conclusions adopted by the Experts' favours Special Tribunals and while noting that these tribunals might make the working of social insurance more complex, enumerates several advantages which are connected with 'specialization'.

We do not underrate the strength of these arguments, but the case in favour of the retention of the present system of County Court administration is, to our mind, stronger still. They are speedy: no more than one month need elapse between the date on which a case is set down for trial, and the hearing. There are in the U.K. 58 County Court judges and 14 sheriffs principal: that is to say 72 persons in all with original jurisdiction under the Workmen's Compensation Act. They are assisted by 221 registrars and 49 sheriffs substitute, viz. 270 subordinate officers of the courts. County Courts are held in 484, Sheriff Courts in 54 towns—538 places in all.[2] Access to the courts is therefore easy and inexpensive.

The proceedings of these courts are invariably reported in full in the local press and justice is thus not only done but seen to be done. The cost of proceedings in County and Sheriff Courts is not high: witnesses are seldom brought from a distance, or kept for some days in a hotel awaiting the trial of a case. Consultations between solicitor and barrister, and between solicitor and client, are not difficult to arrange. The County Court judge gets to know those who appear before him, and becomes familiar with the technique of the industries located in his circuit, and with the trade terms and the dialect of those who appear before him.

It is of course true that in tribunals established under the Unemployment and National Health Insurance and Pensions Acts, local 'Umpires', and 'Referees' at Headquarters, decide cases under these Acts with little or no expense to applicants and with a minimum of delay. But the limits within which they are required to exercise their judicial or arbitral functions are narrow. The issues to be decided are seldom complex. The sums at stake are small; most cases are disposed of

[1] Cf. Butterworth, *Cases*, 1938, p. 362.   [2] *Debates H.C.*, June 28th 1939.

without a formal hearing. The 'respondent' is the State, not a private person or a commercial body corporate. The proceedings of these tribunals and their decisions are seldom published in the press: solicitors or counsel have no right to appear on behalf of appellants.

Special tribunals might well have been instituted in 1880 or 1897; to create them now, after a lapse of over forty years would, in our view, involve great dislocation of the existing arrangements with no corresponding public advantage. No one with practical experience of the working of the Acts will question the need for a workman to be assisted in the presentation of his case by a solicitor and generally by a barrister of experience. Without such aid most plaintiffs would be helpless.

It appears to us that the alternative line of progress—apart from the achievement of negotiated agreements between representatives of employers and employees through Joint Committees—will be found in the creation of a Workmen's Compensation Commissioner[1] aided and supplemented by an authoritative Advisory Board on which County Court judges and registrars and the appropriate Ministries would be represented. Such a body might well prepare, to be laid before Parliament, the drafts of Rules and Regulations for the guidance of Registrars and Medical Referees. The local representatives of the Commissioner should, as suggested by the Holman Gregory Committee,[2] be brought into close touch with employers and workmen and, as advisers and arbitrators, deal with a substantial number of disputes with a minimum of formality, delay, and expense. The functions of the Workmen's Compensation Commissioner and his advisers would, in fact, supplement and complement those of the judges.

The adoption of a system of State Administration implies and, indeed, necessitates the creation of a body of men with specialized training as well as with judicial experience. In the German Accident Insurance Scheme an appeal against evaluation of incapacity made by the managing committee of a Mutual Insurance Association lies to the Higher Insurance Office (see before, p. 228) which consists of a director (a civil servant) appointed for life; a certain number of members (also civil servants) appointed for stated periods; and assessors nominated by employers and workmen, appointed from lists by the occupational organizations concerned.[3] The system accords full recognition to the importance of technical knowledge and advice obtainable through regional or trade organizations of *Berufsgenossenschaften*. The Insurance Office of the German Empire (*Reichsversicherungsamt*) has

---

[1] Cf. *Holman Gregory Report*, para. 107.

[2] Cf. ibid., p. 58, to be read in conjunction with para. 107.

[3] The Swedish system has some points of resemblance to that in Germany. Cf. *Evaluation Report*, p. 278.

24 non-permanent members, of whom by far the largest number represent employers and employees. The Higher Insurance Court (*Oberversicherungsamt*) is assisted by 40 assessors (*Beisitzer*) of whom 20 are elected from the employers' and 20 from the employees' ranks. Similar rules apply to the lower Insurance Courts (*Versicherungsämter*).[1]

Methods of claim settlement under Court Administration in the U.S.A. have recently been subject to severe criticism.[2]

The judges seldom have time, in most jurisdictions, either to examine the files relating to Workmen's Compensation claims, or to give special study to Workmen's Compensation legislation and the intricate problems peculiar to this branch of administration. Under court administration there are as a rule no accessible records (outside the private files of the insurance carriers) of the majority of cases in regard to which no court action is sought by the parties. When a claim agreement is presented to the courts for approval, the customary routine is for the clerk of the court to examine the document to see if both parties have signed and acknowledged it in proper form. If so, he 'rubber stamps' it and that is the end of the transaction as far as any public supervision is concerned.

Such criticisms are not applicable to Court Administration in England. County Court judges do not grudge time and trouble; they investigate claims for compensation with great care and a full sense of responsibility. They make full use of all admissible evidence, even at the cost of some delay. Our criticism is, we repeat, not of the judicial administration of Workmen's Compensation in Britain, but of the system itself. Even as regards the registration of agreements in Britain, such complaints as have been made appear to be directed more against the latitude left to registrars by the legislature than to specific omissions on their part (except in Scotland).

If in Britain medical care, physical and vocational rehabilitation and re-entry into industry should, in future, be included in a scheme of Workmen's Compensation legislation, the need of the courts for expert advice will be even greater than under the present system. State insurance institutions can hardly avoid co-opting representatives of employers and employees particularly for evaluation purposes.[3] The objection that the organs of social insurance institutions 'run the risk of having doubt thrown on their impartiality, since the institution which is responsible for paying benefit becomes at once judge and party in the case' is noted but discounted on the understanding that the organ of the institution responsible for evaluating incapacity should be independent of the manager or the managing committee and include

---

[1] Cf. *Reichsversicherungsordnung*, 1938, §§ 39 sqq., 68 sqq., 83 sqq.

[2] Cf. *Claims Administration in Workmen's Compensation*, U.S. Dept. of Labor, 1938. Reprint from *Labor Review* of June 1938, p. 11.

[3] The I.L.O. thinks highly of the intervention of social insurance institutions (official bodies) in the matter of evaluation.

worker and employer members. On the other hand, the I.L.O. *Report* stresses the specialized knowledge and experience of social insurance institutions which guarantees their 'technical and practical competence'.[1]

We thus reach the following conclusions. The judicial administrative machinery of Workmen's Compensation should not follow any preconceived formula or rigid pattern. Where, as in Britain, the sphere of Workmen's Compensation is still relatively narrow, it cannot take the same form as in countries where it covers the entire field of accident prevention, compensation, and rehabilitation. While, therefore, in Britain ordinary Court Administration, accompanied by extended powers (see Registration), may well suffice and may be use fully complemented by such additional machinery as a Workmen's Compensation Commissioner would possess, other countries might find it more appropriate to entrust these functions to special courts and evaluation boards. In countries with State Administration of Workmen's Compensation, 'special' courts, forming a part of the whole system of insurance itself, may prove to be the most convenient form of judicial administration. In either case employers and workmen should have their part in the administration. But they may equally well exercise such functions where judicial administration is in the hands of the ordinary courts, and may play a useful part before and not after a case has actually come up for hearing. Under existing conditions it appears wiser to retain our existing Court Administration assisted by a Workmen's Compensation Commission. The absence of any machinery whereby representatives of employers and employees can co-operate with the courts, even in an advisory capacity, is regrettable; it can only be explained by the traditional background of Workmen's Compensation in Britain with its narrow scope and with its strong desire to leave as much as possible to private bargaining. This was and is one of the main reasons why arbitration by joint committees, possibly advised and guided by State officials, has made so little progress. It is the reason for the still existing structure of judicial administration through the ordinary courts in case agreements by private efforts should fail.

It is sometimes, quite wrongly, assumed that a system of centralized and State-controlled economic administration would supersede the existing system of judicial administration.[2] This point of view

---

[1] Cf. *Evaluation Report*, pp. 361–2.

[2] Cf. *Hetherington Commission*, Q. 3273–4. 'When you speak about setting up a Workmen's Compensation Commission, you mention that it is to have an Advisory Committee? A. (Sir Arnold Wilson, M.P.): Yes. Q. You also say that you do not want to supersede the Law Courts. How do these things fit together?'

is based upon a misunderstanding of the respective functions of the economic and the judicial administration. This distinction is clearly made in the Swiss system of Workmen's Compensation. Here we have the State-controlled (though not State-administered) *Schweizerische Unfallversicherungsanstalt*, an autonomous Institute represented by the insured, the employers, and the Government, handling the whole matter of compensation insurance on monopolistic lines. There is recourse in cases of dispute to a court which each Canton has to designate. These courts are expressly required[1] to choose for the termination of disputes 'a way of procedure as simple and quick as possible', they have also to see that people without means are provided, on their request, with a solicitor and that the costs of expert advice, &c., are remitted. An appeal lies from these courts to a Federal Insurance Court.[2]

So long as the present system of Workmen's Compensation remains in existence, no alternative form of administration by Commission can be initiated except by private initiative or under special schemes made by the Home Office. Under Part III of the Refractories Industries (Silicosis) Scheme of 1931 and the Sandstone Industry (Silicosis) Scheme of 1931 particular provision is made for Joint Committees:

> The question of the award of compensation and apportionment thereof shall, in the absence of agreement between the Company and the workman, be determined, subject to the provisions of the Scheme, by the Joint Committee, and no agreement in regard thereto between the Company and the workman shall relieve the Fund from any liability under this Scheme unless the said agreement shall have been approved in writing by the Joint Committee.

This piece of Workmen's Compensation machinery is almost unique. It is significant that it coincides with the creation of a Compensation Fund with compulsory powers. As to private endeavours it may be mentioned that in coal-mining in the southern and western districts of Yorkshire an arrangement between the management and the workmen includes a Joint Board which, in certain cases, will be called to adjudicate upon cases of nystagmus.[3] But such attempts have hitherto been sporadic and do not of themselves foreshadow any such radical changes in the administration of Workmen's Compensation as in our judgement and, we do not doubt, that of the Hetherington Commission, are now necessary.

---

[1] Cf. *Bundesgesetz über die Kranken- und Unfallversicherung*, June 13th 1911, Sections 120–2.

[2] Cf. *Schweizerische Unfallversicherungsanstalt, Führer durch die obligatorische Unfallversicherung*, edition Oct. 1938, pp. 6–7 and 98–9.

[3] Cf. Chapter IV, pp. 79–80.

CHAPTER XVI

THE MEDICAL SIDE: THE TREATMENT OF INJURY

Apart from its incentive as an accident preventive, probably the most important function of a compensation law is the rehabilitation of the injured workmen and restoration of their earning capacity. This accomplishment requires adequate medical and surgical treatment—a point evidently overlooked by most of the legislatures, and not fully grasped by many compensation commissions. The old idea of indemnity for tortious action on the part of the employer toward his injured workman is all too prevalent. It may not be deemed advisable to pay full compensation benefits, but there appears to be no valid reason, apart from the extra burden placed upon the employer, why adequate and unlimited medical service should not be furnished.

United States Bureau of Labor Statistics, Bulletin No. 203, 1917.

THERE are few aspects of Workmen's Compensation in which a physician or surgeon is not in the foreground. Just as medical questions have a legal side, so the legal questions which may arise very frequently involve medical considerations, whilst the solution of many administrative problems of Workmen's Compensation is often dependent upon the experienced judgement of a skilled physician or surgeon.[1] The doctor's part in Workmen's Compensation is in the main:

1. Medical treatment;
2. Medico-legal diagnosis.

These functions are distinct, and clearly contrasted. In the former, with which alone we are here concerned, the doctor plays an important part in removing or minimizing ill effects of an injury and in alleviating the consequences to the victim, whose future occupational life may depend upon the degree of success which attends his efforts, upon which also depends the amount of compensation he may receive. It is therefore of direct importance to employers and insurance carriers. In a wider field, any measures which reduce the size of the 'industrial scrap-heap', and the number of physically helpless pensioners of industry or the State is in the national interest. The medico-legal functions of the doctor are advisory, viz. to give evidence as a medical referee or certifying surgeon as to the health of the injured person. His diagnosis—and prognosis—is often decisive and always weighty.

The unique status in Britain of medical treatment under Work-

---

[1] Cf. also Marshall Dawson in 'Medical Aid under Workmen's Compensation Laws', *Monthly Labor Review*, Jan. 1939: 'A medical officer who had long experience under workmen's compensation insisted that compensation administration is 80 per cent. medical.'

men's Compensation law is due to the fact that it antedated National Health legislation by many years. Until 1911 the injured person was left to provide his own treatment and to seek such assistance as friendly societies and public charity might afford. From 1911 onwards the N.H.I. scheme began, however inadequately, to fill the gap. The standard it set was not high, but it was progressive and, to the extent that it provided treatment for non-industrial injuries and maladies, it stimulated the demand for improved methods of handling industrial diseases and occupational injuries. The great discrepancies between the benefits offered by more than 6,000 different Approved Societies and independent branches are notorious: those whose occupation entails the greatest risk are, in general, members of Approved Societies which give the smallest benefit. It was intended, and is still declared to be a principle, that members of Approved Societies should manage their own societies. As a matter of fact, this does not happen. A change in such conditions would react beneficially upon the medical administration of Workmen's Compensation, but it is not the place here to discuss such possibilities.[1] In the words of a recent I.L.O. Report:[2]

The *organization* of medical aid is therefore of prime importance at once for the injured workman who wants to regain his ability to work, for the employer or insurance institution whose liabilities are decreased in proportion as the degree of incapacity is less, and for society in general whose interest is to maintain the greatest amount of productive labour and to lighten the burden implied by the existence of invalids who are unable to work. It is therefore not to be wondered at that in almost all countries medical aid is considered as a normal element of compensation, as a right for the workman and a liability for the employer or insurance institution.

In this respect British compensation law, based mainly upon the law of 1906, differs from that of 'almost all countries', whose compensation laws of recent years have deliberately taken a different road.[3] In the U.S.A., for example, Workmen's Compensation laws differ widely from State to State, but all alike provide for medical, surgical,

---

[1] Cf. PEP, *Report on The British Health Services*, 1937, pp. 206 and 207. Also Chapter V, *passim*. Attention may be called also to S. Mervyn Herbert's criticism of the administration of National Health Insurance, cf. *Britain's Health* with a foreword by Lord Horder, 1939, pp. 82 sqq. and 94 sqq. P. 98: 'It may happen that after a panel doctor certifies a man fit for work the Ministry of Labour branch from which he receives his unemployment pay holds that he is not. In such cases he can draw neither health nor unemployment benefit.' P. 95: 'People living in the same street, even in the same house, may find that they receive entirely different benefits.' Cf. also Dr. Norris, *Industrial Accidents*, p. 129.

[2] Cf.I.L.O., *Compensation for Industrial Accidents*, 1925, p. 306.

[3] Cf. the remarks by Dodd, loc. cit., pp. 408–9. Cf. also the *Supplementary Memorandum* of the Authors, *Hetherington Commission, Evidence*, p. 342.

and hospital benefit the cost of which is in most but not all cases met by the employer or insurance carrier. In eight States the workman has to contribute to the cost of treatment; in W. Virginia there are special schemes whereunder the workman himself insures himself by a monthly payment against the cost of treatment in hospital of industrial injuries.[1] In a few States neither the duration of medical benefits nor the cost of the benefit is limited.[2] It is frequently argued that such limits should be abolished: 'There should be no limit to medical attention. It is false economy to give a man medical care for two weeks, a month, six months or a year, and then turn him adrift because, perchance, you have a limit to what you can do in medical cases.'[3] New York has developed an efficient system of medical care under the Act of 1935, whereunder the employer must provide for an injured employee 'such medical, surgical or other attendance or treatment, nurse and hospital service, medicine, crutches, and apparatus for such period as the nature of the injury or the process of recovery may require. If the employer fails to make the necessary provision on the request of the injured employee, such injured employee may do so at the expense of the employer.'[4] Another feature of medical care under Workmen's Compensation laws in the U.S.A. is that a number of industrial organizations such as railroad companies, mining companies, public utilities, and others have directly or through their employee organizations instituted extended medical and hospital services. But these services, again, are to some extent supported by deductions from pay, with or without contributions from the employer, and vary in scope; in some instances special hospitals have been provided, with medical and hospital service for the workers and their families.[5] These schemes are really analogous to 'contracting-out' schemes such as are permissible in Britain under § 31 of the Act of 1925, and have much to commend them.

Whatever the defects of the medical administration of American Workmen's Compensation,[6] the inclusion of medical benefits as an integral part of the insurance system has been wholly beneficial to injured workmen, and has helped to form a practical bond of common

[1] Cf. Norris, *Industrial Accidents*, p. 129; also Dodd, pp. 436 sqq. and *passim*.

[2] Cf. I.L.O., *International Survey of Social Services*, 1936, vol. i, p. 668.

[3] Cf. Joseph A. Parks, Chairman, Department of Industrial Accidents of Massachusetts and President of the International Association of Industrial Accident Boards and Commissions. 1934 Convention, loc. cit., *Bulletin No. 2*, p. 3.

[4] Section 13. Cf. Dodd, loc. cit., p. 446.

[5] Cf. *Medical Service in Industry and Workmen's Compensation Laws*, Chicago, 1938, p. 3.

[6] For details compare Dodd, pp. 489 sqq. and *passim*, about particular undesirable features of the 'commercialization' of medical practice, &c.

interest between workmen and the insurance carriers, or self-insured employers. There is general agreement that 'better organization of medical and safety services means lower costs' and is financially advantageous; one American Insurance Company explains the advantages of

Specialized medical service, which treats injured men with their jobs in mind, aiming to restore their job-holding ability, thus saving their valuable years of experience.[1]

Mr. Joseph Parks states:

Insurance companies have established great clinics, where they have staffs of experienced surgeons and every facility for bringing about recovery of the injured men. In a serious case the man is promptly removed to hospital and given the best care our great hospitals can give.[2]

Injured workmen, he added, were well cared for by the employer 'because neglect may cost the employer money'. A Committee reported that 'the clinics conducted by the insurance companies and the larger agencies [in the State of New York] are on the whole suitably housed and maintained. They have adequate equipment and are staffed with a competent personnel.' Smaller agencies were less favourably viewed. The same Committee noted many deficiencies; Dodd is sceptical of the sufficiency of medical care by the employer or the insurance agencies, which, in his view, mostly relates to a small number of the larger insurance companies.[3] But the system in the U.S.A. is progressive, and improving, which cannot at present be said of Britain. Dr. Norris states that the only complete industrial medical service planned from the happening of the accident until the final stage of recovery is to be found at Pittsburgh.[4]

In Britain the first step in the direction of such medical treatment and service would be to increase the number of fracture clinics,[5] but the need for such clinics within the spheres of National Health Insurance and Workmen's Compensation was not dealt with by the Delevingne Committee nor in the *Stewart Report*, whose concern was mainly with 'medical procedure', which to our mind cannot be divorced from medical treatment. If the doctor who begins, and completes, the treatment of an injured workman knows the whole history of the case or

[1] A recent advt. of the American Mutual Liability Insurance Co. Cf. also *Medical Service*, loc. cit., p. 35.

[2] Mr. Joseph A. Parks, Chairman of the Department of Industrial Accidents of Massachusetts, *Presidential Address before the Convention of the International Assn. of Industrial Accident Boards and Commissions.* Cf. U.S. Dept. of Labor, *Bulletin No. 2*, 1934, p. 3.

[3] The Meyer Committee. Cf. Dodd, loc. cit., pp. 454–5 and 491.

[4] Cf. Norris, *Industrial Accidents*, p. 129.

[5] Cf. *Interim Report of Delevingne Committee 1937.*

specializes in a particular injury or disease, he can play an important part in medico-legal procedure.[1] Model fracture clinics can cover only one part, though an important part, of the whole field of injuries. Specialized hospital treatment may be needed for silicosis or dermatitis or for rheumatism. To get the best results industrial injuries and diseases ought, as in the U.S.A., to be under the care of those concerned with their compensation. Doctors in this country (see page 232) often stress the indifference of insurance offices to the quick and full recovery of the injured workman. They will remain indifferent so long as their interest is rather to make an economical lump-sum settlement than to ensure the recovery or rehabilitation of the injured person. It is, however, clearly impossible to deal with all industrial injuries and diseases in specialized clinics. It is important to treat patients as near as may be to their homes. Special clinics or even hospitals may be desirable where certain maladies or injuries predominate in certain districts, but, in general, the specialized hospital offers only a partial solution of the problem.

Who, then, should treat the injured person and where? Four alternatives present themselves (none of which is practicable under the present British system of Workmen's Compensation):

1. Medical treatment in the injured workman's home, by his panel doctor.
2. Treatment in a hospital.
3. Treatment by the employer's (or insurance carrier's) doctor.
4. Treatment by a doctor or doctors under some official or semi-official administration.

Home treatment at present predominates to a far greater extent than is commonly supposed, and with unsatisfactory results. The Rehabilitation Committee stated that 75 per cent. of all cases of fractured limbs were treated at home,[2] or in out-patient departments or clinics,[3] sometimes with disastrous results. We may quote a case as an illustration:

T.S., aged 67, a ploughman, on August 26th 1936, fell from a ladder and injured both ankles. He was taken by car to a large general hospital, where he had X-ray examination, and was told that this showed a fracture of the left ankle. This was put in plaster-of-Paris and the patient was sent home by car, and on arrival there found that he could not bear his weight on his right foot. He sent for his Panel doctor, who advised him to stay in bed, which he did for two weeks. The

[1] A very detailed discussion of the point of 'history' and the doctor is given by Dr. A. M'Kendrick, *Medical Reports*, pp. 2–5.

[2] 132,702 cases of new fractures were, so far as the statistical data were available, treated in the course of 1935 in the voluntary hospitals as out-patients only, 45,478 as in-patients. Cf. *Interim Report of Delevingne Committee*, p. 5.

[3] Cf. B.M.A., *Report on Fractures*, 1935, pp. 16–17.

Panel doctor saw him once a week, for the next eight months, but gave him no advice or treatment. The patient went back to hospital and back home again, several times. After months and months a fracture was discovered and it was found that one ankle was reduced to about half the normal range while there was little movement in the left ankle.

Dr. Norris, who reports the case, adds that it is by no means unique. He further says that the two doctors concerned, apparently acting in good faith, were both mistaken: 'The hospital doctor seemed to believe that it was a good thing to put fractures in plaster-of-Paris, that is, if they were recognized; but appeared to have little idea of any treatment other than this, or even the proper way to use plaster-of-Paris in the treatment of fractures, while the panel doctor apparently took the view that advice and treatment were none of his business, and that all he had to do was to furnish certificates once a week.'[1] The case is typical: it shows the necessity of fracture clinics, the dangers of two doctors treating the same injury independently, and the need for unification of the medical administration. It also reveals the dangers of treatment at home. Many injuries might be much earlier and better recognized and diagnosed if the injured man could remain in one hospital till his recovery was assured. We do not suggest that all cases should be dealt with in hospital, nor do we underestimate the services rendered by the family doctor and the general practitioner. The best of them are beyond criticism, though the B.M.A. perhaps overestimates their capacity to deal with the very large number of patients upon their panel.[2] They are, as a body, overworked, and seldom able to keep abreast of medical science. It has even been suggested that they would resent official guidance. An official of the Ministry of Health told the Hetherington Commission that panel doctors might feel that guidance from Whitehall on diagnosis and prognosis or aetiology of disease was ordinarily unnecessary (an expression of opinion with which few will agree) and that they would pay hardly any attention to official publications[3] which may be well-founded. Specialists, on the other hand, habitually keep abreast of new developments at home and abroad, and readily make their published contributions to the common stock of knowledge. The B.M.A. notes that the work of the family doctor must often be complemented 'by the specialist in medicine', but it has not developed this thesis in the case of industrial injuries and

[1] Cf. Norris, *Some Medical Problems in Accident Insurance*, reprint from *Transactions of the Hunterian Society*, 1937–8, pp. 16–17. An interesting little pamphlet which also might be consulted on the point is that by F. M. Doughty, *The Legacy of a Fracture*, n.d.; so also Jordan, loc. cit., *passim*. Cf. our Chapter XI.

[2] Cf. *A General Medical Service for the Nation*, 1938, pp. 10–14.

[3] See Q. and A. 1854–6.

in connexion with the 'planned' and unified treatment of such cases suggested by Dr. Norris and others. Their advice to an injured workman to seek special treatment only when his case appears to be complicated, of longer duration than expected, and the results hitherto attained disappointing, is unlikely to commend itself to an injured man, who would prefer to get the best treatment from the outset. The B.M.A. has extracted from the PEP *Report of 1937* a passage which counsels reliance upon the general practitioner, but does not quote a later passage of the same Report, which states that

For a variety of reasons general practitioners are rarely able in existing circumstances to fill the role thus marked out for them . . . . The panel doctor, at any rate in large towns, often has neither the facilities nor the equipment which, as precise diagnosis becomes daily more possible, are necessary to provide adequate service. . . . These tendencies are strengthened where, owing to the low remuneration he receives or the circumstances of the area in which he lives, the practitioner is forced to undertake more work than he can conscientiously perform.[1]

These observations relate to a statement made by the Consultative Board on Medical and Allied Services of the Scottish Board of Health claiming that 'the first essential for the proper and efficient treatment of individual persons is not institutional but personal service such as can be rendered to the people in their own homes only by a family doctor'. The PEP *Report* takes exception to this statement but agrees that 'excessive readiness to resort to specialist services conflicts with their proper functions. If hospital out-patient departments and wards are used by patients who could be as well, or better treated at or near their homes, the valuable specialist services of the hospitals are being wasted and unnecessary expense is being incurred.' But should it be left for the patient to decide? If hospital treatment is necessary, is it available? Is the family doctor always the best judge as to whether hospital treatment is preferable? Are existing hospital facilities sufficient to prompt those in charge to encourage in-patient treatment? 'Very few hospitals are able to keep their patients long enough . . . . Cases [of juvenile rheumatism] treated at home always show more relapses than those receiving institutional treatment.'[2] The same is probably true of most industrial injuries and diseases. The late Sir John Collie was reluctant to advise injured workmen suffering from adhesions in or around the joint to have them broken down under an anaesthetic in the out-patient department of a hospital. 'Experience shows that these small operations are often very unsuccessful. The patient is sent home with the limb in a sling and told to return next

---

[1] Cf. PEP, *Report on the British Health Services*, 1937, pp. 161 sqq.

[2] Dr. Matthew B. Ray, Senior Physician, The British Red Cross Central Clinic for the Treatment of Rheumatism, in his *Chadwick Lecture 1930*, pp. 10–11.

day to have his arm exercised. He thinks he has been in pain quite long enough, and does not return to the hospital for many days.' The condition then becomes 'really worse than it was'. Sir John Collie strongly urged in-patient treatment for such cases which are by no means uncommon.[1] Sir Leonard Hill takes the same view. 'These persons [suffering from affections of the heart] may be quite capable of useful sedentary work, but they break down when put to manual labour or any overstrain. Such cases are made better in hospitals; they return to unsuitable work, and then go back to hospital, *and so on*, entailing needless expense and unhappiness.'[2] In a recent debate it was said:

A patient [suffering from eye injuries] comes for his weekly or fortnightly certificate which is continued indefinitely, owing to rush of work, without sufficient check of correctness. If the patient has kept off work much too long and an issue is brought to court, the judge is then faced with a man who is fit for work but whose own doctor is stretching a point, he thinks, in the patient's interest, and the result perhaps is the decision that the man is not only fit for his work but has been so for some time.

The speaker (Mr. Collyer Summers), in face of such happenings with 'hospital out-patients', recommended that larger hospitals should establish occupational therapy clinics, where patients could go for one month after the loss of an eye and get proper tuition.[3] The same point, in quite another field, is made by Dr. Sheen in *The Return to Work of the Injured Colliery Miner* where he describes the disastrous consequences of men leaving hospitals too early for home treatment although there the necessary methods for adequate treatment are no longer available.[4] The orthopaedic surgeon ought to be an expert in the technique of the manufacture and material of appliances; such knowledge would be 'a definite asset in planning and ordering apparatus for any particular condition'.[5] But how should such knowledge be expected otherwise than from a specialist?

These contentions find ample confirmation in Dr. H. Ernest Griffiths's imposing work on injury and incapacity which mainly deals with fractures. His experience of thousands of cases covering many years shows the value of specialized and differentiated knowledge to secure a complete cure and full occupational rehabilitation. The long list of 'various physical types' which must be distinguished in order to obtain 'accurate knowledge of the physical requirements of the workman engaged in the job under consideration' suffices to show the

[1] Cf. Collie, loc. cit., p. 127.
[2] Cf. *The Daily Telegraph*, June 1st 1939.
[3] Cf. *Proceedings of the Royal Society of Medicine*, 1938, vol. xxxi, pp. 866–7.
[4] Cf. *British Medical Journal*, March 26th 1938, pp. 153 sqq. See also p. 225 above.
[5] Cf. Dr. E. G. Brackett in Jordan, *Orthopaedic Appliances*, 1939, p. vii; also p. 7.

handicap in such cases of the general practitioner without the advantage of specialized surgical and osteological experience.[1]

In connexion with the problem of the choice of a physician a very thorny question arises. The workman has a natural and proper preference for home treatment by a doctor whom he knows, and who knows him and perhaps his family.

If the workman has the selection of his own physician, he feels that he will be given the correct treatment, that he will not be sent back to work before his strength is recovered, and that his compensation interests are in friendly hands. Even if the physician of the employer's selection is more competent than one chosen by the workman and would therefore render better treatment, the employee knows that such a physician depends for his pay upon the employer or insurer whose interests are either actively or potentially opposed to his own.[2]

On the other hand, where there is medical benefit provided by Workmen's Compensation law:

From the standpoint of the insurance company (under which term will also, for the present, be included the self-insurer), it is of enormous advantage to be able to select the physician, specialist, or hospital to treat the employee, for the relations of the carrier and its doctor are close.

Insurance companies in the U.S.A. claim to employ their own doctor on two grounds:

(1) that the party who has to pay for medical care should also control it, and

(2) that the insurer is better able than the workman to obtain the best medical advice.

The importance of the second argument cannot be denied. American insurance offices have,[3] unlike British offices,[4] a specialized medical service, which treats injured men with their jobs in mind, aiming to restore their occupational capacity and their valuable years of experience. But American writers are by no means satisfied with the medical treatment administration as practised by insurance offices. Dodd alleges that insurance offices select doctors for their legal ability in

[1] Cf. H. Ernest Griffiths, *Injury and Incapacity*, 1935, p. 203, and whole of last part. Cf. also for this point Prof. Karl Gebhardt, *Selbstausgleich und Wiederherstellungschirurgie*, Leipzig, 1936, p. 17, and *passim* for the results of similar observations as made by Griffiths. The importance of a systematic treatment under special medical care and supervision of a specialized character is here demonstrated as the result of experiments made in the famous Hohenlychen institute which treats more than 3,500 people in a year, of which about 1,000 undergo an operation, of which again two to three cases belong to *Unfallchirurgie* (accident surgery). Special stress is laid on the 'self-regulation' or self-cure of the injured under medical control.   [2] Cf. Dodd, loc. cit., p. 413.

[3] Cf. *Fortune*, Dec. 1938, Advertisement of the American Mutual Liability Insurance Company.   [4] Cf. Gillespie, loc. cit.

defeating employees' claims rather than for their medical skill, and complains that only 'a few of the larger insurance companies take a more intelligent view of medical problems arising in compensation and regard it as not only good ethics but also good business to supply the best of medical attention for the period it is needed'.[1] This may explain why much variation exists on this point in the various States.[2] Neither the injured workman, nor insurance carriers, can properly be given entire discretion in the matter.[3] The doctor's interest must also be considered; general practitioners or family doctors are naturally reluctant to lose their patients, whom they have known, with their families, for years. Their reluctance is not due solely, or even mainly, to loss of income. They feel that it is bad for the profession as a whole that the activities of the general practitioner should be restricted in every direction until he becomes a mere dispenser of medicine, or a channel of communication between his patient and a score or more of specialists.[4] In rural areas great weight attaches to this line of argument. It is less applicable to industrial areas, and to industrial injuries and diseases. Dodd concludes that 'the choice of physician by the employee from an impartial panel' as in the State of New York, appears to be the most satisfactory solution.[5] This means that between the free choice of the employee, guaranteed to him by new enactments (1935) and the rights of the employer to recommend a physician to the employee, there stands the authority of a State department. The new law prescribes joint control of treatment and care of the injured by the Department of Labor and the medical societies of the State, the most prominent being the Industrial Commissioner, the Industrial Council, and the Medical Society of the County. A medical clinic desiring to practise under the Workmen's Compensation law—including a factory or plant clinic or laboratory—must obtain a recommendation from the Medical Authority of the County, on the strength of which the Industrial Commissioner may license the clinic as a 'Compensation

[1] Cf. Dodd, loc. cit., p. 491.

[2] Cf. *Medical Service*, &c., 1938. Under 'Choice of Physician'. There is in some States absolute freedom of choice for the employee; in others there is an authorized list for selection; in other States there is free choice, but a Commission must approve; again in others the employee may choose from a panel named by the employer; again in others medical benefits are provided by publicly administered medical funds, the managers of which have power to dictate selection of the physicians. In some States the administrators of the State insurance funds have the power to dictate the selection of physician or surgeon. Provision is generally made for free choice of doctor and hospital by an employee at the employer's expense, in case the employer fails to provide such services.

[3] Cf. Dodd, loc. cit., pp. 492–505.

[4] Cf. B.M.A., *A General Medical Service*, p. 12 and *passim*: 'To short-circuit the family doctor is uneconomic, bad for the patient and bad for the medical profession.'

[5] Cf. loc. cit., p. 504.

Medical Bureau'. The legislation thus seeks to mitigate evils arising from commercialization of the medical treatment of industrial injuries, either by inferior commercial clinics, mostly at the service of self-insurers, or by the insurance company's doctors who may be unduly interested in the financial aspects of claims.

This arrangement closely resembles the German system which, through the semi-official *Berufsgenossenschaften*, has always exercised a measure of control over the medical treatment of the injured. As early as 1904 these trade associations were making full use of their right to erect their own clinics and convalescent homes, subject only to the consent of the Imperial Insurance Office, and in many cases these have become model establishments. In that year it was officially laid down that, although the injured had in certain circumstances the right to choose his own treatment, 'home nursing cannot be of the same benefit as hospital treatment, as regards observation, the use of different apparatus and appropriate food'.[1] More recent enactments have pursued the same course: an ordinance of June 19th 1936 requires Approved Societies, at the request of the *Berufsgenossenschaft*, to consult the *Durchgangsarzt*—forwarding doctor—designated by the *Berufsgenossenschaft* immediately after reporting even a slight accident to the Society and, if possible, before seeking the service of the Society's physician. If the injured person cannot do so himself the *Krankenkasse* must do so. This 'intermediate doctor decides' whether the medical care of the Society is sufficient or whether other methods of cure are advisable. In the latter case he at once moves the *Berufsgenossenschaft* to provide the necessary care and cure. There is also the *Beratungsfacharzt* (consulting specialist) to whom responsibility has been entrusted by the *Berufsgenossenschaft* to advise the injured person, possibly before treatment by the medical practitioner is begun. A list of certain injuries is handed to the Approved Societies by the *Berufsgenossenschaften* in this respect—a matter which of course can only be dealt with by bodies so competent with their industry and its risks as the *Berufsgenossenschaften* in their groups are.[2] These and similar arrangements in regard to the administration of the medical treatment of injured workers tend to strengthen their confidence in the medical men in charge of their case,

---

[1] Cf. *Memorandum* for the St. Louis Exhibition of 1904, by Herr Bielefeldt, then President of the Senate of the Imperial Insurance Office.

[2] Cf. *Die Neuregelung der Beziehungen zwischen den Trägern der Krankenversicherung und der Unfallversicherung*, Berlin, 1936, pp. 16–18. The matter is treated by a special order of June 19th 1936, under the head of *Verletzungsartenverfahren*, i.e. procedure as regards types of injury, para. 6. The *Berufsgenossenschaften* are entitled to inform the Approved Societies (*Krankenkassen*) as to types of cases in which treatment will be administered by the *Berufsgenossenschaften*; twenty-three different types of injuries, relating for the most part to fractures, are named in the order. Cf. also *Hetherington Commission*, p. 607.

and help to achieve a uniform and planned treatment, through the controlling interest exercised by the administrative body on the one hand, the collaboration of doctors, conversant with the necessities of the case on the other, and the assistance of specialist advice, if necessary, from the beginning. The Webbs suggest that such continuity of treatment is available in Soviet Russia.[1]

The medical treatment of the injured worker in Britain is in a much more primitive state. Such machinery as we have outlined above does not exist and has not as yet been envisaged. The B.M.A., while recognizing the necessity of co-ordination,[2] contents itself with recommending that specialists should be available for the individual patient 'normally through the agency of the family doctor', but has no suggestions to make as to how to achieve this end, which presupposes, as in Germany and the U.S.A., a State or semi-State organization. The need for specialized treatment is widely recognized: partnerships in general practice of doctors with special qualifications is increasingly common, and of great value to patients, who thus have the benefit of diagnostic apparatus and premises which no single doctor could afford to maintain.[3] Any decisive reform of National Health Insurance whether upon these lines, or otherwise, would automatically benefit sufferers from industrial injuries and diseases, but does not affect the desirability of making medical benefit a statutory obligation under Workmen's Compensation. The case for this reform may be summarized thus:

1. Insurance carriers of Workmen's Compensation should be directly concerned to promote the recovery and rehabilitation of the injured worker.

2. Continuity and uniformity of treatment from first aid to rehabilitation could be better provided if the medical administration of treatment lay with the compensating authority. Where the incidence of

---

[1] S. and B. Webb, *Soviet Communism a New Civilization?*, 1935, vol. ii, pp. 848–9 and 851.   [2] Cf. *A General Medical Service*, p. 8.

[3] Cf. PEP, *Health Report*, 1937, p. 164. In this connexion the matter of 'Group Service' becomes important. A type of group service recommended in the U.S.A. is such where the physician or surgeon, who is licensed and otherwise qualified, establishes and provides continuous and efficient medical service for a group of industrial organizations. In providing this service the physician or surgeon makes periodic visits to the plant. He institutes health preservation measures, including pre-employment and periodic physical examinations, the prevention of infection, and the control or elimination of other health hazards. He arranges for the treatment of employees who become ill or injured in the line of duty by one who is competent in industrial medicine or traumatic surgery and he follows each case until the worker is back at his job. By specializing in this type of work he can achieve better results medically and the *per capita* medical costs by serving large grouped numbers of employees may also fall within reasonable limits. Cf. also *Medical Service in Industry*, Industrial Welfare Society, 1936, *passim*.

injury is particularly 'industrial' or 'occupational', such specialities might be best handled, and their treatment organized, by bodies conversant with such specialities, particularly in the matter of industrial disease. Bodies like the *Berufsgenossenschaften* could provide special schemes of medical administration adapted to the particular conditions and needs of their industries; this, again, would be of particular importance in the case of after-cure and rehabilitation which have to be administered with special regard to specific industrial occupations; rehabilitation, for instance, of nystagmic miners could be effectively dealt with only by a body closely linked up with representatives of employers and employees in the coal-mining industry; associations of this kind, or committees, in the pottery industry would specialize on dust diseases; in the metal industries their particular concern would be focused on eye troubles, etc. All these considerations amply reinforce the case for providing medical treatment as an integral part of Workmen's Compensation. This does not exclude the possibility that fuller use might be made of our National Health Insurance system as an integral part of the medical administration of Workmen's Compensation. Injuries of shorter duration, perhaps for the first forty-five days of injury, might well come within its care, subject to certain exceptions. Whether the costs are borne from the outset by the Workmen's Compensation authority, or by the National Health authorities, subject to reimbursement from the Workmen's Compensation authority at a later stage, is a matter of secondary importance.

NOTE

IN the Memorandum presented to the Hetherington Commission by the British Hospitals Association (sections 11–12) it is said: 'The position of the insurance companies is admirably explained in a letter received by the Bristol Royal Infirmary from the Federated Employers' Insurance Association Ltd. ". . . Whilst appreciating everything you say, we regret that we are quite unable to do anything in the matter. As an insurance company we are administrators of a fund which is subscribed to purely for the purpose of providing weekly compensation for injured workmen. The rate of this compensation is fixed by an Act of Parliament and the contributions to the fund do not enable us to do anything more than pay the compensation so fixed. Throughout the course of a year we receive thousands of applications from hospitals for maintenance accounts and you can well imagine that the total of them runs into a huge figure making it quite impossible for us to accept responsibility. We entirely agree with you that the position is extremely unsatisfactory from your point of view but it is a matter for the legislature and not for individual insurance companies." In other words insurance companies find themselves obliged, on principle, to refuse to make an *ex-gratia* payment.' Cf. *Hetherington Commission, Evidence,* pp. 1078–9.

CHAPTER XVII

THE MEDICAL SIDE: MEDICAL PROCEDURE

Beware of councils when too full; number makes long disputes.
SIR JOHN DENHAM (1615–69).

THE functions of the doctor in connexion with industrial injuries are by no means exhausted by problems of medical treatment. Of recent years the physician and surgeon have come into their own, and are, in almost every country, given pride of place in the legal and administrative machinery of Workmen's Compensation. Doctors are here employed, not as experts in cure and rehabilitation, but in quasi-judicial capacities, both as to diagnosis and prognosis, alike in contested and uncontested cases. At every stage their opinion is of importance and often decisive, both as to the immediate cause of an injury, and as to the amount and manner and duration of compensation payments. Medical examination and certification of medical referees and certifying surgeons are an important part, but not, as the *Report of the Stewart Committee* appears to suggest, the whole of 'Medical Procedure'. The term should embrace all legal and administrative acts upon which medical opinion is sought, and in which expert medical advice may play a part. The role of forensic medicine begins before the law or either party requires a medical opinion, as evidence in connexion with a disputed claim. In undisputed cases, viz. in the vast majority of all cases, the opinion of a single doctor is sought at the outset, and is accepted without question by both sides. A workman in receipt of weekly payments may be required to undergo examination by his employer's doctor, but only in accordance with Regulations made by the Home Office.[1] Where the facts are not in dispute, the statutory compensation is paid and the workman returns to work when he has recovered from the injury, though, as suggested by the B.M.A., a 'declaration of liability' is not demanded as often or at as early a stage as is desirable, with results adverse to the workman, whose return to work may be unduly delayed.[2]

Under the German system of Workmen's Compensation the injured workman may and should refer at the outset to an independent[3]

[1] Regulations provide (*a*) that the workman may be examined only at reasonable hours, (*b*) that the number of such examinations is subject to certain limits (once a week during the second month, once a month during the third, &c.), and (*c*) that an employer who has commenced proceedings for review may insist upon an additional examination.

[2] Cf. for declaration of liability our former observations on pp. 50 and 190.

[3] Empowered by the *Berufsgenossenschaft*, i.e. a semi-official body under official supervision including representatives of workmen as well as of employers.

doctor. The British workman must look to two medical authorities, his own doctor and his employer's or, more often, the insurance carrier's, whose primary interest is to settle the claim cheaply. Some employers ask a workman when first claiming compensation to produce a medical certificate of incapacity and to agree in advance to pay for it—a practice not justified by the Act, and inconsistent with its spirit and intention. The procedure of examinations as practised by the insurance companies themselves requires careful consideration. However anxious the doctor employed by the insurance office may be to do justice, the mere fact that he is employed by 'the other side' tends to put the injured workman on the defensive and predisposes him to insist upon his 'rights'. An injured workman sent for medical examination by his solicitor, by special arrangement with the insurance office, becomes a plaintiff, under expert cross-examination for the defendant: 'He is always reticent and fears that he may give away important non-medical facts connected with the happening of the accident.'[1] Hence unjustified suspicions, and accusations of malingering.[2] The insurance company's doctor 'knows exactly what to ask the workman. He will ask if the workman can do light work. If he says "Yes", the doctor will so inform the judge; if he says "No" the doctor may give expert evidence to the contrary effect, which may tend to impugn the injured man's veracity.'[3] Any proposal to simplify existing complicated formalities is met with dark hints at 'swinging the lead' and to 'malingering', as practices that would at once become prevalent if precautions were relaxed. Yet not all insurance companies are equally careful to ensure that the injured workman is examined under conditions favourable to the elucidation of his real condition.[4] He may be required to make a long journey to a strange town; he may be kept waiting for a long time; the medical examination may be physically painful, or mentally irritating, particularly in cases of incipient neurosis. In such circumstances the patient may refuse to undergo further examinations and, as a result, be refused further weekly payments.[5] These things were plainly stated in evidence before the Holman Gregory Committee.

Twenty years later Dr. Morgan, speaking for the T.U.C. before the Hetherington Commission, said:

... it is quite common, especially in London, that the workman receives notice to attend for medical examination at a certain place, without even stating the name of

---

[1] Cf. Collie, loc. cit., p. 21.

[2] Cf. vol. i, p. 186; and Norris, *Some Medical Problems in Accident Insurance*, p. 15.

[3] Cf. *John Smith has an Accident*, p. 5.

[4] The T.U.C. Memorandum to the Hetherington Commission states: 'It is the practice of some insurance companies' doctors to make a large number of appointments, with the result that workmen are kept waiting for long periods, and recovery is retarded.' Cf. p. 408 (§ 59).   [5] See our vol. i, p. 154.

the doctor, or the name of the firm, or the name of the insurance company on whose behalf he is to be examined, simply asking him by postcard to attend at a certain address at a certain hour on a certain date for medical examination.

The presence of other doctors is in many cases flatly refused.[1]

The certificate of the employer's doctor may be misinterpreted to the disadvantage of the injured workman.[2] Sir John Collie cites a case in which a workman refused to attend for medical examination unless his solicitor was present, 'as he objected to the behaviour to workmen of the medical man selected by the employer'. The judge could not accept the man's 'dislike of the doctor' as valid ground for refusal to be examined, but acknowledged that in many cases where he had been arbitrator 'the evidence given by the doctor had been very damaging to the workmen and it was natural that workmen should dislike being examined by them'.[3] The *Stewart Report* mentioned similar complaints and noted allegations that the workmen's interests have been adversely affected by the unauthorized disclosure of medical information by doctors who have had workmen under their care and treatment as patients. In such cases, however, disclosure had generally been made by a panel doctor 'acting both as the man's attendant and as adviser to the employer or insurance company', or by the staff of a hospital. The Stewart Committee held[4] that a man's panel doctor should in no circumstances furnish a report on a patient without his previous consent, unless the man is in hospital and the employer not allowed to send his own doctor to examine the workman. We see no good grounds for this exception.

Sir John Collie has discussed at length whether a workman can insist that his own doctor should be present. He cannot do so as of right, though in *Morgan* v. *William Dixon*, 1912, Lord Loreburn, then Lord Chancellor, inclined to the view that in most cases it was quite reasonable for the workman to desire the presence of his doctor, although sometimes it appeared unreasonable because of inconvenience or expense. Lord Shaw on the same occasion held the request to be reasonable. As the law now stands, the County Court or arbitrator has to decide whether such a requirement is reasonable: the necessary application costs money, and causes delay. Doctors employed by insurance companies are loath to communicate with or consult the injured man's doctor,[5] though such consultations would increase the confidence of the injured workman and might prevent

---

[1] Cf. *Hetherington Commission*, Q. 4055-7. Dr. Morgan's evidence: 'they do not want me there even though I propose to go at my own expense.'

[2] Cf. *Hills Patent Glazing Co. Ltd.* v. *Douglas*, Court of Appeal, April 1937.

[3] Cf. Collie, loc. cit., p. 49.   [4] Cf. *Stewart Report*, p. 56.

[5] Cf. also Brend, loc. cit., p. 65.

neurosis. Sir John Collie held that a workman might reasonably insist upon examination at his own place of abode or at the residence of his own doctor[1] and not in a solicitor's office. In the absence of a State-managed organization the problem of medical examination of uncontested cases appears insoluble. It is often referred to in American text-books.[2] Dodd follows Carl Hookstadt, urging that

Constant vigilance to protect the rights of the claimant is necessary under any system of administration. It is probable that none can be devised which would secure complete justice to every employee. But the success of compensation administration depends primarily upon adequate safeguards to the injured employee in the uncontested case—the one place where he is most likely to suffer in his relation with the employer and insurance carrier.

In Britain it is generally assumed that the workman's interests require protection only in disputed cases which go before an arbitrator. It is assumed that if a case is not contested it is because the workman is satisfied, and no intervention is therefore called for. In the U.S.A. the potential evils of such a system are well recognized. Thus Dr. Hatch, formerly Member of the New York Industrial Board, explained in 1935[3] that the choice by the interested parties of attending physicians or examining physicians as the primary source of medical evidence should be made from 'a medical staff selected and maintained by the compensation authority itself', which would 'make available to the administrator exactly the kind of evidence he requires'. The State of New York formerly permitted direct settlements such as are still in use in most American States. Complaints led the Governor to initiate an investigation by a Commissioner who selected at random, and reinvestigated through the courts several hundred cases that had been finally settled by direct negotiation. The revised awards showed in the great majority of cases very large increases. After this 'rather disastrous experience' the legislature so amended the law as to provide that no compensation claim could be closed without giving the claimant an opportunity to be examined by impartial physicians and to be heard by independent referees.[4] This is known as 'the special unit system'.[5] The procedure is entrusted to a central Department in New York City, and the Claims Division of this Department is composed of nine departments or 'units' for disability cases, one unit for fatal cases and

[1] Cf. Collie, loc. cit., p. 51.　　　　　　[2] Cf. Dodd, loc. cit., pp. 117–85.

[3] Cf. 1935 Convention, &c., The Necessity for Medical Staffs in Compensation Administration, Bulletin No. 4, 1936, p. 138. His remarks seem to be based not on theory but on practice.

[4] Cf. V. A. Zimmer, New York Dept. of Labor, Should Hearings be held in All Cases when Disability exceeds One Week? Bulletin of the U.S. Bureau of Labor Statistics, No. 511, 1930, pp. 302–3.

[5] Cf. described in detail by Dodd, loc. cit., pp. 148 sqq. and 173 sqq.

for claims which are not insured. Each unit is composed of 8–12 men, under an examiner-in-charge. Every compensation claim is indexed by the claimant's surname and dealt with by the disability unit to which it is assigned, on an alphabetical basis.

An analogous arrangement exists under the Ontario law of Workmen's Compensation. Within three days of an accident the employer must send a report to the Workmen's Compensation Board. In cases requiring only medical attention no further report from the employer, and none from the employee, may be necessary. In the cases eligible for compensation a fuller report is required both from the employer, the workman, and the doctor concerned. When the employer's report of a statutory accident is received, the workman is at once sent two forms to be completed and posted by himself and his medical attendant respectively. Eight or nine out of ten of the claims received are 'straight' cases, as to which no dispute arises.[1] But they are not less important on that account, as is sometimes suggested in Britain, and it may well be that the procedure adopted tends to obviate dissatisfaction on either side and, therefore, disputes. Where, as in Germany and in Switzerland, such cases are dealt with by a public authority,[2] there is little or none of the friction apt to arise where the doctors of both sides are facing each other. The views of Dr. Hatch, former member of the N.Y. State Industrial Board, in this connexion deserve close attention:

The solution of this problem as to medical evidence . . . is to be found in a medical staff selected and maintained by the compensation administration authority itself. . . . Such a staff, being *an agency of the State itself can have no interest in a claim*, except that of an impartial justice, offsets to any element of bias in evidence coming from other sources. Its unbiassed character is obvious and inspires confidence in the impartiality of decisions guided by its reports or testimony. It supplements, if need be, the employer's resources for medical evidence, ensuring that his interests shall not suffer thereby.[3]

The 'uncontested' or 'undisputed' case has hitherto received no attention in Britain, where Parliament and the Home Office have acted upon the principle of *quieta non movere*. The principle that no compensation case shall be closed without giving both sides an opportunity to be heard and of maintaining an official check upon the correct settlement of undisputed claims seems to us to merit inclusion in any future legislation. British insurance offices have not as yet been asked to make their records available for inspection, and have, indeed, hitherto stressed their confidential nature. Dr. Griffiths (loc. cit., p. v) records

---

[1] Cf. *Ontario Procedure of Workmen's Compensation Claims*, U.S. Dept. of Labor, Washington, 1936, p. 6.   [2] Cf. *Evaluation Report*, loc. cit., pp. 258–9.

[3] Cf. *1935 Convention*, loc. cit., p. 138.

the difficulties he encountered in seeking the history of the cases in which he was interested for his inquiry (see before, p. 275), as insurance offices, with one important exception, were, in general, 'averse to having their private records searched'.

The position of doctors in 'contested' cases, with particular reference to medical referees and certifying surgeons, so far as their testimony assumes importance in later litigation, has been much discussed. Medical referees have various duties. They may be asked to give a certificate in cases referred to them under § 19 of the Act as to the condition of the workman, his fitness for employment, and/or whether, or to what extent, his incapacity is due to accident. They may decide an Appeal under § 43 (1) (*f*) of the Act, when such an appeal is made by either side against the decision of an examining surgeon to give, or withhold, a certificate of disablement, &c., on account of a scheduled disease. They may sit as assessors with the County Court judge, either at his instance or at the request of a party under Schedule 1 (5). Any committee, arbitrator, or judge may require them to report on any matter material to an arbitration under Schedule I (II). They may report to a registrar or County Court judge under § 23 (3) (*b*) of the Act, i.e. where a memorandum of a lump-sum agreement is submitted for registration and the registrar or judge considers that the information as to the workman's condition is insufficient or conflicting. Lastly, the referee may give a certificate under § 16 of the Act in cases where the workman desires to receive his compensation abroad. The functions of the examining surgeon are of less importance to our subject; they principally relate to § 44 of the Statute where, in the case of industrial diseases, examining surgeons are required to testify to the connexion of the injury with the occupation. The examining surgeon does not, however, necessarily enter the picture, as the employer may agree with the workman that he is liable for compensation without requiring the workman to obtain a certificate under § 44 (2).

In our first volume[1] we dealt briefly with the subject of medical referees, calling attention to some long-standing complaints which await a remedy, such as the proposed substitution of a Medical Board for a single referee. The Stewart Committee concluded that 'the advantages of the existing system outweigh its disadvantages', but proposed that the decision of a referee under §§ 19 and 43 (1) (*f*) (see above) of the Act should be subject to appeal, that the panels of practitioners qualified to act as referees should be enlarged and strengthened, and that the rules laid down for the purpose of securing impartiality should continue to apply. The Stewart Committee further suggested that Medical Tribunals should be instituted and that medical issues

[1] Cf. pp. 221–2 and 266.

should usually be decided by a referee or, on appeal, by the Medical Tribunal.

The *Evaluation Report* of the I.L.O. dealt at length with the importance of establishing the impartiality of the doctors and drew attention to the conflict of interest latent in the existing system, noting that the intervention of doctors 'cannot give rise to any objection provided that they are experts who have given proof of their competence to give an opinion on the cases submitted to them and are quite independent'.[1] This is indeed the crux of the matter. How can 'independence' be guaranteed so as to satisfy both sides and, in particular, the injured workman? The I.L.O. probably had in mind mainly such conditions of medical procedure as exist in countries where a State or semi-official body is entrusted with the evaluation of incapacity and other matters concerning medical administration. Its observations are even more applicable to systems whereunder the liability is thrown wholly upon the employer or private insurance bodies, disputed cases being referred to referees who are not 'officials' in the proper sense, or to County Courts.

Every effort has been made to ensure the efficiency and impartiality of referees. Yet the difficulties remain. The Home Office is at pains to secure medical men of the highest qualifications: this is not always easy, because the appointment in many areas is not well paid, and may disqualify the holder for more remunerative work.[2] The Home Office do not appoint as a medical referee a doctor who holds an appointment to an industrial undertaking, or who acts as a medical officer to a Workmen's Club or Friendly Society, or who is regularly employed by, or on behalf of, an insurance company or mutual indemnity association in connexion with cases under Employers' Liability or Workmen's Compensation. The impartiality of the referee is further safeguarded by § 38 (1) of the Act which debars a medical referee from acting as such in a case in connexion with which he has been employed as a medical practitioner on behalf of an employer or workman or by any insurers interested. Referees are further advised to avoid, in their private practice, cases which may afterwards come before them in an official inquiry. But the position is not yet satisfactory, as the *Stewart Report* suggests, and as the evidence given before them would have proved, had it been printed. It would wear a different aspect if referees acted under an official or semi-official body whose impartiality and breadth of view is universally recognized. The Holman Gregory Committee thought that 'so long as the Medical Referees are allowed to engage in private practice they will be subject

---

[1] Cf. *Evaluation Report*, 1937, p. 364. Also pp. 255 sqq.

[2] Cf. *Stewart Report*, pp. 53–4.

to a certain amount of distrust and suspicion' and adumbrated the appointment of whole-time officers by the Ministry of Health under the National Health Insurance Acts, who would also be medical referees.[1] Nothing was done: the subject is not mentioned in the *Report of the Royal Commission on National Health Insurance*.[2]

The Stewart Committee took the view that the small percentage of cases where the referee is called for—perhaps 2 per cent.—indicated that the matter was of secondary importance, as 'the vast majority of cases are settled by agreement and without difficulty',[3] though 'that in the aggregate these cases amount to a considerable number and may involve questions of very great difficulty'. The difficult cases are the important ones; the sense of injustice of an injured workman is not allayed by the contemplation of percentage figures. The Stewart Committee did not ask why medical referees are not employed more frequently in the courts. The following reasons, among others, are relevant. The party exercising the right to summon a medical referee has to pay his fee, and will not do so unless he thinks it is to his advantage. A litigant with a strong case may feel that it is unnecessary to incur the expense; one with a weak case may feel that he has a better chance without a medical assessor. Not all judges welcome them, and not all assessors are helpful.[4]

The *Stewart Report* has placed on record some, at least, of the objections made to them against the present system: we record them below.

1. Several witnesses, and more particularly those speaking for workmen, have contended that Medical Referees, who are required to exercise quasi-judicial functions, do not always act in such a manner as to be immune from any suspicion of bias or prejudice of one side or the other. It is alleged that, in areas immediately adjoining those for which they are appointed, certain Referees frequently appear in Court as expert witnesses for one side or other. . . .

2. A further point of criticism emerging from the evidence of several witnesses was that qualifications of the medical practitioners appointed to act as Medical Referees in particular areas are rarely sufficient for an effective decision in every type of case.

The creation in each area of panels of specialists in the various classes of disease was recommended by witnesses.

3. By far the most common ground of criticism of the Medical Referee was based on the fact that under certain conditions he had power to give a final decision; and it was contended that in matters of such vital importance to the workman the decision ought not to rest with one man. . . . These considerations assumed even greater importance when it was realized that the Medical Referee was often called upon

---

[1] Cf. *Holman Gregory Report*, pp. 62 and 78.
[2] Cf. *Report of the Royal Commission on National Health Insurance*, 1928, pp. 256–9.
[3] Cf. *Stewart Report*, p. 70. [4] Cf. Brend, loc. cit., pp. 73–6.

to give a decision on issues which were not purely medical. . . . It was pointed out that, in arriving at a decision, the Medical Referee was assumed to be endeavouring to apply accepted theories of medical science in regard to a particular disease or a particular form of injury to the circumstances of an individual case; and that the possibility of mistake was greater when it was left to a single Referee to say the last word.

4. In the event of a reference to a Medical Referee under § 19 of the Act the Referee may be required to give a certificate 'specifying where necessary the kind of employment for which' the man is fit. It was stated that considerable doubt exists as to the precise meaning of the expression 'where necessary' in this clause; but it was clear that the Medical Referee does in fact frequently certify a man to be fit for some particular job, and some witnesses declared that it was right and proper that the certificate should take that form since nobody but a medical man could decide what work a man was fit for.

The Stewart Committee, after recording these complaints, noted that 'lack of confidence . . . prompts one party or the other in certain areas to avoid reference to a Referee *as far as they can*'; but found 'consolation' in the fact that only 2 per cent. of all claims were disputed. They did not inquire what the percentage would be but for the admitted 'lack of confidence'.

In making this observation we make no reflection upon referees, whose competence and objectivity are not in question. We agree with Dr. McKendrick[1] that 'it is a difficult matter when we attempt a prognosis—or the assessment of the degree of disability present and future'. The report of a referee who hesitates to give a definite opinion may be set aside by the judge[2] or repudiated as 'ambiguous' because it certified the workman as 'fit for his present employment with the proviso that the dislocation may recur at any time, however light the work'.[3] In this case

(a) the County Court judge held that the workman was fit for his present work and continued compensation as for partial incapacity;

(b) a doctor called in evidence for the employers said the certificate indicated that it was clearly a case where only a declaration of liability was required;

(c) a doctor called in evidence for the workman declared that the

[1] Cf. M'Kendrick, loc. cit., p. 12.

[2] Cf. also Prof. Earl D. McBride, 'Disability Evaluation', in the *American Journal of Surgery*, 1939, p. 841: 'The court often insists upon definite answers to medical questions that are at best controvertible, hypothetical and equivocal.' He suggests 'fundamental training' on how to meet such exigencies and how to present medical subjects publicly to 'non-medical inquisitors'.

[3] Cf. *Riley* v. *Bickershaw Collieries, Ltd.*, April 23rd 1937, Court of Appeal. The case was remitted to the same referee for a fresh certificate. For a discussion of the difficulty of 'prognosis' in such cases, see Norris, *Some Medical Problems*, p. 18.

certificate was unambiguous, and the man was not fit for any work, while

(d) Slesser L.J. found 'great difficulty as to what the medical referee decided' and that he had 'added confusion by adding a proviso'.

Such cases may deter workmen from risking any medical procedure at all and prompt them to accept an early if disadvantageous 'settlement'; a new 'undisputed' case is then recorded, to be quoted as evidence that the existing system gives satisfaction.

'The main trouble', writes Mr. H. M. Eaton in the *Journal of the Chartered Insurance Institute*, 'in connexion with certificates by Medical Referees has arisen when the Certificate is framed in ambiguous terms'. Much waste and trouble, he contends, would be saved if medical referees would 'simply' state 'that the workman has recovered from the accident and is fit for full work, or that he has not fully recovered, and then the work for which he is fit'.[1] Few experienced doctors can state 'simply' whether and for what employment a given workman is fully or partially fit. A doctor who says too little may be suspected by one party of bias and even of ignoring certain symptoms. If he says too much—alleviating his conscience by a proviso—he may not only be suspected of bias by one party but be rebuked by the court for ambiguity. This state of affairs cannot be radically changed in present circumstances. Dr. Brend takes a serious view of 'the great diversity of view among doctors as to the causation of these [mental] disorders, the flat contradictions between medical witnesses on apparently fundamental points being very puzzling to lay members of a court, dealing as they are with cases presenting mainly subjective symptoms'.[2] A judge, a barrister, or a lay juryman can form a good idea of the effect of a crippled limb or the loss of a finger or foot, but not of 'shock' or 'nervousness'; 'he may attach meanings to these words derived from his own personal experience which may be seriously misleading.' Writing of 'Medical Witness in Civil Actions' Dr. Brend says:

One of the doctors called for the plaintiff in action for damages or compensation is usually the plaintiff's ordinary medical attendant and as such, whether he be an insurance practitioner or not, has ties of interest with the plaintiff, and is often his personal friend. The doctor on the other side is generally representative of an insurance company and is fully alive to the fact that his interests and those of the company are identical. . . . This is why we see doctors strongly opposing each other

---

[1] Cf. vol. xxxiii, 1930, p. 237: 'The Legal Process in Connexion with Workmen's Compensation Claims.'

[2] Cf. Brend, loc. cit., pp. 63–4. Among the cases he cites: 'I have heard a doctor state in the witness-box that there were two inches of shortening of a leg, while his opponent maintained that there was no shortening at all.'

in the Courts of Law on questions on which they would readily come to an agreement if acting together, for instance on a Medical Board, for often each is well aware that he is straining his views to meet the claims of his own side.

We shall revert to this matter when, at a later stage, we refer to the somewhat superficial treatment accorded by the Stewart Committee to complaints of 'bias' made by several witnesses.

From these complaints two points of importance emerge:

1. The medical referee *qua* doctor may make bona fide medical mistakes: these may arise from lack of general, or of specialized knowledge, whether of the particular injury, or disease, or of the nature of the 'light work' offered or available.

2. The medical referee may err *qua* 'arbitrator' in cases referred to him for final decision. This raises the question as to whether the parties should have the right, as at present, to 'a more or less free choice between a medical and a non-medical Tribunal—the Medical Referee and the County Court—for the purpose of reaching a medical decision upon a medical issue'.[1] The Stewart Committee answered this question in the negative.

The first point might be met by substituting a Medical Board for a single referee, as recommended to the Stewart Committee by 'some insurance interests',[2] by the B.M.A., and by some legal and judicial witnesses. Several private members' Bills have of late years contained this recommendation.[3]

The Stewart Committee stopped short of a positive recommendation. They agreed that a Board would represent 'a much wider range of experience than a single Referee' and that the opportunity afforded for discussion by several doctors would 'minimize the risk of positive error'; whilst a Board would 'inspire more confidence than the single individual'. But it adduced counter-arguments: A single Referee could work quicker and be cheaper 'in the majority of cases'. But the small minority of cases are all important. They are the doubtful cases, in which the workman is fighting 'for life and death'. The substitution of a Board for a referee will not add to the length or cost of litigation. On the contrary, it is reasonable to suppose that its verdict would carry great weight and deter both parties from appealing to a higher court. As to questions of relative cost, any measure designed to diminish the period of disablement or its consequences would, on a long as well as on a short view, be financially economical, particularly in

---

[1] Cf. *Stewart Report*, p. 71.

[2] Cf. ibid., p. 65.

[3] Cf. Workmen's Compensation Bill (Mr. John Jones) of Oct. 29th 1937, § 6; Workmen's Compensation Bill (Mr. Mainwaring) of Nov. 6th 1936, § 19 sqq.; Workmen's Compensation Bill (Mr. Ridley) of Nov. 18th 1938, § 6.

the matter of long-term 'recurrences'.[1] So far as a Board is more likely than a single referee to supply a correct diagnosis and prognosis much man-power might be saved. Experience of the Ontario system in Canada demonstrates that a Board-system may develop 'a brisk claims routine', which is both speedy and economical.[2] In the U.S.A., where doctors differ upon such subjects no less than in Britain, the hearing officer, as soon as medical controversy begins, refers the injured worker to an impartial medical expert for examination.[3] Here, too, the single-doctor-system is discredited, and preference is shown for a system whereunder, as in New York and Massachusetts, decisions are reached by a Board or Committee of experts.

The State medical staff in New York City has fifteen or more full-time physicians, distributed among the various branch offices, whose duty it is to examine and report impartially upon the condition of compensation claimants to the Board which conducts the compensation hearings. Over 50,000 medical examinations are annually made by the State physicians.[4] On this system, if they knew of it, the Stewart Committee is silent, but their *Report* mentions that the cost of a Board would be 'formidable'. With 'State' doctors there might be less delay, but they would cost money and might also be deprived 'of current experience in practice, hospital and otherwise', and not be able to maintain their 'efficiency'. These arguments disregard the high standard of efficiency of State or semi-State doctors in other countries, and overlook the fundamental fact that, in respect of diagnosis and prognosis, 'treatment' must be distinguished from 'medical procedure'. Some link between Board and specialists is desirable. In Massachusetts the law permits any member of the Accident Board in his discretion to appoint an 'impartial' physician, who is in practice a specialist, to examine and report upon the condition of an injured workman. The law of 1935 provides that a list of registered physicians shall be prepared by the Board of Registration in Medicine and a claim for compensation for injuries due to industrial disease must be referred for diagnosis to three impartial physicians

---

[1] Cf. *Stewart Report*, pp. 82–3.

[2] Cf. for details: *Ontario Procedure in Settlement of Workmen's Compensation Claims*, reprint from *Monthly Labor Review*, Jan. 1936, p. 6: 'The thoroughness of the labor of the clerical staff, medical officers, and claims officers is attested by the very small number of cases which require field investigation.' Further: *Claims Administration in Workmen's Compensation*, reprint from *Monthly Labor Review*, June 1938, p. 3. The importance of the Ontario system was minimized by questions put by Mr. Boyd and Mr. Williams to witnesses before the Hetherington Commission on the ground that it mainly relates to big industries. But the deficiencies in claims procedure under the British system relate as much to the 'big' industries as to the smaller employers (Q. 5034–8).

[3] *Claims Administration*, p. 17.   [4] Cf. Dodd, loc. cit., pp. 447–8.

chosen therefrom. The use of three physicians as industrial disease
referees is compulsory and their diagnosis is binding upon all parties.[1]

Owing perhaps to their restricted terms of reference the Stewart
Committee, like the Holman Gregory Committee, seem to have been
determined to 'maintain the system'. Their *Report* merely recommended an enlargement and strengthening of the panels of referees.
Such an enlargement together with revision of the duties of such
referees (numbering some 280 in Britain) is certainly desirable, but it
in no way disposes of the well-grounded complaints against the single-
referee system, and should not be allowed to divert attention from
the benefits that might accrue from the collaboration of a Board of
three doctors or two doctors and a medico-legal expert, with power
to obtain specialist advice.

We now come to our second point, viz. the position of the referee
not as a doctor but as an arbitrator. The *Stewart Report* criticized the
present state of the law which 'permits' a settlement either by a medical
or a non-medical authority, i.e. either by the medical referee or by
arbitration. They were in favour of abolishing the option which an
employer or an employee now enjoys of securing the determination of
disputes on medical questions either by obtaining a reference to the
medical referee or by initiating arbitration proceedings under the
review procedure.

This recommendation greatly commends itself to us. Litigation
under Workmen's Compensation, which may often be a medical issue
de facto, remains a legal issue *de jure* and should be so treated.[2] The
Stewart Committee favoured the retention of the single referee, subject to an appeal to Medical Tribunals to be established in twelve
large centres, the members being drawn from local panels of qualified
practitioners. They suggested that the Tribunal should consist of
three members, of whom one at least would be an appropriate specialist.
They made careful proposals as to procedure before these Tribunals.[3]
The idea of a Medical Tribunal of Appeal (though without final
powers) deserves careful attention. It seems to have been advocated by
the Stewart Committee as a possible compromise which would help to
retain the single referee in most cases, particularly if 'the cost should
fall on employers and workmen' (with a contribution from the Ex-
chequer). But here lies the danger, particularly from the workman's
angle. His reluctance to prolong the case by further proceedings might

---

[1] Cf. Dodd, loc. cit., pp. 471–2. For these matters also cf. *Medical Service in Industry*,
passim.

[2] Cf. *Stewart Report*, pp. 68 and 78. The T.U.C. Memorandum to the Hetherington
Commission stresses the same point, see p. 418 (§ 64): 'Many medical referees themselves
admit that the powers conferred on them are too great, and that they would like to see
them reduced.'   [3] Cf. ibid., pp. 79 sqq.

be increased by such an arrangement, his doubts as to the advisability of going another step farther to the Tribunal might be enhanced by increasing costs and further delay while, on the other hand, large employers and insurance offices might welcome an appeal to such a Tribunal.[1] We therefore doubt whether, when the worker is the appellant, recourse to a Tribunal of Appeal would be of practical value. We should prefer to see the single referee replaced by Medical Boards, whose weight would endow them with authority and inspire confidence. This solution should not exclude the creation of a Medical Tribunal as envisaged by the Stewart Committee, to which certain cases might be referred.[2]

Only a Medical Board with several members could, in our view, adequately discharge the additional duties which the Stewart Committee sought to place upon the single referee. The Committee suggested that the medical referee should indicate, when he upholds the contention of an employer that the worker has in part recovered and has some degree of earning capacity in the general labour market, any limitations of function as well as any particular work which the worker could suitably, or should not, undertake. The medical referee would further be responsible for examining and reporting upon cases about to be settled by payment of a lump sum 'in any case of doubt'.[3] In all these cases not only would the volume of work be increased, but it would require expert differentiated and special knowledge which no one man could, but a Board might, supply.

The functions of the certifying surgeon, whose duties precede those of the medical referee, relate to scheduled industrial diseases and therefore are of less general importance than those of medical referees. Before an employee can recover compensation in such cases, he must produce a certificate from a certifying surgeon from whom he can appeal to a medical referee. Certifying surgeons were not less freely criticized than medical referees. Though the Stewart Committee took

[1] Dr. Brend writes, loc. cit., p. 85: 'With great respect to the efforts of the Committee this scheme (Medical Tribunal) seems to me to be slow and cumbersome. It involves delay in matters in which a quick decision is always desirable, necessitates witnesses and representatives travelling to the centre and has elements of possible hardships to employers . . . and to workmen. . . .'

[2] Cf. A. G. Erskine-Hill, K.C., M.P., 'Industrial Dermatitis from the Legal Standpoint,' in *The British Journal of Dermatology*, 1937, pp. 427 sqq. He notes that the medical referee 'who is seldom a specialist' has to reach 'a final and binding decision of fact in each case. . . . The difficulty might, in a sense, be lessened by the decision being referred to an arbitrator with a specialist medical assessor.' But 'the cost of procedure' and 'the delay necessarily caused to the workman' suggests that the present system should be retained, and enlarged by a wider panel of specialists.

[3] Cf. *Stewart Report*, pp. 100 and 112.

the view that 'witnesses generally' supported the present system, we gather from the *Report*[1] (in the absence of the evidence) that

1. One or two witnesses expressed the view that the 'reputation for independence in certain areas' of certifying surgeons was not of the best.
2. Several witnesses complained that certifying surgeons are sometimes perfunctory in the performance of their duties.
3. It was asserted 'from several quarters' that the certifying surgeon is not sufficiently often a specialist in the industrial diseases most likely to arise in a given locality.[2]

The number of certificates given by certifying surgeons in the years 1933–5 is increasing, so is also the number of appeals made to the medical referee, and the proportion of successful appeals.

	1933	1934	1935
Certificates given . . .	11,880	13,287	14,411
Appeals made . . .	1,686	2,063	2,141
Appeals allowed . . .	650	742	910
Percentage of Appeals allowed to number made* . .	38·55	35·96	42·5

* Cf. *Stewart Report*, p. 51. For particulars of procedure in this matter by the registrar cf. Willis, loc. cit., pp. 845 sqq.

The Stewart Committee's recommendations in this connexion were meagre. They proposed extension of the time for appeal and a greater measure of supervision by the Home Office over certifying surgeons. It is clear that in present circumstances, for whatever reason, neither certifying surgeons nor medical referees, as a body, inspire complete confidence,[3] and that, in some cases at least, there is a lack of specialized knowledge. The last defect is ascribable not to the medical men concerned, but to the system under which their services are utilized. This is equally true of the question of confidence; it is not the existence but 'the suspicion of bias' which matters.[4] It is not the inadequate medical knowledge of some particular doctor in a given case which matters,

[1] Cf. *Stewart Report*, pp. 57 sqq.

[2] The problem appears particularly related to dermatitis. See p. 58 of the *Stewart Report*. An interesting case relating to an error made by the certifying surgeon is reported in *The British Journal of Dermatology*, 1937, pp. 419–20, by Dr. H. MacCormac. Here the error was unfavourable to the worker who, in fact, had no dermatitis; the case should impress employers with the fact that specialist knowledge by the certifying surgeon as well as medical referees might be as much in their interest as in that of the worker. Dr. MacCormac suggests that all contested cases should be brought before a County Court judge assisted by a medical assessor chosen—in this differing from the present procedure—from a panel of 'experts'.

[3] See *Hetherington Commission*, T.U.C. Evidence, § 60, p. 418.   [4] Cf. ibid., p. 72.

but the suspicion that he is not fully competent. Confidence is vital to cure. It is more likely to be inspired by a Board than by one man, however competent.

The advent of a system of Medical Boards would soon revolutionize the use and repute of professional medical witnesses, who would be chosen more for their professional status than for their skill in 'masked advocacy'.[1] Little good can come from piecemeal changes and minor modifications in the present system, whence are derived the principal evils to which we have drawn attention. Only official or semi-official bodies can be free from the 'suspicion' inherent in the present system, under which conflicting views are thrashed out by the representatives of private interests on the one hand, and those of the injured person on the other.

The T.U.C. Memorandum to the Hetherington Commission added much useful evidence to the point. It also stresses the fact that

the present system directly encourages litigation. Arbitrators rely to a considerable extent on expert medical witnesses. At present the handsome rewards received by medical practitioners as expert witnesses encourages the greatest possible conflict of medical evidence. The object of such witnesses is to assist the side which pays them.[2]

A semi-official body such as an official Medical Board is above such suspicions, particularly if specialist assistance is at its disposal. To repeat the words of the *Evaluation Report* of the I.L.O. (1937): the intervention of doctors 'cannot give rise to any objection provided that the doctors are experts who have given proof of their competence to give an opinion on the cases submitted to them, and are quite independent'.[3] To reach this goal involves, in Britain, a new system of administering Workmen's Compensation; this, in turn, involves economic and social considerations which we will now proceed to examine.

[1] Cf. Brend, loc. cit., p. 93.
[2] Cf. *Hetherington Commission*, p. 419; we may also refer to the particular case cited in A. 4051.   [3] Cf. p. 364.

NOTE

EVIDENCE before the Hetherington Commission presented by a solicitor of great experience in compensation practice, Mr. W. H. Thompson, has confirmed many of our observations relating to the medical administration of Workmen's Compensation. It was too late to embody the relevant passages in the text, but attention may be called to the following point (cf. *Hetherington Commission*, pp. 1000 sqq.): 'The examinations . . . are often perfunctory and unsatisfactory. Men have complained to me over and over again that they have not been examined at all.' 'Many doctors who give evidence . . . are prepared to put themselves forward as experts on almost every conceivable question.' 'The workman is often sent to one doctor after another, presumably in the hope that at some stage of the itinerary the ideal evidence will be obtained.' 'In London the average specialist who does this work wants three guineas for a report and ten to fifteen guineas for attending Court.'

CHAPTER XVIII

THE ECONOMIC AND SOCIAL SIDE: COMPULSORY INSURANCE AND FINANCIAL SECURITY

To rely on the individual being, with us, the natural leaning, we will hear of nothing but the good of relying on the individual; to act through the collective nation on the individual being not our natural leaning, we will hear nothing in recommendation of it. But the wise know that we often need to hear most of that which we are least inclined.
MATTHEW ARNOLD, *Culture and Anarchy*, chap. iii.

The surface of Society is always satisfactory.
C. F. G. MASTERMAN, *The Condition of England*, chap. v.

ALMOST sixty years have passed since the inception of social insurance schemes of Workmen's Compensation in European countries—a period long enough to clarify many of the economic and social advantages and disadvantages attached to the various systems, including the relative merits of optional or compulsory insurance. Before discussing their application to Workmen's Compensation we must be clear as to the underlying principles.

Compulsory insurance is based upon the simple principle that 'no employer may employ an uninsured workman'. This principle is not bound up with State insurance: it has been applied, in Britain, to motor vehicles and drivers, under a system of private insurance, as also to miners, under the Nicholson Act of 1934, the insured workman's rights being safeguarded by elaborate statutory devices.[1]

Germany, the pioneer of social insurance, adopted the principle of compulsion from the outset in 1884. It may well have been regarded as a natural development of the tradition of the industrial gilds in which masters and men played their parts in the control of industry;[2] it was in harmony with, and was a natural extension to, industry of the co-operative movement then gathering strength in Germany.[3]

In Britain, on the contrary, the legislature was most reluctant to admit even the principle of Employers' Liability, and twenty years of argument were necessary to establish the principle of compensation independently of the negligence of either party. The legislature even then was content to rely upon self-interest as an inadequate incentive to the employer to insure against his liability. As in the case of old age

---

[1] See our vol. i, p. 261.
[2] See our vol. i, pp. 9 and 40.
[3] Cf. Schwedtman and Amery, loc. cit. (1911), pp. 7–8 and *passim*; also Manes, loc. cit., *passim*.

pensions, in the eyes of many enraged individualists,[1] so in the case of Workmen's Compensation, almost any amount of destitution and injustice to working men and women seemed preferable to the dread alternative of compulsory insurance. It was in vain that factory inspectors reported, and that conservative majorities on Royal Commissions and radical politicians joined forces in urging, the need for State intervention. The Act of 1934 remains an exception, though the principle of compulsion has found legislative expression in some of the special schemes by which industrial diseases are covered, such as those for the refractories industries and the sandstone industry.[2] Here then is a beginning of compulsory insurance coupled with valuable provisions for certain financial instruments, including a General Compensation Fund. This takes the form of a Limited Company; all payments of compensation under the Scheme and other prescribed expenses are borne by the Fund, which recoups itself by a levy from the employers concerned. It is a significant fact that statutory compulsory compensation has taken root in the coal-mining industry and, by schemes under the Workmen's Compensation Acts, in certain occupations which are apt to lead to dust-diseases.

The coal-mining industry has a relatively high accident-rate and is characterized by occasional 'catastrophic' disasters involving large numbers of men and thus attracting public attention. Dust-diseases are protracted: they occur mainly in the mining industry, in which the trade unions are strong and the owners well organized. But workmen in other industries equally need and deserve protection and, to our mind, workmen in the seven great groups of industries and in the building trade are equally entitled to such protection as compulsory insurance would afford. Apart, however, from the exceptions we have noted, Workmen's Compensation in Britain still relies upon voluntary insurance in contrast to the majority of social insurance laws in general of the principal industrial countries and the British Dominions which have adopted the compulsory principle. The I.L.O. wrote in 1936:

Legislation based on the principle of compulsion is to be found in nearly every country . . . under every political, economic or social system, whether liberal or authoritarian, collectivist or capitalist, compulsory social insurance is recognized as an essential factor of any rational social policy.[3]

So far from the introduction of a compulsory system of insurance into British Workmen's Compensation, involving new or revolutionary principles, it would only harmonize with those now governing social

[1] Cf. Hermann Levy, *Economic Liberalism*, 1913, pp. 122–3.
[2] Cf. vol. i, pp. 264–5.
[3] Cf. *The International Labour Organisation and Social Insurance*, Geneva, 1936, p. 4.

insurance abroad, and would be in no way inconsistent with those underlying the British social services.

More important, perhaps, is the fact that in the international sphere of Workmen's Compensation legislation Britain is among the few countries which have no compulsory accident insurance. A list, also drawn up by the I.L.O. in 1936, shows that of all compulsory social service schemes existing at present those of Workmen's Compensation show an overwhelming majority. They number 130 and relate to 54 countries. Sickness and maternity compulsory schemes number 45 in 31 countries. Invalidity, old age, and widows' and orphans' compulsory insurance schemes number 75 in 30 countries. In such circumstances the absence of compulsory Workmen's Compensation in Britain becomes still more striking.[1]

The *Report* of the I.L.O. mentioned above concludes that certain voluntary institutions may render valuable service in well-organized occupations and in industries which are exceptionally concentrated or have long been prosperous. In such cases, adequate and well-managed insurance funds may be found, financed by large contributions from employers, and paying valuable benefits. 'But', continues the Report,[2]

they are rare and, . . . on the whole, voluntary social insurance has failed to protect the workers against various risks and particularly against premature invalidity and early death.

The *Report* also notes that economic depression after 1931 did not delay application of the compulsory principle, and that from 1934 onwards 'the movement gained renewed force and made substantial progress'. In the U.S.A. the trend of legislation is towards compulsory insurance.[3] Of the 52 Compensation Acts existing in 1936 only 18 were compulsory and 34 were elective. The compulsory feature is found in States which have also an exclusive State Fund, though there are also competitive State Funds which provide for compulsion.[4] But, as Dodd explains, 'to the extent that the employer is coerced to come under the law by the abrogation of common law defences, the law is in fact compulsory'.

The Holman Gregory Committee advocated compulsory insurance,[5]

---

[1] Cf. *The International Labour Organisation and Social Insurance*, Geneva, 1936, p. 188. [2] Cf. ibid., p. 3.

[3] Though the Acts may be distinguished as being 'compulsory' or 'elective', by the latter being meant an Act which permits the employer to reject the Act, but which abrogates his common law defences if he does so. Cf. for particulars Dodd, loc. cit., pp. 31–5 and 747. It should be noted that under the so-called elective Acts there is again a wide variation of types. See ibid., p. 748.

[4] Cf. for details *Handbook of Labor Statistics*, Washington, 1936, pp. 1118–19.

[5] Cf. vol. i, p. 163 and *passim*.

and would doubtless have pressed it more strongly but for an argument, still advanced to-day, brought forward by Mr. Trickett, of the Treasury, in a dissenting Memorandum dealing exclusively with compulsory insurance.[1] He had studied the evidence of witnesses dealing with the risks of voluntary insurance and found out that such witnesses had for the most part declared that the losses to workmen *known to them* by failure on the part of employers to insure were small. The Holman Gregory Committee estimated uninsured employers to number 250,000[2] in 1919: they are probably as numerous to-day. It is the small employer, declared the *Holman Gregory Report*, 'who is most likely to be in default'. He is protected from proceedings by his want of means, and consequently his default 'rarely emerges into the light of day'. Further 'cases occur where a smaller sum than is due is accepted by the workman, owing to the employer's threat of bankruptcy if the full amount is insisted on, or where claims are not pressed because the employer is not worth fighting'. Judge Ruegg himself cited three cases.[3] To ascertain their number is quite impossible, declared the Committee, but Mr. Trickett drew his conclusions without any regard to these 'unseen' or 'unheard' cases. Here is another case where percentages or references to 'relatively' small numbers are of no value, and are apt to lead to false decisions. The number is 'relatively' large: their importance is 'relatively' small; but justice is not concerned with percentages.

It is to be regretted that the Departmental Committee on Compulsory Insurance under the Chairmanship of Sir Felix Cassel, having as its Secretary one so conversant with all matters of social insurance as Mr. G. D. Stockman of the Treasury, was at pains not to inquire into the matter of non-insured employers under the Workmen's Compensation Acts.[4] It restricted its recommendations to the question 'whether any, and if so what, changes in the existing law relating to the carrying on of the business of insurance are desirable in the light of statutory provisions relating to compulsory insurance against third party risks and by employers against liability to their workmen', and interpreted this as relating only to the matter of financial safety and security in regard to the existing laws and schemes of compulsory insurance, but did not think fit to deal with the matter of non-insured employers. They assumed that questions involving 'extensions of compulsory insurance' such as whether 'Workmen's Compensation should be made compulsory other than in coal mining' were beyond their terms of reference.

[1] Cf. *Holman Gregory Report*, p. 77.   [2] Cf. vol. i, p. 161.
[3] Cf. *Holman Gregory Report*, pp. 17–18.
[4] Cf. *Report of the Deptl. Committee on Compulsory Insurance*, July 1937, Cmd. 5528, 1937.

This is the more regrettable as there was some interesting evidence in regard to this point. Mr. G. R. A. Buckland from the Home Office made it clear that information as to the possibilities of extension of the Act of 1934 to other employments had been asked for, but that the Home Secretary thought it advisable to see how it worked before going farther.[1] He was careful to remind the Committee that the Government had decided in 1919 that 'compulsory insurance was going too far', but did not add that since then compulsory insurance by motorists had been introduced. The Corporation of Insurance Brokers in a Memorandum to the Committee declared that

compulsory insurance [of employers against liability to their workmen] is as necessary in the interests of the public as compulsory insurance as applied to liability of personal injuries in connection with road traffic.[2]

The Chairman replied that this was 'outside the scope' of the terms of reference of the Committee.[3] The T.U.C. also regretted the exclusion from discussion of 'the principle of compulsory cover of risk throughout industry in respect of Workmen's Compensation, and the method of giving effect to it'.[4] An outstanding opportunity of discussing the problem was thus missed. In a Debate of November 19th 1937, on a private member's Compensation Bill, the House of Commons was told of two cases where workmen—the one having lost his eye through industrial accident, the other being a youth of 16 who had a leg amputated—were left without compensation by non-insurance of their employers; a third case was mentioned of a man who got an award of 30s. per week which was not met by the uninsured employer who was soon afterwards buried in a pauper's grave. 'There are many other cases of that kind', declared Mr. T. Williams, pointing out that an inquiry into the matter was as necessary as the information was available.[5] Nothing was done: the matter had been 'ventilated'; the members interested 'blew off steam'; the House of Commons served once more as a useful 'safety valve', but the grievances remained unremedied.

A few months later Mr. Dingle Foot, M.P., told of the widow of a miner who had died of silicosis. She received no compensation as the company was not insured and went into bankruptcy.[6] The case showed how little practical importance attaches to § 7 (c) of the Act (Insolvency of the Employer) which gives compensation claims priority among the debts of a company when a receiver is appointed. There were no funds

[1] Cf. *Cassel Report*, A. 1686–7. No case has in fact yet been brought to the courts under this Act.   [2] Cf. ibid., p. 211.   [3] Cf. Q. 4208–9.
[4] Cf. p. 303 and Q. 6039.   [5] Cf. *Debates H.C.*, Nov. 19th 1937, p. 815.
[6] Cf. ibid., Feb. 8th 1939, pp. 1064–7.

from which outstanding claims could be met. The widow got £28 instead of the £280 which was due to her. This case happened in one of the tin mines of Cornwall, notorious for silicosis, a risk to be anticipated by any mining company. One can only agree with Mr. Higgs, a Conservative M.P. and a large employer, who observed that compulsory insurance would be justified if it were only for 'the one case cited'.[1] Further evidence of such cases is to be found in the Memorandum of the T.U.C. to the Hetherington Commission, which strongly urged compulsory insurance of all employers (§ 90) and declared that the Congress 'had experience of many cases where injured workmen have been unable to obtain any compensation or have to put up with less than the amount to which they were entitled because of the employer not being in a position to pay, and not having covered the risk by insurance.

Several typical cases were cited. In questioning Sir Walter Citrine on the point Judge Stewart admitted that his own experience was that, in certain cases, 'terrible hardship resulted to the workman because of the bankruptcy of the employer', though he knew only 'a very few cases of that kind', doubtless because they had not come before him in court. We do not know how many injured workers year by year have to abandon or compound their claims lest their employers should go bankrupt and they themselves might lose a job. Judge Stewart weakened his position by declaring that 'he was not sure' whether in fact the Nicholson Act of 1934 was passed to remedy such cases; reference to the Debates in the House of Commons would have dispelled his doubts.[2]

After general compulsory insurance, the 'security' or financial safety of the existing institutions insuring liability under Workmen's Compensation is of outstanding importance. Experts such as E. T. Elbourne have frequently emphasized that only 'offices of a very strong standing' should be allowed to take this business at all. He states that in order to secure 'a lower rate', firms often insure with 'a weak insurance company, which has been wound up and the employer saddled with the payment of compensation without any means of redress'.[3] In such cases the ultimate loser may be, and often is, the injured workman. In the absence of compulsory insurance the obligation of the State to satisfy itself as to the security offered to the insured is greatly diminished. In the words of Sir Felix Cassel, K.C., 'once the State has said that people who do certain things must insure against risks which those acts involve then it is necessary to take every precaution to ensure that the insurer should be solvent and able to meet his

---

[1] Cf. ibid., Mr. Higgs, p. 1068.
[2] Cf. *Hetherington Commission*, pp. 422, 441, 464. See also our vol. i, pp. 258–60.
[3] Cf. E. T. Elbourne, *Factory Administration and Cost Accounts*, 1929, p. 53.

liabilities'.[1] The Clauson Committee took this view when it endorsed the argument that 'as under the existing law, an employer is at liberty to insure or not at his free will against liabilities to workmen, no argument drawn from the position of the workman can be legitimately employed'.[2] On the other hand, the Clauson Committee as well as the Cassel Committee on Compulsory Insurance saw no reason why Mutual Indemnity Associations should not in future be required to furnish accounts and information as to their business and financial position in the same way as any other insuring body. The Clauson Committee, however, thought that 'responsible employers' might be excused by the Board of Trade from the obligation to make deposits, while, on the other hand, it stated:

> It is said that the constitution of some of these bodies is such that, if a member becomes insolvent or (if a company) liquidates, the benefit of the insurance is lost, and thus the workmen who would have (in effect) a claim, through an insolvent employer, against a company insuring him, may find themselves detrimentally affected by the employer belonging to such a mutual association instead of being insured in an ordinary company.

As, however, existing legislation gives a workman a first charge on his employer's assets for payment of any compensation due, his position is to that extent improved though not secured, and the *Clauson Report* spoke, with good reason, of 'responsible' employers; but where does the distinction in practice begin? The Cassel Committee held that Mutual Indemnity Associations should be placed under the same obligation to furnish accounts and information as insurance companies.[3] Though the former unsatisfactory practice with many indemnity associations 'that if a member became bankrupt or went into liquidation, membership was cancelled and the Association immediately ceased to be responsible for all claims by the member's employees' had been replaced by new arrangements in regard to reserve funds and the continuation of the obligation of the Association, 'the reforms in some instances had not yet advanced far enough'. The reliability of Mutuals was also discussed before the Hetherington Commission. Mr. Bannatyne asked whether want of funds was the reason why, in some cases, Mutuals had 'failed to pay what should have been paid'. He explained, with particular reference to conditions before the Nicholson Act, that some employers were not insured; in some cases the Mutual did not insure the employer against all risk; in others an employer on going bankrupt automatically ceased to be a member of the Mutual. (There

---

[1] Cf. *Cassel Report*, Q. 4210.

[2] Cf. *Report of Departmental Committee appointed to inquire and report what amendments are desirable in the Assurance Companies Act 1909*, 1927, pp. xi–xii.

[3] Cf. pp. 39–41, 43–4, and 45.

is no reason to doubt that such conditions prevail in other industries, but he did not touch upon this point.) 'It is not easy to find out much about Mutuals', said Sir W. Citrine, 'but . . . we believe that they are very easy to form, and very difficult to control, so that possibility of security is weakened'.[1]

Again, there is a gap in the Nicholson Act, the essence of which was already described in our first volume (see p. 261). An employer is not *obliged* to insure against the first 26 weeks of disablement. The insurer must, however, assume liability for compensation in the event of a member becoming bankrupt or going into liquidation or of the appointment of a receiver or manager by debenture holders. The reason given by most witnesses representing Mutual Associations for not insuring in these cases is that the colliery owner is more likely to find light work for men disabled for a short period if he is not insured and that he is kept more closely in touch with his workmen if he is liable for the payment of compensation to them.

We doubt whether this explanation or 'defence' of non-insurance is acceptable. The *Cassel Report* might usefully have reflected upon the relevant statistics. In 1937 the number of terminated cases of accidents in mines (coal-mines and others, which do not come under the Nicholson Act) in which compensation (exclusive of lump-sum payment cases) was paid and which lasted more than 26 weeks, was 3,586 out of a total of this class of cases of 133,206, while the cases under 26 weeks where lump-sum payments were made was small, 4,415. Apart from the seriousness of cases, reflected by their long duration, the field left open to non-insurers despite the Nicholson Act must thus be very wide. The *Cassel Report* emphasized that certain insurers had argued before the Committee that the limitation of 26 weeks was undesirable, as 'from a strict insurance point of view' it is preferable that the insurer should have the absolute conduct of cases from their inception, seeing that liability in a proportion of these cases may fall upon him, and it was mentioned that in view of this some mutual indemnity associations have actually handled all claims from the outset, even though many of them will not result in a charge to the Association's compensation funds. The Nicholson Act further imposes on the insurer the liability to pay compensation in all cases in the event of bankruptcy or liquidation of the owner, and it is therefore difficult for the insurer to assess accurately the premium which should be charged, or the reserve to be held, for such a risk.[2] The Committee thought that the matter should be 'reviewed', apparently meaning that the 26 weeks' limitation was better to be eliminated.

Further recommendations were made to strengthen the security of

---

[1] Cf. *Hetherington Commission*, Q. 4703–5.　　　　[2] Cf. *Cassel Report*, p. 49.

compensation insurance. It is evident that a difficult position may arise in the case of coal-mining disasters. Here very heavy sums may be suddenly involved. Some Mutuals reinsure against such a contingency. The cover obtained generally reinsures payments in excess of sums of £2,000–£5,000 in respect of death claims in any one accident with a maximum of £100,000–£300,000. The Gresford Colliery disaster, resulting in £86,000 in death claims, had been reinsured with Lloyd's. Other associations do not reinsure and the danger of security of payment in big disasters remains, although it may be remote. The Cassel Committee did not accept this contention and held that the sound course for all coal-mining firms and their Mutual Indemnity Associations respectively was to reinsure against disasters through 'a central re-insurance Association' to cover the whole coal-mining industry of the country 'in one organization'.[1] This proposal would bring much nearer a centralization of the entire compensation insurance business as we envisage it. Technical progress has not removed the danger of grave disasters in coal-mining. New safety devices, while diminishing old risks, always created new dangers.[2] Mr. J. W. Fidoe, a mining engineer, has lately drawn attention to the point again. Intensive mechanical mining has completely altered the physical conditions of the pits. The modern conveyer face exudes gas at a rate never contemplated in the days of hand-worked coal, and may reach danger point during part of the coal-filling shift. Ventilation is limited by the layout of the colliery workings, and the air velocity men can tolerate. These facts are 'guessed at or known to colliery managers, but it is not policy for officials to raise an outcry'. The author urges that it is necessary to take precautions both in mining methods and finance, including, we may add, reinsurance.[3] The findings of the Royal Commission on Safety in Coal Mines should lead to the same conclusions in respect of the desired greater financial security as presented by the *Cassel Report*.[4]

---

[1] Cf. *Cassel Report*, p. 42.   [2] Cf. vol. i, pp. 17 and 21.

[3] Cf. *Mine Disasters, The Case for Safety in Coal Mines.* Supplt. to *Compressed Air Engineering*, Dec. 1937, p. 37.

[4] Cf. *Royal Commission on Safety in Coal Mines Report*, 1938, pp. 366 sqq. and 497–8 and *passim*. As regards Explosions and Fires, the recommendations of the Report clearly show the present still existing danger points: (1) the law regarding the use of safety lamps as a precaution against explosion should be recast; (2) the use of substitutes for explosives should be encouraged; (3) the general elimination of electricity from 'safety lamp' mines is not necessary *if* 'a high standard of ventilation is maintained'; (4) more attention should be paid to the prevention of the formation of coal dust. It may be mentioned that the American experience shows in the same direction. Mr. John Roach, Deputy Commissioner of New Jersey, has dealt with the matter elaborately in a paper on *Mechanization in the Coal Industry* before the International Association of Industrial Accident Boards, 1930. Cf. U.S. Dept. of Labor, *Bulletin of Labor Statistics No. 536*, Washington, 1931, pp. 180 sqq. He describes the risk which might be created by mecha-

The Cassel Committee was at pains to investigate the actuarial security of the insurance carriers. As a result of the provisions of § 9 (4) of the Statute of 1925, as amended by the Act of 1931,[1] workers only partially disabled may become entitled to full compensation in the event of their being unable to obtain suitable work from their own or other employers, where the failure to obtain employment is a consequence wholly or mainly due to the injury. There is therefore a further contingent liability where compensation is being paid at partial rates only and this contingency may arise not only as a result of the physical deterioration of the worker, but also from changes in the state of the labour market. One of the stronger motives in regard to the settlement of claims by lump-sum payments on the part of employers is to get rid once and for all of claims in their books. Apart from the matter of accountancy there is another, an actuarial reason which points in the same direction. The methods of dealing with such contingencies differ widely.[2]

The same position arises where injured and fully recovered workers make claims in respect of recurrence of sickness or disease. The *Cassel Report* draws attention to the hypothetical fact that all members of an Association might cease business. In such a case there would be little chance of employing men in light work. A difficult position may arise: 'the claims payable by an Association as a going concern are almost certainly less than they would be if it were wound up.' The Committee concluded that if an obligation were imposed upon Mutual Associations to strengthen their reserves to some minimum standard, little risk would be incurred if, subject to proper safeguards, a reasonable time—not exceeding five years—were allowed within which the additional money as revealed necessary by proper valuation of the outstanding liabilities would be provided. Britain has not yet gone through such severe depressions as the U.S.A. have experienced, when the position of many insurance carriers and thereby workers was in grave danger.[3] Further strengthening of the security appears to

nically operated fans if placed underground; he stresses the fact that about 90 persons are killed in a year in the U.S.A. in coal-mines by coming in contact with electricity; he points to the increasing dangers to workers 'massed around machines' in coal-mines, and arrives at the conclusion that mechanical coal-mining will only mean 'increased safety' if 'the requisite amount of personal effort is expended in really trying to bring about increased safety'.   [1] See our vol. i, p. 256.   [2] Cf. *Cassel Report*, pp. 37-9.

[3] Cf. *Methods of Financing Workmen's Compensation Administration and Funds*. Reprint from *Monthly Labor Review*, March 1936, pp. 4 sqq.: *Effect of the Depression in Impairing Workmen's Compensation Service*. The article declares: '. . . the depression years 1929–34 have made a distinct contribution to the development of workmen's compensation administration in the United States by so exaggerating certain existing defects in the law and administration as to compel attention to the necessary remedies.'

be desirable. There is no good reason for not applying to Mutual Indemnity Associations transacting compulsory Workmen's Compensation business the rule which applies to insurance companies, as already recommended by the Holman Gregory Committee.[1] Associations transacting compulsory Workmen's Compensation business should be brought within the Assurance Companies (Winding Up) Acts, 1933 and 1935, and if other Mutual Indemnity Associations are required to make returns to the Board of Trade they also should be brought within the scope of the Acts.[2] Similar conditions should be imposed upon the 'Compensation Trusts'. Special care is, as the Cassel Committee noted, required in the case of small concerns, since the smaller the concern the greater the risk of insolvency—a strong argument in favour of a concentration of such Funds. The necessity of such strengthening measures appears the more necessary as under the system of free competition of insurance offices the danger is always imminent that, in order to secure a lower insurance rate, employers may insure with weak firms which may be wound up.[3]

Under another system of Workmen's Compensation insurance the whole actuarial position might be different. Where a State or semi-State organization and administration of Workmen's Compensation exists there is, apart from the arrangements regarding the forming of reserve funds, the 'guarantee of the State', as Mr. Wotzel pointed out in his Report to the Workmen's Compensation Committee in 1905.[4] This does not mean, as Mr. Knowles mistakenly told the Holman Gregory Committee,[5] that under the German system there are no reserve funds to be accumulated. On the contrary: the German system has from its very inception made what Mr. Wotzel rightly called 'elaborate provisions' for the accumulation of such funds by the *Berufsgenossenschaften*, including a sliding scale diminishing with the development of the insurance funds. Under the present law[6] these funds or *Rücklagen* are to be accumulated from additional payments to be made in respect of weekly payments (not of any lump-sum payments, so far as these are made under the German law). This reserve fund must amount to 300 per cent. of the *Entschädigungsbeträge*, i.e. the sums to be paid for claims. Certain exceptions are to be granted by the Imperial Insurance Bureau on application by the *Berufsgenos-*

[1] See our vol. i, p. 167.   [2] Cf. *Cassel Report*, p. 45.

[3] Cf. E. T. Elbourne, *Factory Administration and Cost Accounts*, 1929, p. 53.

[4] Cf. *Home Office Memorandum on Foreign and Colonial Laws relating to Compensation for Injuries*, Cmd. 2458, 1905, p. 36.

[5] Cf. his evidence before the Holman Gregory Committee, Q. 1058: 'The German legislation does not think it necessary to capitalize reserves for the purpose of meeting future claims.'

[6] Cf. *Reichsversicherungsordnung. Gewerbe-Unfallversicherung*, paras. 741–8.

senschaft. Mr. Wotzel observed that while the Act of 1897 in England left the workman entirely dependent upon the solvency of the employer, 'the most complete and thorough-going treatment of the question is found in the law of Germany'.

This is still true. At the end of the year 1936 the *Rücklagen* amounted to RM. 106,746,800 for the industrial *Berufsgenossenschaften*, an increase of 14·31 and 19·40 per cent. respectively against the preceding year.[1] Under an official scheme of Workmen's Compensation insurance the danger of insecurity for the workers is greatly lessened, though the strength of a reserve fund is still of importance. Dodd observes, with reference to the 1931–4 crisis in the U.S.A., that 'irrespective of any political juggling of insurance rates or of the efficiency or inefficiency of administration, state funds have, during the period of depression, been subject to the same type of financial strain as have private insurance companies'. An actuarial audit of the Ohio Fund in 1934 showed it to be solvent, but with a surplus reduced from 2,500,000 dollars in 1931 to 115,908 dollars in 1933. But, he adds, 'No loss to injured employees is likely to result from a state fund, either competitive or monopolistic; and this is true whether the solvency is or is not guaranteed by the State. . . . Where a state fund is monopolistic, a deficit may be met by higher rates, placing upon industry in future a burden of accident cost that should have been borne in the past.'[2]

This does not mean that actuarial responsibility of insurance carriers should be lessened where State administration exists; but it may mean a safeguard for the employee. State administration should not weaken the principle, recognized by the Cassel Committee, that it should be made a condition of every licence that the Association should operate on a strict insurance basis including a charge of a sufficient premium to meet the capitalized value of all claims arising during the period of coverage.[3] It would be easier to impose such conditions if industries were grouped into central bodies and their liabilities covered by a collective Compensation Fund. If the Cassel Committee could not agree to recommend such a Fund in regard to already existing compulsory insurance schemes, and under the Nicholson Act, it does not follow that the example set by this Act should not be followed by all other

[1] Cf. *Amtliche Nachrichten für Reichsversicherung*, Dec. 1937, no. 12, p. 428. As war and inflation had greatly devastated the accumulated fund which in 1913 had been even above the level prescribed by para. 743 of the law, these figures do not correspond to the 'three-times' amount. They have been gradually rising since the end of the inflation period and amounted in 1936 to 23·67 per cent. with the industrial and 8·71 per cent. with the agricultural indemnity associations of the prescribed sum of three times the amount of the 'rents' or pensions.

[2] Cf. Dodd, loc. cit., p. 551.   [3] Cf. *Cassel Report*, p. 47.

industries in which at present the conditions of security for the payment of claims under Workmen's Compensation do not provide the fullest security for the injured workman. The best remedy appears to be the creation of a collective compulsory organization of employers for the purpose of accident insurance and the accumulation of the necessary reserve funds.[1] This would entail a fundamental change in the British system of Workmen's Compensation, on lines outlined in our next chapter.

[1] Cf. also *Hetherington Commission*, A. 7227 (M. E. Williams, Compensation Secretary of the South Wales Miners' Federation): '... the Committee we envisage would be a Committee *under a general fund* which we propose should be established'.

CHAPTER XIX

THE ECONOMIC AND SOCIAL SIDE: THE
PRINCIPAL SYSTEMS ANALYSED

I hold every man a debtor to his profession; from the which as men of course do seek to receive countenance and profit, so ought they of duty to endeavour, by way of amends, to be a help and ornament thereunto.　　　　　BACON, *Maxims of Law*, Preface.

THE 'system' of Workmen's Compensation colours its every aspect and affects, as we have shown, all concerned, from the humblest workman or small employer to the Law Lords in the highest of the King's Courts. The view taken by the courts of the accident, its psycho-physical interpretation, and indeed the outlook of the sufferer himself may be affected by different types of administration. Weekly payments, the review of weekly payments, and the payment of lump sums are alike influenced by the various systems of Workmen's Compensation. The forms of legal or medical procedure, and of other aspects of administration are closely dependent upon the system which the legislature has thought proper to prescribe. The scope of Workmen's Compensation, whether limited to 'compensation' proper or extending to rehabilitation or accident prevention will depend upon the system adopted as a basis; the method and principle of compulsory insurance will likewise vary with the system of which it is a feature, rather than an integral part. The student of the different systems existing in Workmen's Compensation administration and organization is confronted with a perplexing variety of types which it seems almost impossible, at first sight, to present in schematic or systematic form. There are systems of State insurance and private insurance, and combinations of both. In some countries Boards administer Workmen's Compensation; in others this is done by a single Commissioner; others again administer Workmen's Compensation through existing trade organizations. Some compensation funds endow administrators with wide powers in various fields; others contain only supervisory and quasi-judicial provisions. Some systems are restricted to cash compensation only; others, whether State or private, cover accident prevention and vocational rehabilitation. In the judicial sphere procedure varies from ordinary court administration to that of Commissions with judicial functions while, under other systems, the State itself may create an Insurance Office with the status of a Ministry and the powers of a High Court of Justice. The variety of systems has indeed given rise to a new terminology: in the U.S.A. there are 'monopolistic' and competitive' 'State Funds; in Canada a distinction is made between 'collective' and 'individual' liability schemes.

The only clear distinction relates to the extent to which executive as well as administrative authority is exercised by the responsible organization (whether State or semi-State). A workmen's Compensation law might be limited in scope, but with a strong element of official administration; the scope of another may be wider, but the element of official administration smaller.[1] On this basis the characteristics of the principal systems may be summarized as follows:

1. *The system of Private Insurance proper.* The law merely provides for compensation payable in cash or otherwise. Employers are left to insure themselves against claims with insurance offices or through mutual associations[2] of a purely collective *private* character. This system may be one of compulsory or voluntary insurance.

2. *The system of administering or supervising the economic and social working of Workmen's Compensation law by official or semi-official bodies*, such as Committees, Commissions, Boards, or a single Commissioner. This does not relate to legal procedure only; it may embrace many sections of the Workmen's Compensation complex such as, for instance, accident prevention, and re-employment schemes, rehabilitation, &c., &c., for it leaves the door open to private insurance as well as to self-insurance.[3]

3. *The system of complete State Insurance*, and comprehensive economic and social administration by State bodies or their nominated official representatives.

In contrast to (2) above this system is monopolistic, and does not allow for optional or eligible private insurance; it is compulsory, though judicial procedure varies and may include either special courts in addition to or in lieu of the ordinary courts of justice.

1. *The system of Private Insurance* is that now existing in *Great Britain*. Insurance is optional. The administrative responsibility of the Government, as compared with other systems, is an irreducible minimum. The scope for official administration would not have been so restricted but for the limited scope of British Workmen's Compensation itself, which excludes accident prevention, medical care, rehabilitation, and re-employment. Official administration is thus strictly limited on *laissez-faire* lines. The social evils of the system, which have

---

[1] Cf. I.L.O., *Memorandum to Hetherington Commission*, pp. 585–605, which contains an interesting account of the different systems; it stresses differences in *financial* structure, but pays little regard to the *social* aspects of the different systems.

[2] Also Committees under certain schemes, see p. 312.

[3] Self-insurance is defined by the I.L.O. as 'the bearing of his risk by the individual employer who gives evidence of his ability to pay any probable compensation claims'.

been obvious since its inception (as shown in our vol. i) and have remained a constant source of distressing complaints (as shown in detail in this volume) and debates covering hundreds of hours in Parliament, are in the main an outcome of these limitations. They have been, as we have seen, scarcely remedied by certain duties laid upon Registrars and the recording of agreements. An extension of such powers, even if (as is not at present the case) they were effectively and uniformly administered, would not be an effective means of reform and would certainly not alter the system. The duties of Registrars are merely protective and passive, devoid of any active, i.e. decisive, or even advisory, character. Registrars prevent gross deception or injustice in most cases, but they are not 'administering' the system. The arrangement between the Home Office and the Accident Office Association for a minimum sum to be returned in benefits out of paid contributions is an exception to the general rule of 'non-interference'. It has not curtailed the development or the profits of the system of private insurance, though it might have done both.

In *France* Workmen's Compensation generally resembles that of Britain. Employers are not bound to insure. There is, however, a National Accident Insurance Fund, limited to the risks of permanent incapacity and death, in which employers may take out an insurance, if they do not prefer to insure with private institutions placed under the control and supervision of the administrative authorities, such as fixed premium companies, mutual associations, associations binding their members jointly and severally for the payment of compensation, and agricultural mutual insurance funds. In the case of insolvency on the part of the insurer or of an employer who is not insured, the compensation due to the injured workers or their dependants is paid out of a Guarantee Fund administered by the Government Deposit and Trust Fund; employers, whether insured or not, must make certain contributions to the Guarantee Fund.[1]

The system in *Belgium* resembles that of France. Fixed premium insurance companies and insurance funds by employers on a mutual basis are alone authorized, after approval by the Government, to carry on industrial accident insurance. Such authorization may be limited to accident insurance, in which case the insurance carrier is required to deposit the capital value of its liability for pensions with a specially approved establishment. Alternatively, it may be extended

[1] The information used in this chapter in regard to Workmen's Compensation in foreign countries is derived in general, and where not quoted otherwise, from the I.L.O. *International Survey of Social Services*, 1933, vols. i (1936) and ii (1937). For France compare also: Dr. C. Chauveau, *Loi sur les Assurances Sociales*, Paris, 1928, *passim*.

to cover pension insurance from accidents, in which case the insurance
carrier pays the pensions for which he is liable.[1]

While most British Dominions and Colonies have adopted some
sort of State administration this has not been the case in *South Australia*,
Tasmania, and *Western Australia*. Here a system very similar to that of
Britain prevails, although insurance is compulsory (in Tasmania since
1933). The system contrasts sharply with other provinces of the
Commonwealth of Australia, as also with the law relating to the employees of the Commonwealth, as here the Commonwealth carries its
own insurance, all matters and questions arising under the Statutes
(of Aug. 14th 1930 and Nov. 10th 1930) being determined by the
Commissioner for Employees' Compensation (i.e. the Secretary to the
Treasury).

In *New Zealand* insurance is neither compulsory nor is there any
official administration of insurance. Compensation is payable by the
employer who is individually liable. For claims of lower amounts (not
exceeding £50) the magistrates' courts decide in cases of dispute and
their decision is final and conclusive. Other cases are decided in a Court
of Arbitration and no appeal lies from the order of this Court. There
have been, of late, many improvements in regard to Workmen's Compensation law in New Zealand, but the administrative organization has
remained unchanged.[2]

It is noteworthy that the system of private and individual insurance
in Britain has been encroached upon by the Refractories Industries
Scheme of 1931[3] less by the creation of a 'General Compensation
Fund' which as such, would not necessarily imply a change in the
system of Workmen's Compensation administration, than by the creation of 'Joint Committees' (see Part III of the Scheme) representative
of both employers and workmen, presided over by an independent
chairman, which exercise jurisdiction in certain matters relating to
Part I of the Scheme. The determination by a Joint Committee of any
question assigned to it is to be final on matters of fact; in areas where no
Joint Committee has been formed another Joint Committee may act
selected by the Home Secretary.

Similar arrangements exist in Belgium, where compensation for
occupational diseases is a responsibility of a special Welfare Fund
administered under the Ministry of Labour and Social Welfare by a
governing body of five members appointed by the Crown, including
representatives of masters and men. A technical committee, comprising

---

[1] Cf. for further particulars: *Rapport relatif à l'Exécution de la Loi sur la Réparation des
Dommages résultant des Accidents du Travail*, Bruxelles, 1938.
[2] Cf. New Zealand Department of Labour, *Report* of Aug. 1st 1937, p. 16.
[3] S.R. and O., 1931, no. 345.

medical practitioners, employers, and workers respectively, is further empowered to make recommendations to the Ministry of Labour and Social Welfare on matters relating to industrial disease claims, schedules, contributions, and other questions. So even within such systems which, as a rule, adhere closely to the principle of individual liability and effort, the trend is towards collective security and administration.

2. *System of partial administration by official or semi-official bodies.* This type of Workmen's Compensation administration predominates in the *United States of America*, where at the inception of Workmen's Compensation opinion was much influenced by the German schemes (see vol. i, p. 194), whilst Ontario adopted another plan, which also departed from the British system and took its direct initiative from Sir William Ralph Meredith's critical views on the subject of private insurance and court administration. Had this matter been governed by federal legislation a uniform and far more complete system of Workmen's Compensation coming nearer to the type of administration to be discussed under (3) might have developed in the U.S.A. As things are, uniform development has been impossible either in regard to judicial administration (see Chapter XIV) or in regard to compulsory or non-compulsory insurance. The existence of State Funds does not itself connote those general supervisory and administrative functions of the State with which we are concerned here and which may involve more than the mere control of the effecting of insurance and its security.

The American systems are bewildering in their variety; it is 'impossible to give an accurate generalized summary of the various state compensation laws due to their differences of expression and administration'.[1] Of forty-six States (including the District of Columbia and the United States Employees) six had neither a Commission nor a Board. In one of these six States (Alabama), while the law is administered by courts, a Superintendent of Insurance has some powers of supervision; in another (Louisiana), the Secretary of State approves insurance policies; in another area the Commissioner of Labor supervises 'election' of the Act (New Hampshire); again in another there is some supervision by District Courts and the Labor Commissioner (New Mexico); again in Tennessee there is some supervision given by the Commissioner of Insurance and Banking and by the Superintendent of the Workmen's Compensation Division of the Department of Labor; and in Wyoming the State Treasurer supervises the Act and the State Fund. Where there are Commissions or Boards we find the following different types: an 'Industrial Commission', an 'Industrial

[1] Cf. *Medical Services in Industry*, N.Y., U.S.A., 1938, p. 43.

Accident Commission', 'Five Workmen's Compensation Commissioners' constituting 'district' authorities, an 'Industrial Board of the (State) Department of Labor', an 'Industrial Commissioner', a 'Compensation Board in the Department of Industrial Relations', a 'State Industrial Accident Commission', 'Industrial Accident Boards', a 'Workmen's Compensation Court', 'Workmen's Compensation Bureaux', a 'Director of Labor' administering Workmen's Compensation, a 'Commissioner of Industries' in the same capacity, a 'Director of Labor and Industries through Division of Industrial Insurance'. There are indeed almost as many different types—though many similar in functions—of administrators as there are States—showing what decentralization of administrative schemes may lead to in regard to lack of administrative uniformity in a country.[1]

The functions of these Boards and Commissions vary widely; they may be

(a) administrative,
(b) quasi-judicial,
(c) judicial, or
(d) they may embrace all these functions.

The administrative functions proper may consist in such matters as the enforcement of requirements that accidents be reported, the investigation and approval of agreements to settle uncontested cases (see before, p. 283), supervision of a financial character and of the necessary security of insurance. Of recent years Boards and Commissions have been largely concerned with matters of cure and rehabilitation. In several jurisdictions special rehabilitation funds controlled by the Workmen's Compensation Commissions have been accumulated. There is a strong movement in favour of a draft model Workmen's Compensation Act which would provide that all Workmen's Compensation Commissions should not only decide compensation claims but be responsible for measures of accident prevention and in rehabilitation of injured workers by providing so-called 'second-injury funds' and 'rehabilitation' funds.[2]

Close contact has been established between the rehabilitation agencies which exist in the great majority of American States and the

[1] Cf. also Dodd, loc. cit., p. 104: '... the patterns into which this type of administration fell in the different states were almost as diverse as the employments included or the benefits granted under several laws.'

[2] Cf. *Co-operation of Workmen's Compensation Administrations with Rehabilitation Agencies*, reprint from *Monthly Labor Review*, Feb. 1936, pp. 4–5. The Federal vocational Rehabilitation Act of 1920 undertakes to make sure of such co-operation by making it one of the conditions of receiving federal aid that a plan be formulated between the compensation authority and the rehabilitation authority.

compensation commissions or other administrative bodies. These agencies (in New York under the State Educational Department) have also been utilized by Commissions and Commissioners for pronouncing upon proposed lump-sum settlements which come to the compensation administration authorities.[1] The further question whether the administration should be carried on by a single Commissioner or by a Board has also been much ventilated.[2] Even such writers as Dodd hesitate to express a definite opinion. Much may depend on political changes; to which cause is ascribed the high 'mortality rate' of such commissioners in the U.S.A.[3] In countries with other political institutions and a greater uniformity of law this may be avoided and the system of a Commissioner with a competent staff or Advisory Committees for his guidance may be preferable to that of Boards though they are of value for special administrative tasks, particularly in matters of medical procedure. What emerges clearly is the general recognition of the necessity for some unified power and control. The 'major issues of administration' are, as stated by Dodd:

The administration of Workmen's Compensation involves the functions of office supervision, investigation, and adjudication. These functions are closely related to each other, and are also closely related to the other activities of a State with respect to accident prevention, rehabilitation, insurance control, and free employment offices.

The neighbouring Dominion of *Canada* is frequently quoted as being in fortunate enjoyment of a particularly valuable system of Compensation Insurance,[4] viz. the 'Ontario' system, which is often compared with those in vogue in the U.S.A. to their disadvantage. This system is a very interesting type of judicial administration. The 'brisk claim routine' dependent upon it deserves attention, but claims paid in Ontario, amounting to about £1 million a year (inclusive of medical aid and rehabilitation) are small in comparison with the £6·5 millions paid in England for seven big industrial groups alone; whilst the structure of industry is far less differentiated in Canada than in England, and facilitates standardization of compensation administration. Apart from this, however, the Ontario system cannot be classified as a scheme of complete official administration and it is not representative of Canada

[1] Cf. U.S. Dept. of Labor, 1930, *Bulletin No. 511*, pp. 166 sqq. and 171. The experiences reported by Mr. R. Jarnegan, of the N.Y. Rehabilitation Bureau as regards the administrative relationship of lump-sum payments and rehabilitation agencies deserves particular attention in regard to coming schemes in England.

[2] Cf. Dodd, loc. cit., pp. 783–7.

[3] Cf. ibid., p. 800.

[4] Cf., for instance, 'Claims Administration in Workmen's Compensation', *Monthly Labor Review*, U.S. Dept. of Labor, June 1938, Serial No. R. 734 for details of such comparison.

as a whole. Workmen's Compensation there differs in as many respects in the Provinces as in the U.S.A. in the States. There are:

1. *Collective Liability schemes* whereunder employers of the industry contribute to an accident fund or accident funds established for different risk classes out of which compensation is paid. Here we have some sort of 'group'-arrangement not unsimilar to the German *Berufsgenossenschaften*. There are Workmen's Compensation Boards or Commissions to administer these schemes, with various functions. The Board is a body corporate: it consists in general of three members appointed. An appeal on questions of law and jurisdiction is allowed to the Supreme Court in New Brunswick and Nova Scotia. In some provinces the Board is entitled to contract with doctors, nurses, and hospitals or other institutions for any medical aid required. In other provinces under such schemes medical aid is directly furnished by the Board; in others again medical aid at least as favourable as that provided by the Act may be approved by the Board.

2. *Individual Liability schemes*, found in the provinces of Ontario and Quebec, Alberta and Saskatchewan. Under these schemes the employer remains individually liable to pay the prescribed compensation. Here again the structure of administration is not uniform. In Ontario and Quebec employers in certain industries considered capable of bearing their own risks are excluded from the Accident Fund. But the schemes are both administered by the Workmen's Compensation Board (commission). In Alberta and Saskatchewan compensation is mainly recovered by actions in the ordinary courts with certain appeals to be allowed to go to the Court of Appeal.

From these features it emerges that Canada, though possessing schemes which in some respects approximate to State administration, has not yet got a comprehensive and unified system.

This is also true of *Australia*. In some of its provinces the system of Workmen's Compensation is still that of private insurance proper, the official organs merely supervising the execution of the Acts, though Commonwealth employees are dealt with by a Commissioner (under the Secretary of the Treasury) for Compensation. In New South Wales there is compulsory insurance with companies licensed for the purpose. Under the Workmen's Compensation Commission are Medical Boards appointed by the Commission, including specialists of all branches; the Commission also sponsors an *ad hoc* Conciliation and Information Bureau, where legal advice and assistance are rendered without charge. There are also special Medical Boards for occupational diseases in the Broken Hill Mine, viz. lead poisoning and silicosis.

In *Queensland* administration is almost fully official. Insurance is administered by a single inter-occupational institute, the State Insurance Office, managed by a permanent official appointed by the Governor in Council, the Insurance Commissioner (thus avoiding the 'political' instability of such appointments in the U.S.A.). There are also Special Boards for lead poisoning in the Mount Isa Mines.

In *Victoria* there is an alternative system. Insurance may be entered with the State Insurance Office in Melbourne, managed by an official (Commissioner) appointed by the Governor in Council; employers may also insure with any private institution approved by the Government. Litigation is, however, conducted before a judge of first instance. We shall state later how the competition between the two administrations—private and official—finds its expression in the matter of costs.

In the *Union of South Africa* the administration generally resembles that of Britain, but there are special regulations for Miners' Phthisis (= Silicosis) and a Miners' Phthisis Administration Board, which is composed of a chairman and three to six members appointed by the Government. A special Bureau deals with medical matters connected with this disease and certifies claims for compensation. Further, the Government has appointed a special Medical Appeal Board consisting of a chairman and two medical practitioners with special knowledge of the diseases of the lungs and respiratory organs to deal with appeals by persons dissatisfied with the decision of the Bureau. In other respects the arrangements are analogous to those for British coal-mining under the Nicholson Act and the Refractories Scheme. Only the recent inauguration of a Workmen's Compensation Commissioner differentiates it decisively from the British type of administration. The Commissioner derives his powers from §§ 17 and 18 of the Workmen's Compensation Act of 1934.[1] These relate to investigations to be made into claims and the settlement of disputes by agreement; to hear complaints from workmen or employers and insurance offices; to certain financial safeguards for workmen; and to medical treatment provided by an employer under §§ 53–9 for a period of one year.

In the *Netherlands* a semi-State system is in existence. Benefits under Workmen's Compensation are fixed and paid by the State Insurance Bank. But employers may also cover their own risks or insure with joint-stock insurance companies or mutual insurance companies responsible to the Bank. Since March 1st 1934 the administration of legislation is also entrusted to Labour Councils consisting of a president appointed by the Crown and four members, two being employers and two workers, which replaced the former Insurance Councils of ten members.

[1] Cf. *Union of South Africa, Workmen's Compensation Act 1934*, Pretoria, 1936, pp. 22–4.

In *Sweden* there is likewise some alternative system; the employer must insure his liability with the State Insurance Institution or with a mutual insurance company set up by employers, for the liabilities of which the members are severally responsible to an unlimited extent. If an employer fails to fulfil his duty, his workers are automatically deemed to be insured with the State Insurance Institution. In case of dispute the final decision lies with the Insurance Council. It should be added that there are Northern Countries Workmen's Insurance Meetings, held as a rule every fourth year, where representatives of the Scandinavian countries discuss questions primarily connected with accident insurance.[1]

In *Denmark* under the new Act of October 1st 1933 the Insurance Institutions may be employers' mutual insurance societies or Danish or foreign insurance companies recognized by the State; in exceptional cases and with special authorization there is self-insurance for private undertakings, but all persons employed at sea must be insured with the Shipowners' Mutual Insurance Society or the Mutual Insurance Society of the Fishing Industry. Central administration of insurance is entrusted to the Accident Insurance Directorate under the Ministry of Social Affairs, an appeal in regard to compensation claims lying to the Accident Insurance Council. It is noteworthy, particularly in a country so largely governed by socialistic ideals, that the State assists employers by contributions amounting in certain cases, i.e. with small employers, to two-fifths of the insurance premiums due from an employer on account of his workers and himself.

As a last form of the type considered under this head we may mention *Argentina*. The accident section of the National Pension Fund is here responsible for the payment of compensation due to persons injured as a result of industrial accidents and to their dependants, the insurance carrier being obliged to pay the capital corresponding to such compensation into this Fund within thirty days from the date of the accident. Employers may, however, insure themselves or through duly recognized insurance companies or employers' Mutuals. The National Pension Fund also pays any compensation which insurance carriers are unable to pay as the result of insolvency—a point which British legislators should note.

A system of partial State administration, though compulsory, prevails in *Spain*.

As may be gathered from our synopsis, systems of partial State administration may vary very widely. The necessity for State control is proportionate to the scope of Workmen's Compensation and grows with it. This necessity leads to new organizations, such as Boards and

[1] Cf. *Social Work and Legislation in Sweden*, Stockholm, 1938, p. 120.

Commissions or a State Commissioner. As a whole the system represents, in our view, a compromise between private and State administration, but it also shows the general tendency of development which is everywhere to strengthen State administration in every direction.

3. *The System of State Administration.* The prototype of this system is that of *Germany.* We have already noted various features of this system, particularly as regards benefits, claims, medical treatment and rehabilitation services, the relations between National Health insurance and Accident insurance, &c., and we have described[1] how the special features of the German compensation law and administration were studied by American investigators and compared with the system of private insurance to the detriment of the latter.

In 1905 Mr. Wotzel, of the Labour Department of the Board of Trade, described the German insurance system as 'the most complete and thoroughgoing treatment of the question'.[2] We have dealt with several aspects of the system elsewhere: our task at this point is to adjust the German system to the general picture of Workmen's Compensation administration.

We must first dispel a misapprehension. The German system is by no means an achievement of 'Socialism' but the reverse, as is to be expected from the political predilections of its sponsor Prince Bismarck. The idea sprang from co-operative (*genossenschaftlich*) ideals older by far than the first accident insurance law of 1884 and than the German Liberal Party, which like the Manchester School of *laisser faire laisser aller*, opposed all attempts to regulate the hours, conditions of life and labour, housing or pay of workers. The principle of the present system was expressed as early as 1881 in a Bill which did not become law owing to Liberal and Social Democratic opposition but contained the following preamble:

Starting from the principle, that the burden caused by industrial accidents as other parts of commercial costs should be considered as costs of production, and that in view of the differences in the danger-risk within different branches of industries every group ought in fairness to bear its own burden, it appears as the most natural and the most just way, to compensate all industrial accidents, so far as they were not caused by intent, and to place the burden of insurance on the entity of employers. By such a measure the liability of the single employer would be altered into an economic burden of the entire group of industry, which the single undertaking would be asked to bear according to its own risk.[3]

The principle of compulsory insurance on the basis of collective liability of which the *Berufsgenossenschaften* became the carriers is

[1] Cf. our vol. i, p. 152–8.
[2] Cf. *Memorandum to the Committee on Compensation for Injuries to Workmen*, Cmd. 2458, 1905, p. 36.
[3] Cf. *Handwörterbuch der Staatswissenschaften: Unfallversicherung.*

clearly set forth. On these Mutual Indemnity Associations the present German law still rests. They are bodies with legal personality (*Körperschaften des Öffentlichen Rechts*) and possess the widest possible administrative powers. Their activities, apart from administering the payment of cash benefits and pensions, include provision of medical attendance, hospital treatment, vocational rehabilitation inclusive of retraining and placing in employment. They also administer accident prevention and first aid and are thereby the organ of 'accident-prophylaxis'. They are required to administer all ordinances relating to the prevention of accidents;[1] they are entitled and in some cases obliged to have at their disposal industrial inspectors for this purpose, they may inspect the books of undertakings and scrutinize the wage limits; they are also obliged to direct such accident prevention in regard to certain building work which may not be for commercial purposes and in regard to the keeping of riding horses and vehicles of all sorts. The *Berufsgenossenschaft* is also obliged (see paras. 677 sqq.) to regulate the *Gefahrenklasse* (Danger Class) and how the Danger Tariff has to be carried on, and it must take steps to secure the payments of contributions due by an employer who may stop his industrial activities. The impositions on the *Berufsgenossenschaften* for efficient safety appliances are far-reaching.[2]

The *Berufsgenossenschaften* must take care that having regard to the technical development and that of medicine and to the economic strength of production accidents are avoided and that in the case of accidents the injured is provided with an effective First Aid.

Members of the *Berufsgenossenschaften* are required to fulfil the safety orders of these organizations and may be fined up to RM. 10,000 (= £500) for default. The obligations in regard to medical care and rehabilitation, as described in Chapters XI and XII, also show how wide is the scope of the *Berufsgenossenschaft*. The idea of the legislation being to create mutual collective security by groups of trade, most *Berufsgenossenschaften* display this characteristic. They exist for all industries, trades, and services. Two main divisions are (*a*) industry and (*b*) agriculture. In 1936 there were 63 industrial and 35 agricultural mutuals and since 1930 25 accident-insurance associations of the *Communes*. The industrial associations again embodied 183 branch associations (*Sektionen*) and 14 special institutions (*Zweig-Anstalten*) for public works carried on by the Reich, the States, and further by the *communes* or federation of *communes*, under certain conditions, in particular for operations carried out on their own account in connexion with building work and the keeping of vehicles and animals for riding otherwise than

---

[1] *Reichsversicherungsordnung*, para. 874 sqq.
[2] Cf. §§ 848 sqq. of the *Reichsversicherungsordnung*.

by way of trade.[1] The agricultural *Berufsgenossenschaften* embodied 481 branch associations. Mining is represented by the *Knappschafts-Berufsgenossenschaft*.[2] But *Berufsgenossenschaften* need not be formed according to the grouping of trades within the whole Reich; they may be formed if considered expedient, upon a regional basis.[3] The administration of the *Berufsgenossenschaften* and their management are regulated by a Statute which has to be agreed upon by the *Genossenschafts*-assembly and which must receive the sanction of the highest State department for insurance, the *Reichsversicherungsamt*.[4] A directorate called *Vorstand* represents the management of the *Genossenschaft*. The *Vorstand* is advised by the law to elect among its members such as have had some continuous experience in their trade groups and also to ensure that in industries with largely differing units of production the interest of the large, medium, and small units should be sufficiently represented. The Statute may also provide for the election of insured workers to the *Vorstand* (directorate) or into that of sectional associations. In the mining groups such representatives of workers are expected to be the 'elders' of the industry (see para. 687). Representatives of the insured, i.e. the workers, must be invited to assist in drafting and execution of safety regulations (see para. 853). The *Berufsgenossenschaften* are moreover obliged to provide in their Statutes for participation by at least one representative of insured persons in the formal assessment of benefits (*förmliche Feststellung der Leistungen*).[5]

Considering the many safeguards which the German system provides for the insured workers in regard to medical and administrative factors, we do not wonder when high German officials assert that litigation, the curse of the British system, is small. Asked about the frequency of disputes under the German insurance system, Dr. H. Lauterbach, Director of the National Association of Industrial *Berufsgenossenschaften*, told the Hetherington Commission[6] that few such cases were brought to Court 'because the professional associations are generally generous in their treatment'. This observation is equally applicable to Arbitration Committees set up by Employers' Mutuals and Trade Unions as in Durham (see Chap. XX).[7]

The German system of State administration was not unique. In

---

[1] For figures cf. *Amtliche Nachrichten für Reichsversicherung*, Berlin, Dec. 25th 1937, pp. 397 sqq.

[2] Cf. vol. i, p. 8. The name *Knappschaft* indicates the gild-origin of the *Berufsgenossenschaften*.

[3] We find *Berufsgenossenschaften* to which the adjective *Norddeutsch* or *Süddeutsch*, or *Sächsisch* or *Rheinisch-Westphälisch* is added, and also such of certain towns as the *Hannoverische* or *Hamburgische* or *Magdeburgische Baugewerks-Berufsgenossenschaft*.

[4] Cf. *Unfallversicherung*, para. 675 sqq.   [5] See Note at end of this chapter.

[6] Cf. loc. cit., Q. 6377–8.   [7] *Hetherington Commission, Evidence*, A. 6865–6.

Austria a very similar system prevailed. Three territorial institutions applied the principle of mutual, apart from one corporative institution, that of the Austrian railways, covering both public and private railway systems. One-third of the members of these institutions are elected by employers and one-third by the insured persons, the remainder were nominated by the Minister of Social Administration and expected to have particular experience in economic conditions.

In *Poland* the system existing in Germany and Austria was closely copied. Insurance was compulsory and administered by public institutions which had the monopoly of insurance in their own area.

Workmen's Compensation in *Czechoslovakia* closely followed Austrian and German precedents. The insurance scheme was compulsory and was administered by two territorial institutions at Prague and Brno. The managing committee of each institution was composed of equal numbers of employers' representatives, insured persons' representatives and persons acquainted with the economic situation of the district and appointed by the Minister of Social Welfare. These institutions which much resembled the *Berufsgenossenschaften*, but on a territorial basis, were subject to State supervision.

Luxemburg with its 300,000 inhabitants, of whom, however, 50,000 are industrial and 50,000 agricultural workers, has also as in Germany two sections, an industrial and an agricultural, both parts of the Accident Insurance Association, which again forms part of the Social Insurance Office. Insurance is compulsory. Workers' delegates are attached to the governing body and sub-committees when the amount of compensation is to be fixed or rules to be drawn up concerning accident prevention. The members of the Association, as in Germany, are required to take the necessary measures for protecting workers against accidents.

In *Italy* until 1933 there was no single compulsory system. The National Industrial Accident Institute existed side by side with voluntary accident associations grouped in a federation and with four compulsory mutual insurance associations. Since June 1933 these have been merged in the Fascist National Industrial Accident Insurance Institute. Only maritime transport workers have their own territorial compulsory associations, and the former compulsory association for workers employed in the sulphur mines of Sicily was transformed into a special section of the Institute in 1934. The Institute is managed by a governing body consisting of five employers' representatives, two accident insurance experts, one representative of the Fascist Party, the Chairman of the Fascist National Social Welfare Institute, two representatives of the Ministry of Corporations and one representative each of the Ministry of Finance and the Ministry of the Colonies.

Norway possesses a complete system of compulsory State Insurance represented by the National Insurance Office, a Government institution. Local agents of the schemes are the sickness insurance funds or local inspectors appointed by the State Insurance Office on the recommendation of the local authorities. Norway has thus adopted State insurance.

Rumania enacted in April 1933 some new legislation unifying and co-ordinating the provisions for meeting risks of sickness, accident, maternity, invalidity, and death throughout the country. Accident insurance is governed by special regulations under this comprehensive social scheme, whether arising in connexion with employment or otherwise. There is a Central Social Insurance Fund, a Higher Supervisory Board, and a Government Commissioner supervising the management of the Central Fund. Insurance is, of course, compulsory.

The system is similar in some respects to that of the *Union of Soviet Socialist Republics* where also Social Insurance is under one unified central management and control, formerly administered by eleven occupational federations as regards industry and by territorial schemes in other branches of occupation. Since 1933 the administration of insurance has been handed over to the General Council of Trade Unions and its forty-seven affiliated associations. Later their number was raised to 163, when the federations were divided into smaller units. Stress is laid on the fact that the structure of insurance is based on the branch of economic activity. The central committee of the trade unions federations and their local organs (district or regional) are responsible for administering the schemes, and the General Council of Trade Unions of the U.S.S.R. for the general management of insurance, i.e. the supervision of the unions, the issue of instructions, and the submission of the social insurance estimates to the Council of the People's Commissaries of the Union for approval.

In *Switzerland* the Swiss National Accident Insurance Fund is responsible for the application of compulsory insurance. It is an independent establishment working on the mutual aid principle and enjoying full legal personality. It has head-quarters in Lucerne and district branches. We have seen before that the law is wisely arranged, in particular as regards the provision of payments of benefits (see 107). Apart from this Institute, i.e. the *Schweizerische Unfallversicherungsanstalt*, there is judicial administration of disputes[1] by courts. The *Anstalt*, as the Institute is generally called, is composed of three organs:

A. The *Verwaltungsrat*, an administrative Council composed of

(1) 12 representatives of the compulsorily insured (the Institute

---

[1] See p. 266.

also deals with self-insurers for other than industrial accidents, *Nicht-Betriebsunfälle*, i.e. accidents not happening in
'industrial units'); further

(2) 16 representatives of private undertakings employing insured workers;

(3) 4 representatives of the facultative insurers (see bracket
above); and

(4) 8 representatives of the Federal Government.

Further organs are:

B. The management (*Direktion*), and

C. The agencies (each Canton is entitled to one agency).[1]

As a last country in this category we may mention *Yugoslavia* which
had its first Social Insurance Act in 1922. The scheme is administered
on a compulsory basis by the Central Workers' Insurance Institution
and its local bodies, consisting of seventeen local workers' insurance
offices and three insurance funds for commercial employees. The
central institution is a public body under autonomous administration.
Its administrative bodies consist in the general meeting in which employers and employees are represented in equal numbers; the managing
committee consisting of twenty-four members elected half by the employer members and half by the insurer members of the general
meeting; the supervising committee is elected by the general meeting
and consists of three representatives of the employers and three representatives of the insured. The organs of the local bodies are organized
in the same tripartite fashion. The rate of contribution which the employers have to pay is fixed according to a scale approved by the
Minister of Social Affairs and Public Health on the proposal of the
central institution and drawn up with reference to the coefficient of
risk of the undertakings covered by the scheme. The gainfully occupied population of Yugoslavia is almost 6,000,000; this carefully
framed scheme should not be overlooked by investigators studying the
administrative structure of Workmen's Compensation in foreign
countries with a view to reform at home.

The following conclusions appear to emerge from our analysis of the
systems applied all over the world to the administration of Workmen's Compensation.

The great majority are to some extent State-administered, though
they often retain, like slowly atrophying organs, in varying degrees,
an element of private insurance, and of collective responsibility of
trade groups. The countries in which private insurance and individual

[1] Cf. Fuehrer, loc. cit., pp. 74–5.

liability prevail are found almost only among the English-speaking countries, viz. Great Britain and some of her Dominions and a few of the States of the U.S.A. In many countries, not least the U.S.A., the tendency has been of late to quicken the pace at which the unification and centralization of compensation insurance is proceeding. The trend towards State administration is also towards a wider conception of the scope of such official activities: it embraces accident prevention, first aid, systems of rehabilitation, and re-employment provisions. This involves the inception of a system of control, inspection, and of continuous administrative improvement which oversteps the facilities and responsibilities of private institutions and still more of the single 'self-insurer'. Yet the example of State administration may stimulate private insurance carriers, as in the U.S.A., to improve their own organization. British Workmen's Compensation has never had to face competition of this kind. The activities of private insurers, companies, or mutual associations have been limited to cash compensation payments only; intervention in such matters as accident prevention or rehabilitation, or re-employment measures, has been sedulously avoided by insurance companies or mutuals in general. It is doubtful whether their administrative organization could cope effectively with any additional responsibilities.

Our survey also shows that State administration should not involve a system of centralized insurance administered by a single State institution, but calls rather for a decentralized system of administration in which existing industrial or social organizations would be fully utilized. Such organizations may be co-operative associations, as the *Berufsgenossenschaften*, trade unions, or district or regional standing Joint Committees where a system of grouping according to industrial branches is not preferred. Wherever State administration has developed, representatives of the insured workers have a responsible part to play in the administration. They may sit on committees or boards, and help to adjudicate upon contested cases; and some members of such committees may be elected by their votes. The British system of private and individual insurance makes no provision for such representation, although it is found in certain contracting-out[1] schemes.

The advantage of dealing with compensation matters by committees of expert knowledge, also fully conversant with *local* conditions of men and work, was emphasized by witnesses before the Hetherington Commission speaking for a Mutual Protection Association and the Durham Miners' Association; the Committee in question was that (formed in 1898) between the Durham Colliery Owners' Protection Association and the Durham Miners' Association, thus having em-

[1] See vol. i, pp. 281, 286, 290.

ployers' and workmens' representatives and coming very near continental types of *Berufsgenossenschaften*. A case of a one-eyed man was mentioned which was settled according to certain classifications by an Arbitration Committee. One of the witnesses declared: 'I am sure you will appreciate that on technical mining issues we can dispose of the matter in ten minutes which on exactly the same point before a Court might take two hours in going through the technical details and putting it to a man not accustomed to the working in that pit.'[1]

It now remains to discuss the economic and social advantages or disadvantages of the different systems. The problem of costs must always be of outstanding importance. On the expense ratio depends what proportion of the amount payable in contributions will be returned to the worker in the form of benefits. The cost of the system will be a deciding factor in any changes that may be made in the near future. The strongest argument against any reform of the system has always been the anticipation of an unbearable burden of higher costs. A reduction or better management of costs may therefore have a decisive influence on matters of principle.

[1] Cf. *Hetherington Commission*, pp. 713–14, A. 6853 and 6870.

NOTE

A DECREE of December 29th 1934 requires *Berufsgenossenschaften* to set up Pension-Committees (*Renten-Ausschüsse*), consisting of the head of an undertaking (*Betriebsführer*) and an insured person. If they cannot agree, the Manager of the *Berufsgenossenschaft* or his representatives must decide. A 'formal' assessment of benefits may be instituted on application either of the insured person or by order of the supervisory authority. This extends to the provision of continuous payments (*Renten*), review of payments, medical and hospital care, and lump-sum settlements. These 'formal' assessments take place where the benefits of accident insurance are not related to matters as medical benefits under National Health Insurance as described before and in case of short-dated regular payments, sick benefit, burial money, or widows' allowances, which are more or less automatically regulated by the *Berufsgenossenschaft* or the *Genossenschaftsvorstand*.

We have already referred to the institutions of the *Versicherungsamt*, the *Ober-Versicherungsamt*, and the *Reichsversicherungsamt*. In certain cases, specified in the law, the *Versicherungsamt* must call upon assessors who are chosen in equal moieties from the ranks of employers and employees (para. 40 of the *Reichsversicherungsordnung*). The principal official, however, is the Imperial Insurance Office (*Reichsversicherungsamt*) whose activities are referred to in almost every section dealing with the higher administration. It has power to assume charge of a *Genossenschaft* which is in default or whose status is dubious (para. 689). It consists of 32 permanent and non-permanent members; of these 12 are chosen to represent employers and 12 as delegates of employees (para. 87). Its duties are very wide: they extend not only to final legal and judicial procedure, but to general supervision. It can also take cognizance of disputes within or between *Berufsgenossenschaften* in regard to the administration of property (paras. 624, 627 *a*, and 636); it plays an important part in the medical provisions touching accident insurance and the care for the injured by its authority under National Health Insurance (*Krankenversicherung*) (paras. 368, 370, 372, and *passim*), and it exercises final authority in the matter of accident prevention through its control over the regulations made by the *Berufsgenossenschaften*. The Reich Insurance Office is the representative of the State in German accident insurance legislation. The *Berufsgenossenschaften* are its chosen local instruments in close touch with local industrial life and with local industrial groups. They have refrained, on official advice, from embarking into the formation and administration of hospitals on their own account. The few existing ones are mainly concerned with medical treatment for the mining industry; they are located in Halle, Bochum, and Gelsenkirchen, all mining centres, and generally bear the name of *Bergmannsheil* (Miners' Welfare). There is one hospital in Berlin owned by the *Berufsgenossenschaft* for the north-eastern iron and steel trade group. Overlapping organization has thereby been prevented.

The organization of German Workmen's Compensation administration is comprehensive and complete, extending from the happening of the accident or disease until the final stage of a possible recovery or rehabilitation including re-entry into employment. Administration is entrusted to bodies especially conversant with the widely different economic and social conditions in various groups of industry, agriculture, mining, seafaring, and other occupations, and provides for representation of all parties interested. Control, supervision, legal and judicial decisions in many fields where constant vigilance and suggestion is required are left to higher and central authorities. Accident prevention is within its scope as one of the best means of diminishing claims for injury.

This short description of the German system of administration was written before the authors had seen Paper No. 17. B of the *Evidence of the Hetherington Commission*, presented by the I.L.O. as a Supplementary Memorandum on certain arrangements of the German administration of accident insurance. This Memorandum gives a number of interesting details, and should be studied in conjunction with our observations.

CHAPTER XX

THE ECONOMIC AND SOCIAL SIDE: COSTS

We first survey the plot, then draw the model; and when we see the figure of the house,
then must we rate the cost of the erection.

SHAKESPEARE, *King Henry IV*, Second Part, Act I, Scene 3.

WORKMEN'S Compensation as practised in England is a costly business. Every committee that has ever sat has been unanimous on this point. One result of the Holman Gregory Committee, as we have seen, was an arrangement in 1923 between the Home Office and the Accident Offices Association, fixing the so-called loss-ratio, i.e. the proportion which the total amount paid or set aside in respect of claims bears to the premiums. The sums yearly paid out in claims,[1] as recorded by the Home Office for the seven groups of industries, only represent the actual total sum paid to workmen or their dependants as compensation, and not the total charge to these industries. To compute the total charge it would be necessary to take into account:

(1) administrative expenses incurred by the offices,
(2) medical costs of employers,
(3) legal costs of employers or insurance companies and mutual indemnity associations,
(4) amounts placed in reserves, and
(5) a credit balance for distribution as profit.

Some such figures are available for insurance companies and mutual indemnity associations though in an imperfect form. The official statistics suggest to the inexpert eye that only 20·6 per cent. of the compensation was paid in 1936 by or for employers insured with insurance companies, compared with 61·3 per cent. by or for employers belonging to Mutual Indemnity Associations and 18·1 per cent. by employers not belonging to either of the two categories. These figures are often cited in support of the view that insurance companies play a secondary part in Compensation Insurance, and that their expense-ratio is therefore of correspondingly little significance. But these percentages are in fact very unevenly spread over the whole industrial field and afford no trustworthy basis for conclusions. Shipping (84·6 per cent.) and Mining (81·8 per cent.) are mainly responsible for the high percentage figure for Mutuals; Industry 'proper', i.e. factory employment, displays a very different picture:

[1] See vol. i, pp. 165–7. Cf. also *Debates H.C.*, Feb. 8th 1939, cols. 1044 and 1075.

insurance companies preponderate decisively in many groups and have a moiety of the total business, viz. 47·8 per cent. as against 43·4 per cent. for Mutuals. The percentages in 1937 were:

Industrial Group	Mutual Indemnity Associations	Insurance Companies
	per cent.	per cent.
Cotton	78·3	20·0
Wool, &c.	34·1	63·1
Other textiles . . .	28·8	70·8
Wood	26·0	68·5
Metals (extraction) . .	71·2	15·9
Engineering and shipbuilding .	65·5	18·9
Other metal work . . .	60·4	27·6
Paper and printing . .	22·1	67·3
China and earthenware . .	56·0	41·2
Other factory industries . .	30·8	56·6

In quarries and constructional work the percentage of companies was 59·5 and 47·1 respectively. It would be interesting to ascertain why Mutuals have been able to obtain a footing in some industries and not in others. The contrast between the cotton and woollen branches of the textile industry is particularly striking. So long as such differences exist and are unexplained no general conclusions as to causes are valid. The evidence of the T.U.C. before the Hetherington Commission helped to dispel the misleading conception of the relatively secondary part which companies play in Workmen's Compensation as contrasted with Mutuals. Mr. Hillwell agreed that insurance companies only have 'a small share in the insurance of industries organized *in large units*', but did not deny that of 17 million workers covered by the Compensation Acts, the 9 millions not included in Home Office statistics 'are those for whom the insurance companies largely cater'.[1]

The annual statistics of the Board of Trade[2] throw light on some of the items which figure in the administrative costs to the companies. The following statement shows the percentage which certain expenses bear to the premium income, i.e. receipts in net premiums, increased by the unearned premiums (or reserve for unexpired risks) at the end of the previous year and diminished by the corresponding

[1] Cf. *Hetherington Commission*, A. and Q. 5023–5. Also I.L.O., *Memorandum*, p. 587, which mentions that private companies' clients include comparatively few large employers.

[2] Cf. *Assurance Companies Returns*. Statements of assurance business under the Assurance Companies Act, 1909, 1938. The figures apply to all industries, and not merely to the seven groups scheduled under the Act.

amount at the end of the year of account.[1] To show the wide gap
between the highest and lowest of such percentages is very significant.

1937

	Tariff companies (number: 40)	Non-tariff companies (number: 22)	Mutual (non-tariff) companies (number: 7)
PREMIUMS EARNED	£5,575,954	£1,171,597	£1,969,253
CLAIMS PAID	£3,597,558	£775,718	£1,594,029
Per cent. of premiums earned .	64·5	66·2	80·9
Highest and lowest percentages .	123·5 and 4·6	109·5 and 11·2	86·5 and 65·2
COMMISSION:			
Per cent. of premiums earned .	7·0	10·0	5·7
Highest and lowest percentages .	13·2 and 1·8	27·6 and 0·4	15·4 and 0·7
EXPENSES OF MANAGEMENT:			
Per cent. of premiums earned .	22·4	19·9	12·7
Highest and lowest percentages .	52·6 and 6·5	32·0 and 8·9	24·1 and 8·5
PROFIT MARGIN OR (—) DEFICIT:			
Per cent. of premiums earned .	6·1	3·9	0·7
Highest profit percentage . .	42·8	38·4	11·3
Highest loss percentage . .	—59·7	—55·4	—8·1

These widely divergent figures are of more value than the grand
totals which show:

Premiums earned	£8,716,804	
Claims paid	£5,967,305	
Per cent. of premiums earned . .	68·5	
Commission:		
Per cent. of premiums earned	7·1 ⎫	
Expenses of management: . . .	⎬ 26·9 ⎫	
Per cent. of premiums earned .	19·8 ⎭ ⎬ 31·5	
Profit or loss margin	plus 4·6 ⎭	

The figures relating to claims paid represent the scheduled item 'payments under policies, *including medical and legal expenses in connexion
therewith*', after deduction of sums reinsured; and the figure is adjusted
by necessary calculations. Legal and medical expenses are stated (on the
authority of certain insurance offices) to average $4\frac{1}{2}$ per cent. of the sums
placed under 'claims' or payment for compensation and damages.[2] This
figure is for members of the Accident Offices Association and is included in the claims heading. Legal and medical expenses incurred in
connexion with the settlement of claims are, as Mr. Buckland observed,

[1] The percentage computation is made by the *Post Magazine and Insurance Monitor*,
Oct. 1st 1938, pp. 1926-7.

[2] Cf. *Workmen's Compensation Statistics*, 1939, p. 7, n. 1.

'on the claims loss side of the expenses side', so that if the loss ratio is $62\frac{1}{2}$ per cent. *the amount actually spent* on claims would average 58 per cent.[1]

The two tables show that Workmen's Compensation insurance is neither inexpensive nor profitable. The Prudential, for instance, spent in 1937 59·8 per cent. of the earned premiums in claims, 8·8 per cent. in commission, 32·2 per cent. in management and showed a loss of 0·8 per cent. of the premiums earned. Most companies with the heaviest rates of loss or profits and other items do little Workmen's Compensation or Employers' Liability business and are not typical, but substantial divergences are common, and deserve close inquiry.

There is nothing here to justify an attitude of complacency. Administrative costs are high. The exclusion of medical and legal expenses incurred by the companies from expenses of management is calculated to mislead. It is no part of the sum paid to injured persons in the form of 'claims': it has not been incurred for their benefit or with their consent. The Tariff Office with the highest premium income in 1937 (over £900,000) returned in claims about £560,000, i.e. not more than 61·5 per cent., while commission and expenses of management absorbed over 37 per cent. Another, with a premium income of somewhat under £100,000, returned 55·6 per cent. in claims and spent *over 44 per cent.* in commission and management. Workmen's Compensation costs the seven main groups of industries about £8 millions a year: the total charge to all employments and industries under the Act is estimated at something like £13 millions.[2] The proportion devoted to the payment of commission and the expenses of administra-

---

[1] Cf. *Hetherington Commission, Evidence,* Buckland, A. 2123. The following figures illustrate the trend of costs of recent years:

Percentage of premiums expenses

			Payment of compensation or damages	Commission	Expenses of management	Profits
1933 ·	·	·	61·66	9·32	25·85	3·17
1934 ·	·	·	63·76	9·36	25·91	0·97
1935 ·	·	··	64·34	8·79	24·35	2·52
1936 ·	·	·	63·66	9·01	24·30	3·03
1937 ·	·	·	64·87	8·79	24·17	2·17

The figures relate to the premium income of insurance companies in connexion with employers' liability insurance in Great Britain and Northern Ireland expended respectively on payment of compensation or damages (including legal and medical expenses incurred with the settlement of claims), payments for commission, expenses of management, and profits; the figures apply to all industries. Cf. *Hetherington Commission,* Paper No. 1. D.

[2] Described by Mr. Buckland before the Hetherington Commission as 'a sort of a very rough attempt in the Annual Statistics'. As to how this figure was reached see A. 813.

tion is clearly high, and, having regard to the cost ratio in certain foreign countries, should be susceptible of substantial reductions.

We often hear that the competitive commercial system in vogue in this country is cheaper than any 'bureaucratic' system. Accurate comparisons are impossible. Where systems vary so greatly the structure of costs and charge must also vary, but wide and marked differences in the cost of administration may have some value for purposes of comparison. The *Holman Gregory Report* devoted only a few sentences to the relative costs of private and State administration: it mentioned that the trade unions were in favour of a monopolistic State Fund 'mainly on the ground that the money which goes in profits to the insurance companies would be available for the workmen'. It is not, however, 'profits' but the high cost of commission and management which deprives workmen of larger benefits. On the other hand, the Holman Gregory Committee stated that the employers and their representatives 'were unanimously against a monopolistic State Fund, urging that it would be more expensive than the present (British) system'.[1] The Committee accepted this contention without comment or criticism. The following observations may be of use for purposes of comparison.

The most interesting example in this respect is probably that of Germany with its wide administrative scope and many ramifications. *Berufsgenossenschaften* and central administrative insurance bodies are linked up with medical services; they have to prepare and to supervise the execution of measures of accident prevention and precaution against industrial disease, to undertake litigation in some cases, to make judicial decisions in others and to receive, invest, and disburse vast sums. The German accident insurance statistics take this into account and analyse costs as follows:

Payment of claims.
Administrative costs of accident prevention.
Legal expenses.
Financial management (*Finanzdienst*).
Administrative expenses proper; subdivided thus

(*a*) those of a personal character (*persönlicher Art*) and
(*b*) those of a material character (*sachlicher Art*) such as the upkeep of offices, correspondence, &c.

Premiums, which we shall now compare with these costs, are collected in the form of a levy or call (*Umlagebeiträge*). This method resembles that adopted by many Mutual Indemnity Associations in England which maintain a reserve fund considerably less than the capitalized value, and make periodic 'calls' on the constituent members to cover

[1] Cf. *Holman Gregory Report*, p. 10.

the estimated liability in respect of claims arising during the period covered by the call.[1] The income, which consists mainly of these contributions, is further increased by certain very small amounts of 'premium'; by interest on capital, and other sources, which costs taken all together do not represent more than about 8 per cent. of the total income.

The following table gives a comparison of costs of administration to income in 1936.[2]

	RM. 000	RM. 000
Income		392,242
Expenditure:		
CLAIMS		285,003
ADMINISTRATIVE COSTS:		
Cost of accident prevention . . .	8,696	
Personal costs of administration . .	28,998	
„ (material costs) . . .	7,132	
Other costs (see above)	19,230	
		64,056
Total expenditure (RM. 000)		349,059

The sum of RM. 64 millions of administrative costs represents about 16 per cent. of the income of accident insurance, though the administrative scope of the scheme is far greater than those of any British insurance companies; for these are only concerned in payment of claims, which again are, to a large extent, settled by one final payment made, as we have seen with the object of reducing both the sum paid in claims and the cost of administration. Of RM. 362 millions contributed in 1937 not less than RM. 285 millions, or about 80 per cent., went back in benefits.

Costs of administration in the U.S.A. are set out in our first volume (p. 166) which shows that the costs of monopolistic State Funds are lower than those of stock companies, mutual companies, or even of State Funds in competition therewith.[3] Dodd asserts[4] that 15 per cent. of benefits suffices to administer an exclusive State Fund. In 1933 in New York the expense ratio of the State Insurance Fund (ratio of expense to earned premiums) was 17·2 per cent.; of mutual insurance companies 26·2 per cent.; of stock companies 47·2 per cent. Even when State Insurance Fund premiums are calculated on the basis of the discounted rates used by the Fund, its 1933 expense ratio was less

[1] Cf. *Hetherington Commission*, p. 422. Also Q. 4912.

[2] Cf. *Amtliche Nachrichten für Reichsversicherung*, 1937, no. 12, pp. iv, 429.

[3] No substantial change has taken place since this table was prepared, soon after 1920, by the well-known actuarial authority Mr. Miles M. Dawson. Cf. also *U.S. Bureau of Labor Statistics Bulletin No. 301. Comparison of Workmen's Compensation Insurance and Administration*, Washington, 1922, p. 10. [4] Cf. loc. cit., p. 557.

than half that of the companies.[1] 'In contrasting the cost of compensation insurance underwritten by different types of insurance carriers', writes Dodd, 'the monopolistic state fund seems to cost employers the least, with the competitive state funds and mutuals next in line, *while insurance in the private stock company is the highest priced of all.*' Low administrative costs must of course be examined with reference to the efficiency of services given.[2] Nevertheless, these impressive figures deserve close attention.

American experience does not stand alone. Another country where State administration competes with private insurance carriers is the State of Victoria, whose Accident Insurance Commissioner of this State, Mr. W. H. Holmes, puts the expense ratio for the year ending June 1938 at 9·7 per cent. as compared with one of 39·6 per cent. for commercial offices. Unlike other insurance offices with which it is in competition, the State institution provides free medical treatment and ambulance and hospital service. Any saving by exemption from income-tax on 'profits' is here much more than off-set by the lower rate of interest earned by its investments.[3]

In Switzerland, where the Swiss National Insurance Fund administers Workmen's Compensation, the total income from insurance against occupational accidents was approximately 50 million francs in 1933. The benefits granted in cash and in kind amounted to 32 million francs. The administrative expenses were fr. 4½ millions or, as in Victoria, about 9 per cent. of the income. Of the employers' contributions of 27 million francs, about 90 per cent. reached injured workmen as benefits in cash and in kind.

In France the cost of administration of French fixed premium companies has been as follows:

Percentage of premium to income

	1933	1934
Acquisition	13·5	13·8
Settlement of claims	2·4	2·5
General administration	15·3	15·5
Other	0·5	0·2
Profit	2·3	5·6
Total	34·0	37·6

[1] Cf. Elmer F. Andrews, 'Exclusive State Fund Needed for Compensation Insurance', *American Labor Legislative Review*, vol. xxiv, p. 168, Dec. 1934. Quoted by Dodd, loc. cit., p. 558; cf. also the interesting statistics presented by the I.L.O., *Hetherington Commission*, pp. 725–6.

[2] Cf. *Methods of Financing Workmen's Compensation*, U.S. Dept. of Labor, Serial No. R. 360, Washington, 1936, pp. 2–4.

[3] The State Institution receives from the Treasury on its deposit 2 per cent. interest. Cf. *Report of Victoria State Accident Insurance Office*, Melbourne, 1938, pp. 2–3.

The expense of Mutuals in France were lower, i.e. 29·2 and 27·0. Yet the figure appears enormous when compared with the expense ratio of official and non-private systems of administration.[1]

In Belgium, where industrial accident insurance is mainly effected by so-called 'fixed' premium companies, and the balance by mutual coal-mining and other funds, commissions and administrative costs (*frais généraux*) amounted in 1933 to 14 and 18 per cent. respectively of premium income; that of the mutual funds (*caisses communes*) averaged 12–13 per cent.; in coal-mining only 8 per cent.[2]

In Canada, where private insurance in respect of employers' liability is limited through the collective liability schemes and the specific organization of Workmen's Compensation administration, the expense ratio in 1934 was 36·56 per cent. The net premiums written by companies were Can. Dollars 349,213.[3] The costliness of compensation business, when in private hands, was emphasized when Sir William R. Meredith put forward his scheme of Workmen's Compensation for Canada—though he stressed the fact that such business was not 'successful' notwithstanding 'the large percentage of premium money applied by companies in expenses'.[4] The high expense ratio of private companies contrasts unfavourably with the administrative expenditure under the Ontario system, which was 7·11 per cent. in 1935.[5]

Expense ratios of different nations and systems are not, of course, strictly comparable; but this low expense ratio appears to us to be an achievement which cannot be explained away by any difference between the structure of Canadian industry and the scope of the Ontario Workmen's Compensation Law as compared with corresponding conditions in Britain or elsewhere.[6] The facts here set forth should suffice to discount 'unanimous', but unsupported, allegations to Committees by 'Employers and their representatives' that State administration

[1] Cf. *Hetherington Commission, Evidence*, p. 445 and p. 726.

[2] Cf. Royaume Belgique, *Rapport relatif à l'Exécution de la Loi sur la Réparation des Dommages résultant des Accidents de Travail*, Bruxelles, 1938, pp. 14–15.

[3] Cf. *Abstract of Statements of Insurance Companies in Canada*, Ottawa, 1935, p. 125.

[4] Cf. *Interim Report on Laws relating to the Liability of Employers*, Toronto, 1912, pp. 104–6.

[5] Cf. *U.S. Dept. of Labor, Ontario Procedure*, reprint, Washington, 1936, p. 5. The amounts awarded or paid by the Workmen's Compensation Board of Ontario in 1934 were as follows:

	Canadian dollars
Compensation	3,657,968
Medical aid	841,738
Accident prevention	146,065
Rehabilitation	10,627
Administration expenses	322,458

[6] Cf. *Hetherington Commission*, Q. 5034–8 and 4978–9 (Mr. Boyd).

would be more costly than the 'present English system' such as those made before and accepted without comment by the Holman Gregory Committee.[1]

The 'high expense ratio' has not escaped the attention of professional insurance writers. In a very interesting study of the subject made in 1923 Mr. Norman M. Walker, Managing Director of the British General, asked his hearers: 'What should we think of a banker who, upon our depositing our money with him, explained that about 40 per cent. of it would need to be spent in expenses?'[2] Another writer comments on the 'seriousness of the present expense ratio', but consoles himself with the reflection that high charges are the rule in the distributive trades of the United Kingdom,[3] though he is silent as to the much lower expense ratio to be found in other countries. Relative comparisons, however, are of little use: what is needed is an investigation of causes and of means to remove them. Insurance experts do not regard the published allocation of 'costs', or the percentage figures, as absolutely reliable. Costing procedure is not uniform and allocation within an office of general expenses is not an exact science. Broadly speaking, however, costs may be analysed as follows:[4]

1. Items over which the management has practically no control: rents, rates, taxes, postage and telegraph, health and other insurances.
2. Items under partial control: salaries, commissions, medical and legal (solicitors') fees.
3. Incidental expenses: advertising, stationery, travelling, general expenses.

American publications stress the 'wide variation' of all these charges; certain factors may, without increasing efficiency, enhance expenses far above those of a centralized and unified State administration, for example:

(*a*) duplication of service among the competitors;
(*b*) excessive competition leading to excessive pressure for getting business by employing still more agents, i.e. over-staffing;

[1] Cf. *Holman Gregory Report*, p. 10. The I.L.O. prepared, while we were working at the same problem, a Memorandum to the Hetherington Commission (*Evidence*, pp. 588 sqq. and 725) which compares several types of accident insurers and reaches the same conclusion as we have done, noting that the rates of statutory funds competing with private insurers in certain countries are 'substantially lower than that of fixed-premium companies'.

[2] Cf. Walker, 'The Expense Ratio of an Insurance Company', *Journal of the Chartered Insurance Institute*, vol. xxvi, 1923, p. 258.

[3] Cf. Herbert G. Hurren (Phoenix Assurance Co.), 'The Expense Ratio', *Journal of the Chartered Insurance Institute*, 1933. [4] Cf. Walker, loc. cit., p. 263.

(*c*) small volume of business of small undertakings in proportion to fixed overhead costs;

(*d*) regional geographical factors, which may vary widely. Such factors are more severely felt in times of depression, as was proved by the depression in the U.S.A. and its influence upon compensation business.[1] The question of agents awaits study by insurance research institutes and by British economists, who have hitherto ignored the sociological aspects of insurance. The commission system offers an easy target. 'Our Agency system', writes Mr. Norman M. Walker,[2] 'is all wrong, and wants reconstructing from the top to the bottom'. Whether or not medical and legal expenses should be reduced depends upon whether and how far litigation could be reduced in the future without detriment to the interests of injured claimants. 'The main trouble in connection with certificates of Medical Referees has arisen where the certificate is framed in ambiguous terms. . . . An enormous amount of expense and trouble would be saved if Medical Referees would simply state that the workman has recovered from the accident and is fit for full work, or that he has not fully recovered, and then the work for which he is fit.'[3] The procedure envisaged under the present system is not so 'simple' as may be imagined. It would be different if a semi-State-administered body or Board representative of and enjoying the confidence of both sides, or an impartial Workmen's Compensation Commissioner, were empowered to reach a decision as to the actual capacity of the injured person and his prospects of re-employment. So far as litigation is a cause of the high expense ratio, neither employers nor insurance offices have done much to discourage it.

One way to surmount the difficulties of a high expense ratio is to impose a statutory or other limitation of expenses or, alternatively, to require a certain proportion of premiums to be devoted to benefits, as proposed by the *Cohen Report* in the case of Industrial Assurance.[4] Such a proposal inspires doubts as to whether the private competitive system of insurance is, as often claimed, the cheapest and simplest. Wherever State or quasi-State administration has been introduced decentralization has followed, with due regard to the particular needs

[1] Cf. for all the points mentioned referring to the expense ratio: *Methods of Financing Compensation Administrations and Funds*, U.S. Dept. of Labor, Serial No. R. 360, 1936, p. 4.

[2] Cf. loc. cit., p. 271. See also I.L.O., *Memorandum to Hetherington Commission*, p. 587: 'They employ a force of agents to solicit business.'

[3] Cf. H. W. Eaton, 'Legal Process in connection with Workmen's Compensation Claims', *Journal of the Chartered Insurance Institute*, vol. xxxiii, p. 237.

[4] For a detailed criticism of this proposal cf. Wilson and Levy, *Industrial Assurance*, 1937, pp. 368, 373–4, 376, 409–11, 415, 448, 454, 460.

of industrial groups. The Home Office agreement with the Accident Office Association was a forward step, in that it tried to counteract excessive costs of management; but it does not follow that it has been effective, or that it was wise to make the lucky or wise office pay for the unlucky or unwise.

The loss-ratio is that of the whole of the Offices who are parties to the agreement. If, therefore, with wise underwriting and good fortune, any Office is below the general average, the difference is increased profit. On the other hand, if an office has the misfortune to be above the general average they will still have to pay their rebate ascertained by taking the experience of the whole of the Offices. Thus the undertaking has not eliminated any of the necessity for wise underwriting— indeed by restricting the amount available for commission, expenses and profit, it has increased the need for careful consideration.[1]

If the stronger members are called to pay, in some form or other, for the continuous (not accidental) mismanagement of others, such collective arrangements lose much of their object.

In the U.S.A. such attempts have been severely criticized. In a recent official publication, 'specific limitations of administrative expense written into workmen's compensation acts' are said to have been responsible for a deterioration of the service rendered by certain institutions; in one State 'the commission was compelled to drop from its working force all the referees'.[2] Such drastic limitations may bring about a reduction of administrative charges, but they may also lead to economies at the expense of those for whom the system exists, viz. the injured workmen.

The fact is that no considerable reduction of costs is possible under the present system which, in spite of the meagre benefits it affords, is barely profitable. Why, then, are insurance offices anxious to retain it under their control? At the last Annual General Meeting of Shareholders of the Commercial Union Assurance Company Ltd. the Chairman, Sir Bertram Hornsby, said:[3]

We have transacted Workmen's Compensation business from the commencement of the first Workmen's Compensation Act, and although the profit is, at the best, very small, it is in the general interest of the great insurance enterprise of this country that the companies should continue to undertake it.

No question of prestige arises, for at no other point is insurance so open to criticism. Nor does the volume of such business add appreciably to the general profits of a company by reducing overhead charges of the business as a whole. But there are other and wider considerations to be taken into account. Accident insurance is a charge

---

[1] Cf. Herbert G. Hurren, loc. cit., p. 299.
[2] Cf. *Methods of Financing*, &c., loc. cit., pp. 11–12.
[3] Cf. *Economist*, May 20th 1939, p. 460.

upon industry and a burden upon the whole structure of national economic life, proportionate to the number and severity of industrial accidents. Every injured workman who is partially or wholly incapacitated increases the burden to be borne. The fewer injured, the more restored to full working capacity, the less the burden. The present system of Workmen's Compensation in Great Britain does little to reduce the number of the one or to improve the physical capacity of the other.

As to the second point little need be said. The existing gaps are fully displayed in our chapters dealing with medical matters and particularly with rehabilitation. Where Workmen's Compensation includes no medical provisions and where no rival State management enters this field, private insurance companies cannot be expected to make experiments. The position of Mutual Indemnity Associations is somewhat different. Endeavours are made by some of them to promote the medical treatment and cure of injured workmen.[1] Even under a system of Mutuals based, as in Britain, entirely upon the interest of employers, a witness for a Textile Trade Federation explained the medical facilities provided by the Federation by declaring that '. . . it is naturally in our interest, as well as in that of the workmen, that they should be made as good and as efficient as possible'. But, he added, single employers would not be 'disposed to accept such a responsibility'.[2] Where a corporate spirit develops, as in the case of such federations or associations, the welfare of the workers employed in that branch of trade, even from the employer's view-point, cannot be overlooked. Where it is a matter between the insurance company and the individual employer such considerations are excluded so long as medical treatment remains outside Workmen's Compensation. The idea of undertaking medical treatment and rehabilitation on sociological grounds and in order to conserve man-power for industry is not one which could be seriously entertained by insurance offices in Britain.[3]

As regards accident prevention the Holman Gregory Committee[4] noted how accident prevention and Workmen's Compensation were linked up in other countries, particularly in the U.S.A., and called attention to merit-, experience-, and schedule-rating, all designed to interest the employer in lower costs of insurance by making safety measures more efficient. But for the opposition of Labour representatives to insurance in any form, lest it should prejudice their shortsighted demand for greater protection for life and limb[5] some measure of safety provision might have been embodied in compensation legislation, thus encouraging insurance offices to control and supervise closely

---

[1] Cf. *Holman Gregory Report*, Q. 6260–79, 7641, and 50967–85.
[2] Cf. ibid., A. 20967–8   [3] See also note on p. 279.
[4] See vol. i, p. 169.   [5] Ibid., pp. 53–4.

and, above all, initiate improvements, if only in order to reduce costs. In the absence of such provisions the impetus has been lacking. Mutual associations have done more in this field and made greater efforts,[1] but the evidence of the Deputy Chief Inspector of Factories, Mr. (later Sir) Gerald Bellhouse, C.B.E., as to accident prevention in relation to insurance offices, was revealing:

Q.: You apparently consider that the employer covers his risk by insurance and ceases to interest himself in safety. Is not that going a long way?

A.: I do not want to exaggerate too much. What I rather mean is that he insures himself and he troubles very little more about his accident risk.

Q.: Do you think that, apart from the question of insurance, he recognizes that even from the selfish point of view it is to his interest to keep his workers fit and well?

A.: I am afraid when I have talked with employers on this subject, a good many of them said to me: We are insured, and we do not worry about the risk.

Asked whether in such circumstances compulsory insurance would not be 'a mistake', Mr. Bellhouse, whose evidence clearly impressed the Committee, replied in the negative, provided that employers were 'required to maintain certain standards'.[2] The clauses in insurance policies relating to safety were not even read by some employers, and many employers had to pay claims out of their own pockets because they had not carried out all the regulations.[3] He suggested that a central body, including insurance companies, should be set up under the control of the State, with power to fix standards for different trades, compliance with which would entitle the factory occupier to obtain special discounts. When the standards had been fixed for any particular industry, and its representatives co-opted to the central body, it should be the duty of the insurance companies to allow the discount to all employers who reached these standards, subject to appeal by any aggrieved employer to an independent tribunal.

Sir Gerald Bellhouse was following the path taken a hundred years ago by Tremenheere. Factory inspectors were, as in 1906 before the Farrer Committee, in favour of compulsory insurance. The Holman Gregory Committee was confident that the arrangement between the Home Office and the Accident Offices Association would bring a change; for under § 9 of the Scheme it was agreed that members of the Association would co-operate with the proposed Commissioner 'in bringing gradually into being a system of discounts from normal rates in consideration of approved safety devices or provisions'.[4] The Com-

---

[1] Cf. *Holman Gregory Committee*, Index, vol. ii, under 'Mutual Associations, accident prevention'.

[2] Q. 22305–7.   [3] Q. 23310–14.

[4] Cf. *Holman Gregory Report*, pp. 68 and 83.

missioner never appeared and the Section remained a dead letter. Accident insurance might at least be linked with the existing 1,246 Safety Committees which, in the view of the Chief Inspector of Factories should include representatives of workmen, as in Germany and elsewhere,[1] a view not yet accepted by such committees. So long as the Act itself makes no provision for medical benefit or for safety and so long as there is no comprehensive and compulsory scheme covering all working occupations inclusive of small employers, insurance offices cannot be expected to reduce costs and damage to national interest attendant upon industrial injuries by introducing special inducements such as 'rating' coupled with an incentive to apply safety precautions to the greatest possible extent.

Nor can insurance companies be expected to show an active interest in rehabilitation, so long as medical charges are not borne by them. The system of lump-sum settlement militates against effective measures to reduce the burden of continuous weekly payments. The two main possibilities of reducing constantly and progressively the costs of insurance are therefore absent from the British system. J. W. Fidoe, A.M.I.E.E., a mining engineer, draws attention to the fact that 'most of the collieries are now held by combinations so that serious financial disaster would show that the insurer has been, in fact, paying his premium to himself'. Apart from further enactments he urges that Lloyd's underwriters and the insurance companies accepting catastrophic risks should insist that the pits, individually, shall be insured. To make this effective the premium rate payable must be determined by the underground condition of each colliery owned by a company. 'The mere fact of a high rate having to be paid would draw attention to the conditions alleged to prevail, and probably lead to improvement in the pit concerned, with a consequent *reduction in the cost of insurance*.'[2]

Merit-rating has not been recommended, however, by the Home Office. The Holman Gregory Committee recommended a system of 'schedule rating' whereby the careful employer would have been benefited. The Home Office Memorandum to the Hetherington Commission took exception to the introduction of any such system,[3] attributing it to the relative lack of safety legislation in that country.[4] The highly mechanized industrial system of the U.S.A. may have predisposed employers and Compensation Boards to combine compensation

[1] Cf. *Annual Report of Chief Inspector for 1937*, p. 35: 'A keen workman member would be, in effect, a voluntary safety officer in his own part of the factory.'

[2] Cf. *Mine Disasters*, loc. cit., Dec. 1937, p. 37. The recommendation corresponds to the American system of cost-reduction.

[3] Cf. loc. cit., paras. 458–65. [4] Cf. Q. 2211–12.

insurance with accident prevention; apart from this, however, the arguments adduced against introducing merit-rating into this country do not appear to us to be valid. The Memorandum declares that a very high percentage of industrial accidents is due to the personal factor and to accident proneness of the *worker*. This statement, so far as it is scientifically established, is not an argument against merit-rating, for it is certain that careful administration can and does reduce accidents due to these factors. Accident proneness should not, as we have shown in Chapter II, be charged against the workman only: there are accident-prone employers, foremen, factories, and machines. No judgement can be passed as yet upon their relative responsibility or that of climate, light, environment, and similar factors.

It has been clearly demonstrated by Mr. E. I. Evans, Actuary Industrial Commissioner of Ohio, in a recent lecture that 'a comprehensive experience merit-rating plan brings before the individual employer in concrete form the proposition—prevent accidents or pay . . . experience merit-rating is an incentive for accident prevention'.[1] In the face of such expert testimony, it is surprising that the Home Office should state that 'it is doubtful whether a system imposing additions or giving reductions of premium, within such limits as are found practicable, would have very much real effect in stimulating employers to improve their plant and otherwise to promote safety in their works'.[2] The same Memorandum notes the possibility of overlapping between factory and mines inspectors and those concerned with merit- or schedule-rating; the logical deduction is that under the present British system of individual liability no such methods can be introduced. They are clearly linked up with collective organization and administration, with insurance funds, compulsory insurance, and mutual controlling bodies. Under the German system, which combines accident prevention with Workmen's Compensation, there is no such overlapping and we have not heard of such complaints from the U.S.A. On the other hand any substantial diminution of risks and, therefore, of injuries from such rating systems would automatically diminish the costs of Workmen's Compensation through the medium of lower premiums or bonuses. Even where private insurance carriers still exist, but Workmen's Compensation legislation provides for medical benefit and where further private companies may compete with official insurance carriers, the incentive to private insurers to reduce costs by

[1] Cf. *Merit Rating and Accident Prevention in Discussion of Industrial Accidents and Diseases, 1934 Convention*, &c., Washington, 1935, pp. 209 sqq.

[2] See also Mr. Buckland's evidence, A. 2214, where the influence of compensation on a 'worker's safety' is discussed. Cf. also the very instructive discussion on 'experience' rating and 'schedule' rating, ibid., Q. 5592–8. For the system in Germany cf. ibid., p. 588.

effective measures of accident precaution and rehabilitation services may play a very important part.

Such is the teaching of the experiences in the U.S.A. It finds expression wherever to-day costs and accident insurance are discussed. The Actuary of the Industrial Commission of Ohio has recorded his conviction that 'experience merit-rating is based on the principle of providing a profit motive to the employer for eliminating accident cost'.[1] 'Compensation is determined by the severity of the injury, the length of the disability, and the amount of permanent disability. It is evident that compensation is increased by the quality of service. Hence only the best pays.'[2] The Chairman of a Commission dealing with Workmen's Compensation explained in a recent address that as the Act provided for safety activities on the part of the Commission, 'this matter, besides being one which we regard as an obligation to the employers and employees of the State, has developed into a hobby with the commission'.[3] This being so, it is not surprising that private offices have thrown themselves enthusiastically into the propagation of these cost-saving schemes. The American Mutual Liability Insurance Company issued recently a publication showing that twelve companies saved nearly $1\frac{1}{2}$ million dollars in the last twenty years by dividends returned each year on premiums paid, the actual rate of injuries having been less than anticipated. 'Through the prevention of industrial accidents policy-holders have lowered their insurance costs and the indirect expenses of accidents which amount to several times insurance costs.' The effect has also been to reduce insurance rates; carefully prepared tables compared the Average Manual Rate with the 'Average Actual Rate', the latter being much lower than the former to the advantage of the Company's clients.[4] The recommendation of the T.U.C. that the 'Board' should charge differential rates of premium, based on the degree of 'accident risk' in different classes of industry, and to reward the employer who takes all precautions for safety was, however, criticized by Sir Hector Hetherington. 'To attempt to create a fund which will make the good lives pay for the bad and at the same time to give a premium to employers who, either by good fortune or by merit are exceptionally favourably placed, seem to me to be

---

[1] Cf. *1934 Convention*, &c., 1935, pp. 209 sqq.

[2] Cf. Dr. J. A. Britton, *1936 Convention*, 1937, p. 203. Cf. also *1934 Convention*, pp. 217 sqq.: *Progress made in the Prevention of Industrial Injuries*, by James L. Gernon, Director of Division of Inspection, Dept. of Labor, New York. Cf. further U.S. Dept. of Labor, *Bulletin No. 536*, 1931.: Gregory C. Kelly, *Classifications and Accident Reports as a Means to reasonable Compensation Insurance Rates*, pp. 106–9.

[3] Cf. *1936 Convention*, 1937, p. 40.

[4] Cf. *How Twelve Companies made Dollars 1,461,939·01*, American Mutual Liability Insurance Co., Boston, 1938.

rather difficult things to combine.'[1] This, as the American example shows, is by no means the case. It is simply a question of creating and managing the fund according to certain average results of accident claims and recompensing the careful employer for his better results, which are seldom due to luck. This involves no actuarial inconsistency or unfairness. It is analogous to the 'no claim' bonus system in motor insurance. Fire premiums are lower where 'sprinklers' are installed throughout a building.

In Ontario 9,900 plants have set up accident prevention associations. The costs are distributed fairly among the employers generally and the costs of safety measures and insurance are thereby diminished.[2]

The Final Report of the Delevingne Committee on Rehabilitation seems to have missed the real connexion between the costs of medical service to be borne by the insurers and the problem of rehabilitation. The Report mentioned a suggestion that 'the Accident Insurance Companies, as parties presumably having a financial interest in the methods and results of treatment of accident cases, should be called upon to contribute towards the support of fracture clinics', and dismisses it as a 'misconception' as 'any charge, placed upon an insurance company, is in effect placed upon those who insure with the company, as it would be necessarily reflected in the premiums'.[3] This is a misconception. In countries where insurance companies cannot discharge their duties by lump-sum payments and where medical care is compulsory it pays offices to reduce *as quickly and as far* as possible the *period* of rent-payments. This cannot be done unless and until the injured workman has been rehabilitated and re-employed. Had the Committee asked why this has been the policy of so many American insurance offices instead, as they did, of simply stating the fact, the Committee might, after $3\frac{1}{2}$ years' deliberation have done more than express their pathetic inability to make any recommendation.

In America experience as to the lowering of the costs of risk to workmen has led to a movement which even goes beyond the circuit of the occupational unit. Schemes have been set up to insure workers for disabilities from non-industrial injuries and illnesses by group insurance. In an automobile accessory plant employing more than 3,000 workers the result has been remarkable. In 1929 the benefit payments in respect of such insurance had been 21·63 dollars per worker. A more complete medical service was then instituted including pre-employment and periodic physical examinations and a close follow-up

[1] Cf. Q. 3841–5. Also pp. 443, 511, and 519.
[2] U.S. Dept. of Labor, *Bulletin No. 536*, 1931.
[3] Cf. Final Report of the Inter-Departmental Committee on the Rehabilitation of Persons injured by Accidents, 1939, pp. 100–1 and 102.

of cases. Absenteeism and benefit payments decreased during the next three years, until the latter reached 8·05 dollars in 1933. It is stated that many other American companies have reported similar results which are praised not only as a great social achievement but also as being in the commercial interest of producers.[1] Thus in the U.S.A. the relationship between the frequency of industrial injury and a comprehensive and active system of insurance has been fully recognized and costs of Workmen's Compensation have been reduced. Merit-rating on the one hand, giving an incentive to the manufacturer to increase safety, close supervision of safety by the insurance carrier on the other, have been a great economic step forward wherever applied. The *social* effects have not been lacking. 'Workmen's Compensation in itself is not a means of accident prevention, but it affords opportunity for substantial aid to accident prevention',[2] and may, under a proper system, do much to promote the reduction of the costs of industrial injury.

We may conclude this chapter by a reference to evidence given before the Hetherington Commission as to the possible economy in 'costs'. It was stated on behalf of the Committee formed by the Durham Colliery Owners' Mutual Protection Association and Durham Miners' Association that there are very few direct expenses. Members get a fee for attending, possibly the miners get something similar. The legal bill of the Mutual Association, which pays the bulk of the costs, was estimated at £500–£600 a year, a negligible sum if divided over the whole of the cases. 'On the other side of the account', so the witness explained, 'we save 400 cases of commutation going to Court, which would be £2 and 10 sh. per case; the 80 fatal cases would go to Court, and we save £7 and 10 sh. each in Court fees; there are 250 non-fatal cases; altogether there would easily be a saving of some thousands of pounds in Court and legal expenses to set against that very rough estimate of £500 or £600.' The cost of running the Committee is 'negligible'.[3] No better illustration could be available to show how far the high cost of Workmen's Compensation in Britain could be reduced by an intelligent change in the principle of administration through collective efforts.

[1] Cf. *Medical Service and Workmen's Compensation Laws*, Chicago, 1938, p. 37.
[2] Dodd, loc. cit., p. 711.
[3] *Hetherington Commission, Evidence*, A. 6865–70. In Alsace-Lorraine, where, after 1919, the system of compulsory insurance and the administration by trade associations were retained, the expenses of administration are only from 9 to 10 per cent. of the premium income. This compares very favourably with the high expense ratio of most of the private companies in France. Cf. *I.L.O. International Survey*, i. 225, 267.

CHAPTER XXI

THE ECONOMIC AND SOCIAL SIDE: THE ADVANTAGES OF A COMPREHENSIVE SYSTEM OF PUBLIC ADMINISTRATION

The English Legislature, like the English People, is of slow temper; essentially conservative. In our wildest periods of reform, in the Long Parliament itself, you notice always the invincible instinct to hold fast by the Old; to admit the minimum of the New; to expand, if it is possible, some old habit or method, already found fruitful, into new growth for the new need. It is an instinct worthy of all honour; akin to all strength of wisdom. . . . The English Legislature is entirely repugnant to believe in 'new epochs'. Nevertheless new epochs do actually come; and with them new imperious peremptory necessities; so that even an English Legislature has to look up, and admit, though with reluctance, that the hour has struck. The hour having struck, let us not say 'impossible'; it will have to be possible! For Time, all-edacious and all-feracious, does run on; and the Seven Sleepers, awakening hungry after a hundred years, find that it is not their old nurses who can now give them suck!

THOMAS CARLYLE, *Past and Present* (1843).

WORKMEN'S Compensation in Great Britain to-day is no more than an attempt to recompense an injured workman by a sum of money. Alternative methods have seldom been discussed and never seriously considered by the legislature. Workmen's Compensation in Britain remains on the Statute Book in substantially the original tentative, almost embryonic, form, in which it first appeared. Accident prevention, which might have been linked up with Workmen's Compensation, was left to *ad hoc* factory inspectors. They have always been pioneers of progressive methods of preventing injury to workers, but have not been able to use the lever of financial stimulus to accident prevention offered by the prospect and practical experience of lower compensation payments. As no National Health Insurance system existed in Britain when Workmen's Compensation began, the treatment of injured workmen was left to other agencies. Consequently, means whereby the injured workman might be restored to his pristine physical capacity await general adoption.

The tendency in all progressive industrial countries is to widen the scope of Workmen's Compensation: the need of a 'complete and effective program' is everywhere emphasized.[1] British Workmen's

---

[1] Cf. an instructive article by Marshall Dawson of the U.S.A. Bureau of Labor Statistics, *Labor Information Bulletin*, Oct. 1937, pp. 7 sqq.: 'Problems of Administering Workmen's Compensation Laws'. He notes the following points as criteria of the completeness of a system:

Compensation lacks anything of the kind. In spite of the great diversity of insurance carriers, which include Insurance Companies and Mutual Indemnity Associations, individual non-insured employers number some hundreds of thousands. Approved Societies reluctantly play an undefined and unfruitful part in helping *or* compelling their members to prosecute their claims in the courts. Registrars of County Courts have widely different views on questions of administrative practice. The interests and views of solicitors and doctors of the parties on the one side, and single referees and certifying surgeons in cases of litigation on the other, differ very widely. Some trade unions can and do advise and assist their members to secure their just dues, by direct negotiations with employers or through the courts, but at least 12 million workmen have no such protection.[1]

The financial soundness of insurance carriers is subject to supervision by the State in some cases, but not in others. Compulsory insurance is required in some industries, but not in the vast majority. Re-employment of injured persons is occasionally dealt with by employers' organizations, but is usually left to chance. Some but not all workers are covered by the law, some for part only of the period during which they are exposed to hazards, and for some but not all of such hazards; many are not covered at all by their employers. Rehabilitation is left to chance or charity except in a few large enterprises. Such, in brief, is the chaotic state of Workmen's Compensation Administration in Britain, as revealed in the evidence tendered to the Hetherington Commission, and by our own studies.

No scheme of patchwork reform will suffice. Our aim is to set forth a system best suited to our needs and to suggest how it should be administered. To this end we have surveyed at length the legal, administrative, and financial structure of Workmen's Compensation in Britain; we have provided, for the first time, thanks to the admirable ground-work performed in the international sphere by the I.L.O., a full statement of the practice of leading industrial countries which, despite an appearance of diversity, display an almost uniform trend which, during the past decade, approaches to something like unity in aim and uniformity in principles though not, of course, in administration.

There is general agreement abroad that the link between insurance and compensation claims should be strong and direct. Employers are

'1. Systematic and continuous endeavours by responsible authorities, employers and workers to determine and eliminate the causes of accidents.

'2. Immediate and adequate medical treatment when injuries occur.

'3. Prompt and equitable payment of compensation benefits.

'4. A plan for rehabilitating workers who, because of their injuries, are no longer able to follow their former occupation.'

[1] Seventeen million employed persons, of whom about 4 millions are full trade unionists.

not less solicitous for their employees' safety because insurance carriers enforce merit-rating and supervise safety precautions under a system of compulsory insurance. Some insurance carriers are required to make substantial deposits to ensure their financial soundness. Others, like Mutual Indemnity Associations, are almost unregulated in that respect. Most employers please themselves whether they will insure their liability or not and about 250,000 employers are uninsured. Compulsory insurance seems to us a necessary preliminary to any substantial change in the system.

The words 'in the course of and arising out of' employment have given rise to much litigation and to decisions which have defeated the original intentions of the legislature. Our view is that the operative words should be so comprehensive as to cover any accident or injury within the occupational unit or undertaking in its widest sense (inclusive of the journey thither).

A comprehensive system of Workmen's Compensation should not be regarded as the fad of social reformers with collectivist leanings and tidy minds. It has deep and fundamental justification in long experience in foreign countries. The linking of accident prevention with Workmen's Compensation has been shown to lessen accidents, and to reduce insurance premiums. A factory inspector cannot properly urge that the application of certain safety precautions would have this effect, any more than a private insurance company could urge safety measures in the interests of humanity. Yet both motives are creditable and in the national interest.

The main object of including medical care and rehabilitation within the scope of Workmen's Compensation is to ensure the best available treatment of injured men, particularly those with serious incapacity which is likely to be of long duration. Such treatment is seldom if ever available under the N.H.I. Acts save for trifling injuries, and there could be no question of occupational rehabilitation under the N.H.I. Acts. In the words of Mr. Neville Chamberlain when introducing the Contributory Pensions Bill in the House of Commons on May 18th 1925 (col. 76):

There is undoubtedly something very attractive in the idea that you should have one single contribution on one single card which would entitle the contributor to all the benefits comprised in the existing scheme of national insurance *combined with Workmen's Compensation,* widows' pension, and old age pension. . . . The Government thought it necessary to give very serious and prolonged attention to the various suggestions that have been made for all-in insurance, and to see whether and if so how far it was practicable to devise a plan of that kind.

We have come to the conclusion that it is impossible to include Workmen's Compensation in a scheme of all-in insurance. To begin with, the risks in various trades vary very greatly. A varying rate could not come into a general scheme; a flat rate would be very unjust to the safer trades and would take away from the employer one incentive to reduce risks and, therefore, his liability. We think it very desirable to maintain that incentive. The whole burden of Workmen's Compensation now falls on employers: they accept it and we see no reason to put the burden elsewhere. There are other objections into which I need not enter. Taken together, they seemed to us overwhelming.

It may well be desirable, however, to link up curative treatment of injured workmen with that available for other members of society.

Some industrial injuries may be almost peculiar to a particular occupation. Tardy recognition of this fact has given rise to special schemes for certain industrial diseases, with *ad hoc* Medical Boards and compulsory medical examinations of workmen, compulsory precautions by employers, and compulsory compensation funds. The system might with advantage be very widely extended, e.g. to nystagmus and to certain industrial neuroses specifically connected with industrial accidents, if only to ensure competent handling by specialists. But in such cases the pathology of the case is peculiar to a particular industrial environment. Another type of condition is that created by accident and negligence proneness. If the studies in regard to multiple accidents, for instance, are to bear practical fruit they should be linked with accident prevention and with diagnostic and prognostic medicine. 'Trivial accidents are indicators of unsafe people whom the record of the ambulance room can be employed to discover';[1] but only if there is an expert link between the ambulance room and Workmen's Compensation. No such link at present exists even in theory.

A further reason for linking up medical benefits with Workmen's Compensation is to ensure *continuity of treatment*. We have dealt with the technical side of this point very fully. We have seen the importance attached to continuity in Germany, for instance by instituting 'forwarding doctors'. The inclusion of provision for continuity of medical treatment in accident insurance law does not prevent a particular voluntary or State institution from making use of the existing general facilities for treatment. But it does provide such institutions with the facilities for power to insist upon such continuity.

This applies also to placement and re-employment of seriously injured workmen in suitable capacities in their former or, on rare occasions, in another industry though perhaps in a different occupation therein. This process, itself of great social importance, should have a legal basis. Little can be achieved so long as it is a matter solely for the individual employer, but 'one employer cannot search the market

[1] Major Greenwood, M.D., and Hilda Woods. Cf. Medical Research Committee, *Report of the Industrial Fatigue Research Board*, 1919, p. 11.

for a single man'.[1] The witness, the Hon. Solicitor to the Scottish Federation of Friendly and Approved Societies, observed that the representatives of insurance offices were in a better position as they had many more cases to handle. But the matter is not one which even the largest insurance offices can handle with advantage. It can best be dealt with by some corporate body representative of a whole industry such as, for example, the Miners' Welfare Fund, in intimate co-operation with Employment Exchanges. The main point is that placement in industry of injured men should be a statutory part of the system of Workmen's Compensation. An employer cannot be compelled to re-employ a man, but he can be required to do his best to do so, and it can be made financially advantageous to him to succeed.

We may note, in concluding this summary, that all progressive systems of Workmen's Compensation administration provide for a measure of participation by the workmen themselves. It is not accidental that the schemes for industrial diseases, such as the Refractories Industries Scheme of 1931,[2] provide for joint committees 'representative of both employers and workmen' under an independent chairman. The I.L.O. Conference of 1925 resolved that it was advisable 'to establish through comprehensive mutual insurance institutions administered *by the employers and workers directly interested, or by the State in collaboration with them*, an organization designed to encourage thrift and to improve the conditions of life of insured persons', and in this connexion expressly mentioned Workmen's Compensation.[3]

The movement to secure a comprehensive system of Workmen's Compensation is common to all industrial countries. It is not the outcome of collectivist aspirations, nor a consequence of technical changes in the organization of industry. It arises from the recognition of the fact that Workmen's Compensation, or industrial accident insurance, is a permanent feature of modern industrialism which requires legislative treatment as a whole and not in sections. The prevention of accidents, the provision of first aid, treatment, and cure, rehabilitation and re-employment are successive facets of a single problem and should be treated as such and if possible under one roof. This is now admitted, even in Britain. The sole reason why so little has been done to bring it about is the tradition of *laisser-faire* and the desire to avoid administrative labour. Upon this tradition the existing system was initiated. It

---

[1] Mr. Baird to the Hetherington Commission. Cf. A. 2644.

[2] See Part III, Section 25.

[3] Cf. *International Labour Organization and Social Insurance*, Geneva, 1936, pp. 122 and 130. Recommendation No. 23 suggested special boards of arbitration comprising an equal number of employers' and workmen's representatives, not to replace but to assist the courts.

has been maintained not on any ground of principle but because any other system involved changes more fundamental than any government or political party has hitherto been prepared to make.

This leads us to our second thesis. If the principle of a comprehensive scheme for Workmen's Compensation is accepted, how should it be administered? It is not a coincidence that almost all countries which have a comprehensive scheme of Workmen's Compensation no longer rely upon or utilize commercial or private enterprise as an integral factor in administration. This does not mean that the State must assume the role of sole administrator; medical care, for example, is administered by private undertakings in the U.S.A. and Ontario and in certain other countries, and medical rehabilitation could be dealt with on the same lines. But, especially in the U.S.A., the pace has been set by coexistent State or public agencies, whose example[1] private insurance carriers felt bound to emulate.[2] The inclusion in a system of Workmen's Compensation of medical benefit and rehabilitation does not involve *ipso facto* the eclipse of private insurance carriers. But behind these competitive methods there is, in the U.S.A., nearly always a Commission or Board with powers of supervision and initiative, as also in Ontario, where company liability schemes are in existence and employers in certain industries are individually held liable to pay compensation. The Workmen's Compensation Board to which, as a rule, compensation is paid here and elsewhere in Canada, determines the necessity, character, and efficiency of medical aid and benefits.[3]

Some degree of centralization of medical services for injured workmen is in general advantageous. It is well that a central authority should lay down certain principles, and exercise some supervision. It by no means follows that such public bodies should become the owners and managers of hospitals, sanatoria, &c., for the purposes of the Act. In the U.S.A. commercialization of medical service under Workmen's Compensation has led to many complaints, not always justified. Dodd concludes that

---

[1] Some interesting facts are found in the *Wisconsin Physical Examination Program* published by the Industrial Commission of Wisconsin, Madison, 1939, pp. 6–7. The Commission deals among other things with accident prevention and safety measures; with experience rating; with a wide range of questions relating to 'physical examinations in industry'; with insurance companies which try to persuade or encourage employers to refuse arbitrarily or unreasonably employment to or to discharge employees. 'The commissioner of insurance may, upon complaint of the industrial commission, revoke the licence of such corporation.'

[2] Cf. Dodd, who cannot be said to be in any way prejudiced, who declares: 'Both public and private organizations have sought to set up something in the way of definite standards both for the content and for the administration of Workmen's Compensation.' Cf. loc. cit., p. 828.   [3] Cf. *International Survey*, vol. i, pp. 150, 152, 156.

all insurance clinics and all commercial clinics or other organizations which are operated to treat industrial cases for private profit should, by law, be abolished, and the treatment of all compensation cases except those requiring first aid should be exclusively confined to the members of a panel of physicians and surgeons and specialists nominated by the officers or a committee of the medical society in the county or area concerned.[1]

This verdict should be recalled if and when medical treatment becomes an integral part of British Workmen's Compensation and if private insurance carriers, companies, or Mutuals should seek to limit their new obligations by entering into agreements with private commercial clinics.

This is also true of rehabilitation. The Federal Vocational Rehabilitation Act in the U.S.A. withholds federal aid in the absence of an adequate system of co-operation between the compensation and the rehabilitation authorities.[2] Insurance carriers in Britain could, however, not possibly administer an adequate medical service for injured persons, and duplication would unduly increase costs. Public administration, therefore, seems unavoidable, but it should be upon lines which would ensure co-operation with *ad hoc* regional bodies representing industries, and with centralized institutions such as the Miners' Welfare Fund or existing contracting-out schemes.

The same considerations apply to safety measures and accident precaution. If new Workmen's Compensation law included such provisions there is no *a priori* ground why private insurance carriers or Mutuals should not undertake the task. But the *Holman Gregory Report* noted of insurance offices: 'There is no systematic inspection; the existence of a safety or welfare committee is not a factor.'[3] H.M. Inspector's Report of 1938 points the same moral: 'Safety organizations cannot be really effective unless the management is keenly interested in safety and is willing to help in any possible way.'[4] In any case private organizations do not, in practice, seem effective. A witness for a Mutual Association told the Holman Gregory Committee that his Association had power to repudiate liability if the machinery was not fenced, 'but we have never exercised it'.[5] The question would wear a different aspect if the law required employers to apply safety measures under the general control of a public authority (which need not be a State department). Mutual associations could do the work well, if properly authorized. Commercial organizations have had plenty of time to show 'interest', but have shown none. Dodd notes of the U.S.A. that a 'purely monopolistic state fund has perhaps the best opportunity in

[1] Cf. Dodd, loc. cit., pp. 494–5. Cf. also ibid., pp. 445, 447, 452–6.
[2] Cf. ibid., pp. 718–19.   [3] Cf. p. 67.
[4] Cf. *Report for 1937*, p. 35.   [5] Cf. *Holman Gregory Committee*, A. 21045.

the field of accident prevention, because it carries all risks within the state and may effectively co-ordinate accident prevention and merit rating, and also because those in control of the fund can also control the establishment and enforcement of state safety codes'. This is the sort of 'interest' which Sir Duncan Wilson declares to be fundamentally necessary for the execution of industrial safety measures.

He recently reminded an expert audience that dangers from gas explosions to which workers in chemical factories were particularly prone depended much less on the worker than on those responsible for the design, construction, and maintenance of the plant. Other speakers who followed him agreed that responsibility should rest with the management as well as with the workers who, as a safety officer declared, were given more than their share of blame. Posters appealed almost exclusively to the workmen and sometimes warned workers against hazards which it was the business of the management to eliminate. Such discussions show the value of the close collective collaboration between management and workers in the administration of accident prevention which might form part of a new system of Workmen's Compensation.[1] In his latest Report the Chief Inspector of Factories records the collaboration of employers and trades unions by Joint Standing Committees, notably in the cotton spinning and weaving trades. The Report of this Committee declared lately that 'the safety provisions require the evolution of new methods of working as well as the devising of new safety appliances', and praises the 'active assistance of all parties, and the machinery of the Joint Standing Committee'.[2]

Dodd agrees that progress on these lines is possible under a competitive system in well-defined areas (e.g. coal-mining). Even the private company which 'concentrates on a single industry or in a single area has as good an opportunity to do effective safety work as has a large private company writing insurance covering all occupations in a wider area' but, he adds, results 'depend not so much upon the type of insurer as upon insurers having sufficient business to sustain an adequate safety service'.[3] To eliminate the smaller insurance offices or organizations is not practicable: the remedy lies in a decentralized grouping of employers so as to make them bear collectively the costs, to apply their special trade-group knowledge to safety measures, with a Commissioner or Board to enforce their rules on their behalf. This compulsory community of interest would serve to give the widest effect to any desirable precautions whilst reducing costs by pooling

[1] Cf. *The Times*, Apr. 21st 1939. Speech at Conference arranged by Soc. of Chem. Engineers.
[2] Cf. *Report of Chief Inspector for 1938*, p. 35.   [3] Cf. Dodd, loc. cit., pp. 562–3.

interests. Such Joint Committees or Mutual Indemnity Associations with a collective and State-controlled character might be formed under the supervision of the Government wherever local and divisional groups of industry exist with common problems in regard to the in-cidence, frequency, or special kind of accidents and injuries. For example, the South Wales anthracite coal-field produces only one-fortieth of the United Kingdom output of coal, but has 50 per cent. of certified silicosis.[1] The South Wales mine-owners and miners acting jointly could deal with this matter comprehensively leaving silicosis in other districts, where it is much rarer, to an association covering the rest of the kingdom. Methods and grouping must vary, but the object should be: 'To provide means of minimizing the number of accidents in industrial pursuits.'[2] It is this principle, in contrast to the administration which separates insurance from accident preven-tion, which matters; ways to realize it are easily to be found if once it is adopted.

Compulsory insurance is possible without having State administra-tion, but commercial insurance offices may regard it as commercially unremunerative. They have in practice hitherto opposed it, presum-ably because it would saddle them with responsibility for 'undesirable' risks with which Workmen's Compensation abounds. They would have to insure all small employers and plants which might be on the danger line. The problem is particularly urgent where compulsory insurance goes hand in hand with private administration of compensa-tion; it has proved very intractable under the competitive systems in the U.S.A. The difficulty of apportioning undesirable risks which commercial companies would normally decline to assume is formid-able.[3] It can only be avoided where compulsory insurance is an integral part of the public administration of compensation.

The inescapable conclusion is that 'for the uniform distribution of the burden of undesirable risks, some governmental compulsion appears to be necessary'.[4] Compulsion facilitates efficiency in adminis-tration as well as in medical treatment by decentralization to regional or industrial units centralizing administration by groups or areas responsible to a central Department, which would make it possible to adjust and distribute risks by such devices as merit-rating, the results of which far surpass the best which can be effected by private under-takings.

The Home Office is alive to the advantage of 'pooling' risks under

[1] Cf. *The Times*, May 4th 1939. Mr. Geoffrey Lloyd, Sec. for Mines.
[2] Cf. *Workmen's Compensation Law*, Wisconsin, 1911. *Preamble, Wisconsin Physical Examination Program*, Madison, 1939, pub. by the Industrial Commission of Wisconsin, p. 20.   [3] Cf. Dodd, loc. cit., pp. 570–3.   [4] Cf. ibid., p. 571.

compulsory insurance. It has, for instance, made it possible to abolish the 'time limit' for compensation in the case of industrial disease.[1] 'The abolition of the time limit [in the case of industries in which silicosis is of common occurrence] depends largely on whether arrangements are made, through compensation funds or in connexion with compulsory insurance, to pool the risk', in which case 'it would not be necessary to establish a claim against a particular employer under whom the workman worked many years before'. This is the fundamental principle of the German system of collective insurance. What is true of silicosis is true of all other injuries. The importance of pooling risks and of collective effort is widely recognized.[2] 'The formation of a Medical Committee, working in co-operation with industry and the Home Office authorities, in the improving of protective devices and evolving sufficient eye protection is a question of urgent importance.' But an organization must first be formed to represent an 'industry'. To such bodies medical committees, however specialized, may be attached. The same applies to matters of rehabilitation and re-employment of the one-eyed worker, the absence of which Dr. Minton deplores.

A system of Workmen's Compensation should inspire trust and confidence in those for whose benefit it exists. That this is admittedly not the case in Britain to-day is no reflection on judicial administration. On the contrary: judges frequently express in very strong terms their regret that the law they have to administer so often does less than justice to the injured worker. We can recollect no case in which the judge thought the employer was hardly used. Our judges have tried to make the best of what they clearly regard as a defective law and a bad system of administration which cramps and fetters them in the effort to do justice. These difficulties will be increased by any attempt to widen the scope of Workmen's Compensation. The present system of Workmen's Compensation is distrusted by workmen because it involves too often a contest between two parties of unequal strength. The help of the trade unions is of inestimable value, but it is available only for a minority of workmen.

It is often urged that the number of cases of litigation is relatively small, but the system of private insurance necessarily involves 'bargaining', i.e. an attempt to compel 'agreement' without recourse to judicial action. This has, in practice, led to lump-sum settlements with all its attendant evils. This device is characteristic of all systems of private accident insurance. It is designed to reduce benefits to workmen and to save costs to employers, for it is cheap to work. State

[1] Cf. *Home Office Memorandum to Hetherington Commission*, para. 457 (2) and (3).
[2] Dr. Minton. Cf. *Transactions of the Ophthalmological Society*, 1939.

administration would rarely have recourse thereto. The system of lump-sum payments is often unfair, but suits insurance offices. An inherent defect of the present system is that it ties insurance offices and single employers alike to a wholly unregulated evaluation. It involves *ad hoc* decisions, based on arbitrary 'bargaining', against a dubious and complicated legal background. Under a new system of evaluation, industrial group associations or committees might (*vide* Chapter IX) succeed in relating wages or earnings to incapacity upon a basis which would disregard the difference between pre-accident and post-accident wages of the injured person and take into account only his professional status under normal conditions. In County Durham, District Compensation Committees seem to have overcome all the difficulties of assessing normal average earnings in the mining industries. There are standards for the short-time worker working three days, and for married and single men, and even for a boy under 21 who has been six months in the mine.[1] Conditions among miscellaneous employments of course vary more than in coal-mining,[2] but more than half all insured persons are engaged in specialized industries. Disability schedules, likewise, are only possible under State administration.

The outstanding feature alike of the 'review of weekly payments', of incapacity or non- or partial incapacity, and of light work is the litigation entailed; 'uncontested' or 'undisputed' cases are frequently settled on a basis unfair to the worker and to the detriment of society at large. There has been as yet no systematic inquiry as to whether the agreements embodied in such uncontested cases are fair to the worker. Injured persons are pressed by insurance offices to accept early settlements, optimistically termed 'agreed bargains'. If provision is made in new legislation for control or inspection of any agreed payments or settlements, an extension of public administration is inevitable and would certainly be justified by results.

Existing safeguards are admittedly inadequate. Neither registrars nor judges have, in general, the facilities or the training required. Court administration can usefully remain. But a Workmen's Compensation Board, or a Commissioner or group-association having Joint Committees for such purpose, might evolve a far truer picture of the actual conditions relating to incapacity, partial incapacity, light work, and all the other items entering matters of evaluation and of review than is

---

[1] Cf. *Hetherington Commission*, Q. and A. 2227; for a similar Committee in Yorkshire cf. *Debates H.C.*, 30 January 1940, col. 1074.

[2] Cf. Hermann Levy, *The New Industrial System*, 1936, pp. 87–114. The Home Office Memorandum to the Hetherington Commission well recognized the fact that by the creation of flat rates fewer questions which necessarily lead to litigation would arise. Cf. *Memorandum*, para. 474.

now possible. An injury is a social as well as a medical matter, but no 'social referee' has ever been suggested. A Board or a Compensation Commissioner might fulfil such a function, and might enable a judge to deal adequately with the highly specialized features of industrial injuries. Only thus can the injured workman's suspicion be removed; it is bound to flourish under a private system. So far as it exists in Britain in regard to certain industrial diseases it has been wholly successful.

State or Board administration can and, in practice, does dispel disadvantages and evils inherent in systems of private insurance; it alone makes possible fruitful co-operation between organized industry, labour organizations, and the public administration. Mutual Indemnity Associations, whose interests are not wider than those of their members, are unlikely to grapple with the social needs of their particular industry, though such a body as the Miners' Welfare Association might do so. Such excellent bodies as the Medical Research Council and the Industrial Health Research Board would be far more useful if there existed some agency whose object it was to practise what they preach. In the words of the Collect for the first Sunday after the Epiphany we 'both perceive and know what things we ought to do'; what we lack is 'grace, *and power*, faithfully to fulfil the same'. The bitter experience of the war of 1914–18 was necessary in order to gain 'much valuable knowledge on the effects of hours of work on efficiency'.[1] The Industrial Health Research Board was set up 'to secure the co-operation of industries in making widely known such results of research work as are capable of useful application to practical needs'.[2] After a lapse of twenty years the Board claims that 'some of the conclusions have already (!) been translated into practice', e.g. short rest pauses and the use of spectacles for very fine work—obvious devices which not merely cost nothing but are directly reflected in output. Of multiple accidents, accident and negligence proneness, and other matters dealt with in Chapter II of this book we hear too little. Scientific research has not thrown enough light upon such diseases as nystagmus or silicosis and has done nothing to encourage re-employment, light work, &c., whilst injured workers suffering from traumatic mental disorders owe nothing to the Medical Research Council, though it is financed by the National Health Insurance Fund. The war of 1914–18 provided unparalleled opportunities for studying the effect of every variety of shock;[3] but the valuable experience of

[1] Cf. Medical Research Council, *Eighteenth Annual Report of the Industrial Health Research Board*, 1938, p. 1.
[2] Cf. ibid., p. 59.
[3] Cf. Brend, loc. cit., pp. 8, 34, and *passim*.

the Ministry of Pensions has had as yet no effect whatever upon the administration of Workmen's Compensation. The requisite administrative link, backed by State or semi-State bodies, is missing. The Ministry of Labour has unequalled experience and up-to-date knowledge of the labour market, which plays so important a part in regard to the question of partial incapacity, light work, and the review of weekly payments, but plays no part in the administration of Workmen's Compensation. Only a centralized body or a body at least locally centralized or centralized by groups can achieve permanent results in this direction. Only a public or collective body can link up accident prevention, the treatment of injury and disease, rehabilitation or re-employment. *Ad hoc* measures relating and restricted to particular aspects of particular injuries or diseases, such as nystagmus, or fractures, or silicosis, will of themselves achieve little. The Final Report of the Rehabilitation Committee, published in the summer of 1939 after 3½ years' consideration, concentrates one-sidedly on fractures; but it shows incidentally that while fractures are not a typical form of 'industrial' accident, there are some injuries and several diseases which are almost peculiar to certain trades. Industrial fractures may best be dealt with under a general scheme, but other industrial injuries and diseases urgently require *ad hoc* treatment, notably nystagmus and eye injuries. Rehabilitation schemes have little chance of success if not backed up by organized industry and labour. As the Wisconsin Industrial Commission noted recently:

Occupational hazards in industry are so numerous and constantly changing that it has been almost impossible for medical knowledge to keep abreast of changes in formulating specialized examination techniques for the determination of exposures of workmen.

It is for this reason that the Commission urges 'concerted efforts'.[1] *Has meus ad metas sudet oportet equus.* This too should be our aim.

Difficulties would disappear if boldly faced. British employers, in spite of 'individualism', have never refrained from 'association' when it appeared to be in their interest.[2] Under the present system of Workmen's Compensation no such necessity exists. That the apparent simplicity of the British system merely shows lack of comprehensiveness was early recognized by American investigators and by Mr. A. A. Wotzel of the British 'Labour Department' and Sir Leo Chiozza Money[3]

---

[1] Cf. *Wisconsin Physical Examination*, loc. cit., p. 12.

[2] Cf. Hermann Levy, *The New Industrial System*, 1936, first chapters and *passim*.

[3] Cf. Leo Chiozza Money, *Insurance versus Poverty*, with an introduction by the Rt. Hon. D. Lloyd George, 1912, pp. 53–4: 'It appears to me that the German method of dealing with employers' liability is infinitely superior to ours. . . . The employers' accident insurance associations draw up strict safety rules in each trade, and enforce them among

(see vol. i, pp. 76 and 79). That the present system is costly, and that a comprehensive system might be cheaper, we have already demonstrated. By avoiding competitive duplication, by making insurance universal, by concentrating administration in groups and areas under unified control, the new order might be much less costly than the old and would set large sums free every year for the purposes of rehabilitation and cure.

It should not be difficult to form associative indemnity associations.[1]

Collective liability systems [wrote Sir William Meredith in 1912][2] are uniformly conceded to be the most satisfactory both in theory and in practical results. The type system, that of Germany, is the outstanding example of a successful solution of the problem of accident compensation . . . the collective system is simple, direct and economical in its operation. By eliminating the element of contest between the employee on the one hand, and the employer and the insurance company on the other, practically the whole of the waste is eliminated and the expenses of administration reduced to a minimum. The collective system does not afford the same incentive for discriminating against older or practically disabled workmen. No rule supporting such a discrimination could be justified in the face of public sentiment. The elimination of a direct clash between employer and employee removes a source of friction and tends to more harmonious relations.

Sir William Meredith, after comprehensive investigation,[3] expressed

their members. Any employer who breaks the rules is obviously unfair to his fellow-employers as well as to himself; need we wonder that the system naturally brings about an ever-rising standard of safety and comfort?'

[1] In the Workmen's Compensation Bill for Ontario which was drafted in 1913 the matter of 'formation of associations' comprised not more than two small sections of which one merely related to the schedule which indicated the industries in which the employers were to be liable to contribute to the Accident Fund. Of these sections Section 97 (2) appeared to be the most important, empowering the Workmen's Compensation Board to approve the rules of such associations and so make them binding on all the employers included in the class. Cf. Sections 97(1)–(3) and 98 of the Bill in *Final Report on Laws relating to the Liability of Employers*, Toronto, 1913, p. 52.

The Reports in which Sir William Meredith described the different systems of Workmen's Compensation administration, giving full credit to the German *Berufsgenossenschaften* are what a recent official American publication called 'the most valuable documents in compensation literature'.

[2] Cf. *Interim Report on Laws relating to the Liability of Employers*, Toronto, 1912, p. 91.

[3] It was after a full scrutiny of 'some systems' that Sir William Meredith drew his conclusions in favour of what later became the Ontario system. He described and criticized the 'English system' and contrasted it with that of Germany, Washington, Norway, Ohio, and Massachusetts. His praise of the collective system was not less elaborate than his criticism of those of 'individual liability'. The main points in regard to the latter were: (1) An individual system affords no assurance of solvency. (2) The individual system handicaps the smaller employer. (3) An individual system affords very little direct incentive to prevention of injury. (4) It is 'extremely wasteful'. (5) It does not afford proper facilities for the administration of periodical payments. (6) It militates against the employment of older and partially incapacitated workmen. (7) It involves a direct contest inimical to harmonious

his conviction that the original aim of the British legislature was to inaugurate a system similar to that of Germany 'but on a voluntary instead of a compulsory basis', but that 'this hope had been entirely dispelled and the tendency was 'rather towards the extinction of those schemes which existed before the passing of the Act'.[1]

Reform of Workmen's Compensation requires continued co-operative effort. In the words of Mr. L. Clinton Robinson:[2]

As the German poet Heine once said, 'Every age has its problem, by solving which humanity is helped forward', and if our age were to be remembered for no other achievement in its economic development than the perfection of the co-operative system of the unfortunate victims of industrial accidents, it would merit the grateful thanks of posterity.

Sir William Meredith concluded his recommendations with the following words:

In these days of social and industrial unrest it is, in my judgment, of the gravest importance to the community that every proved injustice to any section or class resulting from bad or unfair laws should be promptly removed by the enactment of remedial legislation and I do not doubt that the country which is quick to discern and prompt to remove injustice will enjoy, and that deservedly, the blessing of industrial peace and freedom from social unrest. Half measures which mitigate but do not remove injustice are, in my judgment, to be avoided. That the existing law (of Workmen's Compensation) inflicts injustice on the working man is admitted by all. From that injustice he has long suffered, and it would, in my judgment, be the greatest mistake if questions as to the scope and character of the proposed remedial legislation were to be determined, not by the consideration of what is just to the working man, but what is the least he can be put off with; or if Legislature were to be deterred from passing a law designed to do full justice owing to groundless fear that disaster to the industries of the Province would follow from the enactment of it.

This plea is as cogent to-day as when it was written. It is the judgement of a great British subject. With it we take leave of our readers.

---

relations. Sir William had carefully studied the investigation by Schwedtmann and Emery (see our vol. i, pp. 157–8), which apparently escaped the attention of the Holman Gregory Committee eight years later. His *Final Report* is a masterpiece of institutional research which should remain a lasting example of classic and comprehensive research. For the above point cf. *Interim Report*, loc. cit., pp. 89–90 and 94–100.

[1] Cf. ibid. p. 88. Cf. also our vol. i, pp. 62, 115, and 275 sqq.; for the utter insufficiency with which the German system was treated by the Holman Gregory Committee, see ibid., p. 193.

[2] 'The Development of the Ideal of Workmen's Compensation', *Journal of the Chartered Insurance Institute*, 1934, vol. xxxvii, p. 302.

BIBLIOGRAPHY[1]

I. BOOKS, PAMPHLETS, REPRINTS

ALLEN, R. G. D., and BOWLEY, A. L. *Family Expenditure.* 1935.

American Mutual Liability Insurance Company. How 12 companies made Dollars 1,461,939·01.

ANON. *John Smith has an Accident.* Published by the T.U.C. n.d.

BELL, LADY. *At the Works.* 1911.

BLANCHARD, R. H. *Workmen's Compensation in the U.S.A.* Geneva, 1926.

BOWLEY, *see under* ALLEN, R. G. D.

BOYWINDT, DR. HANS. *Die Berufsgenossenschaft der Neuzeit.* Berlin, 1921.

BRAY, M. B. *The Treatment of Rheumatism* (reprint).

BREND, DR. W. A. *Traumatic Mental Disorders in Courts of Law.* 1938.

BRIEGER, E. *After-Care and Rehabilitation.* 1937. (International Union against Tuberculosis.)

British Encyclopaedia of Medical Practice.

BUTTERWORTH'S *Workmen's Compensation Cases.*

CHAUVEAU, DR. C. *La Loi sur les Assurances Sociales.* Paris, 1928.

CHAVERNACK, *see under* IMBERT.

COHEN, JOSEPH L. *Workmen's Compensation.* 1923.

—— *Social Insurance Unified.* 1924.

COLLIE, SIR JOHN. *Workmen's Compensation. Its Medical Aspects.* 1933.

COLLIS, E. W., and GREENWOOD, MAJOR. *The Health of the Industrial Worker.* 1921.

DAWSON, W. H. *Social Insurance in Germany.* 1912.

DODD, WALTER F. *Administration of Workmen's Compensation.* New York, 1936.

DOUGHTY, F. M. *The Legacy of a Fracture.* 1937.

ELBOURNE, E. T. *Factory Administration and Cost Accounts.* 1929.

EMERY, *see under* SCHWEDTMANN.

Encyclopaedia Britannica.

FARMER, ERIC. *The Cause of Accidents.* 1932.

FLORENCE, P. SARGANT. *Economics of Fatigue and Unrest.* 1924.

FORGUE, DR., and JEANBRAU, E. *Guide pratique du médecin dans les accidents du travail.* 1924.

FOX, DR. FORTESCUE. *Arthritis in Women.* 1936.

Fuehrer durch die obligatorische Unfallversicherung. (Swiss.) Oct. 1938.

[1] For publications relating to the historical development of Employers' Liability and Workmen's Compensation the bibliography of vol. i, pp. 268 sqq., may be consulted.

GEBHARDT, PROF. DR. KARL. *Selbstausgleich und Wiederherstellungschirurgie.* Leipzig, 1936.
GREENWOOD, *see under* COLLIS.
GREIG, E. C. *Industrial Welfare.* 1937.
GRIFFITHS, E. H. *Injury and Incapacity.* 1935.

HACKETT, J. D. *Health Maintenance in Industry.* Chicago, 1925.
Handwoerterbuch der Staatswissenschaften. Jena.
HAYHURST, E. R., and KOBER, G. M. *Industrial Health.* Philadelphia, 1924.
HERBERT, A. P. *Misleading Cases in the Common Law.* 1927.
HERBERT, S. MERVYN. *Britain's Health,* with a foreword by Lord Horder. 1939.

ICKERT-WEICHSEL. *Grundriss der sozialen Medizin.* Leipzig, 1932.
IMBERT, LEON, ODDO, C., and CHAVERNACK, P. *Guide pour l'évaluation des incapacités.* Paris, 1923.

JEANBRAU, *see under* FORGUE.
JORDAN, HENRY H. *Orthopaedic Appliances.* New York, 1938.

KESSLER, H. H. *Accidental Injuries.* New York, 1932.
KOBER, *see under* HAYHURST.

LANZA, A. J. *Silicosis and Asbestosis.* 1938.
LAUBER, W. *Praxis des sozialen Unfallversicherungsrechts der Schweiz.* Bern, 1982.
LAUTERBACH, DR. *Die dritte Verordnung ueber Ausdehnung der Unfallversicherung auf Berufskrankheiten.* Muenchen, 1936.
LEGGE, SIR T. *Industrial Maladies.* 1934.
LEVY, PROF. HERMANN. *Economic Liberalism.* 1913.
—— *The New Industrial System.* 1936.
—— *see also under* WILSON.
LIEK, DR. ERWIN. *Die Schäden der sozialen Versicherung.* Muenchen, 1927.
LOEBEL, DR. J. *Gesundheitslexikon.* Berlin, 1930.

M'KENDRICK, ARCHIBALD. *Medical Reports* (reprint). 1937.
MANES, PROF. ALFRED. *Versicherungswesen,* vol. iii. Leipzig, 1932.
Men without Work. A Report made to the Pilgrim Trust. 1938.

NEWSHOLME, SIR ARTHUR. *International Studies on the Relation between the Private and Official Practice in Medicine,* vol. iii. 1931.
NORRIS, DR. D. C. *The Nervous Element in Accident Claims.* 1932.
—— *Effects of Injuries upon Earning Capacity* (reprint). 1936.

ODDO, *see under* IMBERT.

Reichsversicherung mit Anmerkungen. Berlin, 1930.
—— *Handkommentar zur,* 1914.
—— herausgegeben von Dr. Eichelsbacher. Muenchen, 1938.

RUEGG, HIS HON. JUDGE A. H., and STANES, H. P. *Workmen's Compensation Act 1906.* 1922.

SCHWEDTMANN, FERDINAND, and EMERY, JAMES A. *Accident Prevention and Relief.* Published for the National Association of Manufacturers of the U.S.A. New York, 1911.

SCHWENGER, R. *Die betriebliche Sozialpolitik in der westdeutschen Grossindustrie.* Muenchen, 1934.

Social Work and Legislation in Sweden. Stockholm, 1938.

STANES, *see under* RUEGG.

STAFFORD, C. H. *The Legal Aspects of Industrial Diseases.* 1934.

TRINCA, A. J. *Hernia and Workmen's Compensation Acts.* Melbourne, 1939.

VERNON, H. M. *Accidents and their Prevention.* 1936.

WEBB, SIDNEY and BEATRICE. *Soviet Communism, a new Civilisation.* 1935.

v. WEIZSAECKER, PROF. *Soziale Krankheit und soziale Gesundung.* Berlin, 1939.

WILLIS, W. ADDINGTON. *The Workmen's Compensation Acts,* 30 ed.

WILSON, SIR ARNOLD, and LEVY, PROF. HERMANN. *Industrial Assurance.* 1937.

—— —— *Burial Reform and Funeral Costs.* 1938.

—— —— *Workmen's Compensation,* vol. i. 1939.

WOODBURY. *Workers' Health and Safety.* New York, 1936.

II. REPORTS, OFFICIAL DOCUMENTS, HANDBOOKS, ETC.

Departmental Committee on Workmen's Compensation. (Holman Gregory Report.) 1920.

Report of the Dept. Committee appointed to inquire and report what amendments are desirable in the Assurance Companies Act 1909. (Clauson Report.) 1927.

—— —— Committee on Compulsory Insurance. (Cassel Report.) 1937.

—— —— Dept. Committee on Certain Questions arising under the Workmen's Compensation Acts. (Stewart Report.) 1938.

Interim Report of the Inter-Dept. Committee on the Rehabilitation of Persons injured by Accidents. (Delevingne Report.) 1937. Final Report, 1939.

Royal Commission on Safety in Coal Mines. 1936–8.

—— —— on Workmen's Compensation. Minutes of Evidence. (Hetherington Commission.) 1939–40.

Annual Reports of H.M. Chief Inspector of Factories.

—— —— the Secretary for Mines.

—— —— Industrial Research Board (Medical Research Council).

—— —— Royal Surgical Society.

Annual Report of Unemployment Assistance Board, 1937.

Reports of the Chief Medical Officer of the Ministry of Health.

Interim Report on Laws relating to the Liability of Employers. Toronto, 1912. Final Report, 1913.

Royal Commission on National Health Insurance. 1928.

Report of the Joint Conference of the Invalid Children's Association and the Central Council for the Care of Cripples. 1935.

PEP Report on the British Health Services. 1937.

Report of the Chief Registrar of Friendly Societies. 1937.

—— New Zealand Department of Labour. August 1937.

—— Government Actuary on the 5th Valuation of Approved Societies.

Registrar General, Decennial Supplement. Occupational Mortality. 1938.

Rapport relatif à l'exécution de la Loi sur la Réparation des Dommages résultant des Accidents du Travail. Bruxelles, 1938.

Union of South Africa Workmen's Compensation Act 1934. Pretoria, 1936.

Assurance Companies Returns. 1938.

Report of the Victoria State Insurance Office. Melbourne, 1938.

Industrial Commissioner of Wisconsin. Wisconsin Physical Examination Program. Madison, 1939.

Home Office. Memorandum on Foreign and Colonial Laws relating to Compensation for Injuries. (Mr. Wotzel.) 1905.

—— Memorandum on Silicosis and Asbestosis. 1935.

—— —— on the Workmen's Compensation Acts, 1925–31. 1936.

—— Workmen's Compensation Statistics.

—— Dept. Committee on Compensation for Industrial Diseases. Reports of 1932, 1933, and 1936.

—— How Factory Accidents happen. 1 July 1937.

—— Lighting in Factories and Workshops. (Welfare Pamphlet.) 1937.

—— Dept. Committee on Lighting in Factories and Workshops. 1915, 1921, 1922, 1938.

—— A Guide to the Factory Acts. 1938.

—— Report of the Dept. Committee on Compensation for Card Room Workers. 1939.

International Labour Office. Silicosis, 1930.

—— International Survey of Social Services, 1933. 2 vols. 1936, 1937.

—— —— of Legal Decisions on Labour Law. (Various issues.)

—— Occupation and Health. 1930, 1934.

—— International Labour Organization and Social Insurance. 1936.

—— The Evaluation of Incapacity for Work in Social Insurance. (Evaluation Report.) 1937.

—— Industrial Accidents Statistics. 1938.

U.S.A. Department of Labor. Division of Labor Standards. Discussion of Industrial Accidents and Diseases. 1935.

—— Convention of the International Association of Industrial Accident Boards and Commissions. (Various publications.)

U.S.A. Department of Labor. Safety Practices Pamphlets.

Survey of the Merseyside. 1934.
London Charity Society. Memorandum on Rehabilitation. n.d.
League of Nations. The Problem of Nutrition. 1936.

British Medical Association. Report of Committee on Fractures. 1935.
—— On the Diagnosis and Certification of Miner's Nystagmus. 1936.
—— A General Medical Service for the Nation. 1938.
Medical Research Committee and Department of Scientific and Industrial Research. Reports of the Industrial Fatigue Research Board. No. 4 (Multiple Accidents). 1919.
Medical Research Council. First Report on Miner's Nystagmus. 1922. Third Report, 1932.
—— Sickness Absence and Labour Wastage. 1936.
American College of Surgeons. Medical Service in Industry and Workmen's Compensation Laws. 1938.
Industrial Welfare Society. Medical Service in Industry. 1936.

Statistical Abstract of the United Kingdom.
The Census of Great Britain. 1931.
The Census of Production. 1935.
Bulletins of the Bureau of Labor Statistics (U.S.A.).
Handbook of Labor Statistics. Washington, 1936.

Das Reichsversicherungsamt und die Deutsche Arbeiterversicherung. 1910.
Entscheidungen und Mitteilungen des Reichsversicherungsamtes. 1935.
Die Neuregelung der Beziehungen zwischen den Traegern der Krankenversicherung und der Unfallversicherung. Berlin, 1936.

House of Commons. Debates.
House of Lords. Debates.

III. NEWSPAPERS, REVIEWS, AND JOURNALS

The Times.
The Daily Telegraph.
Industrial Welfare.
Industrial Safety Bulletin.
Archiv fuer Sozialwissenschaft.
Proceedings of the Institute of Mining Engineers.
Transactions of the Ophthalmological Society of Gt. Britain. 1939.
The Law Journal.
Law Quarterly Review.
Juristische Wochenschrift.
Transactions of the Hunterian Society.
British Journal of Dermatology. 1937.
The Lancet.
Bath and Wiltshire Chronicle. 1935.
The Journal of Industrial Hygiene.
The Insurance Mail.
The Economist.
The Landworker.

The Charity Organisation Society Quarterly.

U.S.A. Monthly Labor Review.

The Journal of the Royal Statistical Society.

Proceedings of the Royal Society of Medicine.

Proceedings of the Insurance Institute of London.

American Journal of Surgery. 1938.

British Medical Journal.

Amtliche Nachrichten für Reichsversicherung.

British Journal of Tuberculosis.

Reichsarbeitsblatt.

Zentralblatt für Psychotherapie.

Berliner Medizinische Wochenschrift.

Occupational Psychology. 1939.

British Journal of Psychology. 1933.

Journal of the Royal Institute of Public Health and Hygiene. 1938.

Journal of the Royal Army Corps, 1938.

Modern Law Review.

Labour.

Toynbee Outlook.

U.S. Labor Information Bulletin.

Post Magazine and Insurance Monitor.

Journal of the Chartered Insurance Institute.

INDEX

[Acts of Parliament will be found under 'Legislation'.]

PRINTED IN
GREAT BRITAIN
AT THE
UNIVERSITY PRESS
OXFORD
BY
JOHN JOHNSON
PRINTER
TO THE
UNIVERSITY